FIVE CENTURIES OF SIKH TRADITION

Ideology, Society, Politics and Culture

FIVE CENTURIES OF SIKH TRADITION

Ideology, Society, Politics and Culture

* * *

ESSAYS FOR INDU BANGA

Edited by
REETA GREWAL & SHEENA PALL

MANOHAR
2005

First published 2005

ISBN 81-7304-653-0

Published by

Ajay Kumar Jain *for*
Manohar Publishers & Distributors
4753/23 Ansari Road, Daryaganj
New Delhi 110 002

Typeset at

Digigrafics
New Delhi 110 049

Printed at

Lordson Publishers Pvt. Ltd.
Delhi 110 007

Distributed in South Asia by

FOUNDATION BOOKS

4381/4, Ansari Road
Daryaganj, New Delhi 110 002
and its branches at Mumbai, Hyderabad,
Bangalore, Chennai, Kolkata

Contents

Preface

Talking to some of her young students in the Department of History, Professor Indu Banga casually remarked that she had done enough of teaching for one life and would now like to retire from the Panjab University to devote herself entirely to research. They were a little shocked to realize that she was old enough to retire. As a token of their gratitude for what she had done for her students and researchers they thought of presenting a suitable tribute to Professor Banga and consulted Dr Reeta Grewal, a former student of Professor Banga and now a colleague in the Department; she approved of the idea of a felicitation volume with papers contributed by Professor Banga's students and colleagues.

We approached Professor J.S. Grewal for advice. He liked the idea, and suggested that some senior scholars, who knew Professor Banga and her work, could also be invited to contribute papers. We wrote to senior historians on behalf of the research students and colleagues of Professor Indu Banga for contribution to a volume on the Punjab to be published in appreciation of her lifelong commitment to the discipline of history and her contribution to the study of regional, urban and Indian history. The response was very encouraging. Professor Juergensmeyer responded promptly that he 'would be honoured' to have his article included in the volume honouring Professor Banga. Dr Mohinder Singh wrote that such a tribute was 'much overdue' and that he would write a new article 'because of his personal regard for Professor Banga'. Professor Chattopadhyaya said that if his Punjab History Conference address could merit inclusion in the proposed volume, he should feel honoured. Dr Lafont wrote that he would be glad to contribute a fresh article. Professor Iqtidar Alam Khan wrote that he would deem it a privilege to have his article included in a volume planned in appreciation of Professor Banga's contribution to the history of the Punjab.

Coming within four weeks of our request, these responses encouraged us to goad the students and colleagues of Professor Banga to send their contributions before the end of 2004.

Eventually, when all the contributions came in we realized that the volume would become extraordinarily large. Therefore, we decided to publish two volumes. After much thought and consultation, we thought of one volume as *Precolonial and Colonial Punjab: Society, Economy, Politics and Culture* and the other as *Five Centuries of Sikh Tradition: Ideology, Society, Politics and Culture*. We are happy to acknowledge that Sasha, Kuldeep Grewal and Karamjit Malhotra were always there to help us at all stages to prepare the two volumes for the press. Professor J.S. Grewal was graciously accessible for consultation and advice. Gulshan Katoch was there to expedite typing and retyping with Savitri's help. Shri Ramesh Jain took personal interest in the publication. We are thankful to them all for their distinctive contribution towards the publication of these two volumes.

We regard these volumes as a suitable tribute to Professor Indu Banga and we hope that, like the *Five Punjabi Centuries* she edited, these two volumes would be appreciated by scholars interested in Punjab and Sikh studies.

REETA GREWAL
SHEENA PALL

Indu Banga, the Historian

SHEENA PALL

The recent award of Hem Chandra Roychaudhari Birth Centenary Gold Medal to Professor Indu Banga by the Asiatic Society for her 'outstanding contribution to the field of Indian history' symbolizes in a way her national and international recognition as a historian.

Indu was born on 7 September 1945 at Dagshai, now a part of Solan district in Himachal Pradesh. Her father, with a degree in engineering from Edinbrugh, had joined the Military Engineering Service and was posted at Dagshai. He belonged to Bannu in the North West Frontier Province. Indu's mother, from the Sialkot district of West Punjab, was one of the early women graduates of the Punjab University at Lahore. Her father was in judicial service.

Indu started her primary education at the Saint Patrick's, a Roman Catholic School at Jodhpur. From Jodhpur she went to Gwalior and Jaipur, and eventually to Pilani where she completed her higher secondary education from the Birla Balika Vidyapeeth in 1961. She recalls with a certain degree of nostalgia that she participated in all the extra-curricular activities of the school. She was editor of its house magazine, a sports champion, an NCC under-officer and she directed plays and organized cultural functions. With her happy experience in Birla Balika Vidyapeeth, Indu insisted on going to the Birla Arts College at Pilani. Her mother wanted her to join the well known Sophia College at Ajmer, but Indu had her way and got her B.A. degree from Pilani in 1964 with History, Economics, Political Science, English, Hindi and General Science.

Her father was now posted at Kasauli, and Indu decided to join the Panjab University at Chandigarh for the Master's degree in History. Ever since her childhood she had been drawn to history. As she recalls, at the age of ten she had read not only her own history textbook but also the history books of the senior classes. She was an avid reader of fiction too, reading short stories and novels, sometimes scanning through two to three books in a day. When she joined the Department of History at Chandigarh her aspiration was to compete for administrative services or to become a journalist. The inspiration for journalism came from her maternal uncle, Krishan Bhatia, a well known journalist and the author of *Indira Gandhi* and *The Ordeal of Nationhood*. Since her school days, she had been writing occasionally for newspapers and magazines. However, Indu became interested gradually in historical research. She attributes this change in her thinking to the influence of Dr J.S. Grewal who was then teaching in the Department of History, Panjab University. Dr Grewal's teaching involved detailed discussions with his students, encouraging them to read and think for themselves. She still remembers how Dr Grewal enabled her to see a clear distinction between Indian Nationalism and Hindu Nationalism. These discussions induced Indu Banga to think of research and teaching as a profession.

The turning point finally came when Indu Banga attended a History Teachers Seminar at the Department of History after she had appeared for her M.A. examination in April 1966. This seminar was organized by Dr John C.B. Webster, then a Lecturer at Baring Union Christian College, Batala, in collaboration with the Department of History, with active participation of Dr Ravinder Kumar and Dr J.S. Grewal. Several historians who later gained eminence in the field acted as resource persons. Apart from Tapan Raychaudhuri, who was already a known entity, there were Parthasarthi Gupta, Romila Thapar, Ravinder Kumar, J.S. Grewal, and W.H. McLeod. Indu Banga was inspired the most by Romila Thapar who became her role model.

During one of the lunches in the course of the seminar, Indu Banga happened to share the table with Dr John C.B. Webster and Dr W.H. McLeod. They chatted about history. She did not realize that she was being informally interviewed for lectureship at the Baring Union Christian College, Batala. Soon she received a letter from its Principal, Dr Ram Singh, asking her to meet him in the waiting room of the railway station at Ambala Cantonment where her father was posted. Somewhat reluctantly, and without disclosing it to her parents, she went for an interview conducted over a glass of *nimbu pani*. Within a week, she received an appointment letter. Dr Grewal advised her to take up teaching for at least a year, saying that it would help her, among other things, to make up her mind finally about research and teaching as a profession. Indu Banga was able to persuade her parents to let her join the college for a year in July 1966. A year's stay at the Baring Union Christian College turned out to be an instructive experience for her, especially her interaction with Webster and McLeod as her colleagues. By the end of the year she was firmly committed to research and teaching.

Professor Gurinder Singh Mann, who was a student of the Baring College then, goes down the memory lane to tell us that, with a small circle of teenage friends, he would sit on the stairs of the college library to watch the tall gracious young Lecturer in History, wrapped up in her camel coloured cardigan returning from her class, feeling that their home town poet Shiv Kumar had sung of her beauty and grace in a poem which they remembered by heart.

Dr John C.B. Webster recalls:

> Dr Indu Banga had just completed her M.A. in History at Chandigarh when I met her at a History Teachers Seminar I had organized in the Department in 1966. At the time she was thinking of taking the I.A.S. examination but our three weeks seminar seems to have convinced her to pursue history instead. I then persuaded her to come to Baring Union Christian College, Batala and for 1966-67 she joined Dr W.H. McLeod and myself in the History Department there. She has been an excellent colleague right from the onset and has remained a good friend as well, helping me in some of my research, as well as providing excellent hospitality and intellectual stimulation whenever I came to Chandigarh. She is one of the people to whom I dedicated my book, *Studying History*.

Indu Banga resigned from Baring College in 1967 to become a Research Fellow at the Panjab University. After a year she got the UGC Research Fellowship, and in July 1970, she was selected as a Junior Lecturer in the Department of History, Panjab University. In July 1971, Indu Banga joined the Department of History, Guru Nanak Dev University, Amritsar, as a Lecturer.

She was to spend nearly twenty years of her academic life at Amritsar.

II

One clear link between Chandigarh and Amritsar was provided by Indu Banga's doctoral research. The area in which she wanted to pursue research was the social and economic history of medieval India. Initially she had thought of the Khalji period, and started learning Persian. Later on, however, she decided to work on the agrarian system of the Sikhs. For one thing, the discovery of *madad-i ma'ash* documents by Professor B.N. Goswamy, later published as *The Mughal and Sikh Rulers and the Vaishnavas of Pindori: A Historical Interpretation of 52 Persian Documents*, translated and edited by B.N. Goswamy and J.S. Grewal, suggested the possibility of more such documents being discovered to make the study of the agrarian system of the Sikhs feasible. The revenue records of Ranjit Singh, known as the Khalsa Darbar Records, available in the Punjab State Archives at Patiala was another favourable factor. The agrarian system of the Sikhs was entirely an unchartered field, and the great work published by Dr Irfan Habib on the agrarian system of the Mughals in 1963 could serve as a model. However, some senior historians of the Punjab were sceptical about the possibility of such a work. Professor Sri Ram Sharma asked in fact whether the Sikhs had an agrarian system at all. It was assumed by many that whatever was worth saying on the subject had already been said by Sita Ram Kohli. Indu Banga refused to be bogged down. Much to her delight she began to find fresh evidence on the subject in the early British and contemporary Urdu and Persian sources.

Indu Banga recalls with gratification Professor Nurul Hasan's remark during her Ph.D. *viva* in 1974. He observed that 'one could not make out the social or religious identity of the scholar'. Indu Banga took it as a compliment. The thesis was revised and published in 1978, with a foreword by Professor Nurul Hasan, referring to the work as 'invaluable for a meaningful study of the agrarian relations in the Punjab'. Jean-Marie Lafont found it 'immediately of great use' in understanding Maharaja Ranjit Singh's agrarian policy. Professor Sukhwant Singh recollects: Dr Indu Banga was 'the first historian to highlight the agrarian history of the Punjab'. After going through the book, says Dr Surya Kant, 'I realized that here was a scholar who examined history geographically'. 'For my own researchers', says Dr Veena Sachdeva, 'I keep Professor Banga's *Agrarian System* handy to tell them how footnotes are given and how bibliographies are prepared. Her work serves as a model.'

Ten years earlier, Indu Banga had presented her first research paper at the Indian History Congress Session at Patiala on Ahmad Shah Abdali. She fondly recalls Professor Barun De's favourable comments which were a source of delight and encouragement. Then in 1969 she attended the first conference on medieval India at Aligarh on the occasion of the quincentenary celebration of the birth of Guru Nanak. She presented a paper on 'Continuity and Change Under Sikh Rule', with Professor Satish Chandra as Chairman of the session, in a state of nervousness, reading it almost in one breath. Gradually, however, she discovered that her papers were well received. She gained confidence and poise. The *Agrarian System of the Sikhs* was written and revised with a cool confidence.

III

Dr Indu Banga was selected as Reader in 1974 and as Professor in 1982. Professor Sukhwant Singh, who worked with Dr Banga for his doctoral research, remembers her as 'an excellent teacher', with 'clarity of thought and expression' and 'deeply respected by the students'. Another research student, Dr Sukhdev S. Sohal, appreciates her as a teacher and a historian: 'she is, as a person, considerate and conscientious to the core. Lending help to a needy student is her *forte*. Soft-spoken, sophisticated, she is equally demanding of her students in academics. Her penchant for minute detail in research is beyond belief. She is a quintessential scholar who takes care of intricate layers of historical evidence, nuanced interpretation and methodological subtleties'.

In the seventies and eighties, Professor Banga was actually involved in a number of academic programmes, besides teaching and guiding research. Her association with the Punjab History Conference had begun before she came to Amritsar. She contributed papers to the Conference regularly in the seventies. She was invited in 1980 to preside over its Medieval Section.

Dr Mohinder Singh recalls: 'While I had heard a lot about Professor Banga's qualities as an inspiring teacher and a devoted scholar, it was only during the successive sessions of the Punjab History Conference in Patiala that I watched Professor Banga and her team of young scholars rather closely to appreciate what she was doing'. Professor K.L. Tuteja says that she set a fine example of 'deep academic and professional commitment'. As Dr Chetan Singh graciously put it, a new school of historical studies was coming up at Amritsar.

As we noticed earlier, Professor Banga's association with the Indian History Congress had started in 1967. Attending its sessions regularly and contributing papers, she became a member of its executive committee in 1980-3 and in 1985-6. She acted as the Local Secretary of the 46th Session of the Indian History Congress at Amritsar in 1985. In 1988, she was elected President of its Modern Section. Already, the wide scope of Professor Banga's historical interests had become known, and she was elected President of the History Section of the Social Sciences Congress at Aligarh in 1984.

Professor Banga's association with the University Grants Commission began in 1973 as Deputy Director of its Summer Institute at Guru Nanak Dev University. In 1976 she was Deputy Director of the UGC Zonal Workshop in History Syllabi. In 1982 she was Local Secretary of the UGC Workshop on National Integration at Guru Nanak Dev University. She was associated with the UGC NET in its formative years. In 1983-5, she was a member of the UGC panel in History and Archaeology. In 1988, she became Research Scientist-C (Professorial) of the University Grants Commission. During all these years, Dr Indu Banga organized a number of seminars, conferences, symposia and workshops sponsored by the Indian Council of Historical Research as well as the UGC.

Indu Banga's organizational skills and desire for perfection made such assignments a welcome challenge. She personally went into the nitty-gritty of every aspect to ensure flawless programmes, be it water for the speakers on the podium, fresh flowers, papers for distribution, arrangements for the participants to be met at the railway station or the bus stand, and for their stay. Dr Veena Sachdeva, then a Research Associate at Amritsar, recalls:

I was struck by Professor Banga's exceptional flare for organizing seminars and conferences. All details were worked out and reduced to writing for members of the various committees. It was a pleasure to work with her on such occasions.

Professor Banga's association with the UGC had one peculiar significance. In 1976-9, she was Deputy Director of a UGC project on 'Urbanization in the Upper Bari Doab, 1600-1947'. A seminar on urbanization in India was held at Amritsar in connection with this project. Its proceedings, co-edited by Dr Banga, were published as *Studies in Urban History*. Furthermore, an Urban History Group was formed at the end of the seminar in 1978, and it developed subsequently into the Urban History Association of India on the pattern of the Indian History Congress. Dr Banga was its Treasurer from 1981 to 1987 and its Secretary from1987 to 1990. A number of seminars, symposia and lectures were organized by the Urban History Association of India, often in coordination with the Indian History Congress. The Association brought out a number of publications. Dr Banga prepared *Bibliography of Urban Studies in India* which was published by the Association in 1981. The books edited by Professor Banga for the Association have been particularly well received: *The City in Indian History* (1991) and *Ports and Their Hinterlands in India, 1700-1950* (1992).

These were not the only publications of Professor Banga. The *Early Nineteenth Century Panjab*, a translation of the description of the Punjab by Ganesh Das in his *Char Bagh-i Punjab*, was published in 1974. The *Civil and Military Affairs of Maharaja Ranjit Singh: A Study of Over 450 Orders in Persian* was published in 1987. Over a score of articles were published in the seventies and eighties. Professor Banga's publications during her stay in Amritsar cover polity, economy, society, the state, the ruling class, the *jagirdari* system, *dharmarth* grants, rural-urban interaction, and ecology and land rights. The *Journal of Regional History* was edited in the early 1980s. At this time, she also wrote history textbooks for class VII and class XI for the Punjab School Education Board at Chandigarh.

With her varied interests, Dr Indu Banga could interact with a number of social scientists, both Indian and foreign. Lafont recalls:

On deputation to the Punjab University, Lahore, in 1972, I started working on the French officers in the service of Maharaja Ranjit Singh and I used to regularly cross over the border to Amritsar, Patiala, Chandigarh and Delhi, either alone or with my family, for research and exchanges with Indian scholars. I and my wife quickly met with Indu Banga, and we remember with pleasure our quiet exchanges in her GNDU residence at Amritsar when her mother was so kindly receiving us. She helped me a lot, giving me her connections and introducing me to several scholars who in turn became friends. My appointment in India in 1987 gave us some more opportunity to meet, in Delhi and Chandigarh that time. Meeting Indu is always refreshing because of her scholarship as well as her grace and kindness in sharing with us her knowledge as well as her intuitions.

Professor Banga was invited to international seminars at Berkeley and Toronto in 1987. In the year following, she participated in conferences at Toronto and Vancouver. During these years she utilized the opportunity to work in the British Library (then Commonwealth Relations).

Amritsar was also the place to provide experience of administration for Professor Indu Banga. She was Head of the Department of History from 1981 to 1986, and then in 1989-90. She was Chairperson of the Board of Studies in History during these years. She was member of the University Senate and Syndicate, its Academic Council and its Planning Board. She was Dean of the Faculty of Arts. Had she stayed on in the University she would have become its Dean of Academic Affairs as one of the senior most Professors. In many respects, thus, the two decades at Amritsar proved to be rich and rewarding in terms of academic and administrative experience. Indu Banga, the historian, had emerged from this experience. According to Dr Mohinder Singh, Professor Banga 'not only continued the good work started by her illustrious teacher and distinguished historian, Professor J.S Grewal, but also succeeded in bringing the History Department on the national map'.

Professor Harish K. Puri looks back at the Amritsar decades in a mood of calm appreciation:

We have known Professor Indu Banga as a deeply loved and respected friend of our family since the time she joined Baring Union Christian College, Batala as a Lecturer in History in 1966. Later we were together at Guru Nanak Dev University for about 20 years as colleagues, friends and neighbours. This was the place, a newly established University, where some of us were from 1971-2 quite passionately involved in building the basic institutional structures and infrastructure and in creating a conducive intellectual and cultural environment for teaching and research. The moving spirit behind all this effort was Professor J.S. Grewal.

It is good to recall what I closely observed about Indu Banga. We noticed in her a capacity for untiring hard work and the ability to enable a large number of colleagues, including teachers from affiliated colleges to join in updating syllabi, develop a habit of studying in the library, guiding young researchers, organizing seminars, writing papers and participating in discussions. It was possible to establish fairly high standards of teaching and research and she herself grew into a historian of high standing.

The most endearing qualities which enabled Indu Banga to achieve so much, were the grace and charm with which she went about her work. Blessed with an exceptionally caring disposition towards relatives, friends and students she was not only sensitive to the emotional needs of dear ones but also able to show problem-solving readiness. Thereby she was able to bring courage to her own life and that of many others. We wish her a long life of good health and satisfaction of a life well lived.

IV

In August 1990 Professor Indu Banga joined the Department of History, Panjab University, Chandigarh. Dr Mohinder Singh recalls:

> When she decided to leave Guru Nanak Dev University to take up Professorship at the Panjab University, Chandigarh, we thought that was the end of the History Department at Amritsar. But this was not so, mainly because she had created a line of succession. It is not surprising to find younger faculty members continuing Professor Banga's tradition of teaching combined with scholarship.

Much of Professor Banga's activity at Chandigarh was in continuation of her interests in Amritsar. She was elected to the executive committee of the Indian History Congress in 1992 and again in 1997-9. On invitation from the Congress, she co-edited *History and Ideology: The Khalsa over 300 Years* in 1999, a book that has been reprinted and also translated into Punjabi. For her association with the UGC, she acted as a resource person for its Refresher Courses in History at regional and national centres in the 1990s. From 1993-9, she was again a member of its History and Archaeology panel. She is now a member of the Indian Council of Historical Research. In 1991-2, she became Vice-President of the Urban History Association of India. Since 1993 she has worked as its Secretary. She has recently edited *Urban Phenomena in Indian History* for the Association. The pattern of her visits abroad has continued since the Amritsar years. Besides working in the British Library from 1990 to 2001, she has participated in seminars and conferences at Coventry and Santa Barbara several times from 1994-2001. She is on the Editorial Board of *The Journal of Punjab Studies* which has been started from Santa Barbara in continuation of the *International Journal of Punjab Studies* from Coventry. Some of the other activities of Professor Banga were related to the NCERT regional committee for the contemporary history of India of which Professor Banga was the convenor in 1996. In 1992, she was a member of the state steering committee for Joint Preliminary Test for Eligibility for Lectureship in the University and colleges of the Punjab and Chandigarh.

In the early 1990s Professor Banga participated in the programmes of the Indian Institute of Advanced Study at Shimla and edited several volumes: *Philosophy of Science* (1992), jointly with Jayant Narlikar, *Causation in History* (1992), on her own, and *Cultural Reorientation in Modern India* (1996), jointly with Jaidev. She was associated with the team project on Cultural Networks and Socio-Religious Movements in Indian Civilization, working specifically on the emergence of Hindu consciousness in colonial Punjab. Another institution in which Professor Banga has played a very active role is the Institute of Punjab Studies. It has organized a number of seminars, with financial support mainly from the ICHR. She has edited the proceedings of a few of these seminars: *Punjab in Prosperity and Violence* (1998), and a volume on gender relations, an area in which she developed interest in the 1990s. Another volume that she has edited is entitled *Five Punjabi Centuries* (1997). It is a felicitation volume for Professor J.S. Grewal on polity, economy, society and culture of the north-western India from 1500 to 1990. It turned out to be a standard reading for researchers and teachers in the area of Punjab studies and has been reprinted.

Professor Banga has worked on her own and joined other scholars in a common academic endeavor. The historian with whom she has collaborated over the decades is her own teacher and senior colleague, Professor J.S. Grewal. Their first joint work appeared in 1974 as the *Early Nineteenth Century Panjab*, followed by *Maharaja Ranjit Singh and His Times* in 1978, *Studies in Urban History* in 1981, *Civil and Military Affairs of Maharaja Ranjit Singh* in 1987, *Punjab in Prosperity and Violence* in 1998, *History and Ideology: The Khalsa over 300 Years* in 1999, *Lala Lajpat Rai in Retrospect* in 2000, and *Maharaja Ranjit Singh: The State and Society* in 2001. Their book entitled *Paramountcy, Patriotism and the Panth: A Political Biography of Maharaja Ripudaman Singh of Nabha* is being prepared for the press as a study of nationalism in princely India. Professor Grewal feels happy over this long collaboration in which Professor Banga's contribution has increased with passage of time. But for her deference for a former teacher, she would have been the senior author or editor. He regrets that she does not formally appear as a co-editor in *The State and Society in Medieval India* (Part I of Volume VII of the *History of Science, Philosophy and Culture in Indian Civilization*), published by the Oxford University Press in 2005, nor in the forthcoming second part, *Religious Movements and Institutions in Medieval India*. However, in view of Professor Banga's contribution towards the preparation of these volumes, they are dedicated to her.

Professor Indu Banga's teachers, colleagues and students are an extended fraternity for her. The loving care she showers upon her students, makes her an unforgettable teacher. Dr Veena Sachdev recalls:

> For over a decade now I have seen one permanent fixture on her table: the *Concise Oxford Dictionary*. She uses it herself and more than that she asks her students to use it in her presence. She provides reading materials to students at her own cost in order to ensure that they are left with no excuses. Deeply committed to the discipline, she feels depressed sometimes to see teachers and students with negative or indifferent attitudes.

Professor Banga's objective as a teacher is to enable her students to develop their critical faculty. She ridicules dictation of notes in the classroom as a fraud on the students. Laying emphasis on understanding rather than information, she structures her teaching in a way that conveys a sense of connection between the past and the present, creates an awareness of the allied disciplines, helps the students to acquire a secular liberal outlook and to broaden their social sympathies, particularly towards the underprivileged sections of the society. She encourages researchers to write with clarity, and to present their research with confidence.

By now, Professor Indu Banga has two generations of researchers. Many of her earliest students have become Professors, guiding research in their own and new areas of research. Dr Reeta Grewal in the Department of History, Panjab University, has guided a large number of researchers as a former student of Professor Banga and now a colleague. The youngest researchers of Professor Banga are the most appreciative of her mature guidance and her personal interest in their work. I am one of them, a great admirer of Professor Banga.

Kuldeep Grewal has this to say about her supervisor:

> In my long association with Professor Indu Banga as a researcher, I have come to look upon her as my role model. She is meticulous, magnanimous and gentle. Her guidance has enabled me to hone my skills to bring out the best in me. I feel extremely fortunate to have a mentor who is both a friend and a guide.

The youngest student of Professor Banga is Karamjit Malhotra. She says:

> Professor Indu Banga has influenced me deeply as an M.A. student and a young researcher. I feel inspired by her dedication and commitment to the discipline of history. She is largely responsible for showing me the way to historical research. Her sympathetic attitude makes her a friendly guide. For me she has become a role model. With her earnestness and clarity of thought, she has inspired others like myself to take up research with the idea of teaching history.

Finally, we may quote Professor Mark Juergensmeyer's appreciative assessment of Professor Indu Banga as a historian:

> One of the things that impresses you most about Professor Banga is that she has the right personality to be a good historian. More than anything else, careful history requires not only diligent research but also thoughtful reflection. What Professor Banga brings to her research is a temperament

of patience and sensitivity that resists easy conclusions and pat answers. The truth is always more complicated than that. She is willing to let the research sit for a while, let the conclusions emerge rather than be forced on the data, and persists in asking questions even when everyone else thinks they have found the answers. She embodies the best of the historian's mind and moods, a pattern of both sensitivity and sensibility.

We share Dr Mohinder Singh's view that Professor Banga 'carries her eminence lightly', and we join him in wishing 'her long and meaningful life in the service of history and culture of the Punjab'. Lafont feels sure that 'the present volume will be a "bouquet de fleurs", diverse, beautiful and colourful from the scholarly community of historians celebrating a great friend as much as a leading scholar in the various fields of history'. We are grateful to the contributors who have made it possible.

PUBLICATIONS

BOOKS

Urban Phenomena in Indian History, ed. (forthcoming).

Maharaja Ranjit Singh: The State and Society, ed. (conjoint), Guru Nanak Dev University, Amritsar, 2001.

Lala Lajpat Rai in Retrospect: Political, Economic, Social and Cultural Concerns, ed. (conjoint), Panjab University, Chandigarh, 2000.

History and Ideology: The Khalsa over 300 Years, ed. (conjoint), Indian History Congress/ Tulika, New Delhi, 1999.

Punjab in Prosperity and Violence, 1947-1997, ed. (conjoint), Institute of Punjab Studies/ K.K. Publishers, New Delhi, 1998.

Five Punjabi Centuries: Polity, Economy, Society and Culture, c. 1500-1990, ed., Manohar, New Delhi, 1997. Reprint, 2000.

Cultural Reorientation in Modern India, ed. (conjoint), Indian Institute of Advanced Study, Shimla, 1996.

Philosophy of Science, ed. (conjoint), Indian Institute of Advanced Study, Shimla, 1992.

Causation in History, ed., Indian Institute of Advanced Study, Shimla, 1992.

Ports and Their Hinterlands in India, 1700-1950, ed., Manohar, New Delhi, 1992.

The City in Indian History, ed., Manohar, New Delhi, 1991. Reprints 1994, 2005.

Civil and Military Affairs of Maharaja Ranjit Singh: A Study of over 450 Orders in Persian, ed. (conjoint), Guru Nanak Dev University, Amritsar, 1987.

Textbook of History for class XI, Punjab School Board, Chandigarh, 1983. *Textbook of History* for class VII, Punjab School Board, Chandigarh, 1982.

Studies in Urban History, ed. (conjoint), Guru Nanak Dev University, Amritsar, 1981.

Maharaja Ranjit Singh and His Times, ed. (conjoint), Guru Nanak Dev University, Amritsar, 1980.

Agrarian System of the Sikhs: Late Eighteenth and Early Nineteenth Century, Manohar Publications, New Delhi/South Asia Books, USA, 1978.

Early Nineteenth Century Panjab, ed. and tr. (conjoint), Guru Nanak Dev University, Amritsar, 1974.

ARTICLES

'Gender Relations in Medieval India', *The State and Society in Medieval India*, vol. VII A (ed. J.S. Grewal), History of Science, Philosophy and Culture in Indian Civilization, Oxford University Press, New Delhi, 2005.

'State and Society in the Punjab, 1765-1845', *The State and Society in Medieval India*, vol. VII A (ed. J.S. Grewal), History of Science, Philosophy and Culture in Indian Civilization, Oxford University Press, New Delhi, 2005.

'Urban-Rural Interaction: The Upper Bari Doab (*c.* 1500-1900)', *Five Thousand Years of Urbanization: The Punjab Region* (ed. Reeta Grewal), Manohar, New Delhi, 2005.

'Swami Dayanand's Aryavarta', *India: Studies in the History of an Idea* (ed. Irfan Habib), Munshiram Manoharlal, New Delhi, 2005.

'Ecology and Land Rights in the Punjab', *Journal of Punjab Studies*, Santa Barbara, 2004, vol. 11, no. 1.

'In the Service of Hindu Nationalism: Banerjee's *Evolution*', *The Khalsa: Sikh and Non-Sikh Perspectives* (ed. J.S. Grewal), Manohar, New Delhi, 2004.

'Khalsa Ideology and Politics: Banda Bahadur to Ranjit Singh', *The Khalsa and the Punjab: Studies in Sikh History to the 19th Century* (ed. Himadri Banerjee), Indian History Congress/Tulika, New Delhi, 2002.

'Lajpat Rai on the Arya Samaj: An Insider's View', *Lala Lajpat Rai in Retrospect: Political, Economic, Social and Cultural Concerns* (ed. J.S. Grewal and Indu Banga), Panjab University, Chandigarh, 2000.

'Pakistan, Khalistan and Partition' (conjoint), *The Partition in Retrospect* (ed. Amrik Singh), National Institute of Punjab Studies/Anamika Publishers, New Delhi, 2000.

'Jallianwala Bagh Tragedy: The Official Attitude and its Significance' (conjoint), *Jallianwala Bagh Massacre* (ed. V.N. Datta and S. Settar), Indian Council of Historical Research and Pragati Publications, New Delhi, 2000.

'Equality and Political Order', *Relevance of Khalsa Value System in the 21st Century* (ed. G.S. Cheema and I.S. Sandhu), Anandpur Sahib Foundation, Chandigarh, 2000.

'Ritual in the Arya Samaj Movement', *Organizational and Institutional Aspects of Religious Movements* (ed. Joseph T. O' Connell), Indian Institute of Advanced Study, Shimla, 1999.

'Arya Samaj and Punjabi Identity', *Punjabi Identity in a Global Context* (ed. Pritam Singh and Shinder Thandi), Oxford University Press, New Delhi, 1999.

'The Sikhs and the Prospect of Pakistan', *History and Ideology: The Khalsa over 300 Years* (ed. J.S. Grewal and Indu Banga), Indian History Congress/Tulika, New Delhi, 1999.

'Formation of the Sikh State, 1765-1845', *Five Punjabi Centuries: Polity, Economy, Society and Culture, c. 1500-1990* (ed. Indu Banga), Manohar, New Delhi, 1997.

'The Ideology of Swami Dayanand', *Cultural Reorientation in Modern India* (eds. Indu Banga and Jaidev), Indian Institute of Advanced Study, Shimla, 1996.

'Socio-Religious Reform and Patriarchy', *Women in Indian History: Social, Political, Economic and Cultural Perspectives* (ed. Kiran Pawar), Vision and Venture, Patiala, 1996.

'Karachi and its Hinterland under Colonial Rule', *Ports and Their Hinterlands in India, 1700-1950* (ed. Indu Banga), Manohar, New Delhi, 1992.

'Historical Causation', *Philosophy of Science* (ed. Jayant V. Narlikar et al.), Indian Institute of Advanced Study, Shimla, 1992.

'The Emergence of Hindu Consciousness in Colonial Punjab', *Self-Images, Identity and Nationality* (ed. P.C. Chatterjee), Indian Institute of Advanced Study, Shimla, 1989.

'Social Structure, Religious Ideology and Political Articulation: The Sikhs of the Punjab', Presidential Address: Modern Section, Indian History Congress, 49th Session, Dharwad, 1988.

'Crisis of Sikh Politics, 1940-47', *Sikh History and Religion in the*

Twentieth Century (eds. Joseph T. O' Connell et al.), Centre for South Asian Studies, University of Toronto, 1988.

'Custom, Land and Law in the Pre-Colonial Punjab: A Note', *Proceedings Indian History Congress*, Amritsar, 1985.

'Ranjit Singh at Work', *Maharaja Ranjit Singh: Politics, Society and Economy* (ed. Fauja Singh and A.C. Arora), Punjabi University, Patiala, 1984.

'Perspectives on Peasantry in India', *Journal of Social Science Research*, Panjab University, 1982, vol. VII, nos.1-2.

'Formation of a Regional State in Medieval India', Symposium on the State in Indian History, *Proceedings Indian History Congress*, Kurukshetra, 1982.

'The Ruling Class Under Ranjit Singh', *Journal of Regional History*, Guru Nank Dev University, 1982, vol. III.

'Agrarian Roots of Urbanization: The Case of Medieval Batala', *Proceedings Indian History Congress*, Bodh Gaya, 1981.

'Sikh Polity during the Eighteenth Century', *Proceedings Punjab History Conference*, Patiala, 1981.

'The Maharaja Orders: A Study of 462 Parwanas', *Journal of Regional History*, 1981, vol. II.

'Bibliography of Urban Studies in India', *Newsletter: I*, Urban History Association of India, 1981.

'Polity, Economy and Urbanization in the Upper Bari Doab, 1700-1947', *Studies in Urban History* (ed. J.S. Grewal and Indu Banga), Guru Nanak Dev University, Amritsar, 1981.

'Social Mobility in the Punjab Under Maharaja Ranjit Singh', *Maharaja Ranjit Singh and His Times* (ed. J.S. Grewal and Indu Banga), Guru Nanak Dev University, Amritsar, 1980.

'State Formation Under Sikh Rule', *Journal of Regional History*, 1980, vol. I.

'Presidential Address: Medieval Punjab', *Proceedings Punjab History Conference*, Patiala, 1980.

'The Jagirdari System of Maharaja Ranjit Singh in the Light of His Orders', *Proceedings Indian History Congress*, Waltair, 1979.

'Ala Singh: The Founder of a State', *The Panjab Past and Present: Essays in Honour of Dr. Ganda Singh* (ed. Harbans Singh and N. Gerald Barrier), Punjabi University, Patiala, 1976.

'The Agrarian System of Ranjit Singh', *Proceedings Indian History Congress*, Aligarh, 1975.

'Sikh Revenue Administration: The Framework', *Studies in Local and Regional History* (ed. J.S. Grewal), Guru Nanak Dev University, Amritsar, 1974.

'Nature of Sikh Rule', *Proceedings Punjab History Conference*, Patiala, 1972.

'Religious Land Grants under Sikh Rule', *Proceedings Punjab History Conference*, Patiala, 1971.

'Ranjit Singh, the Suzerain', *Proceedings Punjab History Conference*, Patiala, 1970.

'Ahmad Shah Abdali's Designs over the Punjab', *Proceedings Indian History Congress*, Patiala, 1967.

Introduction

REETA GREWAL

In the history of the Punjab during the past five centuries, the Sikhs have emerged as a conspicuous component of the society. Understandably, therefore, a number of papers we received related to Sikh themes. They cover Sikh ideology, society, politics and culture. These are the aspects of Sikh tradition in which Professor Banga has taken academic interest to gain eminence as one of the few non-Sikh historians of the Sikhs. We are thankful to the contributors who have made this volume possible as a tribute to Professor Banga.

I

Four papers relate essentially to the precolonial phase of Sikh history. Professor J.S. Grewal argues that Sikhism arose as a new faith from its very beginning in the early sixteenth century. Bhai Gurdas projects the path of Guru Nanak as transcending the paths of both Hindus and Muslims living in a state of constant confrontation. However, Guru Nanak does not talk in terms of Hindu-Muslim confrontation. He is more concerned with their common or peculiar limitations. The political domination of Muslims was embodied in the Turko-Afghan rule which was oppressive, corrupt, and discriminatory. Guru Nanak is critical of both the rulers and the ruling class. However, the ruling class was not entirely Muslim: it had a component of Khatris and Brahmans also, besides the non-Muslim *chaudharis* and *muqaddams* in the countryside. There was no difference between the Hindu and Muslim orthodoxies, both alien to the idea of loving devotion. The Sufis were better than the *mullas*, but they too were closely aligned with the state and depended on its patronage. The Jogis were better than the traditional Shaivas but their asceticism and renunciation, coupled with their presumption that self-effort alone could lead to liberation, made them irrelevant for Guru Nanak. The Vaishnava *bhaktas* were no better than the Pandit: their belief in incarnation, their idol-worship, the song and dance as a mode of worship among them, made them ridiculous in the eyes of Guru Nanak. The only set of people appreciated by Guru Nanak in general terms were *sadhs* and *sants*. However, the view put forward by W.H. McLeod that Guru Nanak was a Sant, like Kabir, is not tenable. They do share some common concepts but even so the differences of emphasis are quite pronounced. Guru Nanak rejects asceticism and renunciation but Kabir accepts both. Kabir lays emphasis on *ahimsa*, but Guru Nanak does not. Kabir showed no interest in institutionalization on the basis of his ideas; Guru Nanak laid the foundation of all the important Sikh institutions: the Guru, the *Granth*, and the Gurdwara. Professor Grewal concludes that Guru Nanak founded a new faith as the basis of a new kind of social order.

Karamjit Malhotra has translated and analysed the earliest dated manual on the Sikh way of life in the context of the study of a distinct genre of Sikh literature known as the *rahitnama*. Called *Nasihatnama*, this manual, dated 1718-19, is a copy. W.H. McLeod has argued that the original could have been composed within a few years of Guru Gobind Singh's death in 1708. This in itself is a very important inference. Most of the scholars had believed till recently that the earliest *rahitnamas* were composed several decades after the death of Guru Gobind Singh. Karamjit suggests that there is nothing in the *Nasihatnama* to go against the assumption that it was actually composed in the lifetime of Guru Gobind Singh between 1699 and 1708. The manual relates to the religious life of the Sikhs, their ethical values, and their political aspirations. The first two are clearly linked with the earlier Sikh tradition: worship of one God, dedication to the Guru, veneration for the Shabad, Nam and Gurbani (the *Granth*), the daily participation in *kirtan* and *katha* in the *dharmsal*, the ideal of *nam*, *dan* and *isnan*, equality, earnest living, charity, and goodwill for all. The third feature is new: the duty of the Khalsa is to bear arms, to ride horses, to fight in the van, and to subdue the enemy. The objective before the Khalsa is to establish sovereign rule. Indeed, there is the well-known prophecy which has become a part of the Khalsa anthem: *Raj Karega Khalsa* (the Khalsa shall rule). If Karamjit Malhotra's understanding of the *Nasihatnama* is correct, and there is no reason to believe that it is not, her discovery is not only dramatic but revolutionary in its own small but significant way.

Professor Iqtidar Alam Khan presents some fresh insights into the martial and political culture of the Khalsa. The initial steps in the direction of organized power were taken by Guru Arjan by appointing *masands* and compiling the Holy Granth. Rejecting many of the prejudices that divided Hindus and Muslims as well as the high and low castes among them, the Sikhs came to believe that they were neither Hindu or Muslim, and their preceptor was the true king. The growing importance of the Sikhs was acknowledged by Akbar, Prince Khusrau and Jahangir in their own way. The martyrdom of Guru Arjan triggered off the process of militarization. The increasing hostility of the Mughal state, particularly under Aurangzeb, provided the manifest aim of overthrowing the Mughal rule in those parts of the Punjab where it was vulnerable from the proximity of the recalcitrant hill chiefs. Already in the time of Guru Hargobind, armed bands were organized, on a pattern taken from the adversaries, with a certain ratio of horsemen and musketeers. Professor Khan points out that the musket was next in importance to the sword from the very beginning. The use of cannon was adopted in the time of Guru Gobind Singh and Banda Bahadur. The Khalsa of Guru Gobind Singh were not mercenaries but devoted followers in faith. Their distinctive culture seems to have survived down to the late eighteenth century. The contemporary Nur Muhammad praises their chivalry, integrity and their regard for women, irrespective of their age or creed. In the art of musketry the Khalsa had no match. Having learnt the art of using musket from horseback, they used their light cavalry with devastating effect. Finally, Professor Khan points out that the Khalsa are wrongly presented as defenders of Hinduism against the onslaught of Islam. In the *Zafarnama*, Guru Gobind Singh criticizes Aurangzeb as a ruler, but he does not criticize Islam. If anything, he criticizes Hinduism in a sense when he says in the *Zafarnama*: 'I have killed the recalcitrant hillmen who worship images and I am a breaker of images'.

Professor B.N. Goswamy has written a comprehensive paper on painting, bringing out the role of state patronage. Painting in the Punjab plains goes back to the sixteenth century. In the seventeenth-eighteenth centuries, painting flourished in the hills as well. There is credible evidence that some Pahari painters worked for the early Sikh chiefs and then came to Lahore in the time of Maharaja Ranjit Singh. William Barr saw paintings that adorned the walls at Lahore, Patti, Wazirabad, Gujranwala and Peshawar. The Maharaja and his courtiers patronized painting. The Sikh themes included idealized portraits of the ten Gurus. Portraiture in general was done on a considerable scale, but there was a great deal of other work too. There was no sharp demarcation between Sikh and Hindu themes. While sets of portraits of the great Gurus and *janamsakhi* series were produced in the hill areas, works based on Sanskrit and Hindi texts were made by painters active in the Punjab plains. Apart from the kingdom of Lahore, the states of Patiala, Nabha, Jind and Kapurthala patronized painters from Rajasthan and the hills. Professor Goswamy describes the art of painting in Patiala in fascinating detail. Builders, painters, poets and musicians were patronized at several places. Nearly all activity was marked by a catholicity of approach, and a decided liberality of outlook. In a remarkable painting of procession apparently of Maharaja Narinder Singh, the focus of the artist is on *Guru Granth Sahib* and the Maharaja is only a follower in the procession. Professor Goswamy points out that, during the second half of the nineteenth century, some of the eminent Sikh painters successfully met the challenge from European art, placing the same marked emphasis on close observation and correspondence.

II

Five papers relate to the colonial period. Anurupita Kaur has analysed the early census reports, pointing out that the first striking feature of the data is the increase in the number of Sikhs from less than 1.8 million in 1868 to nearly 2.7 million in 1901, their percentage in the total population going up from 6.5 to nearly

14. The largest number of Sikhs were in the districts of Amritsar, Lahore, Jalandhar, Ludhiana and Ferozepur. The numbers increased in all these and several other districts. However, even the highest percentage of Sikhs in the total population in a district remained less than 30. Only a small proportion of Sikhs, less than 7 per cent, lived in towns or cities. The ratio of females to males was also remarkably adverse, less than 770 females per 1,000 males, though the figure varied from caste to caste. By far the most dominant caste among the Sikhs was that of the Jats who numbered over a million. The Tarkhans and Chuhras, who were next to the Jats, were not much more than 100,000. The Khatris and Aroras together were about 75,000. The Kalals, Mahtams and Banias were less than 10,000 each. Information on the Sikhs in the princely states was much less detailed, but the broad demographic trends were rather similar. The Sikhs were generally seen divided into the followers of Guru Nanak and Guru Gobind Singh, that is Nanakpanthi Sikhs and Khalsa Singhs. For the purpose of the census till 1901 only the latter were regarded as Sikhs. In 1911, for the first time, all Sikhs were enabled to return themselves as Sikhs. Consequently, there was an extraordinary increase in the number of Sikhs, more than 37 per cent. Obviously, the Nanakpanthi Sikhs, who were not returned as Sikhs earlier, swelled the ranks. Their insistence on being returned as Sikhs had a close bearing on the issue of identity: not only the Khalsa Singhs but also the Nanakpanthi Sikhs, by and large, had come to regard themselves as distinct from Hindus. There were a large number of identities within each of the two broad categories of Nanakpanthi Sikhs and Khalsa Singhs. The number and proportion of the latter, on the whole, was much larger than the number and proportion of the former. The rise of the Singh Sabha movement tended to reinforce this trend.

Professor Joginder Singh has analysed the Sikh periodical literature of the first two decades of the twentieth century to depict very clearly the transition from the socioreligious concerns of late nineteenth century to the explicitly political concerns of early twentieth century. The number of Sikh weekly, fortnightly and monthly periodicals in the first two decades of the twentieth century was more than thirty (in Punjabi, Urdu and English). Associated with them were teachers, lawyers, physicians and servicemen who were directly or indirectly linked with the Singh Sabhas. The periodicals like the *Khalsa Samachar* and the *Khalsa Advocate* emphasized the importance of the Khalsa *rahit*, the observance of the Sikh rites of birth, marriage and death, and the distinct identity of Sikhism and the Sikhs. Nearly all the periodicals emphasized the importance of Anglo-Sikh education for boys and girls, attaching special importance to Punjabi language and the Gurmukhi script. They pleaded with the government that the medium of primary education in the Punjab should be Punjabi. Mismanagement of the historic Gurdwaras attracted the attention of all the Sikh periodicals. The demolition of the wall of Gurdwara Rakabganj in Delhi led to an agitation against the government. Implicit in this anti-British stance was rejection of the loyalist politics of the Chief Khalsa Diwan. After the Lucknow Pact between the Indian National Congress and the All India Muslim League in 1916, the Sikh periodicals advocated separate representation and weightage for the Sikhs. In due course, a political organization, the Central Sikh League, was launched, inaugurated in the Bradlaugh Hall at Lahore on the day of protest against the Rowlatt Bills, 30 March 1919. It was a momentous political event, providing an alternative to the Chief Khalsa Diwan. Sikh resurgence had clearly acquired a political forum before the end of the second decade. The Akalis had appeared on the scene towards the end of 1920.

Dr Darshan S. Tatla has illustrated some aspects of the Sikh resurgence at the beginning of the twentieth century through the activities of Teja Singh who was one among several Sikh reformers to play a prominent part in creating new consciousness among the Sikhs. With M.A. and LL.B. degrees from the Punjab University he became Vice-Principal of Khalsa College at Amritsar in 1904 where he came into contact with Sant Attar Singh during the latter's visit to Amritsar. Inspired by Sant Attar Singh, Teja Singh went abroad in 1907 for higher education. He returned to the Punjab in 1913 with a Master's degree from Harvard to become the founder-principal of Akal College at Mastuana. Teja Singh also associated himself with the school for girls established at Bhasaur by another well-known Sikh reformer, Babu Teja Singh. During the Gurdwara Reform movement, Principal Teja Singh remained associated with the Shiromani Gurdwara Prabandhak

Committee. For some time, he acted as the Jathedar of the Akal Takht. He was closely associated with Maharaja Ripudaman Singh of Nabha who was removed from his *gaddi* in July 1923 for his prolonged resistance to the paramount power. However, politics remained subordinate to Teja Singh's interest in religion and education. Dr Tatla has given a detailed account of his activities in Europe and North America for over five years, establishing three important Gurdwaras, countering the media stereotype of Sikhs as ignorant rural peasants, rallying them for a common cause, and forcing the Canadian politicians and administrators to take South Asian concerns seriously.

Dr Mohinder Singh takes up the controversial issue of the involvement of the Shiromani Gurdwara Prabandhak Committee (SGPC) in the 'abdication' of Maharaja Ripudaman Singh. There is no doubt that the Maharaja had a close affiliation with the Akalis, but the general impression that he was deprived of his throne mainly because he championed their cause is only partially correct. Ripudaman Singh had acquired an independent and nationalistic outlook as a prince. In the Viceroy's Legislative Council in 1907-8 he openly aligned himself with non-official members like Gopal Krishna Gokhale and Rash Bihari Ghose. His speeches in the Council reflected his nationalist thinking on almost all issues. With regard to his accession to the throne in 1912, he raised strong objection to the practice of placing Indian princes on their *gaddi* by an agent of the British Government. He looked upon his accession as valid without any official sanction or ceremony. As a ruler too he challenged the authority of the British officers whenever he could. He resented unwarranted interference of the Government of India in the internal affairs of his state. He had thus incurred serious displeasure of the British officials who found the opportunity to settle the score during his dispute with Maharaja Bhupinder Singh of Patiala. The Enquiry Officer, Justice Stuart, held both the rulers guilty of one or the other offence. However, while the Maharaja of Patiala received indemnity, Maharaja Ripudaman Singh was made to abdicate in favour of his minor son and removed to Dehradun on 9 July 1923. Dr Mohinder Singh observes that the Maharaja's association with the Akalis hastened his fall, but his dissociation from them could not have saved him. The SGPC was not competent to take up a political issue like the restoration of Maharaja Ripudaman Singh but the 'extremist' Akalis were not bothered about technical or legal niceties, taking the plea that his removal from Nabha was 'a side-attack' on the Akali movement. The government treated the whole issue as a matter of prestige and adopted unjust, illegal and violent measures to suppress the *morcha* which was prolonged due to the obstinacy of the Akalis as well. Eventually, the national and Sikh leaders advised the Akalis to give up agitation over the restoration of Maharaja Ripudaman Singh. The SGPC adopted a lukewarm attitude. The Maharaja also realized the weakness of the Akalis and dissociated himself from the agitation. In this situation, the Gurdwaras Act was passed in 1925, but the issue of restoration was virtually given up. The long agitation stiffened the attitude of the government towards the Maharaja; he was removed to Kodaikanal early in 1928. Neither the Maharaja nor the Akalis gained anything from the prolonged Jaito Morcha.

The indictment of Patiala was in a sense a sequel to the Nabha affair. Kuldeep Kaur Grewal places the Patiala Enquiry of 1930 in the context of the control of the paramount power over princely states in India. Political, legal or statutory enquiry could be instituted for serious crimes or maladministration in a princely state. In the case of Patiala, however, the initiative did not come from the Indian Government but from Indian politicians. The Indian States' People's Conference (ISPC) appointed an Enquiry Committee to go into the charges levelled against the Maharaja of Patiala by the 'citizens' of Patiala and the leaders of the Punjab Riyasati Praja Mandal. The report of the Enquiry Committee, published as the *Indictment of Patiala*, was submitted to the government as presenting a *prima facie* case for a formal enquiry. Maharaja Bhupinder Singh of Patiala was Chancellor of the Chamber of Princes at this time, having subserved imperial interests for two decades. Lord Irwin, the Viceroy, felt that the charges were too serious to be ignored. The Agent to the Governor-General, J.A.O Fitzpatrick, was all out to help the Maharaja. Eventually, a way out was planned in consultation with the Secretary of State for India. Fitzpatrick himself was appointed to conduct the enquiry on a formal request from the Maharaja himself. As expected, Fitzpatrick exonerated the Maharaja of all charges. In the process, he blamed Maharaja Ripudaman Singh of actively planning agitation against Maharaja Bhupinder Singh, and recommended curtailment of his allowance as a political prisoner in Kodaikanal. Kuldeep Grewal gives a fascinating account of the whole affair on the basis of documentary evidence. It was a telling comment on the working of the paramountcy. A prince who was loyal to the British was rescued from a grave situation through an enquiry that was merely a farce. The crucial consideration for the paramount power in its relations with the Indian princes was political, and not constitutional, legal or moral.

III

The paper by Professor Gopal Krishan links the colonial period with contemporary times. Two other papers relate to contemporary history. The last paper by Professor Gurinder Singh Mann covers the entire span of Sikh history.

Professor Gopal Krishan points out that Sikh population in 1881 was 1.85 million and in 2001 it was 21 million; in 1881, the Sikhs formed 0.9 per cent of the total population of India and their percentage in 2001 was 1.9; in 1881, 93 per cent of the Sikhs lived in the Punjab, and in 2001 their percentage was 76. In 1881, the number of Sikhs outside India could be counted in thousands and in 2001 nearly 2 million Sikhs were living outside India. Professor Gopal Krishan has studied these changing patterns in fascinating detail in two broad phases: the first from 1881 to 1941, and the second from 1951 to 2001. He has paid special attention to the process by which the Sikhs have settled abroad. The distributional pattern of the Sikh population can now be described as 'high concentration coupled with wide scattering'. In 1881, the Sikh population was concentrated mainly between the rivers Ravi and Ghaggar. A large number of Sikhs settled in the canal colonies beyond the Ravi during the colonial period. The distributional pattern of the Sikhs underwent a phenomenal change after 1947. By far the largest majority settled in the Indian Punjab and their concentration in a number of contiguous districts carried the possibility of creating a state with Sikh majority, which was realized in 1966. A large number of Sikhs are living in the adjoining states of Haryana, Rajasthan and

Uttar Pradesh, and Sikhs have migrated to capital, industrial and cantonment cities of the eastern states, Maharashtra, Gujarat and Rajasthan. Even more striking than migration within India is the Sikh migration to other countries, especially to Great Britain, Canada and the United States. The Sikh population in India constitutes less than 2 per cent of its total population, but the percentage of Sikhs among the Indians abroad is no less than 7.

Dr Shinder Singh Thandi has studied the impact of foreign remittances on the agrarian economy of a few Sikh villages in the Jalandhar district in the late 1960s and the early 1970s. All these villages had adopted the technology of green revolution and all of them had a substantial proportion of its landholders living in UK. Evidence gathered from fieldwork strongly indicates that remittances and their utilization enhanced the process of capitalist differentiation of the peasantry, increased land values, and resulted in concentration of holding in landed property. However, there were difficulties involved in accumulation through expansion of the physical area of farms. The alternative, therefore, was 'capital intensification'. Rich peasants were able to establish themselves as the dominant tenants. Adequately backed by overseas remittances, they emerged as full-fledged capital farmers, hiring permanent labour particularly from the eastern states. Dr Thandi concludes that overseas migration undoubtedly facilitated the emergence of a class of dominant tenants who were already socially, politically and economically powerful. Migration and remittances fuelled the process both in terms of increasing economic concentration and the newly emerging property relations.

After a brief review of literature on the Punjab problem, Professor J.S. Grewal points out that in the world of politics and scholarship the term generally used for Sikh politics is 'communal' or 'fundamental'. No distinction is made between the constitutional movement for greater autonomy for the states in India and the militant movement for a sovereign Sikh state, called Khalistan, presumably because both get related to Sikh identity. Professor Grewal himself elaborates the point of Khalsa or Singh identity shared by the Akalis and the protagonists of Khalistan, and how this identity has evolved historically. Outlining the history of the Akalis, he underscores the point that their politics, though vociferously based on Sikh identity, have been constitutional or agitational and never militant, and their objective has been territorial reorganization to ensure for themselves the largest possible share in political power within the Indian union of states. Occasional deviation was more or less tactical or wholly visionary. The movement for Khalistan is generally associated with Sant Jarnail Singh Bhindranwale, but it started actually after his death in the Operation Blue Star in June 1984, and it gained momentum after the failure of the Rajiv-Longowal Accord. Professor Grewal hammers the point that, though it may be tempting to see the objective of autonomy leading logically to the objective of sovereign rule, historically there is no inevitable link between religious identity and political sovereignty.

Professor Gurinder Singh Mann's paper covers the entire span of Sikh history for outlining the Sikh educational heritage. By the end of the Guru period in 1708, the Sikh educational heritage contained literature in five different areas: *Guru Granth*; the writings of Bhai Gurdas as the core interpretative literature; the rudimentary statements pertaining to *rahit* emerging as an autonomous genre called the *rahitnamas*; the *janamsakhi* literature; and the poetry recorded in the *Dasam Granth*. The three middle categories developed further in the eighteenth century, especially the *gurbilas* as an extension of interest in the lives of the Gurus. In the early nineteenth century, Ratan Singh Bhangu's *Guru Panth Prakash* went beyond the Janamsakhi and the Gurbilas as a work of history; the works of Bhai Santokh Singh became a sort of transition to the later period. After annexation of the Punjab in 1849, more attention was given to *Guru Granth* and the *rahitnama* literature was systematized; the *janamsakhi* and *gurbilas* literature began to be published. However, the literary and historical context of the literature produced in the time of Guru Gobind Singh has yet to be firmly understood. In the pre-colonial period, Sikh heritage was transmitted by the Gurus and their representatives, the mother in the family, the village Gurdwara, and large Sikh centres of learning at Amritsar and Talwandi Sabo. Even independent scholars were available to teach. The schools attached to Gurdwaras slowly went out of existence during the colonial period but the Gurdwara itself survived. The need of *granthis* for the Gurdwaras increased, and Sikh seminaries continued to train individuals as *granthis*. The mainstream Sikh leaders expanded the boundaries of education by incorporating the contents of Western education in schools and colleges for boys and girls. The Khalsa College at Amritsar was an outstanding example. After independence, the Punjabi University and Guru Nanak Dev University were established. The arrival of modernity coincided with Sikh emigration from the Punjab and the community's spread all over the globe. Gurdwaras, summer camps, and Sikh schools transmit Sikh heritage to Sikh boys and girls abroad. Voluntary organizations have been formed for this purpose. The products of the indigenous Sikh education have constituted the primary strand for the dissemination of Sikh education, e.g. Bhai Santokh Singh, Tara Singh Narotam, Giani Gian Singh, Sant Gurbachan Singh, and Jathedar Joginder Singh. Among the other products of indigenous Sikh education are those who moved out of the religious setting like Piara Singh Padam. Another set of scholars have written only in English for a different readership, e.g. J.D. Cunningham, Ernest Trumpp, Max Arthur Macauliffe and W.H. McLeod. These include Sikh scholars trained in Western modes of education like J.S. Grewal. There are still others like Harjot Oberoi who apply Western ideas to the Sikh tradition. Given all these strands, differences of interpretation may be expected. During the twentieth century, particularly in the past few decades, controversies have arisen about the text, message and history of the Sikh scripture, with special reference to the Kartarpur Pothi, the lives of Guru Gobind Singh and Guru Hargobind, the death of Guru Tegh Bahadur, and the authorship of the *Dasam Granth*. The SGPC also gets involved in these controversies. The complex interplay of people and points of view does not get explained by looking at the situation as an attempt of the Sikh religious authority to re-assert itself or as a conflict between traditional and historical scholarship. As the community continues to reflect on the issues of Sikh educational heritage, the Sikh tradition would advance further towards becoming a major actor on the stage of world religions.

1

Foundation of the Sikh Faith

J.S. GREWAL

Tracing what may loosely be regarded as the history of religious dispensations in India, Bhai Gurdas comes close to his own times, the early seventeenth century, and observes that there were four *varnas* among the Hindus and four schools (*mazhabs*) among the Muslims. Engrossed in self-conceit, niggardliness of spirit and pride, they pointlessly pulled in different directions. The Ganges and Benares were sacred to the Hindus and Mecca and Ka'aba to the Muslims. Circumcision was sacrosanct among the Muslims; the sacred thread (*janju*) and the sacred mark (*tilak*) among the Hindus. Giving the name of Ram or Rahim to one God, they ignorantly created two ways. Forgetting the Vedas and the *Quran* (*kateb*) they were led astray by greed and earthly attachment. Locked in a deadly contention, the Brahman and the Mulla missed the truth. They remained subject to the chain of transmigration.[1]

As Bhai Gurdas puts it, the fog of ignorance was lifted by Guru Nanak and darkness vanished with the rising of the sun. Truth was proclaimed in all the nine regions of the earth. At last, the Gurmukh was made manifest in the Dark Age (*kaljug*).[2] Guru Nanak was sent by the Merciful One to save the crying humanity. He showed the path of humility to his Sikhs in the worship of one God; he spread the fully restored *dharma* among all the four *varnas*, making no distinction between the prince and the pauper. True to his mission, Guru Nanak saved the world in the Dark Age by proclaiming the true Name (*satnam*).[3] The true Name is the only means of liberation. They who take refuge in the Guru receive the gift of liberation through the true Word (*sat sabad*).[4]

II

Bhai Gurdas gives trenchant expression to the idea that Sikhism arose in a context of religious contention. But how did Guru Nanak look upon Hindus and Muslims of his day? Guru Nanak refers to the dominance of Islam in the Dark Age when God is called Allah and blue dress is current. The dominance of Islam is intimately linked with the establishment of Turko-Afghan rule.[5] The *shaikhs* are an integral part of this new dispensation. Now that the turn of the *shaikhs* had come, the *ad-purakh* was called Allah; such was now the custom that gods and their temples were taxed.[6] Babur's troops, the marriage party of sin, indulged in the rape of innocent women and the murder of unarmed men (the subject people).[7]

Guru Nanak had no sympathy with the rulers who lorded over the people and indulged in luxuries – fleet-footed caparisoned horses, colourful *harems*, tall mansions, pleasures of all kinds.[8] The *Babur-vani* verses should be read in this context and not only as a kind of nemesis:

> Where are now the sports, the stables and horses, the trumpets and clarions? Where are now the sword-belts, the carriages and the scarlet tunics? Where are now the mirrors and the handsome faces? They are nowhere to be seen.

Again:

> Where are now the mansions, palaces and seraglios? Where are now the soft beds and the beautiful women whose sight banished sleep? Where are the betels and the *harems*? They have all vanished.[9]

The rulers were corrupt. They dispensed justice, not in the name of God (Khuda) but when their palm was greased.[10] The *qazi*, the kingpin of the administration of justice, ate an unlawfully earned food, comparable to dirt.[11] Furthermore, the rulers oppressed the subject people. The *rajas* acted like lions and the *muqaddams* like dogs; they fell upon the *raiyat* day and night. The officials of the state inflicted wounds to kill the prey and 'the dogs', their servants, ate its liver and licked its blood.[12] It must be noted that, even if *rajas* are taken to be the Afghan rulers, all the *muqaddams* could not be Muslim. Obviously, the Hindu *muqaddams* collaborated with the rulers in their oppression of the common people. Guru Nanak leaves no doubt that Brahmans and Khatris were among the collaborators of the Afghan rulers. The *pandit* is asked to discard deceit. He has adopted the manners of the Turks; he reads the *Quran* in public but inside the home he performs *puja*; he wears *dhoti, tikka* and *mala*, but eats the food of those whom he regards as *mlechh*. Above all, he regards the cow-dung as sacred but taxes the cow and the Brahman.[13]

'They who perform *namaz* eat human beings; they who wear the sacred thread wield the knife.' The latter are supposed to be the Khatris in the service of the state. The Brahmans perform services for them and partake of their ill-gotten food. With the sacred mark on their forehead and *dhoti* on their waist, these Khatris wield the knife like butchers; they wear blue dress to become acceptable to the rulers; they eat the food of the *mlechh* but profess to believe in the Puranas; they forbid others to enter their *chauka* (cooking-place) but they themselves eat (*halal*) mutton.[14] Explicitly too, Guru Nanak castigates the Khatri collaborator for adopting the language of the *mlechh* and discarding his traditional *dharma*.[15] Neither the Khatri nor the Brahman was performing his duties in accordance with the *varna* ideal. The ideal stood glaringly infringed and yet the Khatris and Brahmans held on to it. Their position was utterly false, a mere pretence. What made this pretence inevitable was their willing acceptance of an unjust state.

Collaboration with the state was the flaw of the Sufis as well. It is generally believed that Guru Nanak had great appreciation for the Sufis. We have noted already that the *shaikhs* stand allied with those who tax gods and temples. They stand bracketed with the other categories of Muslims who claim exclusive veracity for Islam: along with *qazis* and *mullas*, the *pirs* and *shaikhs* continue to pray for blessings but 'Allah does not consult anyone when He makes or unmakes; He alone knows his power; He alone is the doer. He watches everyone and bestows His grace on whomever He wills.'[16] Elsewhere, however, the *ulama* who expound the *shari'at* are told that only he who becomes God's slave is a true Musalman.[17] Indeed, to be a true Musalman one should adopt the path of the *auliya*, cultivate detachment, and willingly accept what is decreed by God, but the *shaikh* suffers from *haumai* (self-centredness) as much as the *qazi*.[18] Presumptuous of his own place of honour with God, the *shaikh* gives this assurance to others as well. His position is compared to that of the rat which is too fat to enter the hole and yet ties a winnowing basket (*chhaj*) to its tail. He does not have trust in God either: he receives revenue-free land from the state (which is unjust).[19]

III

Guru Nanak's view of contemporary Hindus is not much different. The Shaktas are summarily condemned (possibly for a ritual that involved drinking of alcohol and indulgence in sexual intercourse) – like the Jain monks who are denounced primarily for their atheism. The *pandit* is a blind follower of tradition, devoid of any serious thinking.[20] He himself does not know, but he teaches others; he runs his shop on falsehood.[21] He is comparable with the spider that weaves its web all the time, living and dying upside down: he talks of the Vedas and the Shastras but pursues worldly occupations; this pretence does not cleanse his inner dirt.[22] The sacred thread and the sacred mark are of no avail.[23] They are useless or irrelevant in the eyes of Guru Nanak. On the authority of the Vedas, the Shastras and the Puranas, the *pandit* tries to uphold much that has become irrelevant, useless or harmful – social customs and ceremonies as well as religious beliefs, rites and practices.

The *jogis* are often mentioned with the *pandit* and the *pir*. One cannot get rid of pride (*garb*) by smearing the body with ash.[24] Like blind fools, the *jogi* lives in the wilderness or sits in the cremation ground. He begs for food and clothing. He sits in meditation and yet indulges in wrangling every day. He hankers after supernatural powers.[25] He does not know what is real *jog*:

> *Jog* does not lie in the cloak, nor in the staff, nor in smearing the body with ash; it does not consist in ear-rings, nor in shaving the hair, nor in blowing the horn; it is attained by living pure amidst the impurities of attachment.[26]

Guru Nanak castigates the *jogis* for their lack of concern for the people and their assumption that they can attain to the state of *sahaj* with self-effort alone, without the grace of God.

It may come to some scholars as a surprise that Guru Nanak

thinks of the representatives of Vaishnava *bhakti* as no better than the *jogis*.[27] But there is nothing surprising in this. In the first place, Vishnu is not God for Guru Nanak. Secondly, Guru Nanak does not subscribe to the idea of incarnation. Therefore, whatever their greatness, Rama and Krishna are human beings in his eyes. Their worship cannot have any merit. The impersonations of Krishna and Rama in dance and song, which were somewhat popular in the time of Guru Nanak, elicit no appreciation from him. In fact, they are noticed for ridicule. In the first place, acting or dancing as a profession has no moral merit.[28] Yoked to the service of religion, they become a demerit.

> The disciples play on musical instruments and the *gurus* dance; they move their feet and they move their head; dust rises to fall in their hair; people laugh and go home. They dance for bread and fall on the ground, singing of *gopis* and of Kahn, singing of Sita and of Ram.[29]

From the statement of Bhai Gurdas about the emergence of Sikhism in response to Hindu-Muslim strife we have moved into a much more complex situation in which Guru Nanak appears to approve of neither the Sufis nor the *ulama*, neither the *pandits* nor the *jogis*, and not even of Vaishnava *bhakti*. The only category of people whom Guru Nanak positively appreciates are the *sants*. For example, 'there is no access to the company of *sants* without the Guru'.[30] Quite obviously, the company of *sants* is cherishable. However, the '*sants*' of Guru Nanak have to be carefully identified.

IV

W.H. McLeod places Guru Nanak squarely in the *sant tradition* as a synthesis of elements drawn from Vaishnava *bhakti* and the *hatha-yoga* of Nath *jogis*, with a marginal contribution from Sufism. Among the *sants*, McLeod mentions Namdev, Ravidas and Kabir. For him, the pattern evolved by Guru Nanak is 'a reworking of the Sant synthesis'; it does not depart far from the Sant sources 'as far as its fundamental components are concerned'. Guru Nanak uses *sant* categories and *sant* terminology and affirms *sant* doctrines. However, the *sant* synthesis is amplified, clarified and integrated in considerable measure by Guru Nanak, particularly through his concepts of the Shabad, the Nam, the

Guru, and the Hukam. What we find in his works is an 'expanded and re-interpreted' *sant* thought. Within the pattern of *sant* belief Guru Nanak's synthesis possesses 'a significant originality' and 'a unique clarity'. It possesses also the quality of survival.[31]

McLeod has been criticized for his hypothesis about Guru Nanak's relationship with the *sant* tradition. However, he has not discarded his hypothesis, arguing that, whereas for a believer it may be natural to believe that his religion is a revealed religion, it is legitimate for a historian 'to explore the surrounding religious landscape and the society in which a particular religion was born'.[32] McLeod underlines the 'unqualified emphasis' of the *sants* on 'the interior nature of spiritual understanding' and 'the discipline' required for *moksha* as 'an eternal equipoise'. The ideas of incarnation, idol-worship, sacred scriptures and pilgrimages are discarded in favour of focus on the Word.[33] The stress is on the irrelevance of caste status as a means of deliverance and on the formless quality of God. The essence of *sant* belief remains loving devotion to a personal deity.[34] McLeod examines the teachings of Guru Nanak and comes to the conclusion that: 'In Guru Nanak, as in Kabir, there is the same rejection of exterior forms, the same insistence on the need for inward devotion and its sufficiency as the sole means of liberation.'[35]

Furthermore, if the question whether or not Guru Nanak was a *sant* is strictly a question of antecedents and influences, 'the answer must be in the affirmative'. This does not mean that there is no originality in the hymns of Guru Nanak. There is much that is 'profoundly original' in them and there is 'an integrated and coherent system no other *sant* has produced; there is a clarity no other Sant has matched'. Add to this the appointment of a successor by Guru Nanak. 'Nothing in the Sant experience can remotely compare to the Panth which was eventually to emerge from that decision of Guru Nanak.'[36]

McLeod dwells on shared terminology and categories of thought, and tends to think in terms of influences and borrowings, but his approach leaves out the creative response of both Kabir and Guru Nanak to their historical situation. Moreover, McLeod does not take into account what Kabir and Guru Nanak *did*, quite apart from what they *said*. Only the entire range of ideas and actions can enable us to see the differences as well as the similarities between Kabir and Guru Nanak.

V

It is true that Kabir uses the terms *nam, shabad, guru* and *hukam* in his compositions but nowhere with the kind of emphasis that we find in the compositions of Guru Nanak. Take for example the concept of *hukam*:

How is Truth to be attained,
How the veil of falsehood torn asunder?
Submit to the *hukam*; walk in its way: Nanak, thus it is written.[37]

The idea of walking in the way of *hukam* to attain Truth is nowhere to be found in Kabir. Even the concept of *hukam* is not so comprehensive in Kabir as it is in Guru Nanak:

The *hukam* is beyond describing. All forms were created by the *hukam*; life was created through the *hukam*; greatness is imparted in accordance with the *hukam*. Distinctions between what is exalted and what is lowly are the result of the *hukam* and in accordance with it suffering comes to some and joy to others. Through the *hukam* one receives blessing, and another is condemned to everlasting transmigration. All were within the *hukam*; none are beyond its authority. Nanak, if anyone comprehends the *hukam*, his *haumai* is purged.[38]

As McLeod himself says, the *hukam* is 'an all-embracing principle, the sum total of all divinely instituted laws; and it is a revelation of the nature of God'.[39] Indeed, Guru Nanak's use of *hukam* carries his thought most obviously beyond the thought of Kabir.[40] Incidentally, Guru Nanak's emphasis on divine grace (*nadar*) also carries him beyond Kabir.[41] It may be pointed out that the divine order (*hukam*) and divine grace (*nadar*) are the obverse and the reverse of the same coin: one underlines God's omnipotence and the other his kindness, without compromising his absolute power and absolute freedom.

Similarly, Guru Nanak's emphasis on the Name (*nam*) is greater than Kabir's, and the concept is more comprehensive:

Through the Name, one can cross the ocean of existence. Through the Name one can obtain the secret of true worship and honour. The Name is one's best ornament, intellect and objective. Through the Name one gets recognition from others; without the Name there can be no honour. All other wisdom is mere pretence; there is no fulfilment without the Name. In the Name is real power, the authority of the *diwan*, the might of the army, and the sovereignty of the *sultan*. Through the Name come true honour and greatness, and the mark of God's merciful grace. The state of eternal bliss is found in the Name, the proper way of adoration. The Name is the nectar that purges the poison (of *maya*). Through the Name descends all happiness upon one's heart.[42]

Add to this stanza the verse:

Whatever God has made is an expression of the Name. There is no part of creation which is not an expression of God.[43]

The Name is the total expression of all that God is: the Name is the Truth. Human beings are called upon to meditate on the Name. For Kabir, too, there is no emancipation without *Ram-nam*.[44] However, we do not get the impression that the Name for Kabir holds strictly the same significance as for Guru Nanak. Indeed, it has been suggested that the Name in Guru Nanak's compositions is the creative and dynamic immanence of God.[45] McLeod himself says that Guru Nanak's concepts of the *shabad* and the Guru, as much as the concepts of the *hukam* and the *nam*, 'carry us beyond anything that the works of earlier Sants offer in any explicit form'.[46] Differences of degree tend to result in a difference of kind.

The differences between Kabir and Guru Nanak appear to arise from their conception of God. It is true that God for them is one, both transcendent and immanent. Both reject the idea of incarnation. Nevertheless, whereas Kabir tends to be monistic, Guru Nanak is emphatic about the attributes of a personal God. This Being is one, creator and sustainer of all things, immanent in his creation, without fear and without enmity, not subject to time, beyond birth and death, himself responsible for his own manifestation and known by the Guru's grace. Kabir however does not celebrate the greatness or the grace of God in the same way as Guru Nanak does:

Having heard of your greatness everyone speaks of it, but only by seeing can you know the immensity of your greatness. No one can know or express your worth. They who tell of you are gathered up into you. Great are you, my lord, ineffable and of excellences beyond comprehending. None can encompass the measure of your greatness. The exegetes gather together and expound the scripture; all extollers of your worth together try to determine that worth; men of understanding and men of contemplation, *gurus* and the *gurus* of *gurus* (who proclaim your greatness) express not even a fragment of your greatness. All truth, all austerities, all goodness, all the impressive works of *siddhas* (owe their existence to you). Without you none has scaled the mystical heights but when your grace is received, no obstacle remains. Yours is a storehouse filled with excellences beyond telling. He to whom you give support does not need any other help. Nanak declares: you are the true one and all is in your hands.[47]

There is no hymn of this kind in the compositions of Kabir, neither in *Guru Granth Sahib* nor in the *Bijak*.

The monistic tendency of Kabir's thought can be seen in some of his hymns included in the *Bijak*:

Pandit, you have got it wrong. There is no creator or creation there, no gross or fine, no wind or fire, no sun, moon, earth or water, no radiant form, no time there, no word, no flash, no faith, no cause and effect, nor any thought of the Veda. No Hari or Brahma, no Shiva or Shakti, no pilgrimage and no rituals. No mother, father or guru there. Is it two or one? Kabir says, if you understand now, you're guru, I am disciple.[48]

This is the state in which Kabir can see the ultimate reality as one. Indeed, Kabir's *Ram* tends to be the name of this ultimate reality.

It's a heavy confusion. Veda, Koran, holiness, hell, woman, man, a clay pot shot with air and sperm.... When the pot falls apart, what do you call it? Numskull! You have missed the point. It's all one skin and bone, one piss and shit, one blood, one meat. From one drop, a universe. Who's Brahmin? Who's Shudra? Brahma *rajas*, Shiva *tamas*, Vishnu *sattva*... Kabir says, plunge into Ram. There: No Hindu. No Turk.[49]

In this hymn the Hindu and the Turk are the same, the Brahman and the Shudra are the same, because they spring from the same impersonal reality. They are pots of the same clay.

There are some other important differences between Guru Nanak and Kabir. Guru Nanak rejects both asceticism and renunciation.

Meditation on the True One brings illumination and so one lives detached in the midst of evil. Such is the greatness of the True *Guru* that even surrounded by wife and sons one can attain salvation.[50]

Indeed, only he who earns with his own effort and spares something for others can recognize the path of liberation.[51] Kabir does not contest renunciation or even begging. If one can sing the praises of God in the company of *sants*, begging for food is preferable to a tall mansion full of gold and beautiful women, and a flag flying on its top.[52] Begging is better than staking a claim to territory and political power.[53] A householder should either practise *dharma* as a householder or adopt *bairag*; if a *bairagi* adopts the life of a householder, it is a misfortune.[54] Kabir's tolerance of mendicancy and renunciation go together: the renunciant has to depend on others for subsistence. This is something that is ridiculed by Guru Nanak in his contest with the *jogis*.

Guru Nanak has no objection to meat-eating but Kabir is strongly in favour of *ahimsa*. It is interesting to note that Kabir rejects the idea of incarnation at one place on the argument that God is too kind to go around killing goblins as a turtle or a fish. Parashuram never slew any princes, *maya* pulled that trick. With cowherds and milkmaids, God did not come to Gokul to kill Kansa. God is gracious, everyone's lord; he does not conquer, does not defeat.[55] One reason for Kabir's condemnation of the Brahman is that he is a slicked-down butcher; he slaughters a goat and rushes for a buffalo; with a sandalpaste on his brow he does a song and dance for the goddess and crushes souls in the wink of an eye – the river of blood flows on.[56] The *qazi* is no different: he slaughters cows.[57] He turns a living soul into a corpse and calls it a holy rite.[58] Kabir tells the *qazi*:

> What kind of work is that, going from house to house chopping heads? Who gave the order for chickens and goats? Who told you to swing the knife? ... Fast all day, kill cows at night, here prayers, there blood; does this please God?[59]

Kabir tells the *pandit* to be kind to created beings and take care of them; without living beings, a living being cannot live; life is the basis of life.[60] There is no doubt that Kabir regards *ahimsa* as a mark of religious piety. To kill is to commit a grave sin:

> Don't murder a poor creature, we all share one breath. Though you hear a thousand Puranas, you won't get free of that death.

This is followed by:

> Don't murder a poor creature, he'll pay you back the same. Make pilgrimage, give a million jewels to the gods, but you won't be saved.[61]

VI

Like Guru Nanak, Kabir addresses himself to Hindus and Muslims, sometimes together. He associates the Turk with *tariqat* or the path of the Sufis, and he associates the Hindu with Veda and the Puranas.[62] What may be regarded as Hindu and Muslim orthodoxies are both denounced by Kabir. He asserts that no one can attain liberation without the Name of God.[63] He has nothing to learn from the *pandit* and the *mulla*.[64] On the other hand, the *pandit* and the *mulla* can follow Kabir by appropriating the Name of Ram to the exclusion of everything else.[65] The Vedas and the *Quran* stand bracketed and rejected as irrelevant for Kabir's purposes. Kabir's *Ram-nam* stands opposed to the known scriptures; the Brahman and the *pandit*, the *mulla* and the *shaikh*, represent the opposite of what Kabir stands for. He ridicules their mutual antagonism as born of ignorance. The *jogi* figures no better than the *pandit*, or the *mulla*, or the *shaikh*. The terminology of the *jogis* is used by Kabir to convey his own message to them. Otherwise their practices are ridiculed and their claim to be on the right path is treated as self-conceit. They too are in need of the Name of Ram.[66]

Kabir denounces the Shaktas, particularly the left-handers who indulge in meat, liquor and sexual intercourse as a religious ritual.[67] He prefers the Vaishnava over the Shakta.[68] But the Vaishnava in his own right is not appreciated: his outward appearance conceals inner falsehood, like the gold ornament filled with *lakh*.[69] Kabir does not approve of any existing system of religious belief and practice. He denounces caste distinctions. However, towards women his attitude is ambivalent: he rejects the idea of impurity associated with the woman who has given birth to a child but he does not contest the idea of woman's subordination. Outside the home, however, she can possibly become a *bairagan*, the counterpart of the male renunciant. On the whole, Kabir's compositions contain a set of ideas which appear to suggest a system outside the system called Hindu and Muslim.

A scholar who has made a detailed study of the *Bijak* makes the following observation:

> Some modern commentators have tried to present Kabir as a synthesizer of Hinduism and Islam; but the picture is a false one. While drawing on various traditions as he saw fit, Kabir emphatically declared his independence from both the major religions of his countrymen, vigorously attacked the follies of both, and tried to kindle the fire of a similar autonomy and courage in those who claimed to be his disciples.[70]

This observation is acceptable so far as Kabir's autonomy or independence is concerned. It also brackets Kabir with Guru Nanak. Their works present systems of inter-related ideas which are independent of all other systems of religious ideas. Their positions are similar not because they belong to the same tradition but because each had a new path to show to his contemporaries. The paths were new but not the same precisely because they were differently conceived from the very beginning.

VII

Guru Nanak tried to give practical shape to his ideals, particularly when his fame had spread and disciples gathered at Kartarpur to learn from him as the acknowledged master, or Guru. Meditation upon the divine Name in the early hours and corporate singing of divine praises (*kirtan*), both in the morning and the evening, formed an essential feature of the devotional life of the disciples (who came to be known as Sikhs in the lifetime of Guru Nanak).[71] The Guru gave instruction to individuals and to regular gatherings of disciples in accordance with the ideas embodied in his compositions. His conception of disciplined worldliness enjoined continuation of normal family relationships. The practice of community meal was introduced at Kartarpur. In other words, the prototype of Gurdwara was established by Guru Nanak with its two essential features: congregational worship in which the *bani* of Guru Nanak was used, and community meal which was maintained with the voluntary contributions from the Sikhs. Before his death, Guru Nanak installed one of his disciples in his place as the Guru in preference to his sons.

A new ideology, the new institutions of guruship and the Gurdwara, and a new socioreligious fraternity can all be clearly traced to Guru Nanak. The Sikh Panth was to develop on the strong basis provided by him. When we turn to Kabir, there is no clear indication that he assumed the formal position of a *guru*, or that he established any formal mode of worship, or that he appointed a successor. It now seems probable that Kabir Panth did not come into existence for more than a century after his death. This would also explain why the Kabir 'tradition' in the *Guru Granth Sahib* is regarded by scholars as not only older but also more authentic than the *Bijak* which began to be compiled in the seventeenth century. In any case, the trajectory of the Kabir Panth bears no resemblance to that of the Sikh Panth. The differences can be explained essentially in terms of what Kabir and Guru Nanak said and did in their lifetime.

VIII

Can we understand the advent of Sikhism in terms of Guru Nanak's response to religious strife? If we listen to Bhai Gurdas, the answer is 'yes'. If we turn to Guru Nanak, however, the answer is much more qualified. In the first place, Guru Nanak uses the terms Hindu and Muslim rather rarely in his compositions, and nowhere talks of Hindu-Muslim confrontation. Nevertheless, he is acutely aware of the religiopolitical domination of Islam. He denounces the policy of discrimination followed by Muslim rulers on the basis of differences in the religious affiliation of their subjects. He also denounces the corruption of the *qazis* who administer justice and association of the Shaikhs with Muslim rule and their dependence on its patronage. Relatively speaking, Guru Nanak appreciates some of the ideas and attitudes of Sufis in comparison with the *ulama*, but both the Sufis and the *ulama* are advised to acquaint themselves with the true path discovered by him.

When it comes to oppression, the Muslim rulers and the Muslim ruling class do not stand alone; they have their collaborators among the non-Muslims, especially Khatris and Brahmans. In addition to their role as the instruments of oppression, they are castigated for the gulf between what they uphold in theory and what they actually practise. The *varna* ideal is of special importance in this context – it has lost justification in the eyes of Guru Nanak. His denunciation of caste distinctions springs from the moral ideal that all human beings deserve one and the same kind of treatment. As against the rich, the powerful and the privileged, he identifies himself with the poor, the helpless and the unprivileged. In the religious sphere he approves of neither the Brahman and his scriptures, nor the *jogis* and their practices, nor the beliefs and practices of Vaishnava *bhakti*.

Thus, Guru Nanak is critical of all major systems of religious belief and practice in his time. If we look closely at the basis of his criticism, we find that he has his own system of ideas which provides the criteria for criticism. In other words, his own ideology and his criticism of other systems are the obverse and the reverse of the same ethicospiritual coin. Guru Nanak claims that his message comes from God. Those who believe in him take his message to be literally revealed. Even metaphorically, Guru Nanak makes it absolutely clear that he invokes for his ideology no earthly scripture or spiritual or religious authority. He is on his own. Essentially, the ideology of Guru Nanak embodies his creative response not to religious strife but to the total political, social and religious situation of his days. His message was meant to transcend all contemporary dispensations. He is silent about Kabir but it is not difficult to imagine that, despite much appreciation, he would not have entirely approved of his system. Guru Nanak founded a new religion as the basis of a new social order.

NOTES

1. Giani Hazara Singh (ed.), *Varan Bhai Gurdas*, Amritsar: Khalsa Samachar, 1962, *Var* I: *pauri* 21.
2. Ibid., *Var* I, *pauri* 27.
3. Ibid., I: 23.
4. Ibid., I: 1.
5. Sahib Singh (ed.), *Asa di Var Steek*, Amritsar: Singh Brothers, 1991 (17th edn.), p. 91.
6. *Guru Granth Sahib*, p. 1191.
7. J.S. Grewal, *Guru Nanak in History*, Chandigarh: Panjab University, 1969, pp. 160-1.

8. *Asa di Var Steek*, pp. 112-13.
9. Cf. J.S. Grewal, *Guru Nanak in History*, p. 163.
10. Ibid., pp. 156-7.
11. Ibid., p. 230.
12. Ibid., p. 157.
13. *Asa di Var Steek*, pp. 105-6.
14. Ibid., p. 107.
15. *Guru Nanak in History*, p. 181 n. 72.
16. Ibid., p. 229.
17. Ibid., pp. 230-1.
18. Ibid., p. 231.
19. Ibid., p. 232.
20. Ibid., p. 210.
21. Ibid., p. 211.
22. Ibid., p. 212.
23. Ibid., p. 213.
24. Ibid., pp. 215, 216.
25. Ibid., p. 217.
26. Ibid., p. 218.
27. Ibid., p. 218.
28. *Asa di Var Steek*, p. 79.
29. Ibid., p. 45.
30. *Guru Nanak in History*, p. 240.
31. McLeod, *Guru Nanak and the Sikh Religion*, Oxford: Clarendon Press, 1969, pp. 152-8, 161.
32. Idem, *Sikhism*, Penguin Books, 1997, p. 88.
33. Ibid., pp. 91-2.
34. Ibid., p. 94.
35. Ibid., p. 101.
36. Ibid., p. 102.
37. McLeod, *Guru Nanak and the Sikh Religion*, p. 200.
38. Ibid., p. 200.
39. Ibid., p. 203.
40. Ibid., p. 191.
41. Ibid., p. 190.
42. *Guru Nanak in History*, p. 237.
43. McLeod, *Guru Nanak and the Sikh Religion*, p. 196.
44. Sahib Singh (ed.), *Steek Bhagat Bani (Kabir)*, Amritsar: Singh Brothers, 1994 (6th edn.), pp. 91, 144, 146, 151, 156, 209, 223, 235.
45. Daljeet Singh, *Essentials of Sikhism*, Amritsar: Singh Brothers, 1994, p. 60.
46. McLeod, *Guru Nanak and the Sikh Religion*, p. 161.
47. Ibid., pp. 176-7.

48. Linda Hess and Shukdev Singh (trs.), *The Bijak of Kabir*, San Francisco: North Point Press, 1983, p. 56.
49. Ibid., p. 67.
50. Bhai Jodh Singh (ed.), *Kabir Bani Steek*, Patiala: Punjabi University, p. 212.
51. Ibid., p. 211.
52. Ibid., p. 239.
53. Ibid., p. 242.
54. Ibid., p. 256.
55. Hess and Singh, *The Bijak*, p. 45.
56. Ibid., p. 46.
57. Ibid., p. 57.
58. Ibid., p. 69.
59. Ibid., pp. 87-8.
60. Ibid., p. 111.
61. Ibid., p. 115.
62. Bhai Jodh Singh, *Kabir Bani Steek*, p. 65.
63. Ibid., p. 22.
64. Ibid., p. 186.
65. Ibid., pp. 184, 219-20.
66. Ibid., pp. 3, 6, 30, 44-5, 47, 122, 124, 14, 163, 167-8, 183, 189, 211.
67. Ibid., p. 89.
68. Ibid., p. 222.
69. Ibid., p. 238.
70. Hess and Singh, *The Bijak*, p. 5.
71. In the *Japji*, for example, the word 'Sikh' is used for both the instruction of the Guru and the person who has received this instruction. The facile suggestion that the word 'Sikh' (*sishya*) means a student or a learner ignores this fact. A Sikh, obviously, is a person who has imbibed Guru Nanak's instruction as his disciple.

2

The Earliest Manual on the Sikh Way of Life

KARAMJIT K. MALHOTRA

While referring to a manuscript in the Library of Guru Nanak Dev University, W.H. McLeod has observed that it was 'a dramatic find'.[1] The manuscript in question is a manual of instructions (*Nasihatnama*) on the Sikh way of life, and forms a small part of a large manuscript numbered MS 770. This manuscript was prepared in Sammat 1775 (AD 1718-19). The *Nasihatnama*, thus, becomes the earliest dated manual on the Sikh way of life. Since it is a copy, the original must have been written earlier, which takes it closer to the time of Gurú Gobind Singh. In the history of the study of *rahitnamas*, i.e. manuals on the Sikh way of life, MS 770 *does* become a dramatic discovery. Its significance can be appreciated in the context of the study of *rahitnamas*.

I

As pointed out by a number of scholars, suggestions and ideas about the Sikh way of life (*rahit*) are found in *Guru Granth Sahib* and in the *Vars* of Bhai Gurdas in the seventeenth century. Such suggestions continued to be included in various kinds of Sikh literature during the eighteenth and the early nineteenth century. At the same time, however, appeared the form known as *rahitnama*. W.H. McLeod has observed that the *rahitnamas* record the Sikh Panth's distinctive code of conduct, and the pattern of prescribed behaviour, attributable to Guru Gobind Singh. These writings have occupied a position of substantial influence in the religious tradition of the Sikhs.[2]

The twentieth century scholars interested in the Sikh way of life, Sikh ethics and gender relations have used the evidence of *rahitnamas* and commented on their nature and character. Some other scholars have studied the *rahitnamas* directly.[3] Analysis of individual *rahitnamas* began in the mid-1960s,[4] and to this interest has been added the study of *rahitnamas* in general.

As Piara Singh Padam points out, the word *rahitnama* is a compound of two words: the Punjabi word *rahit* and the Persian word *nama*.[5] The word *rahit* refers to 'mode of living' and the word *nama* to something written in the form of a letter, document or book. A *rahitnama* therefore is a manual on the mode of living. According to Bhai Kahn Singh Nabha, *rahitnamas* lay down norms for the Sikh way of life in accordance with the principles of Sikhism; they also talk of the acts which infringe those principles and are, therefore, prohibited.[6]

The script of the *rahitnamas* is invariably Gurmukhi and their language generally Punjabi. The *rahitnamas* are both in verse and prose, and their size ranges from eight to fifty pages. In the late nineteenth century, Sikh scholars like Pandit Tara Singh Narotam began to list a large number of writings in the category of *rahitnamas*. Bhai Kahn Singh Nabha refers to a collection of 37 *rahitnamas* made by Pandit Bhagwan Singh. However, Bhai Kahn Singh expressed the view that numerous compositions regarded as *rahitnamas* were not in accordance with the Gurbani and the writings of Bhai Gurdas. Among the well known *rahitnamas*, Bhai Kahn Singh includes the following: *Tankhanama*, *rahitnamas* attributed to Chaupa Singh, Prahlad Singh, Desa Singh and Daya Singh, *Prashan Uttar* of Bhai Nand Lal, and the *Prem Sumarg*. Also included in the list are Gurbani, the *bani* of Bhai Gurdas, the works of Bhai Nand Lal, *Sarabloh Parkash, Gursobha, Mahima Prakash, Gurbilas* of Bhai Sukha Singh, *Gurpartap Surya, Ratanmal (Sau-Sakhi)* and *Wajibularz (Bhagatavali)*.[7] This list includes works which contain norms of the Sikh way of life but are not formal *rahitnamas*. It may be added that Bhai Kahn Singh is not uncritical of formal *rahitnamas*. For example, he states that the *rahitnama* of Chaupa Singh contains many interpolations. The *rahitnama* of Prahlad Singh contains contradictory statements: Guru Gobind Singh was not at Abchal Nagar in 1695, and the Khalsa had not yet been created. The *Prem Sumarg* was composed by a Sikh in the name of Guru Gobind Singh and the *Tankhanama* by a Sikh in the name of Nand Lal.[8]

A number of *rahitnama* texts have been published by scholars. *Bhai Nand Lal Granthavali* edited by Ganda Singh contains two *rahitnama* texts.[9] The *Rahitname* published by Piara Singh Padam contains the texts of 14 *rahitnamas*. Six of the formal *rahitnamas* are the same as those listed by Bhai Kahn Singh Nabha: Bhai Nand Lal's *Tankhanama, rahitnamas* of Prahlad Singh, Chaupa Singh, Desa Singh, Daya Singh, and the *Prem Sumarg*. Two other formal *rahitnamas* are Bhai Nand Lal's *Sakhi Rahit ki* and *Rahitnama*. The other six are: Bhai Sahib Singh's *Rahitnama* and *Muktinama*, Pandit Nihal Singh's *Khalsa Ustat*, Bawa Sumer Singh's *Khalsa Panchasika*, Bhai Buddh Singh's *Khalsa Shatak*, and *Wajibularz (Bhagatavali)*. According to Padam, none of these works is a composition of Guru Gobind Singh. They appear to have been written by Sikhs during the eighteenth century, invoking the name of Guru Gobind Singh to make them authoritative. In their present form, they appear to have been written after 1720, though the possibility of older material being included in them cannot be ruled out.[10]

According to Gobind Singh Mansukhani, the *rahitnamas* were written by some of the devoted Sikhs of the Guru; they contain detail of the Sikh code of discipline. He tries to refute McLeod on the point of five Ks, referring to the evidence of the *Rahitnama* of Chaupa Singh. However, Mansukhani does not actually cite the *Rahitnama*. He concedes that there may be later interpolations in the extant *rahitnamas*. In his anxiety to prove that the formulation of the five Ks has come down from the days of Guru Gobind Singh, Mansukhani adopts an uncritical attitude towards the evidence of the formal *rahitnamas* he uses.[11]

According to Nripinder Singh, the *rahitnamas* constitute a unique body of literature in a style that bears little resemblance to that of the compositions of Guru Gobind Singh in the *Dasam Granth*. Of the several *rahitnamas* two are singularly significant and by far the longest ones: the *Prem Sumarg* and the *Chaupa Singh Rahitnama*. There are eight other *rahitnamas* which are valuable. However, authorships are spurious: Guru Gobind Singh is claimed to be the writer, dictator, overseer or patron of these *rahitnamas*. But they cannot be from the pen of the Guru. Even when their author is supposed to be the same, there are dissimilarities between the *rahitnamas* attributed to them. According to Nripinder Singh, Bhai Randhir Singh has adopted the textual approach in his study of the *Prem Sumarg* and Mohan Singh Diwana the literary approach to deal with stylistic nuances. He goes on to add that J.S. Grewal in his review of the *Prem Sumarg* rejects the claims of Bhai Randhir Singh and Mohan Singh who 'unrealistically exaggerate the role of literature in the development of human destinies and institutions'. Only a handful of students of Punjabi literature and Sikh history have explored the nature of *rahitnamas* in the twentieth century. Nripinder Singh names the scholars who have made some comment on the *rahitnamas* without undertaking a serious study. Among them are Bhai Kahn Singh Nabha, Bhai Jodh Singh, Ernest Trumpp, Max Arthur Macaullife, S.S. Kohli, and Avtar Singh.

Nripinder Singh asserts that the *rahitnamas* form an important part of Sikh religiousness and the ethical concerns which developed within the Sikh moral tradition. 'It is too early in Rahitnama research to attempt any comparative study of the various texts that have come down to us.' Nevertheless, he suggests that, though these writings may not be from Guru Gobind Singh's pen, or even from that of his close associates, there is a possibility that someone or several people from the Sikh community started working on an elementary arrangement of rules of conduct for easy reference, either through suggestion from the tenth Guru or from an inner compulsion at witnessing or participating in the life-style forged through the creation of the Khalsa, especially after the passing away of the Guru in 1708. A larger work bearing on *rahit* must have come into circulation sometime in the middle of the eighteenth century.[12]

Nripinder Singh points out that as religious and moral documents, the *rahitnamas* are not divorced from the political history of the period; they embody and enrich, inform and incorporate the finer elements produced by the struggle of the Sikh people in a particularly tumultuous period of their history. The *rahitnamas* can be read as 'interlocutions wherein the Guru's word prevails in establishing what is appropriate, necessary and required for the formation of the community'. The insistence on uncut hair as part of the *rahit*, for example, is one element in the *rahitnamas*, which acquires a quasi moral status: 'mutually devised action for living the virtuous life required of its members a "common form" that was uniquely their own'. The concept of *tankha*, i.e. penalty for expiation imposed publicly for the transgression of the Sikh religious and moral code, marked out the moral necessity of accepting responsibility for one's actions and indicated the subordination of the individual to the collective will of the community. Gambling, cheating, falsehood and intoxicants constitute a set of moral failures which would endanger the community. The *rahitnamas* condemn these as vices destructive of human association. The *rahitnamas* are a singular literature that informs us of the religious insights of the Sikh community in the eighteenth and nineteenth centuries; they project the positive way in which they contributed to the development of Sikh moral behaviour and character, and they indicate the state of Sikh ethical awareness at the time of their writings. They specify institutional arrangements morally significant for the existence of the Sikh community. The *rahitnama* injunctions on societal inter-relationships, in which they insist on the necessity to break away from the customs and conventions of Hindus and Muslims, were governed by the historical circumstances.[13]

Jeevan Deol looks at the *rahitnamas* as the defining texts of the eighteenth century Khalsa and as the codes of conduct written by and largely for the Khalsa. Their main concern remains the Khalsa, its rituals and the minutiae of its everyday life, though some *rahitnamas* discuss the relationships between Khalsa and non-Khalsa Sikhs or define some of the rituals of non-Khalsa life. Deol takes up three *rahitnamas* which certainly belonged to the eighteenth century: the *Tankhanama* attributed to Bhai Nand Lal (MS 770), the *Rahitnama* attributed to Chaupa Singh, and the *Sakhi Rahit* appended to this *rahitnama*. All these three *rahitnamas* highlight the concerns which were central to the definition of a member of the Khalsa. In the *Tankhanama* the central duties of a Sikh are attachment to the ideal of *nam, dan*, and *isnan* and obedience to the Word (*bani*). At the centre of Sikh identity is the community of believers constituted through worship and commensality. The other two *rahitnamas* insist on the distinctive identity of the Sikhs. By excluding both non-Sikhs and non-Khalsa Sikhs from the Khalsa's sacred universe, the *rahitnamas* butteress its distinctiveness and ensure that it remains the territory of the Khalsa alone. The insistence that every Singh should bear arms and keep his hair long marks out a Singh as a member of the Khalsa community and inscribes a collective narrative on his body. The ultimate meaning of the Khalsa is its pursuit of political sovereignty. The climax of the *Tankhanama* comes with the theme of Khalsa's military prowess and its eventual attainment of sovereignty.[14]

Rai Jasbir Singh is one of the few historians who have written directly on the *rahitnamas*. He states that three *rahitnamas* were attributed to Bhai Nand Lal and one each to Bhai Prahlad Singh, Bhai Daya Singh, Bhai Chaupa Singh and Bhai Desa Singh. All these authors were believed to be attendants of Guru Gobind Singh. It was also believed that these *rahitnamas* were written at the instance of Guru Gobind Singh. For three of these *rahitnamas* even the date of their composition was supposed to be known, i.e. 1695 for the *Rahitnamas* of Nand Lal and Prahlad Singh, and 1700 for the *Rahitnama* of Chaupa Singh. Rai Jasbir Singh argues that the language of the *rahitnamas* is very different from that of *Chandi di Var* and the *Janamsakhi* of Guru Nanak composed in 1733. Therefore, the *rahitnamas* were composed after 1733. Furthermore, the *rahitnamas* give expression to anti-Mughal sentiment, which could be a reaction to the efforts of Mir Mannu to annihilate the Sikhs. Two other things were important for the writers of the *rahitnamas*: one, that the Mughals should not succeed in obliging the Sikhs to deviate from their tenets and two, that the Sikhs themselves should not compromise their tenets. The *Rahitnama* of Bhai Desa Singh refers to the debate among the Sikhs about the authenticity of *Dasam Granth*, which had started in 1740. It also says that Bhai Desa Singh stayed in a Bunga at Amritsar which had been occupied by Jassa Singh Ahluwalia. There is a reference to Abchal Nagar and Muktsar, both of which find mention in Koer Singh's *Gurbilas* composed in 1751. Rai Jasbir Singh concludes that the *rahitnamas* were not written in the time of Guru Gobind Singh. Even during the eighteenth century the *rahitnamas* could not have been composed before 1750. Therefore, in Rai Jasbir Singh's view, these *rahitnamas* were written in the 1750s. But they were attributed to the contemporaries of Guru Gobind Singh, who wrote them at his instance in order to make the *rahitnamas* more authoritative.[15]

Swaran Singh Sanehi states that the available *rahitnamas* provide ample evidence that they did not contain the principles laid down solely by the Gurus; the Sikh congregations or learned Sikhs also added their views to these documents according to the exigency of their times. Though their number is said to range from thirty to forty, only half a dozen writings called *rahitnamas* are actually available. This does not mean, however, that the earlier Sikh literature does not contain injunctions about the Sikh way of life. What we do not find in the earlier literature is the various punishments prescribed for different kinds of offences. The *Rahitnamas* attributed to Bhai Nand Lal present an inferior type of poetry showing no regard for the metre or rhythm. Therefore, the author of these *rahitnamas* could not be the Bhai Nand Lal Goya traditionally associated with Guru Gobind Singh. For similar reasons, the authorship of Bhai Chaupa Singh and Bhai Daya Singh could also be rejected. The *rahitnamas* contain contradictory statements and interpolations. Swaran Singh comes to the conclusion that all the *rahitnamas* were the works of a much later period than what is stated in them. Guru Gobind Singh must have given instructions with regard to the Sikh way of life, particularly after the institution of the Khalsa. However, it is extremely difficult to identify his direct injunctions in the available *rahitnamas*. On the other hand the fact that the *rahitnamas* are not the genuine works of Guru Gobind Singh, or of his prominent Sikhs, does not imply that the *rahitnamas* made no contribution to the religious, literary and social life of the Sikhs.[16]

According to Gurinder Singh Mann, the declaration of the Khalsa created an unprecedented situation. On the one hand, it required a more elaborate *rahit* and, on the other it paved the way for phasing out the office of the Guru, the authoritative figure to answer questions. The result was the creation of manuals of Sikh belief and practice known as *rahitnamas*. The first text of this type, according to Mann, was prepared in 1701. This has not survived but a version seems to have been incorporated in a text attributed to Chaupa Singh. The reference appears to be to the *Sakhi Rahit* appended to the *Rahitnama* attributed to Chaupa Singh. According to Chaupa Singh, the *rahit* recorded by him was by no means comprehensive; the Sikhs could add something to its content while remaining in harmony with the spirit of Sikh beliefs enshrined in the *Guru Granth*. The authority of the *rahit* was rooted in revelation but it was clearly an evolving set of rules designed to meet the needs of the community in changing circumstances. Sikh savants continued to write their versions of the *rahit* which reflected the needs of the Sikh community at various junctures in Sikh history. With the coming of the printing press the need to generate a single authoritative document became clear. Eventually, in 1950, the Shiromani Gurdwara Prabandhak Committee finalized the *Rahit Maryada* which has served as the standard of Sikh belief and conduct.[17]

W.H. McLeod has studied the *rahitnamas* much more systematically and in much greater detail than any other scholar. He published an article on the problem of Punjabi *rahitnamas* in 1982,[18] followed by another in 1986 on the Khalsa *rahit* as a marker of Sikh identity.[19] A year later, he published *The Chaupa Singh Rahit-nama* which contains the texts and translations of two *rahitnamas*, besides a longish introduction and meticulous annotation.[20] More recently, he has published *Sikhs of the Khalsa: A History of the Khalsa Rahit*. This work is not confined to the formal *rahitnamas*; it also contains what McLeod refers to as 'either proto-*rahit* compositions' or the 'the other Rahit material'. His book consists essentially of two parts, the second part containing translations. In the first part there are four chapters which are relevant for any discussion of the *rahitnamas* of the eighteenth century. Apart from the introduction which contains information, among other things, on *rahitnama* manuscripts and printed editions, previous translators, and a summary history of studies concerning the *rahit*, the first four chapters relate to 'the beginnings' upto the time of Guru Gobind Singh, the *rahit* materials of the eighteenth century, and the six *rahitnamas* of the eighteenth century.

The six *rahitnamas* of the eighteenth century identified by McLeod are the following: the *Tankhanama* attributed to Bhai Nand Lal, the *Rahitnama* attributed to Prahlad Rai, the *Sakhi*

Rahit attributed to Bhai Nand Lal, and the *Rahitnamas* attributed to Chaupa Singh, Desa Singh and Daya Singh. The order of their occurrence in the chapter also indicates McLeod's understanding of their chronological order.[21]

About the authorship of these *rahitnamas*, McLeod has argued that Bhai Nand Lal Goya, who is generally associated with Guru Gobind Singh, was not the author of any of the *rahitnamas* attributed to him. It is possible however, that there was a person called Nand Lal in Guru Gobind Singh's entourage, that in fact that there were three or four anonymous authors who acquired this name. 'Whatever the situation, we can at least conclude that Nand Lal Goya was not the author of the *rahitnamas*. They may have been written by a different person called Nand Lal or they may have their name attached to them in order to give them some form of authority.'[22]

According to McLeod, Daya Singh of the Panj Piare can also be eliminated as the author of Daya Singh *Rahitnama*. The traditional linking of his name with one of the Panj Piare is the result either of deliberate deception by the actual author or of the simple coincidence that the author's name was also Daya Singh. McLeod looks upon the *Rahitnama* of Daya Singh as a later work on the argument that it is a lengthy piece of work and that it has been written in a comparatively modern *khari boli* prose. McLeod refers to some of the features of this *rahitnama*, which suggest that the *rahitnama* was written towards the end of the eighteenth century.[23]

Virtually nothing is known about Prahlad Rai. It is unlikely, however, that the author of the *rahitnama* attributed to Prahlad Rai was a person of this name who was a Brahman Sikh courtier of Guru Gobind Singh. The work is said to have been completed on 13 February 1696, but it refers to initiation and also to a Sikh who 'has been a Khalsa of the Guru from birth'. It also contains an injunction against the wearing of red clothing, which indicates a date after the late 1720s. Therefore, McLeod is inclined to place the composition of this *rahitnama* in the 1730s.[24]

Chaupa Singh, who is known as the *khidava* of Guru Gobind Singh, belongs to the Chhibber family of Brahmans, one of whom produced the *Bansavalinama Dasan Patshahian Da* in 1769. The *Rahitnama* attributed to Chaupa Singh bears indisputable evidence of having been written by a Brahman Sikh. It is possible that a portion of this work can be traced to the personal servant of Guru Gobind Singh. Its length and complexity suggest that it came later than the simpler versions attributed to Nand Lal or Prahlad Rai. The earliest extant *Chaupa Singh Rahitnama* has been placed in the period between 1740 and 1765, with the strong probability that it was written during the 1740s.[25]

The *Sakhi Rahit Ki*, according to McLeod, bears all the marks of an early product. However, its contents do not reflect any sign of the turmoil created by Banda. It rather seems to have been written during a peaceful period, being aimed at the Brahmans and not at the Muslim perpetrators of Banda's downfall. This *rahitnama* is always found as an appendix to *Chaupa Singh Rahitnama,* never as an independent work. On the whole, therefore, McLeod is inclined to place its composition in the mid-1730s.[26]

McLeod notices that the earliest extant *rahitnama* manuscript is a copy of the *Nasihatnama* (later erroneously termed *Tankhanama*) as one of the three *rahitnamas* attributed to Nand Lal. It is one of several works, which together bear the date 1718-19, and are numbered MS 770. It was one of the two most popular of the early *rahitnamas*. A much later version appears in MS 234 of the Punjab Languages Department, Patiala, where its date is given as 1825-6. Another copy dated 1856-7 is included in MS 1018 at the Guru Nanak Dev University Library. As *Tankhanama*, this work has been included in several anthologies. One modern version is included by Ganda Singh in his *Bhai Nand Lal Granthavali*, another modern version which is almost the same as the Ganda Singh text is in Piara Singh Padam's *Rahitname*.[27]

McLeod has observed that the scholars who have edited the texts have separated the individual words that were linked in the original manuscripts, and that they may also have corrected the spelling and the grammar of the original. 'In most cases they will have correctly reproduced the meaning intended by the original scribe. In some cases, however, they will have concealed his intentions. They may also have tidied up a style which scholars would prefer to have reproduced in its untidy condition.' McLeod winds up his account of the *Nasihatnama* with a statement which is both meaningful and significant: 'MS 770 still awaits a Gurmukhi edition. It will be very interesting to see what is done with this carelessly executed manuscript.'[28]

II

W.H. McLeod observes that there are numerous errors in the text of MS 770. Several words have been miscopied, and several others have been misspelt; whole lines have been left out at places. A portion of almost ten verses has been missed by the scribe. The scribe's carelessness is important as it means that he was copying an existing text, from which it follows that the *Nasihatnama* contained in MS 770 cannot have been the original one. The original work can be very close to the *Gursobha*, that is, within a few years of Guru Gobind Singh's death.[29]

The text of MS 770 collated with MS 234 and another manuscript in the library of Guru Nanak Dev University, Amritsar, namely MS 29 (dated AD 1831), which apparently has not come to the notice of McLeod, clearly indicates that the errors in MS 770 are even more numerous than what is stated by McLeod. Significantly, almost all the errors get explained if we assume that the copyist was not actually literate in the Punjabi language, or in Gurmukhi script. Incidentally, McLeod is wrong in saying that the word *tankha* or *tankhahia* does not occur in MS 770; the words are spelt as *tankhaee* and *tankhaai*.[30] McLeod's argument in favour of the original manuscript having been written within a few years of Guru Gobind Singh's death does not go far enough: there is no feature of the manuscript which can be invoked against the assumption that the work in question was composed before the death of Guru Gobind Singh.

For his translation of the *Nasihatnama* McLeod has used six texts, including MS 770 and MS 234 (but not MS 29). The structure of his translation is provided by the text of the *Tankhanama* published by Ganda Singh in 1968. In other words, MS 770 has not been used by him as the basic text.[31]

McLeod has classified the contents of the *Nasihatnama* under the following headings: duties and privileges of a Khalsa, doctrine and devotion, dress and outward appearance, bathing and personal hygiene, crime and misdemeanours, social relationships, sexual morality, charity, the *sangat*, *Guru Granth Sahib*, rituals, *karha prasad*, preparation and consumption of food, weapons and warfare, false teachers, attitude towards Hindus, attitude towards Muslims, and sundry prohibitions. McLeod goes on to add that the work concludes with a triumphant couplet in praise of the Khalsa, the mighty Khalsa which though few in number will yet overwhelm the Turks and demolish all enemies of truth. All those who acknowledge its rule shall find eternal liberation. Out of this long list, McLeod mentions six features as of particular interest. These are: warfare, strong opposition to Muslims, attendance at the *sangat*, the distribution of food (presumably in the *langar*) and its consumption in general, the preparation of *karha prasad* and sexual morality.[32] These features relate to the religious life of the Khalsa, their ethics, and their political aspirations. Almost the entire content of the *Nasihatnama* can be appreciated in terms of these three aspects of the Khalsa way of life.

We may note at the outset that several epithets are used for God in the *Nasihatnama*: Har, Jagdis, Gobind, Wahiguru, Khalik (*Khaliq*), and Akal. The epithets Wahiguru and Akal are characteristically Sikh; the others come from the Shaiva and Vaishnava traditions, and from Islam. However, all these epithets occur in *Guru Granth Sahib*. There is no doubt that the unity of God is assumed and, by implication, there is no belief in gods and goddesses of the Indian tradition. Worship is to be addressed only to Wahiguru.

The negative and positive injunctions of the *Nasihatnama* are addressed to the Sikhs. The epithets used for the Sikhs are not without significance: *sikh, sadh, sadh-sikh, khalsa,* and *singh*. The use of the term Singh indicates that the *Nasihatnama* was composed after the institution of the Khalsa in 1699. However, this term is used only once. The term Khalsa is used for those whose duty is to bear arms and to fight. We know that the Singh and the Khalsa were not equated in the time of Guru Gobind Singh.[33] There is a possibility, therefore, that the Khalsa in the *Nasihatnama* is not necessarily equated with the Singh. We may also note that there is no reference to the Khalsa as the Guru, which would not be expected if we assume that the work was composed before 1708. However, the form of salutation used at the end of the *Nasihatnama* is *Wahguru ji ka Khalsa, Wahguru ji ki Fateh*. This salutation is likely to have come into currency before the death of Guru Gobind Singh.[34]

A good deal of importance is given to the Guru, though he is referred to only thrice. At the end of the *Nasihatnama* he is referred to as *Patshahi Dasvin* (The Tenth King). This carries the implication that he is coming after nine predecessors, and that he is just like them if not actually one with them. The Sikhs are instructed to look up to the Guru for everything and never to turn to anyone else. Every Sikh is expected to keep a *golak* in order to accumulate savings for offering to the Guru. Any Sikh who is disrespectful to the Guru in any way is denounced as deceitful. An outsider who slanders the Guru in the presence of a Sikh deserves to be killed by the sword, a duty which the Sikh who hears such a slander should perform. These references to the Guru are indicative of a situation in which he has opponents and slanderers. We know that the institution of the Khalsa had provoked opposition from within the community as well as from outsiders.[35]

There is no reference to *Guru Granth* or to the *Granth Sahib* in the *Nasihatnama*. However, the terms Gurbani, Gurbachan and *shabad* are used in a way which suggests that the references are to the *Granth Sahib*. The Sikhs are expected to bow to the *shabad*, which carries the implication of bowing to the *Granth*. They are expected to sing no song other than the Guru's *bachan*, which again is the word of the Guru and, therefore, the *Granth*. The Sikhs are expected to remain attached to Gurbani, which can possibly refer to the *Granth* in particular.

There is hardly any doubt that the scripture is present in the place of congregation (*satsang*) for which neither the term *dharmsal* nor *gurdwara* is used. However, a Sikh is expected to go to the congregational worship in the morning and concentrate on the praises of God being sung; he should not indulge in talk, while hearing the praises of God; he should not hesitate to seat a poor Sikh beside him; he should not talk without an understanding of the *shabad*; and he should bow to the *shabad* at the end of the performance of *kirtan*. All these details enable us to visualise the performance of *kirtan* and *katha* (which are specifically mentioned elsewhere in the *Nasihatnama*) in a *dharmsal* or a *gurdwara*.

There is hardly any doubt that *karha prasad* was distributed at the end of the performance of *kirtan* and *katha* in the *dharmsal* or the *gurdwara*. The method of preparing the *karha prasad* indicates that a Sikh was expected to be very meticulous in its preparation. All its three ingredients (wheat flour, *ghee* and sugar) were to be taken in equal quantities. The spot where the *prasad* was to be prepared was swept and plastered; the utensils to be used were scrubbed and washed; the person to prepare the *prasad* was expected to bathe and to recite Wahiguru Wahiguru all the time, and nothing else; a new pitcher was to be used for fresh water; when the *prasad* was ready it was to be placed on a four-legged low table and praises of God were to be sung around it. This was the way to receive grace in the preparation of the *prasad*. While distributing the *karha prasad* the person doing so must cover his head. Before eating *prasad*, whether *karha prasad* or food (in the *langar* or elsewhere), a Sikh was expected to utter Wahiguru.

The *dharmsal* or the *gurdwara* was not the only place where a Sikh was expected to perform worship. He was expected to rise early in the morning, take bath with cold water, and recite *Japji* before eating anything. After that he was expected to go to the *satsang*. In the evening he was expected to recite the *Rahiras*, and to praise God before going to sleep at night. Before going to some other place in connection with his business he should go to the *dharmsal* or the *gurdwara* and offer formal prayer (*ardas*) for the success of his undertaking. On his return, he should go to the *dharmsal* or the *gurdwara* to make a suitable offering before going home. The *dharmsal* or the *gurdwara* is thus seen as the most important institution of the Sikhs. The injunction to stick to one's *dharma* in this context appears to be a reference to the Sikh *dharma*. In any case the *Nasihatnama* underscores the importance of following injunctions with regard to the Sikh way of life, both the positive and the negative injunctions.

The *Nasihatnama* underscores the importance of deeds, both good and bad. A Sikh is expected not to indulge in backbiting, slandering, gambling or stealing. He is not expected to appropriate anything that does not belong to him. He is expected to be generous and charitable, especially towards the Sikhs who come to him as guests. He is expected to keep the promise he makes.

He is expected not to blow out a lamp (he should extinguish it by fanning); he is expected not to extinguish fire with water that has been partly drunk by himself or by someone else. Above all, he is expected to avoid the naked state. He should not take his bath naked; he should not eat with his head uncovered; and as we have already noticed, he should not distribute *prasad* without covering his head. Even for the sexual act he should not be in a naked state.

This last injunction is clearly intended to be a curb on sensuality and is related to the conception of proper sexual relations in the *Nasihatnama*. A Sikh is expected to observe strict fidelity to his wife. He must not visit a prostitute and he should not develop sexual relations with another woman.

The injunctions meant specifically for the Khalsa can be appreciated in the context of the foregoing paragraphs. A Khalsa should not indulge in slander; he should practise charity; he should curb sensual pleasures; he should avoid misdeeds; he should discard all false sense of honour, that is, pride; he should flee from a strange woman; he should keep awake at night; he should not have eye on things which do not belong to him; he should remain attached to Gurbani; he should never harm a created being because the Creator of all beings is offended if anyone of them is harmed; he should protect the poor; he should recite the Name and remain attached to it; he should stick to his *dharma* even at the cost of his life. All these injunctions could be, and have been, given to all Sikhs.

However, there are other injunctions in the *Nasihatnama* which are specifically and almost exclusively given to the Khalsa. A Khalsa should fight in the van; he should kill *khans*; he should destroy the enemy; he should attack the opponents; he should ride the horse; he should be ready for fight all the time; he should bear arms; and he should kill the Turks. All these injunctions relate to a situation of political struggle against the contemporary rulers and their supporters who are referred to as Turks. The injunctions not addressed specifically to the Khalsa but related to the political situation can be appreciated in this context. A Sikh is not expected to show any respect for the authority of the Turks. He is not expected to touch iron with his feet, since iron had acquired a certain degree of sanctity through its various uses, especially in the form of weapons. Since the Turks were the enemy, a Sikh was not expected to take meat from a Turk for eating.

The *Nasihatnama* ends with a sure prophecy of sovereignty and rulership. All the slanderers of the Khalsa shall be eliminated, or they shall hide. The rule of the Khalsa shall be established by the Guru who would transform all the four castes into one and worship Wahiguru. They shall ride horses and keep hawks. The Turks shall run away at their sight. Each one of them would fight a lakh and a quarter of the enemy. Anyone of them who dies fighting shall attain to liberation. They shall ride caparisoned elephants and their spears shall wave in the air. At their doors, drums shall be beaten. When the number of Khalsa musketeers reaches 1,25,000, their rule shall become universal. 'The Khalsa shall rule and no opponent shall withstand them; dishonoured, they shall all submit and only they who seek refuge with the Khalsa shall be saved'.

The evidence for the claim of the Khalsa to sovereignty comes from the coins struck in the time of Banda and the inscriptions which they bear. The earliest of these coins was struck in 1710, i.e. within two years of Guru Gobind Singh's death. It is difficult to imagine that Banda Bahadur himself would come upon this idea or have this aspiration. It is more likely, therefore that the idea was conceived by Guru Gobind Singh himself. The view of Ratan Singh Bhangu that the Khalsa was meant to be sovereign from the very beginning may or may not be literally acceptable. But the contemporary evidence available on Guru Gobind Singh leaves no doubt about his political activity. The idea of rulership for the Khalsa harmonizes better with the known personality of Guru Gobind Singh than with the career of Banda Bahadur before he met Guru Gobind Singh. Indeed, if we assume that the *Nasihatnama* was written before the death of Guru Gobind Singh it becomes the most important evidence in support of the idea that sovereignty for the Khalsa was conceived by Guru Gobind Singh.

The essence of the Sikh way of life is given in the very first answer ascribed to Guru Gobind Singh. It is the pursuit of *nam, dan* and *isnan*. All these three terms appear to have acquired a comprehensive meaning in Sikh tradition before the institution of the Khalsa. *Nam* represented almost the whole ideology of Guru Nanak, especially the sum total of his religious teachings and ethics. *Dan* in Sikh tradition had come to represent charity out of the honest earnings of a Sikh; it included not only what a Sikh contributed to the common funds of the community but also what he voluntarily did for others. Similarly, *isnan* represented not only physical cleanliness but also ethical living. The essence of a Sikh way of life was thus meant for all Sikhs, whatever the term used for them. It certainly included the Khalsa. The concern of the writer with the religious and ethical life of the Khalsa, and their political aspirations, comes out clearly in the text.

III

The translation given below is based on the text of MS 770 as reconstructed by collation with MS 234 and MS 29. The reconstructed text is not given here because of the shortage of space. The broad procedure followed in reconstructing the text may however be stated:

1. The cluster of 12 lines at the beginning of MS 234 and MS 29 points to an obvious omission in MS 770. These 12 lines were added to the text of MS 770.
2. Similarly, two complementary lines at different places in MS 234 were added to rectify an obvious omission in MS 770. For the same reason, one complementary line was added from MS 29.
3. There are two lines in MS 770 which are not there either in MS 234 or in MS 29. Both these lines were retained.
4. There are 18 lines in MS 234 and MS 29 which are not there in MS 770. These 18 lines were not added to the text of MS 770. Thus, the total number of lines added to the original text of MS 770 is only 15.
5. There are 14 lines in the three manuscripts which vary. If the line given in MS 770 makes sense, it was retained. Otherwise, it was replaced by the line from MS 234, or MS 29 on the same criterion.
6. There are 18 words in MS 770 which do not make sense in the given context. They were replaced by words from MS 234, or MS 29.

7. At seven places in MS 770 the words are incomplete, whereas in the other two manuscripts these words are complete.
8. There are 10 words in MS 770 in which vowels are missing. There is one word in which a vowel is superfluous.
9. There are 170 words in MS 770 which have different spellings. Since they all make sense in the context, they were retained.

It will be seen that the text of MS 770 as reconstructed for translation remains very close to the original text of MS 770. The changes made are the necessary minimum.

TRANSLATION

Guru ji ki fateh
Nasihatnama[36]

Question by Bhai Nand Lal ji and answers by Guru Gobind Singh ji

DOHRA

Nand Lal ji asked: 'Guru ji! Please tell me which are the commendable deeds and which are not.'

DOHRA

'Listen to me Nand Lal: the Sikh way is to cherish nothing but *nam*, *dan* and *isnan*.'[37]

CHAUPAI

'He who does not go to the *satsang*[38] in the morning is a great defaulter. He who allows his mind to swerve in the congregation shall not find a place in this world or the next. He who indulges in talk while hearing to the praises of God (in the congregation) will go', says Gobind, 'to the abode of *Yama*'. 'He who does not like a poor person to sit beside him is a grave defaulter. He who talks without understanding the *shabad* gains nothing. He who bows to the *shabad* at the end of the performance will attain to God.'[39]

DOHRA

'He who entertains greed while distributing *prasad*, or distributes it unequally, will remain in sorrow forever.'

CHAUPAI

'Now listen to the way of preparing *prasad* in the cauldron:[40] the three ingredients must be in equal quantities; the floor must be swept before it is plastered; the utensils must be scrubbed and washed; the person to prepare the *prasad* must bathe before entering the cooking place; he must recite only Wahiguru all the time; a new pitcher should be filled with fresh water meant for use; when ready, [the *prasad*] should be placed on a *chauki*;[41] praises of God should be sung. The whole point [of this procedure], Nand Lal, is this: the *prasad* gets rightly prepared through God's grace.'

DOHRA

'Listen to me, Nand Lal: he who shows any sign of submission to the Turk,[42] or touches iron[43] with his foot, remains subject to the cycle of death and rebirth.'

CHAUPAI

'He who does not bathe with cold water, who eats food[44] without reciting the *Japji*,[45] who wastes the evening without reciting the *Rahiras*,[46] who sleeps during the night without praising God,[47] who indulges in backbiting to spoil things for others, and who ignores the injunctions of *dharm* – his whole life is futile. He who does not keep his promise', says Gobind, 'finds no place. He who takes meat[48] from the Turk to eat, who sings anything other than the Guru's word,[49] who is lured by women's songs, be sure Nand Lal, will go to hell.'[50]

DOHRA

'He who calls himself *sadh* but does not appropriate *rahit*,[51] commits a fraud; better than his talk, Nand Lal, is silence.'

CHAUPAI

'He who undertakes a journey without performing a prayer,[52] who eats food without making an offering on return, who appropriates an abandoned article, who lies with a woman other than his wife and who does not give charity[53] to the needy will find no place of honour in God's court. He who does not listen attentively to *kirtan* and *katha*, who talks disrespectfully of *sadh-sikh*,[54] and who resorts to slandering, gambling or stealing, will remain subject to eternal suffering. If a Sikh finds any person defaming the Guru, he should use his sword to make an offering of such a person.'[55]

DOHRA

'Listen to this Nand Lal: he who does not keep a *golak*[56] and trades deceitfully,[57] shall suffer in hell a thousand times.'

CHAUPAI

'He who blows out the *deepak*,[58] who extinguishes fire with water that has partly been drunk, who eats without uttering Wahiguru,[59] who visits a prostitute, who develops illicit relations with a woman, is not liked', says Gobind. 'He who deceives the Guru is a great defaulter.[60] He who prays to anyone other than the Guru, who sleeps in a nude state, who indulges in sexual intercourse all nude, and who bathes all naked' (is a great defaulter).[61]

DOHRA

'Besides indulging in these evil deeds, he who eats food bareheaded, and who distributes *prasad* bareheaded, is a great defaulter.'

CHAUPAI

'The *khalsa* is he who abandons slander, who fights in the van, who gives charity, who kills Khans,[62] who subdues the five,[63] who discards evil deeds, who abandons pride,[64] who shuns women (other than his wife),[65] who keeps awake during the night, who does not cast greedy eyes on what belongs to others,[66] who loves Gurbani, and who fights face to face.'

DOHRA

'The *khalsa* is he who recognizes that all human beings belong to the Creator and who does not harm them. When the created beings are harmed, Nand Lal, the Creator is offended.'

CHAUPAI

'The *khalsa* is he who protects the poor, who destroys the wicked, who recites the Name,[67] who fights the enemy, who concentrates his mind on the Name, who is detached from all other ties, who rides the horse, who fights every day, who bears arms,[68] who promotes *dharm*,[69] and who dies for his faith.'

DOHRA

'The proclamation of God shall prevail, and the slanderers [of the *khalsa*] shall not be able to oppose [them]. The slanderers shall be obliged to take refuge in forests and hills; the *khalsa* shall attain to liberation.'[70]

CHAUPAI

'Listen to me Nand Lal ji: I shall verily establish my own rule. I shall merge all the four castes[71] into one, and make them recite the name of God. They shall ride horses and keep hawks; the Turks shall take flight on seeing them. I shall empower each Singh to confront a lakh and a quarter (of the enemy); he who dies fighting shall attain to liberation. Their spears shall wave in the air, and they shall ride caparisoned elephants; drums shall be beaten at their doors. When they acquire fire arms in plenty,[72] they shall rule everywhere.'[73]

DOHRA

'The *khalsa* shall rule and none shall withstand them; shorn of honour, they shall all submit, and only they who take refuge with the *khalsa* shall be saved.'[74]

Here ends the *Nasihatnama*[75] uttered by the Tenth King.[76]

Wahiguru ji ka Khalsa, Wahiguru ji ki Fateh!

NOTES

1. W.H. McLeod, *Sikhs of the Khalsa: A History of the Khalsa Rahit*, New Delhi: Oxford University Press, 2003, p. 68.
2. Ibid., p. 1; idem, *Textual Sources for the Study of Sikhism*, U.K.: Manchester University Press, 1984, pp. 2, 3.
3. For example, Rai Jasbir Singh, 'Rahitnamas: Their Period of Writing', *Punjab History Conference Proceedings*, Thirteenth Session, 1979, Patiala: Punjabi University, 1980.

   Swaran Singh Sanehi, 'Rahitnamas of the Sikhs', *Journal of Sikh Studies* (1984), vol. XI, pt. 1.
4. J.S. Grewal, 'The Prem Sumarg: A Theory of Sikh Social Order', *Punjab History Conference Proceedings*, 1965, Patiala: Punjabi University, pp. 100-11.
5. Piara Singh Padam (ed.), *Rahitname*, Amritsar: Singh Brothers, 1995 (rpt.), p. 43.
6. Kahn Singh Nabha, *Gurshabad Ratnakar Mahankosh*, Patiala: Punjab Languages Department, 1999 (rpt.), p. 1015.
7. Loc. cit.
8. Kahn Singh Nabha, *Gurshabad Ratnakar Mahankosh*, pp. 479, 796, 806, 574.
9. Ganda Singh (ed.), *Bhai Nand Lal Granthavali*, Patiala: Punjabi University, 2000 (rpt.), pp. 186-93.
10. Padam, *Rahitname*, pp. 43, 44.
11. Gobind Singh Mansukhani, 'Sikh Rahat-Maryada and Sikh Symbols', in Jasbir Singh Mann and Harbans Singh Saraon (ed.), *Advanced Studies in Sikhism*, Irvine, CA: Sikh Community of North America, 1989, pp. 178, 179, 182, 184, 185, 186, 188, 189.
12. Nripinder Singh, 'Rahitnamas and Aggrandizement of Khalsa Tradition', in Dharam Singh (ed.), *Sikhism and Secularism: Essays in Honour of Professor Harbans Singh*, New Delhi: Harman Publishing House, 1994, pp. 301-5.

13. Ibid., pp. 308-17.
14. Jeevan Deol, 'Eighteenth Century Khalsa Identity: Discourse, Praxis and Narrative', in Christopher Shackle, Gurharpal Singh & Arvind-Pal Singh Mandair (eds.), *Sikh Religion, Culture and Ethnicity*, Richmond: Curzon, 2001, pp. 35-9.
15. Rai Jasbir Singh, 'Rahitnamas: Their Period of Writing', pp. 116-19.
16. Swaran Singh Sanehi, 'Rahitnamas of the Sikhs', pp. 66, 75, 76, 77, 79.
17. Gurinder Singh Mann, *Religions of the World: Sikhism*, London: Laurence King Publishing Ltd, 2004, p. 78.
18. W.H. McLeod, 'The Problem of the Punjabi *Rahitnamas*', *Exploring Sikhism: Aspects of Sikh Identity, Culture, and Thought*, New Delhi: Oxford University Press, 2000, pp. 103-125.
19. Idem, 'The Khalsa Rahit: The Sikh Identity Defined', ibid., pp. 126-35.
20. Idem, *The Chaupa Singh Rahit-Nama*, New Zealand: University of Otago Press, 1987.
21. Idem, *Sikhs of the Khalsa*, p. 65.
22. Ibid., p. 66.
23. Ibid., pp. 67, 71, 72.
24. Ibid., pp. 67, 70, 71.
25. Ibid., pp. 67, 70.
26. Loc. cit.
27. Ibid., p. 16.
28. Ibid., pp. 16-18.
29. Ibid., pp. 68-9.
30. Ibid., p. 82. In fact, the occurrence of these words in MS 770 could suggest to the later copyists the title *Tankhanama*.
31. Ibid., p. 279.
32. Ibid., pp. 83-7.
33. For example, in a *hukamnama* of Guru Gobind Singh dated 6 February, 1702 the person who is called 'my Khalsa' by the Guru is Bhai Mihar Chand and not Mihar Singh. In another *hukamnama* of the same date the names mentioned are Dharm Chand and Karam Chand as well as Mihar Chand. In yet another *hukamnama* the names mentioned are Bhai Bindraban and Gulal Chand. In a *hukamnama* of 1704, the names mentioned are Sukhia, Mukhia and Parsa. In all these *hukamnamas*, the Khalsa are asked to come to Anandpur fully armed. Ganda Singh (ed.), *Hukamname Guru Sahibaan, Mata Sahibaan, Banda Singh ate Khalsa ji de*, Patiala: Punjabi University, 1967, pp. 168-71, 175, 181.
34. The form of Khalsa salutation used here is not a new thing. There are indications that this form had emerged in the time of Guru Gobind Singh. In his *hukamnama*, dated 3 February 1708, there is a reference to '*Wahguru ji da Khalsa*'. Ganda Singh, *Hukamname*, p. 191. In the

Gursobha, both '*Wahguru ji ka Khalsa*' and '*Wah guru ji ki Fateh*' appear, though separately. Shamsher Singh Ashok (ed.), *Shri Gur Sobha*, Amritsar: SGPC, 1967, pp. 53, 105, 131. For detail, see *The Encyclopaedia of Sikhism*, ed. Harbans Singh, Patiala: Punjabi University, 1998, vol. IV, pp. 400-2.

35. Ashok, *Shri Gur Sobha*, pp. 42-58.
36. The first two *dohras* and the first eight lines of the *chaupai* are taken from MS 234 with some minor changes on the basis of a comparison with MS 29, but the title *Nasihatnama* is retained, which is actually given at the end.
37. For *nam, dan*, and *isnan*, see W.H. McLeod, *Historical Dictionary of Sikhism*, London: The Scarecrow Press, 1995, pp. 66, 109, 146. *The Encyclopaedia of Sikhism*, vol. I, pp. 502-4; vol. III, pp. 159-61.
38. Literally, true association, *satsang* refers generally to Sikh congregation in the *dharmsal* or the *gurdwara*.
39. The term *shabad* appears to refer to the *Granth Sahib*.
40. The word used in the text is *karaha* (cauldron). Since the sacred food (*prasad*) was prepared in it, it was called *karha prasad*. Its three ingredients are wheat flour, sugar and *ghee*.
41. *Chauki* is a four-legged low stool or table. Probably, the idea was to keep it lower that the seat of the *Granth Sahib*.
42. The phrase *mohar turk ki* can refer to the coin of the state headed by a Muslim. It can also mean the royal seal on a *farman* (imperial order). Showing respect to it would symbolise submission.
43. The word *loh* (iron) may refer to weapons of iron. However, iron by itself had sanctity because of its various uses in the Sikh tradition.
44. The word *prasad* is used here obviously for food and not for sacred food.
45. The composition of Guru Nanak known as *Japji* was recited early in the morning apparently since the days of Guru Nanak. In *Guru Granth Sahib*, the *Japji* has 38 *pauris* of Guru Nanak, followed by a *shlok* of Guru Angad. *Shabadarth Sri Guru Granth Sahib Ji*, Amritsar: Shiromani Gurdwara Prabandhak Committee, 2000, vol. I, pp. 1-8. For detail, see *The Encyclopaedia of Sikhism*, vol. II, pp. 347-9.
46. Guru Nanak's composition known as *Rahiras* was recited in the evening since his own times. In the *Guru Granth Sahib*, it has two constituents, *So Dar* and *So Purakh*. *So Dar* consists of five stanzas: the first three stanzas by Guru Nanak; the fourth by Guru Ram Das, and the fifth by Guru Arjan. *So Purakh* consists of four stanzas: the first three stanzas are by Guru Ram Das and the fourth stanza by Guru Arjan. *Shabadarth Sri Guru Granth Sahib ji*, vol. I, pp. 9-12. For detail, see *The Encyclopaedia of Sikhism*, vol. III, pp. 431-2.
47. The word used in the text is *kirat* and not *kirtan*. It refers to the Sikh practice of praising God before going to sleep.

48. The term *halal* is not used in the text but the situation does refer to it by implication. However, the emphasis appears to be on having no relations with the Muslims who wielded power and authority.
49. The word used in the text is *gurbachan*, literally, what is uttered by the Guru. It appears to be synonymous with the *sabad*.
50. The term used in the text is Jampur, i.e. the city or the abode of Yama, which is hell.
51. The use of the word *rahit* in the text does not appear to refer to the formal *rahit* as it is understood today, but it does refer to the Sikh way of life which is inclusive of all commendable practices and beliefs.
52. The word used in the text is *ardas*. It could be used for any prayer. However, there are indications in the *Dabistan-i Mazahib* that the practice of collective prayer by the Sikh congregation had developed by the mid-seventeenth century: *Sikh History from Persian Sources*, ed. J.S. Grewal and Irfan Habib, New Delhi: Tulika/Indian History Congress, 2001, p. 76.
53. The word used in the text is *dan*. The emphasis in the Sikh tradition is on giving something to others rather than receiving anything from others. For details, see *The Encyclopaedia of Sikhism*, vol. I, pp. 502-4.
54. The words *sadh* and *sikh* are used together in the text as synonyms.
55. The word used in the text is *bhetan* (to offer or make an offering). However, the inport is clear: the slanderer must be punished with death.
56. In the *Dabistan-i Mazahib* it is stated that every Sikh according to his resources put together money and took it to the *masand* by way of offering (*bhet*); the *masand* used to take all the offerings to the Guru's establishment: *Sikh History from Persian Sources*, p. 66. In the *hukamnamas* of Guru Hargobind the terms used for offering are *karvar* or simply *kar*: Ganda Singh, *Hukamname*, pp. 65, 67. In the *hukamnama* of Guru Har Krishan the term used is *bhet*. Ibid., p. 73. In the *hukamnamas* of Guru Tegh Bahadur the terms used are simply *kar*, *karbar* and *kar bhet*. Ibid., pp. 83, 88, 89, 92, 93, 96, 97, 98, 99, 101, 104, 105. In a *hukamnama* attributed to Mata Gujri, the terms used are *kar bhet*, *sukh manat* and *ardas*. Ibid., p. 123. In the *hukamnamas* of Guru Gobind Singh the terms used are *kar*, *kar bhet*, *manat*, *dasvandh* and *golak*. Ibid., pp. 132, 133, 135-7 145, 153, 156-7. It appears, therefore, that the term *golak* was used for the first time by Guru Gobind Singh. However, it remained in currency along with other terms. In the *hukamnamas* of Mata Sundari and Mata Sahib Ḍevi the terms used are *golak* as well as *kar*, *kar bhet*, *dasvandh*, *chaliha* and *sukh-manat*: Ibid., pp. 199, 201, 203, 205, 209, 211, 213, 214, 215, 217, 219, 223, 225, 226, 229. All this evidence clearly shows that there were several categories of offerings, and *golak* was one of them.

The use of the word *golak* suggests that a receptacle was kept for voluntary cash offerings in *dharmsals* or *gurdwaras*. Possibly, some Sikhs kept such receptacles in their homes to deposit offerings from time to time, for their eventual transfer to the Guru, a *dharmsal* or Gurdwara.

57. The terms used in the text are *chhal* (deceit) and *vapar* (trade). Therefore, the import can be specific in terms of buying and selling. But it can also be more general: that of conducting any trade deceitfully or dishonestly. It can also mean that not to keep the *golak* is to deceive the Guru.
58. The word *deepak* (or *diva*) refers obviously to the earthen lamp that can be blown out. But it should be extinguished by fanning.
59. By the early eighteenth century, the epithet Wahiguru had come to be used for God as conceived in the *Granth Sahib*.
60. The text is not clear, especially the term *Gur talpi*. Therefore, the translation given here carries only the general import.
61. The words given in bracket are not there in the text but in the context of the *chaupai* there is hardly any doubt that this is the import.
62. The term *khan* refers strictly to a title. However, since this title was conferred on individuals connected with the state, it came to be associated with the holders of power. In the present context it can be equated with 'Turk'.
63. 'The five' are generally believed to refer to *kam, krodh, lobh, moh* and *hankar*. The phrase can also refer to the five senses.
64. The term used in the text is *aan* which can mean honour. However, in the present context it appears to refer to a false sense of honour, or pride.
65. The term used in the text is *par-triya*, literally, 'another's woman'. It appears to carry the import of a woman other than one's wife.
66. The term used in the text is *par-dristi*, which appears to refer both to 'another woman' and things belonging to others.
67. The term used in the text is *nam-jap* which can mean both recitation of the name through Gurbani and remembrance of God.
68. The phrase used in the text is '*sastar ko dharay*', which suggests a certain degree of sanctity attached to weapons.
69. The use of the word *dharm* in the present context leaves hardly any doubt that it refers primarily to Sikh faith.
70. The text is not very clear and it is possible to interpret it differently. However, in the context of the preceding *chaupai*, the import appears to be what is given in the translation.
71. The term used in the text is *char varan* which can be taken to refer to the four main castes of the traditional social hierarchy, i.e. the Brahman, the Kshatriya, the Vaishya, and the Shudra. However, if taken literally, the mass of the people below the rank of Shudras would be left out. The import of the phrase in the present context is 'all categories of people'.

72. The phrase used in the text is '*sava lakh jab dukhe palita*', literally, 1,25,000 matchlocks. It is interesting to note that preference is given to fire arms over the traditional weapons of war. There is evidence of the use of matchlock in the time of Guru Gobind Singh by his warriors. See Iqtidar Alam Khan, 'The Khalsa of Guru Gobind Singh: Its Soldiers and their Arms', in *The Khalsa and the Punjab*, ed. Himadri Banerjee, New Delhi: Tulika/Indian History Congress, 2002, pp. 26-7.
73. The phrase used in the text is *ude ast* (sunrise and sunset). This would mean 'wherever the sun shines' and therefore 'everywhere'.
74. This is the earliest known use of the couplet which became in due course a part of the Khalsa anthem. For detail, see *The Encyclopaedia of Sikhism*, vol. III, pp. 441-2.
    Significantly, however, the victory of the followers of Guru Gobind Singh in the future is prophesied in the *Gursobha* which is believed to have been composed in 1711. Ashok, *Shri Gur Sobha*, pp. 136-7.
75. The use of the term *Nasihatnama* is interesting. It carries the import of being a manual of instructions. By the early nineteenth century, the term preferred for a work of this kind was *rahitnama*, as given in MS 234.
76. The phrase used for Guru Gobind Singh in the text is *patsahi dasvin*. The use of the compound word *mukh-vak* carries the import that the content of this work was actually uttered by Guru Gobind Singh. This may not be taken literally. However, it does not necessarily follow that what is presented here is not in accordance with the ideas of Guru Gobind Singh.

3

Martial and Political Culture of the Khalsa

IQTIDAR ALAM KHAN

While reorganizing the Sikhs on martial lines, Guru Gobind Singh preferred to call them his Khalsa, a Punjabi adaptation of Arabic *khalisa* denoting 'land and sources of revenue reserved for the imperial treasury'.[1] In Guru Gobind Singh's scheme, however, the term Khalsa denoted formation identified with the highest spiritual and temporal authority represented by the Guru and the Holy Granth.[2] The members of Khalsa were not the Guru's mercenaries employed as retainers. They were his devout followers who by giving proof of their complete and selfless devotion to his person as well as to the faith he embodied, had earned for themselves the special status of the righteous warriors in the service of God, the Timeless One (*akal*). That some of them received stipends only indicated that, being householders, they had to take the responsibility of nurturing their families.[3] In the final analysis, all the Khalsa had earned for themselves the Guru's sanction to use with their names the suffix 'Singh' that signified their status as pious warriors. This raised them from the position of the Guru's ordinary disciples to that of a military brotherhood in which all were equals. The only criterion of distinction within the Khalsa was the individual's piety and readiness to sacrifice his all for the larger cause.[4]

It is possible to argue that, as a military system, the Khalsa emerged from the Sikh political and army organization taking shape during the preceding one hundred years. The story of the emergence of the Sikh political and military organization of that early period, as gleaned from the Sikh traditions, is largely corroborated by Persian texts like the *Dabistan-i Mazahib* (1653-6) and Bhim Sen's *Nuskha-i Dilkusha* (1708-9). Even Jahangir's cryptic and hostile notice of Guru Arjan and his followers does not contradict the basic drift of this story on any significant count.[5] This evidence enables us to trace the stages through which the Sikh community evolved in the direction of Guru Gobind Singh's Khalsa.

The author of the *Dabistan-i Mazahib* as well as Bhim Sen implicitly suggest that the initial step in the direction of the Sikhs' emergence as an organized power in the Punjab was Guru Arjan's practice of appointing *masands*, that is, deputies or representatives of the Guru in every town and locality entrusting them with the task of collecting *bhet* (offerings) from the Sikhs with the help of a large staff.[6] Already, at the end of the sixteenth century the number of Guru's disciples was very large. They appeared to be particularly concentrated in the central parts of the Punjab. According to Bhim Sen, 'a majority of the men of Multan, Lahore and those parts have submitted to him' (that is, the Guru). This network of *masands* and the large funds they raised for the Guru appear to have created a general impression by the end of the sixteenth century, that the Guru, in addition to being the spiritual head of a numerous and prosperous sect, was also in command of a considerable power firmly rooted in the civil society of the Punjab.[7]

The Gurus are known to have vigorously preached the path of liberation, rejecting in the process many of the rituals and beliefs of Hindus and Muslims. The most significant manifestation of the resulting doctrines was the compilation of the Holy Granth (1606) by Guru Arjan. As the followers of a new creed, the Sikhs firmly rejected many of the prejudices that divided Hindus and Muslims as well as the high and low castes among them. The religious ideas propagated by the Gurus also paved the ground for the rise of an awareness among the Sikhs that they were neither Hindu nor Muslim and that their own creed bound them as a community of equals headed by their preceptor who was the true king (*sachcha padshah*) for them.[8]

From Akbar onwards, the Mughal rulers were always aware of this special status of the Guru. Of Akbar's reported visits to the abode of the Gurus, one to Guru Arjan is incidentally recorded by his court chronicler, Abul Fazl.[9] Akbar's offer of land to Guru Ram Das (1580), Khusrau's going to Guru Arjan for his blessings and for material help in 1606, and the deep concern with which this development was viewed by Jahangir, go to testify that, already by the end of the sixteenth century, the Sikh Guru had come to exercise an authority that could not easily be ignored by any ruler controlling the Punjab.[10]

Guru Arjan's martyrdom at the hands of the Mughal officials of Lahore, possibly at Jahangir's instigation, seems to have triggered off the militarization of the Sikh community that eventually culminated in the rise of Guru Gobind Singh's Khalsa. In the beginning, no doubt, it was a defensive reaction. But with the increasing hostility of the Mughal state, particularly under Aurangzeb, towards the Sikhs and the widening appeal of their creed among the Jat peasantry of the Punjab, the sweep and militancy of the Sikh resistance continued to grow with the manifest aim of overthrowing the Mughal rule in those parts of the Punjab where it was vulnerable from the proximity of the recalcitrant hill chiefs.

The earliest manifestation of the process leading to this transformation was, perhaps, Guru Hargobind's soldierly lifestyle and his keen interest in hunting that was so very unlike the ways of his predecessors.[11] He was the first Guru to have raised a contingent of armed personnel and to maintain a large stable. Guru Hargobind's personal contingent, according to the author of the *Dabistan-i Mazahib*, comprised 300 horsemen and 60 musketeers.[12] It is likely that Guru Hargobind organized this contingent during the time he was staying at the Mughal court, first for a long period under Jahangir after his release from the Gwalior fort, and subsequently for a short duration under Shah Jahan. William Irvine suggests that during these intervals the Guru held an important position at the Mughal court.[13] It is of interest to note in this context that the ratio of horsemen and the musketeers in Guru Hargobind's military contingent, as reported by the author of *Dabistan-i Mazahib*, was 1:5, that was nearly the same as maintained in the contingents of the Mughal *mansabdars* during the seventeenth century. The strength of the foot-musketeers in the contingent of a senior Mughal noble serving in the Deccan in 1689 was calculated as 17.4 per cent of the number of horsemen actually accompanying him. This would mean that the ratio between the two categories of troops in his contingent was around 1:5.747.[14] Again, it can also be argued that the rates of payment to the cavalry soldiers in the Guru's contingent were not much at variance with those prescribed for troopers in Mughal service.[15] These similarities might suggest that the armed bands led by Guru Hargobind in his fight against the Mughals were organized on the pattern taken from their adversaries. In this connection, it is noteworthy that Guru Hargobind had of course ample opportunity of observing the working of the Mughal military system from close quarters.

II

As compared to the armed bands commanded by Guru Hargobind, the Khalsa of Guru Gobind Singh was a qualitatively new type of organization. It was basically an army of volunteers inspired by the zeal of establishing justice as envisaged by the Guru and the *Granth*. They submitted willingly to the discipline imposed on them by their preceptor, the Guru, and in his absence, by the chosen representatives of the Khalsa. But, at the same time, this novel organization was rooted in the military expertise gained by the Sikhs during the preceding one hundred years or so of their intermittent though mostly hostile interaction with the Mughal authorities. There had survived in the Khalsa army several elements of the army organization reminiscent of the 'Mughal features' of Guru Hargobind's contingent of armed retainers. For example, side by side with the pious warriors who did not expect any remuneration for the service they rendered, many ordinary soldiers who received regular pay from the Guru for their services were also present in the Khalsa army. Sikh traditions mention incidents when some of the Guru's soldiers would clamour for the payment of their arrears in a manner that was not very different from the behaviour of the retainers of the Mughal *mansabdars* in similar situations. But, during Guru Gobind Singh's time, there were a large number of men who preferred not to receive any payment for the military service they rendered; for them the greatest reward of their services was the Guru's approval of their general conduct and performance in the battlefield. It was evidently this section of the Sikh soldiery that contributed the most to the high moral tenor of the Khalsa ethos. This distinctive culture of the Khalsa seems to have survived down to the late eighteenth century. Nur Muhammad, writing in 1764-5, from a manifestly hostile angle about the Sikh resistance against Abdali's repeated incursions into the Punjab, has the following to say about the Khalsa warriors of the period:

> In no case would they slay a coward (*namard*), nor would they put an obstacle in the way of a fugitive. They do not plunder the gold and ornaments of a woman, be she a well-to-do lady or a slave-girl (*kaniz*). There is no adultery among them, nor are these mischievous people given to thieving. Whether a woman is young or old, they tell her, '*Buriya*, go and sit in a corner'. The word *buriya* in the Indian language means 'an old woman'. There is no thief at all among them, nor is there any house-breaker. They do not make friends with adulterers and thieves, though their general conduct is not commendable.[16]

Like the Mughal army, the Khalsa army in Guru Gobind Singh's time was predominantly a cavalry force, though, unlike the Mughal horsemen, the Khalsa soldiers were generally mounted on the locally available light horses.[17] As late as 1707, 300 horsemen that the Guru commanded at the time of his joining Prince Mu'azzam near Lahore perhaps represented the core of the Khalsa army.[18] A reading of Nur Muhammad's *Jang-nama* would suggest that in the late eighteenth century the Khalsa soldiers were mainly horsemen wielding lances, swords and muskets. The description given by him of the skirmishes taking place in 1764-5 between the Afghans and their Sikh adversaries indicates that by that time the Khalsa soldiers had already learnt the art of using muskets from the horseback,[19] an art that apparently, first, came to India from West Asia towards the end of the seventeenth century.[20] These descriptions also bring out the Khalsa cavalry's skills of carrying out irregular warfare in which locally available light horses were used innovatively. In Lepel Griffin's graphic language 'the clouds of horsemen hung on the skirts of the Afghan armies, afraid to venture an attack upon regular troops, but cutting off convoys and endangering the communications of the enemy'.[21] It was a form of warfare that was adopted by the Khalsa army from the very beginning and like the Marathas they used their light cavalry with devastating effect.

In the light of this, it is difficult to agree with some English scholars of the nineteenth century who tend to take a rather poor view of the performance of the Sikh cavalry, not only of their own time, but also of the early days of the Khalsa. Lepel Griffin writes, for example: 'Sikh cavalry were, as a rule, miserably mounted and armed and became more celebrated for taking to flight when attacked than for any display of volour.'[22] Cunningham also seems to suggest that the Sikhs were inferior cavalry soldiers as compared to the Rajputs and Pathans, who, in his estimate, had inherited the traditions of horsemanship from 'Pirthee Raee Jenghiz Khan'.[23] Such estimates of the quality of Sikh cavalry were perhaps not wrong for the nineteenth century, when in the face of musket-wielding infantry trained on European lines, the cavalry of every description had become ineffective. But it is difficult to deny that the Sikh light cavalry played a very significant role in undermining Mughal authority in the Punjab during the early decades of the eighteenth century. It also appears to have contributed significantly towards preventing the Punjab's passing totally under the control of the Afghans following Ahmad Shah Abdali's victory over the Marathas in the third battle of Panipat in 1761.

Lepel Griffin is quite off the mark in observing that the Sikhs did not like the use of gunpowder and 'were never at ease with a musket in their hands'.[24] The impression that the Sikhs had no tradition of using artillery before these were introduced in the army of Ranjit Singh is also equally fallacious.[25] As a matter of fact, the Sikhs appear to have acquired the skill of using muskets from the ground as well as from the back of a moving horse at quite an early date.[26] The author of the *Dabistan-i Mazahib* mentions 60 gunners (*topchis*) of Guru Hargobind's contingent. These were possibly foot-musketeers, most of whom were perhaps recruited from amongst his own disciples. This would suggest that expertise in firearms existed among the Sikhs as far back as the middle of the seventeenth century. This should also explain the inclusion of musket (a firestick) by Guru Gobind Singh among the arms that the members of the Khalsa were expected to carry – the remaining four being a sword, a bow, an arrow and a pike. In the hierarchy of these arms, musket was placed in the second position, next only to the sword.[27] In the notice of the battles fought by the Khalsa army under the last Guru's leadership, there is repeated mention of the use of muskets by the Khalsa soldiers. The *Jang-nama* (1765) speaks of the considerable command that the Sikhs had achieved in the use of musket from horseback. At one place the author mentions the use of muskets by the Sikh cavalry in these words: 'During the battle they take out their muskets (*tufang*) and come galloping (*jaulan kunan*) into the field (all the time) roaring like tigers.'[28] This and similar other descriptions by Nur Muhammad go to fully justify James Skinner's remark in the *Tashrih al-Aqwam* (1825) that in the art of musketry (*fan-i-tufangadazi*) the Sikhs had no match.[29]

It is of course true that before Ranjit Singh, the Sikhs were not particularly interested in maintaining artillery. This was possibly a direct result of the Sikhs, then specializing in irregular warfare, the *chakkarbazi* of James Skinner's description.[30] But in the course of their revolt against the Mughals whenever the Khalsa army was able to bring under its control a fort or considerable township it did not hesitate to deploy for its defence whatever artillery could be procured. To this extent Cunningham's sweeping statement – 'cannon was not used by the early Sikhs'[31] – is not really tenable. Several cases of the early Sikhs occasionally using cannon can be cited. For example, with reference to Sikh traditions, Macauliffe mentions the use of two cannon pieces, *baghan* (tiger) and *bijay-ghosh* (sound of victory), in defence of Anandpur in 1701.[32] Similarly one may also refer to Banda Bahadur's having with him at Lohgarh in 1710 a cannon made out of the trunk of a tamarind tree, which he filled with powder and blew up before vacating that fort.[33]

III

These remarks on the evolution of the Khalsa army also call for a brief re-examination of the thesis that Guru Gobind Singh's Khalsa were the defenders of Hinduism against Islamic onslaught under Aurangzeb. The thesis is sometimes vulgarized to the extent of ascribing to the Guru, a deep hatred for Islam and Muslims. It is maintained that the Guru had proclaimed a general war against Muslims declaring that 'no quarter was to be given to them'. The destruction of Islam was, it is asserted, one of the aims of the Khalsa for whom 'it was unlawful to salute Muhammadans, to associate with them on any terms'.[34] It needs to be noted that this thesis is not supported by the authentic historical evidence that survives in the form of Guru Gobind Singh's own writings, his sayings and stories and anecdotes about him recorded in the contemporary Persian chronicles as also in the Sikh traditions that have been recorded.

Even a cursory reading of Guru Gobind Singh's *Zafarnama* reveals that this thesis amounts to a total travesty of the thrust of his statement therein. In this work, the most stringent criticism is reserved for Aurangzeb's conduct as king, in that he was tyrannical in his behaviour and law or ethics did not regulate the exercise of political authority by him. The Guru's condemnation of Aurangzeb's public conduct was not that he was trying to enforce the orthodox Islamic law in his empire but, on the other hand, that he was not acting in accordance with the true spirit of the *Quran* and the Prophet's tradition. Rebuking Aurangzeb for the false promise by his commanders on one occasion, the Guru writes:

> Thou hast no idea of what an oath on the Quran is, and canst have no belief in Divine Providence ... when thou didst swear by Muhammad and called the word of God to witness, it was incumbent on thee to observe that oath.[35]

The overall tenor of this letter of the Guru is very clear; he is denouncing Aurangzeb's conduct but not his faith, Islam. There is no remark in the Guru's *Zafarnama* that may be considered as directed even obliquely against Islam. On the other hand, the Guru appears to refer to the *Quran* and Prophet Muhammad with respect. This was in conformity with the Sikh spirit of respecting Islam as one of the three great religions of India. The Sikh tradition refers to a saying of Guru Tegh Bahadur to the effect that 'three religions, Hinduism, Islam and Sikhism', shall, 'survive to future ages'.[36] This sentiment apparently permeated the Sikh tradition from the very beginning and carried the added sanction of Guru Tegh Bahadur's prophecy. It does not permit one to imagine that Guru Gobind Singh and his Khalsa were aimed at destroying Islam and Muslims.

Guru Tegh Bahadur's martyrdom, no doubt, strengthened the resolve of the Sikhs to oppose Aurangzeb's bigotry and to work for the overthrow of his rule, but it neither led Guru Gobind Singh to work for the destruction of Islam nor did he come to regard the entire Muslim population of India as the irreconcilable enemies of the Khalsa. While not hesitating to target many of the Mughals and Afghans closely identified with the Mughal empire, Guru Gobind Singh was always willing to accommodate in his army Muslims who were prepared to contribute to his fight against Mughal rule. Khushwant Singh is very correct in saying that Guru Gobind Singh 'made sure that his crusade would not be wrongly construed as one of Sikhs against the Muslims'. According to him, 'the nucleus of the Guru's personal contingent consisted of five hundred Pathan mercenaries'.[37]

Sikh chronicles, reproducing traditions about the Gurus and those relating to early Sikh history, are replete with anecdotes mentioning Muslims serving in Guru Gobind Singh's army pitted against the Mughals or helping him and his followers in different ways. One such instance highlighted in the Sikh tradition is the role played by two of Guru Gobind Singh's Muslim retainers and a Mughal officer sympathetic to him, in the battle of Anandpur (1701). Maimun Khan and Saiyad Beg, the two retainers, are reported to have fought 'like tigers' alongside the Khalsa soldiers. There was a fierce single-handed combat between a hill chief, obviously a Hindu raja, fighting for the Mughals, and Saiyad Beg of the Guru's army. At the end of this combat, Saiyad Beg succeeded in killing the hill chief, but was himself mortally wounded by the Mughal troops that had intervened in this contest on noticing that the Raja was about to be overpowered. On this occasion, Maimun Khan is reported as having charged on horseback in every direction and so creating great havoc among the Mughal troops. Again, we are told that Saiyad Khan, a high ranking officer, who commanded the Mughal troops sent with the hill chiefs to attack the Khalsa army withdrew from the battle while the contest was going on. He acted in this manner out of his friendly feelings for the Guru.[38] Similarly, mention may be made of two Muslims, Ghani Khan and Nabi Khan, who being old acquaintances of the Guru, volunteered their services to him in 1705, when he was being pursued by the Mughals after vacating Chamkaur. These two are reported to have carried the Guru, disguised as a *pir* from Uch, in a litter, from place to place. During the same wanderings the Guru was helped at Lal (near Patiala) by a friendly Saiyad from Nurpur (near Machhiwara), who allayed the suspicions of the Mughal soldiers about the identity of the 'Pir of Uch'.[39]

Some of the families of the Muslim gentry (*ashraf*) in the Punjab claimed with pride till very recently that their ancestors served in the army of Guru Gobind Singh. One such family of Saiyads of Rawalpindi is reported to have preserved in their possession a manuscript of Guru Gobind Singh's letter to Aurangzeb down to 1917. Their claim was that two of their ancestors were employed in the Guru's army and had gone with him to the Deccan in 1707.[40]

As far as the view that Guru Gobind Singh and his Khalsa perceived themselves as defenders of Hinduism against Islamic aggression is concerned, one may cite many of the sayings and edicts of Guru Gobind Singh emphasizing that the Khalsa were to always demarcate themselves clearly both from Hindu as well as from Islamic beliefs and practices. In the *Zafarnama*, he makes the explicit statement that he killed the intriguing hill chiefs who were idol-worshippers whereas he was a breaker of idols.[41] This may not be taken literally but it makes the point clear.

NOTES

1. Irfan Habib, *The Agrarian System of Mughal India*, Bombay: Asia Publishing House, 1963, p. 259.
2. M.A. Macauliffe, *The Sikh Religion: Its Gurus, Sacred Writings and Authors*, Delhi, 1998 (rpt.), vol. V, p. 244. Guru Gobind Singh is reported to have said in his last sermon: 'Henceforth, the Guru shall be the Khalsa and Khalsa the Guru. I have infused my mental and bodily spirit into the *Granth Sahib* and Khalsa.'
3. In 1704, when Guru Gobind Singh was being pursued by the Mughals from place to place and was also facing financial difficulties, he did his best to pay the salaries of his soldiers. Cf. Macauliffe, ibid., p. 217.

4. Ibid., pp. 94-100.
5. *Tuzuk-i Jahangiri*, ed. Saiyid Ahmad, Ghazipur and Aligarh: 1863-4, p. 34. *Dabistan-i Mazahib*, Lucknow: Nawal Kishore, 1904, pp. 223-5, 233-40. Bhim Sen, *Nuskha-i Dilkusha*, MS, British Library, Or. MSS 23, fols. 168b-169a. Cf. Macauliffe, *The Sikh Religion*, vol. II, pp. 271ff, for Guru Ram Das's biography subsequent to his appointing *masands*; vols. III and IV provide information on the lives and works of Guru Arjan, Guru Hargobind and Guru Tegh Bahadur. The bulk of the information used in Macauliffe's work is derived from the Sikh traditions preserved in the *Suraj Prakash* and the *Janamsakhis*.
6. *Dabistan-i Mazahib*, p. 233. Bhim Sen, fol. 168b. Khushwant Singh, *History of the Sikhs, 1469-1988*, 2 vols., Princeton: 1963, p. 11.
7. Bhim Sen, fol. 168b.
8. Apparently the title *sachcha padshah* came to be used for the Guru more frequently from Guru Arjan's time onwards. At least this is the impression given by the *Dabistan-i Mazahib*, p. 233.
9. Cf. Abul Fazl, *Akbarnama*, ed. Agha Ahmad Ali and Abd-al Rahim, Calcutta, 1873-7, vol. III, p. 746. Sikh traditions mention Akbar's two other visits to the abode of the Gurus. The first one was in the lifetime of Guru Ram Das (that is, *c.* 1581), to whom he is reported to have given a land grant. Irvine opines that the name Chak Guru or Guru Chak that continued to be associated with Amritsar till the late eighteenth century indicates that this tract was indeed given by some authority to the Guru as a revenue-free grant. The visit by Akbar noticed in the Sikh tradition is placed sometime after the compilation of Holy Granth by Guru Arjan. On this occasion he is reported to have received complaints from 'Qazis and Pandits' that the Holy Granth 'reviled' the Hindu and Muslim divinities. Akbar had the relevant lines read out to him and firmly rejected the complaints. He personally made an offering of 51 gold *muhrs* to the Holy Granth. Macauliffe, *The Sikh Religion*, vol. III, p. 83. This last must be the same as the meeting with Guru Arjan mentioned by Abul Fazl.
10. *Tuzuk-i Jahangiri*, p. 34. *Dabistan-i Mazahib*, p. 234.
11. *Dabistan-i Mazahib*, pp. 234-5. It is emphasized that Guru Hargobind considered his participation in warfare as a part of his task of educating the people. When he killed someone in battle it was not by way of anger but to teach his adversary as to how the sword was to be used.
12. *Dabistan-i Mazahib*, p. 235. While describing Guru Hargobind's contingent, the author seems to use the term *topchi* in its loose meaning of 'gunners' to denote musketeers. This term in the given context cannot be taken as meaning artillerymen for whom the more appropriate expressions would have been *top andaz / gola-andaz / deg-andaz*.
13. William Irvine, *Later Mughals*, ed. J.N. Sarkar, New Delhi: Oriental Books, 1971 (rpt.), p. 77.

14. Iqtidar Alam Khan, 'The Matchlock Musket in the Mughal Empire – An Instrument of Centralization', *Proceedings of the Indian History Congress*, Patiala: 1998, pp. 200-1.
15. Macauliffe, *The Sikh Religion*, vol. V, p. 217. Guru Hargobind is reported as paying his cavalry troops at the rate of eight annas per day (that is, Rs. 15 per month) that was nearly at par with the payment the Mughal *sih-bandis* received.
16. Nur Muhammad, *Jang-nama*, ed. Ganda Singh, Amritsar: 1937, p. 158. Khushwant Singh, *A History of the Sikhs*, p. 160, n. 48.
17. This, incidentally, is also suggested by the rate of payment to the cavalry troopers of Guru Gobind Singh (Rs. 15 per month). Cf. Macauliffe, *The Sikh Religion*, vol. V, pp. 203-4.
18. Iqtidar Alam Khan, 'Indian Response to Firearms (1300-1750)', *Proceedings of the Indian History Congress*, Bangalore: 1997, p. 252.
19. Nur Muhammad, *Jang-nama*, pp. 105, 106.
20. Iqtidar Alam Khan, 'Indian Response to Firearms', pp. 17-18.
21. Lepel Griffin, *Ranjit Singh*, Oxford: 1905, p. 134.
22. Ibid., p. 134.
23. Joseph Davy Cunningham, *A History of the Sikhs*, ed. H.L.O. Garrett, Delhi: 1915, p. 154.
24. Griffin, *Ranjit Singh*, p. 86.
25. Cunningham, *A History of the Sikhs*, p. 99.
26. Macauliffe refers to Sikh cavalry using muskets from horseback in the battle of Anandpur in 1701, *The Sikh Religion*, vol. V, p. 168.
27. K.S. Narang and P.C. Saxena, *History of the Punjab* (rev. H.R. Gupta), Delhi: 1953, p. 196.
28. Nur Muhammad, *Jang-nama*, pp. 156-7. Ganda Singh's translation (p. 56) of this part of the poem misses the significance of the expression *jaulan kunan* (galloping) in the text. It clearly hints at the Sikhs' wielding muskets from horseback.
29. *Tashrih al-Aqwam*, MS British Library, Add. 27255, fol. 160b.
30. Nur Muhammad's description of the Sikh method of irregular warfare is graphic: 'They were not ashamed of a retreat, they don't fight in an (open) field. They come, fire their muskets from a distance and immediately retire from the battlefield. They are without any shame and modesty. They would come again and again and retire with the same frequency.' *Jang-nama*, p. 165. I have mainly followed Ganda Singh's translation of these lines (p. 63).
31. Cunningham, *A History of the Sikhs*, p. 99.
32. Macauliffe, *The Sikh Religion*, vol. V, p. 173.
33. Irvine, *Later Mughals*, vol. I, p. 116.
34. Griffin, *Ranjit Singh*, pp. 60-114.
35. Macauliffe, *The Sikh Religion*, vol. V, pp. 203-4.
36. Ibid., vol. IV, p. 379.

37. Khushwant Singh, *A History of the Sikhs*, vol. I, p. 79.
38. Macauliffe, *The Sikh Religion*, vol. V, pp. 161-2.
39. Ibid., pp. 192-3.
40. Cf. Nanak Chand Naz's Urdu foreword in his edition of the *Zafarnama* of Guru Gobind Singh, Amritsar, 1952, p. 14. This edition had the explicit blessings of Master Tara Singh.
41. Ibid., p. 134.

4

Sikh Patronage of Painting

B.N. GOSWAMY

Over the years, a very uneven view has come to be taken of painting in the Punjab. A measure of interest seems to attach to it, but it figures with no prominence in the histories of Indian painting; it is believed to be too derivative, with no clear identity of its own; little is understood of its qualities; the rough edge it is sometimes seen to possess is often spoken of with an air of amused indulgence. In fact, the thinking on the subject has moved within certain grooves, with fixed notions having come to be formed in respect of matters that affect our very understanding of it: matters relating, thus, to sources and influences, the quantum of the work done, the levels at which it was patronized, or the taste of the patrons; the range of themes treated of in it; even the period which it covers. But much needs to change, for there is evidence to suggest that these grooves of thought are too narrow, and some of the notions are rooted more in ignorance, or in prejudice, than in fact.

Even though most people tend to think of painting in the Punjab essentially as nineteenth century work of the 'Sikh Punjab', there is little doubt that painting in these parts goes back at least to the sixteenth century, when the *suba* of Lahore flourished under the Mughals. At that time illustrated manuscripts were being produced in the workshops then active here; one knows of painted episodes that place the action in this part of the empire; painters drawn from the region were undoubtedly working in the imperial ateliers. When William Finch, trading in indigo and other merchandise for the East India Company, came to Lahore in 1611 as 'one of the greatest cities of the East', he saw a great deal of painting there and described it in vivid detail.[1] It is with eager eyes that he took in the mural-covered walls inside the royal quarters of Jahangir, with their carved windows and the great *diwan-khana*. In his account, there is an elaborate notice of a painted *darbar* scene, with 'the King's picture, sitting cross-legged on a chair of state; on his right hand Sultan Pervese, Sultan Caroone, and Sultan Timoret, his sonnes; ... next them Emirsee Sheriff, elder brother to Caun Asom', and so on. 'On the left hand of the King stands Rajaw Bowsing, who beats away flyes, then Raja Ramdas, who holds his sword, Cheriff Caun, Caun John, ... Rajaw Bossow, Rajaw Ransing, Majo Kesso and Lala Bersing. Note also that in this gallery, as you enter, on the right hand of the King over the doore is the picture of our Saviour; opposite on this left-hand, of the Virgin Mary.' On the wall of another small gallery in the same royal quarters, Finch saw 'drawne the picture of the Acabar sitting in his state, and before him Sha Selim his sonne standing with a hawke on his fist, ... and by him his (other) three sonnes'. In the women's lodgings, 'where the King useth to sit', he says with some sympathy for the 'poore women' who had to endure these sights, 'are drawne overhead many pictures of Banian dews, or rather divels, intermixt in most ugly shape with long hornes, staring eyes, shagge haires, great fangs, ugly pawes, long tailes, ...'.

Finch's descriptions ring very true, for they conjure up images of work that we know so well from the range of Mughal paintings on paper. It is safe to assume that work in the style associated with the Mughal court must have gone on here throughout the seventeenth and the eighteenth centuries even if its scale is difficult to judge in the absence of clear documentation. It is of interest, however, that evidence, especially on work done in the eighteenth century in the late Mughal style in the Punjab plains, is now beginning to surface. There is for instance that group of inscribed and dated paintings with clear 'Punjabi' themes,[2] like Heer, heroine of one of the classics of Punjabi literature, and Puran Bhagat, a character from a well-loved Punjab legend. These works seem to have been sold for specified sums by one Brijnath to Khudabaksh in 1748 in a small Punjab town. It is again likely that several sets of 'portraits' of the great Sikh Gurus in the late-Mughal style, which one finds scattered in different collections, were also done in the Punjab plains. It is difficult to think of the period as one of studied inactivity as far as painting is concerned.

All this while there flourished, not far from the plains of Punjab, in the belt of hill states stretching from Jammu in the west to Sirmur in the east, the great Pahari styles of painting, northerly branch of what is broadly called the Rajput School. Here, for some part of the seventeenth century, and throughout the eighteenth, work of great sensitivity, at once passionate and restrained, elegant and free of pretence, continued being done in the family workshops of painters active at centres like Basohli, Mankot, Nurpur, Chamba, Kangra, Guler, and Mandi, under the patronage of Rajput chiefs. This Pahari painting is in itself so large and so distinctive a chapter in the history of Indian art that it is treated quite separately from painting in the Punjab. But it is necessary to see the powerful influence it exercised. In fact, it is difficult to fully understand the development of painting in the Punjab plains without a clear reference to it.

The evidence of style had long pointed in the direction of there being a strong connection.[3] Now, however, there is a whole body of documents to which one can refer. One speaks here not only of the portraits of men of power and influence in the plains, men like the governors, Adina Beg Khan and Mir Mannu, done by a great Pahari painter like Nainsukh,[4] but of other evidence, like that yielded by a large and remarkable drawing, showing the spread of the style of the distinguished painter family to which Nainsukh belonged.[5] The drawing takes the form of *ugra* aspects of the Devi, presumably the *ishta*-deity of the painter family, with numerous spidery arms which spread out around her, and end at points where the names of several Pahari states and of three chiefs are inscribed within circles. Interestingly, all the three chiefs mentioned by name are Sikh Sardars active in the second half of the eighteenth century as one knows well from history: Jai Singh Kanhaiya, his son Gurbakhsh Singh, and Jassa Singh Ramgarhia. The chiefs are mentioned by name apparently because they were masters of no named states. But this leaves one in no doubt about the connection between these chiefs and some Pahari painters who must have worked for them, something we get further proof of from the portraits in Pahari hands of these chiefs that have survived, and a fine group-picture showing Jai Singh Kanhaiya conferring with some Pahari rulers including Raj Singh of Chamba, Prakash Chand of Guler and the young Sansar Chand of Kangra.[6] There is an early reference again to a 'picture of felicity' being taken when a meeting took place between some Sikh chiefs, including a forbear of Ranjit Singh, in the environs of Batala. Clearly there was an interest in painting and, with some Pahari painters close at hand, an opportunity. There is a case thus for revising some of the conclusions arrived at by W.G. Archer, in his fine early study of Sikh painting, among them the statement that it was 'the years 1810 to 1830 (which) saw the first approach by hill artists to Sikh patrons and the first expression of interest in painting by Sikhs themselves'.[7]

Besides references, we now have a large, and uncommonly informative, group of documents, which firmly establishes the connection between at least one family of Pahari painters, now based in Rajol, and the Sikh centre of power at Lahore.[8] Most of these, couched in the Persian current at that time at the Sikh court, are in the nature of *parwanas*, being orders issued in favour of or involving members of the Seu-Nainsukh family, among them Nikka, Nainsukh's son, and Nikka's three sons, Gokal, Harkhu and Chhajju. In these figure the terms on which a painter is engaged, the confirmation of an old grant of land, summons to a painter asking him to present himself at the court, even a letter to a hill functionary asking him to help the painter Chhajju out who had been 'falsely implicated' in a case of murder. Not all the documents are issued by the ruler of Lahore himself (many of these bear the seals of the powerful Sandhanwalia Sardars, close relations of the Maharaja) but at least one of them is. The document, with its matter-of-fact tone and its references to past orders, perfectly captures the flavour of the times. It bears the date 1825, is in favour of the painter Nikka, and is addressed to the local Sikh functionary at Rihlu, the *taluka* near Kangra in a village of which the painter family lived. This is how the *parwana*, written in the *shikasteh* script, reads in Persian:

Onkar

[Seal]
May the Immortal (God)
be the Protector

[Personal Seal]
May the Immortal (God)
be the Protector

Ranjit Singh

May the Kardar of Rihlu be hereby informed.

The painter Nikka has been, from olden times, in possession of land valued at rupees one hundred and twenty-five (Rs. 125) per annum.

This grant of land has been confirmed upon him on the recommendation of Sardar Budh Singh ji. It is ordered that the land should be left with him and without his being subject to render any service or *begar*. In this matter this should be treated as a strict injunction.

Written on the 31st of the month of Asuj, S. 1882. Under orders of the Huzur at Camp Rambagh.

[In the margin]
(Conveyed) verbally through Raja Sahib Jio.

Documents such as this, through their sheer routineness of text and phraseology, establish a great deal, for in them one gets a sense of there being nothing unusual about a grant, or an engagement, like this. Almost certainly in the *daftar-i mu'alla*, which is mentioned in one of the Rajol family documents, there must have been such documents. When the members of another prominent Pahari family of artists, Purkhu and Buddhu, establish contact in another document that has survived, there is an almost casual reference to visits to Lahore from where one of the brothers asks the other to get him some material.[9] The records kept by priests at centres of pilgrimage, which have yielded such rich information on Pahari artists, also contain names of artists, among them Deviditta of Basohli, who had come, at least temporarily, to live in Lahore.[10] One gets the feeling of there being a stir of activity within the kingdom, and this through references to the work there of Pahari artists alone. There were, as we now know, many more. And the sheer quantum of work done in the Punjab in the early nineteenth century must have been impressive.

Consider, in this connection, the evidence of a traveller like William Barr, one of those many Englishmen who travelled through Sikh Punjab in the early years of the nineteenth century. Barr was an observant man, taking in and recording all that he was seeing, among them the paintings that adorned walls at place after place: Lahore, Patti, Wazirabad, Gujranwala, Peshawar. His descriptions are elaborate, though not free of wry comment:

> The gateway [of the Maharaja's palace at Lahore] which consists of a tolerably lofty archway with a tower at each side, is covered from its summit to its base with paintings, the greater number taken from the history of Krishna as related to the Prem Sagar, though a few describe the habits and peculiarities of a wandering fakeer. The figures are almost all about one-third the size of life, but with proportions as ludicrous and absurd as they can well be. In some the eye occupies nearly the whole side of a face, and in others the head appears as massive as the body. Here fakeers may be seen with their hands clasped above their heads, and with finger-nails two or three inches long; ... In one compartment, [Krishna] is portrayed with a milkmaid shampooing his great toe, in another, he is perched up in a tree, from the branches of which depend various articles of dress he has stolen from some fair damsels, ... Having satisfied our curiosity at these wonderful embellishments, we passed beneath the archway and came to the inner gate of the palace which we remarked is enriched with paintings of a similar character to those on the first, and though no doubt considered to be in good taste by the Punjabees, to Englishmen they have a most ridiculous appearance.[11]

William Barr's Victorian views on the art do not have to be taken seriously, but passages like this (and there are many in his account) bear witness yet again to the fact of painting flourishing in the state.

It is difficult to imagine that all this could have happened without the encouragement or the approval of the Maharaja himself. Far too much seems to have been written about Ranjit Singh's alleged personal indifference to painting, his holding the art in poor esteem. When he repeatedly puts off the British visitor, Vigne's request that he be allowed to draw a portrait of his, it has been seen as proof of the Maharaja being 'strongly averse to being painted',[12] apparently due to awareness of his own unprepossessing, pock-marked appearance. When in reply to the question about what he does, the same Englishman almost light-heartedly says, 'I can draw', the astonishment of the Maharaja is interpreted as his dismay that so lowly an art as painting be regarded by a white sahib so highly.[13] This, however, is hardly conclusive evidence. And it certainly does not go with other facts that we know: his confirming grants of land upon painters in royal service; his having the royal quarters adorned with paintings covering wall after wall; visiting Europeans speaking of 'the state artist' and his portfolio of drawings, 'some of them very clever'; or the Maharaja issuing orders from time to time to have reception chambers properly adorned with paintings. An entry in the official chronicle, dated March 1834, thus, speaks of the Baradari at Adinanagar, an unimportant little town that was sometimes used as a summer resort, being prepared under the Maharaja's orders by Sardar Lehna Singh Majithia. The Sardar was instructed to carry several improvements out, among them to make the water run in a large volume from the Shahnahar (close to the Baradari). It was further remarked that a painter for the purposes of making figures, pictures and marks, pleasing to the sight, had been sent for and was to be given one rupee a day from the account of the Maharaja.[14]

It seems from all this that the Maharaja is often presented in an unfair light when it comes to his attitude towards the arts. The natural silence of the records in this respect, the sheer tumult of these years, the crowding of events, the preoccupation of chroniclers and foreign visitors with capturing in their accounts the magnificence of his court, its 'savage splendour' seem to obscure much from our view. We see remarkably little of the Maharaja's private beliefs, his inner life, those meaningful moments of quiet. But on the rare occasions that we do when he personally takes interest in the marble ordered from Jaipur for use in the *parikrama* of the Golden Temple, for instance, commissions silver-doors with repousse-work to be made for the shrine of the Goddess at Kangra, chooses the *pashmina* shawls to be sent for the Pandits of Benares and Gaya, or retires in the night to listen quietly to Attar Khan playing upon the flute, a very different picture emerges.[15]

The Maharaja apart, one knows that painting had other patrons in the kingdom. The Sandhanwalia Sardars, mentioned as they so often are in the Rajol documents, were obviously fond of the art, as was Sher Singh, the Maharaja's son who eventually succeeded him on the throne.[16] There is a fair indication that another powerful family, the Majithias, took interest in painting. The redoubtable Dogra brothers, Gulab Singh, Dhian Singh, and Suchet Singh, so close to the Maharaja – belonged to a branch of the Jammu royal family that was associated with the patronage of painting for more than a hundred years. And then there were those foreign officers in the service of the Maharaja – Court, Allard,[17] and Ventura – who were commissioning painters like Imam Bakhsh of Lahore to produce for them illustrated manuscripts[18] when they were not lost in contemplating the 'indecorous' picture adorning the walls of their sprawling *havelis*, or puzzling out the Indian perspective used in painted scenes of a battle.[19]

Whatever the nature and the level of patronage, the area of the greatest confusion, or misjudgement, as far as painting in the Punjab is concerned, seems to be the range of themes treated in it. The view commonly taken is that 'painting in the Punjab' is synonymous with 'Sikh painting', and Sikh painting is in turn 'chiefly an art of portraiture'. In some ways, this is a neat and certainly a convenient formulation, for it sets crisp limits and helps establish a clear identity for the work. However, the more one sees of painting in the Punjab in this period, and the more closely one analyses it, the greater the need one feels to open the issue up and to question these statements. For there is far more to painting in the Punjab than themes that are easily recognizable as 'Sikh', or than portraiture alone.

Among the 'Sikh themes' would easily count sets of idealized portraits of the ten great Gurus, from Guru Nanak to Guru Gobind Singh, and extensive series of paintings or drawings centring upon the *janamsakhis* of Guru Nanak. Undoubtedly, a great deal of work was done on these, and some splendid series were turned out, although it needs to be stated that these themes did not interest the Sikhs alone. Idealized, *lakshana*-based, portraits of the Gurus had already emerged in the Pahari tradition in the eighteenth century – Guru Nanak Dev as a recluse wearing a patchwork quilt, for instance; Guru Hargobind with signs of worldly power surrounding him; Guru Harkishan as a young boy; Guru Gobind Singh as a plumed royal figure on horseback, with a hawk on his hand. The itinerant groups of Kashmiri scribes and painters to whom one owes the production of countless manuscripts in the northern plains had, similarly, started illuminating the sacred text, and illustrating the *janamsakhis* in the eighteenth century; creating their own somewhat innovative variants upon standardized renderings.[20]

Portraiture, which has repeatedly been spoken of as the most favoured theme of 'Sikh painting', was indeed done on a considerable scale, and some very sensitive studies were turned out. Even more than the formal sets like the finely-executed, extensive set featuring likenesses of the courtiers and functionaries at the Lahore Court by the painter Chhajju, now unfortunately scattered,[21] it is the remarkably large number of informal painted sketches or drawings that stand out from this period.[22] It is easy to understand this interest in portraits, for personal achievement needed in some ways to be celebrated, and in a warring unstable world, ephemeral life was seen as worthy of being commemorated. Undoubtedly portraiture received a fillip also from the fact of so many Europeans then living in the Punjab or travelling through it taking strong interest in it, with portraits being an obvious means of recording the characters they were living or dealing with, and turning them into objects of formal exchange between dignitaries. One is struck by the fact that the most penetrating portraits of the times are those that show single individuals rather than groups of people, the groups tending to be somewhat dry and 'official'-looking; but also by the fact that a few scenes filled with authentic figures in *darbar* settings seem to have been executed by the most competent of artists active at the Lahore court. There are of course those studies, done by not the most skilled of hands late in the nineteenth century when the nostalgia for a fallen kingdom swept the Punjab;[23] or work done by visiting Europeans some of it in oils as by Schoefft. But, surprisingly, in the time of the Maharaja himself, little comes one's way in the form of painting that evokes the great splendour of the court, of which there is so much verbal description available from the times, in the manner of Mughal painting, for instance.

In all the animated discussions of portraiture, it needs to be pointed out, however, that a great deal of other work that was done by the painters active at this time in the Punjab seems to be lost sight of. Without doubt portraiture serves the purpose of giving a defining character to Punjab work, for one is able to identify the figures that one knows well from history, but then it also limits its character, making it narrower than it was. There seems to be little doubt that what are, rather unhistorically, defined as 'Hindu themes' as distinct from Sikh, were being treated on an extensive scale throughout the period and the region. The sharp distinction between Hindu and Sikh themes that is sometimes perceived seems in fact to belong almost certainly to a period much later than that of the Maharaja. The evidence in this respect is considerable and worth serious attention. One reads again and again about the widespread reverence paid to the Sikh Gurus and Sikh shrines by Hindus and Sikhs alike, and about the Maharaja and the Sikh nobility paying homage to Hindu shrines and texts: all those devout pilgrimages to Haridwar,[24] the gifts made to the Brahmans of Kashi and Gaya,[25] the offering of silver doors at the shrine of the Goddess (Jwalamukhi), and so on. There is a clear, visual extension of this in the form of lack of any sharp demarcation between Sikh and Hindu themes when one examines the evidence of the murals on the walls of Sikh royal palaces and other structures – all those descriptions of scenes based on the 'Prem Sagar', the vernacular translation of the Bhagavata Purana, of which Barr speaks, or the surviving panels on the walls of the Sheesh Mahal at Patiala with engaging renderings of the incarnations of Vishnu, the many deeds of Krishna, illustrations based on the *Satsai* of Bihari,[26] and so on – whether in the first half of the nineteenth century or the second.

When a view like this is taken, the whole issue opens up, and many things fall into place: the *rasikapriya* series featuring so prominently Radha and Krishna from the Kapurthala collection; the famous 'Kangra' *Gita Govinda* with texts inscribed at back not only in Sanskrit but also translated into Punjabi and written in Gurmukhi characters;[27] illustrated *nayaka-nayika* series;[28] and 'Pahari' looking erotic sets with Sikh figures. It would appear that, at least for a few decades, sets of portraits of the great Gurus and *janamsakhi* series were being produced in as many numbers, and with as much feeling, in the Pahari areas[29] as works based on classical Sanskrit and Hindi texts were being made by painters active in the Punjab plains, and not for Hindu patrons alone.

Later, things were to change, and new winds were to blow. The availability of European models, the obvious attraction wielded by 'realistic works', the coming in of painters like Kehar Singh, Kapur Singh, Kishan Singh, and Bishan Singh, stimulated by the responses to things newer than what tradition held, the harnessing of local talents by officers like Skinner and Fraser for producing work with a very different flavour, the whole phenomenon of the rise of Company painting in this part of the country: all these led to the production of other and absorbing work. But that is another story.

II

If the arts that flourished under Maharaja Ranjit Singh are largely undervalued, or seen through distorting mirrors, those of the other Sikh kingdoms of the Punjab barely even enter anyone's reckoning. And yet they need to be looked at with care. For not only is there, in them, a certain quality capable of sustaining interest; they also raise a different set of issues, and can sometimes be seen as possessed of a distinctive temper.

The Phulkian group of rulers all had Chaudhari Phul as their common ancestor, as the name suggests. The pre-eminent among the Phulkian states was Patiala.[30] There were Nabha and Jind, which were closely related. Then there were other states like Kapurthala which was founded by Jassa Singh Ahluwalia. Their emergence as kingdoms was slow. The energies of intrepid men like Ala Singh – 'gallant, and at the same time prudent', in Lepel Griffin's phrase – and Jassa Singh Ahluwalia, had in the eighteenth century led to the formation of potentially powerful state units; it was, however, only after they entered into a relationship early in the nineteenth century with the British then anxious to contain the growing power of Ranjit Singh across the Sutlej, that a true opportunity of founding stable kingdoms came their way. They could now, without having to look nervously over their shoulders, and without being eyed by Lahore, garner resources, build, absorb, and create systems of governance, and eventually develop their own style.

Of special interest is Patiala, which, after the dissolution of the great centre of power at Lahore, took its rightful place as the pre-eminent Sikh kingdom of the Punjab. Here, after a series of rulers, for one of whom British historians used colourful descriptions like 'a fine specimen of a barbarian – rude, courageous, impulsive, generous and ignorant' – the reign of Maharaja Karam Singh (1813-45) was a period of relative quiet, and of early stirrings in 'the arts of peace'. Fourth in descent from the founder of the state, he occupied himself with internal consolidation and a basis for a durable relationship with the British. But it is under his son and successor, Maharaja Narinder Singh (1845-62), 'the most enlightened ruler that Patiala has ever possessed', who acceded to the throne at the young age of 23, that we see a true, intense burst of activity.[31] Great new building enterprises are undertaken: the security of the Qila Mubarak, the great ancestral fort inside the city, is abandoned for spacious new palaces and related structures outside the city walls, the Moti Mahal, the Sheesh Mahal, the Banasar Bagh, a large man-made lake, the Lakshman Jhoola, and well laid-out gardens. There is much literary activity, and poets drawn from distant centres in northern India, come and settle in Patiala. Distinguished classical singers are invited to the court, the Patiala *gharana* of Hindustani music coming to acquire great fame, with the redoubtable Bade Ghulam Ali Khan becoming in recent times its best known exponent. Murals are commissioned on a very considerable scale, and wall upon wall of palaces, religious establishments, and forts, is adorned; miniature painting flourishes; and an impressive number of illustrated manuscripts of classical texts – the *janamsakhis* of Guru Nanak, the *Sursagar*, the *Sudama Charit*, the *Rukmini Mangal*, the *Mahabharata*, the *Rasikapriya*, among them – are produced. Patiala emerges as a major centre of crafts some of which still distinguish the city. Whole bazaars with row after row of specialist craftsmen playing the same trade, catering partly to princely needs, spring up: jewellers, embroiders, dyers, makers of gold-worked *jutti*-footwear, tailors, *paranda* and draw-string-makers. Suddenly, one is breathing the air of a court that aims at casting itself in the classical Indian mould, not merely a centre of power but a hub of cultural activity and patronage extended to distant quarters. In some ways, what happens under

Maharaja Narinder Singh serves as more than a model for his successors at Patiala; it also influences the rulers of other Sikh kingdoms, Kapurthala, Nabha, Jind, Faridkot, among them. The arts come to be cared for in these places, too, on the same lines if not on the same scale.

It is clear that Patiala was not always the kind of court it came to be towards the middle of the nineteenth century, and after. The early period was marked by too much strife with too little time, or vision. It would, therefore, be of special interest to trace the manner in which the beginnings of sustained artistic activity were made here, a certain acculturation achieved.

One is struck by several things: the range of activity for one, and the pace that it gathered as the century progressed. There is evidence to suggest that, following the fall of the Lahore kingdom, and the ensuing confusion, some of the artists – 'we are like sunflowers', the artists often say – seeking the warmth of patronage, decided to move elsewhere. Of the Pahari artists who had worked for Ranjit Singh and his nobles at Lahore, some returned to their native hills. But Patiala, with its considerable resource, its power intact, and an emerging interest in the arts, must also have been an obvious destination. Some facts are available. An interesting case in point is that of the painter Deviditta, great-grandson of the celebrated Nainsukh of Guler, who had earlier lived with his family at Basohli in the hills.[32] In the *bahi*-records of the *panda*-priests at that great centre of pilgrimage, Haridwar, there are several entries relating to him. In the year 1856, he describes himself as settled in the 'gali of Kanhaiya Kapur, in the Machhihatta area' of Lahore; in 1866, and again in the following year, however, we notice his having come to Haridwar 'from Patiala' where he must obviously have been working. Still earlier, in another *bahi*-record, we find mention of 'the painter Gohi, brother of Rodu and Bibru (Biba), and son of Hardayal, belonging to the town of Haripur-Guler in the hills' coming on a pilgrimage to Haridwar in 1843 from Patiala[33] where he was 'in the service of Maharaja Karam Singh'. Nine years later, Gohi's brother, Biba also comes to Haridwar 'from Patiala', where he was 'in the service of Maharaja Narinder Singh'.

Names of other painters from the hills also surface later: Ghathu Ram, Saudagar, and Kehru. The evidence is brief, almost scrappy – such unfortunately is the nature of all evidence on Indian painters of the past – but one begins to discern in it a pattern: there was work to be found in Patiala, perhaps even discerning patronage. Precise documentation is lacking, but visual evidence raises the strong suggestion that painters converged upon Patiala also from other areas, especially from Alwar and Jaipur. Their hand is visible most clearly in the murals still extant in the glittering Sheesh Mahal, begun in 1847 for Maharaja Narinder Singh.[34] Panel after panel on those walls is done in the recognizable Alwar-Jaipur style, the painters seeming to carry on in Patiala where they had left off in their native Rajasthani setting. The range of themes, the treatment of individual episodes, the figuration, the line, the colouring: nothing leaves one in any doubt about this. Unfortunately no names of these Rajasthani artists have survived. Oral evidence does, however, raise the presumption that it was members of the extended family of a master-builder who was sent for by the court, Udai Ram Jaipuria – the one name that does seem to have stayed in local memory – who might have been responsible at least for the rich floral embellishment in the Sheesh Mahal and other buildings here.[35] Other names, like those of Ganga Baksh and Sheo Ram, float about in the air. The Rajasthani connection was obviously strong, for the records of the priests at Haridwar also speak of families of 'Rajaura Tarkhans' or 'Khatis' of Jaipur living in Patiala.[36] There is a long list of names, and some indication that the family was originally one of 'Jangir Brahmans', before it got reduced to the status of 'carpenter/mason-painters', much like some of the artisan families of the hills that we know so well now.

The Pahari and the Rajasthani painters apart, at least one prominent family of Muslim artists, originating probably from Delhi, was active at Patiala. The name of Allah Ditta figures, on the basis of oral evidence, at the head of this family when it migrated here. The names of Basharat Ullah and Muhammad Sharif, descended from him, are still better documented, for paintings inscribed with their names have survived, one of them, a fine equestrian study of Guru Gobind Singh, rendered by Muhammad Sharif for Sardar Gurmukh Singh, member of the state's 'Honourable Council'.[37] Also travelling through the region as in most of the other parts of northern India, were itinerant Kashmiri scribes and painters, copying and illustrating in their own style manuscripts for those that would commission them. With all this happening, it was natural that there be exchanges between the painter groups, some interface occur between ideas, conventions, and themes be expanded and modified: for no one could possibly have lived in utter isolation, sealed against influences.

Also, all this activity, this rich coming together in Patiala of builders and painters, poets and musicians, from different directions could not but have resulted in a certain momentum being built. Gifted men tended naturally, in the circumstances then obtaining, to gravitate towards the place where patronage, especially warm patronage, was available. One thinks of other places and other patrons as described by panegyrists. The rulers of Patiala that we are speaking of may not have been 'just as Nushirwan' and 'second Akbars in their recognition of men's qualities'. But, as at so many other Indian courts that took true interest in the arts, it would seem that here too 'crowds of people of skill and talent, professional soldiers and those addicted to pleasure' gathered for 'gaining happiness from the rulers' gifts and favours'.

What is striking at many of these centres is the fact that nearly all activity was marked by a catholicity of approach, a decided liberality of outlook. To take Patiala as a case in point once again, during most of the period of growth, there was no narrowness of vision; no fissures along religious or sectarian lines, whether in matters of state or those of the arts, were visible. The rulers themselves were devout Sikhs, but the prime ministers who served as many as four rulers were Muslims, Khalifa Muhammad Hasan whose family came from Samana being the most eminent among them.[38] When building activity on a significant scale is undertaken under Maharaja Narinder Singh, it is not only Sikh Gurdwaras that are built besides palaces and forts but also significant Hindu temples, including Badrinath, Kedarnath, Tung Nath, and Raj Rajeshwari. Quite obviously a text like the *Janamsakhi* of Guru Nanak Dev remains a favourite for illustration, but the painters spend much of their time upon illustrating classics of Hindu mythology or major literary works in Hindi. The walls of the Sheesh Mahal or of the fort at Gobindgarh bear the same aspect as walls in a Rajasthani palace in respect of themes treated in the murals. Here, too, Krishna steals the gopis' clothes, Vishnu assumes his Cosmic form, lovers collide in the dark lanes that Bihari envisions in his *Satsai,* Sudama leaves his poor hut to go to Dwarka. It all looks so natural. Nothing comes as a surprise: neither the rich grants of land in the name of temples, nor the ruler's appearance at them for paying personal homage; neither the power wielded by able Muslim administrators, nor the recitation of the *Ramayana* in the Qila Androon, nor the state celebration of festivals associated with the different faiths. The sense one gets is that all this is rooted in conviction, not policy. The symmetry with Maharaja Ranjit Singh's kingdom comes sharply to one's mind.

Finally, what is striking is the turn that painting took when new challenges appeared for painters in the form of European work at these courts. Work in the European mode in oil or watercolour was not unknown in the trans-Sutlej Punjab, with all those European officers in the Maharaja's service, professional artists and gifted amateurs in such large numbers passing through the region, and gifts brought in by state visitors. Influences had thus started registering on the minds of the Indian painters then active, especially when it came to rendering portraits, a genre already much in favour among Sikh patrons. One even knows of whole sets of paintings – summary renderings – beginning to be turned out in the 'Company' manner at Lahore. But now, in the second half of the nineteenth century, at Patiala as much as at Kapurthala or Jind or Nabha, a whole range of painters seem to have decided to take the challenge up, meeting European art at its own terms as it were, not working in the same medium but placing the same marked emphasis on close observation, and correspondences. Figures like the Sikh painters, Kehar Singh and Kapur Singh, active in the second half of the nineteenth century, and both of them gifted in their own way, seem to set out, from the very beginning, to turn their hands to this kind of work. Some fine studies result,[39] Kehar Singh showing strong interest in endowing his earthy figures with a marked sense of volume, and Kapur Singh laying stress on close observation of character and on capturing resonant detail. The names of these two artists crop up again and again, some of Kapur Singh's studies done on machine-made paper, being inscribed with captions in English. Kehar Singh, possessed of 'a darting, sure brush', seems to have taken his skills around, and we certainly find his work first at Lahore and then at Kapurthala, turning out portrait studies, whole series of craftsmen at work, recording gifts of silverware with engraved messages, even copying European-style coats-of-arm, complete with inaccurately written legends in Latin.

Even more fascinating is the work done by some painters, drawn from Rajasthan but now comfortably settled in Patiala. Obviously sensing a change in the air, aware of the impression that 'realistic' European-style portraits made upon their patrons, and sensitive to new needs, these painters seem to have bent their energies towards recording appearances like never before. In their hands have survived a prodigious number of portraits – small-sized sketches often with the barest trace of colour in them – of persons whom they saw all around themselves in their Patiala surroundings: warriors and petty nobles, performers and tutors, staff bearers and torch-lighters, *farrashes* and *chobdars*.[40] The drawings are done with brush on the usual Sialkoti, and hand-made paper, sometimes two or three on the same sheet, most of them inscribed in a spidery hand in Rajasthani *nagari* identifying the person. But these stand clearly apart from those dreary trades-and-professions sets which were turned out in such large numbers in 'Company' India. These are individual studies, sensitive and warm, live to the touch, produced not in fulfilment of some commission but to keep one's hand in good trim, as it were. One can see in the background of this kind of work not only the rigour of a great tradition but also the desire to move ahead. The studies are sharp, authentic, remarkably fresh.

One cannot catalogue here all the work done in these states: the illustrated texts, rich panels of murals, renderings of the great Gurus, series of royal portraits, sets showing professions and trades and castes. Only the true flavour of the work needs to be caught, and that can be done through turning to some selected examples. A truly representative work is that uncommonly large 'miniature', now in the Sheesh Mahal Museum: the scene of a state procession. It shows an enormous, dense phalanx of men, riders on horseback, accoutred soldiers, bumble footmen in neat uniforms, moving in slow, measured steps from right to left, but staying close to a group of exquisitely decorated elephants ridden by princes and men of obvious rank. The dark, smoky forms of elephants, barely relieved by gold-worked caparisons, keep rising like a cloud till the eye reaches the pre-eminent among them, supporting a dazzling scalloped *howdah* in which one discerns the figure of the Maharaja, Narinder Singh: nimbate, grave and dignified, not oversized and almost unmindful of the panoply of power which surrounds him. A rank of men wearing blazing red turbans walk very close to the royal mount; a forest of vertically held lances and differently inclined ensigns of royalty, held aloft by another group of unseen soldiers, creates one more shield as it were for the royal rider. One is tempted to linger long and admiringly on every detail of this entourage: the serried ranks, the individually studied faces of men packed into this crowd, the glitter of the uniforms, the minutiae of weapons and saddlery and flywhisks. But there is more to the scene than this, for at a slight distance, well ahead of the group around the Maharaja, is yet another file of elephants on the back of one of which, also under a domed *howdah*, is being carried the sacred Sikh scripture, the *Guru Granth Sahib*, neatly covered by a textile, and attended upon by a devout attendant who waves a Yak's-tail *chauri* over it. One realizes then that the procession belongs to the holy book, not to the Maharaja who, despite all the rank and circumstance, is meant to be seen as a humble follower, a devotee, bringing up the rear as it were. The point made is sharp, the impact stunning. The work is packed with other details: the wall of the fortified city well at the back, the European style carriage in the distance, the elegantly carved palanquins carried by *kahar*-bearers on their shoulders. But these add up to little more than harmless diversions. The eye tends to travel again and again to the elephants with the holy book. For *that* is where the spirit of the painting, with its fusion of Rajasthani and Pahari elements, clearly resides.

In another painting, showing a Sikh chief enjoying music, rain and mangoes, and a decisively Pahari feeling, the mood is entirely different.[41] Quiet enjoyment is in the air. The comfortable looking Sikh noble seen in it, seated under a canopy but also holding up an umbrella, for making doubly certain that he stays dry, is difficult to identify, but he could as easily be a figure from these states as from Lahore. There are no signs of royalty around him – no flywhisk bearers, no parasols of the usual kind are to be seen – but status is decisively established: he is the only one seated on a raised *moorha*-like cushioned stool; the musicians perform only for him; the enormous basket of mangoes is placed directly in front of him as if he were the only one entitled to them. The cool marble terrace on which the chief and the performers are seated, the large carpet placed on it, are further indications.

But there are no hints here of the prowess of the Sardar. He does not carry, even as a token, any weapon like a sword or a dagger. All that engages him is the good life that he can live at this moment: the cooling rain of the monsoon months, luscious mangoes, perhaps great, soul-satisfying music. It is more as a *rasika* than as a warrior that we see the chief. With this as his intention, the painter establishes the moment well. The garden at the back, with its plantain leaves and one of the mango trees laden with fruit, and the marble terrace provide the perfect setting. Three musicians, *mirasis* perhaps, sing and play: the principal performer, the man with the greying beard carrying an orange coloured *tanpura,* extends one hand forward as he sings; an accompanist wearing a small tight headgear and carrying another *tanpura*, yellow in colour, sits next to him; the lively percussionist, playing on a large *dholak* drum, sits at the near edge, long flowing hair barely covered by the small turban, and fingers perfectly poised to strike. The threesome may not have the wonderful vivacity that we see in some Pahari work, but they still make for an engaging study. On his part, the chief seems to be totally absorbed in listening, paying, at least at this moment, almost no attention to the mangoes of which a small bunch dangles idly in his right hand. There is relish in the rendering, and informality. Also an artlessness that is endearing. The work seems not to draw upon routine, endlessly repeated pictorial cliches. There is here a directness that takes one by surprise.

At the end, a remarkably simple, unpretentious study of an ordinary man, a peasant perhaps, or some artisan.[42] The painter views him from very close, with a sense of engagement. As he renders him, this bearded man, with uneven eyes, full lips, wearing a commoner's twisted turban, bears no mark of rank but is not devoid of a certain dignity. He seems here to look the viewer straight in the eye, not arrogantly but with an honesty on his face. The work is affecting.

It is also different from the delicate work done by Rajasthani artists that one has spoken of before. For it goes beyond those discreet, held-back studies, and takes one almost to the threshold of photography, as if anticipating it.

NOTES

1. William Foster (ed.), *Early Travels in India: 1583-1619*, Delhi: S. Chand & Co., 1968 (rpt.), pp. 161 ff. William Finch, 'servant to Master Johnson in Cheapside', landed in India in 1608 and remained attached to Captain Hawkins, the valuable record of whose travels has also survived.
2. This group of paintings once in the collection of the art-dealer, Subhash Kapur of New York, seems now unfortunately to have been dispersed. Many of the paintings, done in what can roughly be termed the 'provincial Mughal' manner, carried inscriptions in the hand of a late owner, giving the sum paid for the work.
3. W.G. Archer's distinguished work, *Paintings of the Sikhs* (London, 1966) established this connection almost entirely on the basis of the visual evidence then available. Since then other materials have, however, come to light; interestingly, most of them support some of the conclusions he had arrived at.
4. See the portraits published as nos. 4, 27 and 36 in B.N. Goswamy, *Nainsukh of Guler: A great Pahari Painter from a small Hill State*, Zurich: Artibus Asiae, 1997.
5. This splendid, uncommonly large drawing was first published in B.N. Goswamy, 'Pahari Painting: the Family as the Basis of Style', *Marg*, vol. xxi, no. 4, 1968. For a better, and more detailed reproduction, however, are B.N. Goswamy, 'Of Patronage and Pahari Painting' in *Aspects of Indian Art*, ed. Pratapaditya Pal, Leiden: E.J. Brill, 1972, pls. lxxiv-lxxvi.
6. The painting, bearing no. 250, is in the Chandigarh Museum. It carries at its back a long inscription identifying the personages portrayed in it. A variant version of this work is in the Victoria & Albert Museum, no. I.S. 128-1955. An early 'Assembly of the Sikhs', published by Ananda Coomaraswamy in his *Rajput Painting*, Oxford: 1916, pl. lxxvi, and now in the Museum of Fine Arts, Boston, also shows a Pahari prince – at the bottom right of the painting – who may well be Mian Man Chand, younger brother of Maharaja Sansar Chand of Kangra.

7. Archer, *Paintings of the Sikhs*, p. 31.
8. These documents remain among the most valuable sources of their kind in the history of Indian art. Comprising of a group of twenty *parwanas* and letters, nearly all of them in Persian, they were first published in B.N. Goswamy, *Painters at the Sikh Court*, Wiesbaden: Steiner, 1975.
9. This five-line note is written by Purkhu to his elder brother, Buddhu, and is written at the back of a leaf on which figure three portraits in the form of painted sketches. For a reproduction, B.N. Goswamy and Eberhard Fischer, *Pahari Masters: Court Painters of Northern India*, Zurich: 1992, p. 372.
10. Deviditta, son of Gursahai, and thus great-grandson of Nainsukh of Guler, seems to have come from Basohli – where this branch of the family had come to settle – to Lahore. An entry relating to him as living at Lahore in 'the (quarter called) Macchihatta, the street of Kanhaiya Kapur, the house of Mulaki Misar', in VS 1913/AD 1856. See, B.N. Goswamy, 'Pahari Painting', *Marg*, 1968.
11. William Barr, *Journal of a March from Delhi to Peshawur and ... Cabul etc.*, Patiala: Punjab Languages Department, 1970 (rpt.), pp. 39-40.
12. Archer, *Paintings of the Sikhs*, p. 31.
13. Baron Charles Hugel, who was in Lahore, and spent some time conversing with Ranjit Singh, remarks upon how the Maharaja 'did not seem to comprehend how an art so little esteemed by himself could possibly occupy the time of a great white man': *Travels in Kashmir and the Punjab, etc.*, London: 1845, p. 250. But for a discussion of this and other related points, see B.N. Goswamy, 'A Matter of Taste: Some Notes on the Context of Painting in Sikh Punjab', in *Paroksa*, ed. Gulammohammed Shaikh and Kapila Vatsyayana, Delhi, 1984.
14. Sohan Lal Suri, *Umdat-ut-Tawarikh*, trans. & ed. V.S. Suri, vol. III, Delhi: S. Chand, 1961, pp. 192-3.
15. For a detailed discussion, see B.N. Goswamy, 'A Matter of Taste', in *Paroksa*, 1984.
16. For documents issued in favour of painters by the Sandhanwalia Sardars and Maharaja Sher Singh, see B.N. Goswamy, *Paintings at the Sikh Court*, Wiesbaden: 1975.
17. A portrait of Allard, with his family including his Kashmiri wife, is now in the collection of Stuart Carey Welch.
18. Apart from his other work, some of which was carried back by his French patrons to France, Imam Bakhsh was also responsible for a fine series of drawings of horses, one of which showed Napoleon astride one kind of horse. This series is now dispersed; one or two works from it are, however, now in the collection of the Himachal Pradesh State Museum, Shimla.

19. In the scenes painted on the walls of General Allard's house in the Anarkali in Lahore, William Barr found the perspective 'most ridiculous ... ; at the siege of Moultan, the cannons are turned up on end to enable the gunners to load them, the figures overtop the fortifications and the cavalry seems to be manouvering in the air ...', *Journal of a March*, pp. 69-70.
20. To the work of itinerant Kashmiri painters and scribes so active in the plains of the Punjab in the nineteenth century, and responsible for vast numbers of calligraphed texts now extant, attention is drawn in Karuna Goswamy, *Kashmiri Painting: Assimilation and Diffusion; Production and Patronage*, Shimla: Indian Institute of Advanced Study, 1998.
21. This set seems to have been very extensive, each work a portrait of some prominent figure at the Lahore court in a conventional setting, seated under an arch and resting against a bolster, etc., One of the paintings from this series, bearing the name of the painter Chhajju and dated – as far as one can recall – in the early forties of the nineteenth century, was once offered for sale to the Guru Nanak Dev University at Amritsar.
22. These painted sketches, full of freshness and warm observation, are to be found in many collections, chief among them the Victoria & Albert Museum, the Chandigarh Museum, and the Lahore Museum. Most of these carry brief descriptive captions, identifying the person portrayed, and place the figure against an uncoloured ground, primed in white broadly in the space used for the portrait.
23. Archer's *Paintings of the Sikhs,* contains evocative account of this period of painting in the Punjab.
24. There are repeated references in Sohan Lal Suri's *Tawarikh,* to pilgrimages to Haridwar undertaken by Sikh chiefs and nobles. There is an air of routineness in these descriptions. Thus, an entry dated in the year 1832: 'Bhai Ram Singh presented to the Maharaja *parshad* from Gangaji with some garments and an elephant. ...'
25. Thus, the Maharaja's orders to Diwan Moti Ram to distribute *pashmina* worth Rs. 10,000 to these Brahmans.
26. These panels on the Sheesh Mahal walls, with the usual renderings of the lover and the beloved as Krishna and Radha, are based obviously upon a Pahari miniature series of the same theme, formerly in the collection of the Maharaja of Tehri-Garhwal.
27. This is the series, in the hand of the painters in the first generation after Nainsukh, which was published by M.S. Randhawa in his *Kangra Paintings of the Gita Govinda*, New Delhi: National Museum, 1963.
28. Dispersed leaves from different series with this theme, with an obvious Punjabi flavour, are to be seen in many collections even if it is difficult to think of a complete series that has survived.

29. The set of 'portraits' of the great Gurus, formerly in the collection of Wazir Kartar Singh of Bassa Waziran in Nurpur, or the extensive series of drawings of the Janamsakhi in the Chandigarh Museum serve as cases in point.
30. Even though it is now dated, Lepel Griffin's *Rajas of the Punjab*, first published in 1873 and reprinted by the Punjab Languages Department from Patiala in 1970, presents a connected account of the cis-Sutlej states.
31. Khalifa Muhammad Husain's history of Patiala in Urdu, *Tarikh-i Patiala*, has very useful information on the period. R.P. Srivastava's collection of essays, *Art and Archaeology of Punjab* (Delhi, 1990) and S.P. Srivastava's *Art and Cultural Heritage of Patiala* (Delhi, 1991) contain further useful information on the period.
32. The case of Deviditta, son of Gursahai, and thus great-grandson of Nainsukh of Guler, is of great interest. When he moved from Basohli to Lahore is not exactly recorded, but between 1856 and 1866 the circumstances at Lahore seem to have changed for him. Apparently, the continued availability of patronage at the princely state of Patiala while Lahore had gone into decline, must have been a factor. See B.N. Goswamy, 'Pahari Painting', *Marg*, 1968.
33. This information comes, once again, from the pilgrimage records kept by the priests at Haridwar. For a brief discussion, see B.N. Goswamy, 'Painting at Patiala', *Pushpanjali*, Bombay, 1980, pp. 56 ff.
34. These frescoes are discussed in detail in Karuna Goswamy, 'Frescoes in the Sheesh Mahal, Patiala', *Roopalekha*, vol. xxxviii, nos. 1-2. Also, see Kanwarjit Kang's doctoral dissertation, 'Mural Paintings in 19th Century Punjab', Chandigarh: Panjab University, 1978.
35. 'Mistri' Ude Ram Jaipuria appears to have moved to Patiala in the reign of Maharaja Karam Singh. Most of his work seems, however, to have been done under Maharaja Narinder Singh. See S.P. Srivastava, *Art and Cultural Heritage*, pp. 20-1.
36. There are several entries relating to this Rajasthani group of craftsmen settled at Patiala in the records of Pandit Gopal Toombria at Haridwar.
37. This painting is now in the collection of the Himachal Pradesh State Museum, Shimla. R.P. Srivastava has recorded very useful information from the family to which Basharat Ullah and Muhammad Sharif belonged and which is now settled in Lahore.
38. The two brothers, Khalifas Muhammad Hasan and Muhammad Husain, were sons of Mir Sadat Ali who served as a tutor in Urdu and Persian to Maharaja Narinder Singh. Names of other Muslim administrators and counsellors coming from Lucknow are also remembered with respect. See S.P. Srivastava, *Art and Cultural Heritage*, pp. 6-7.

39. No detailed study of the work of these artists has yet been made. However, there is a brief discussion of them in M.S. Randhawa, 'Kehar Singh and Kapur Singh: Two Punjabi Artists of the 19th century', in *Chhavi*, Benares, 1971; K.C. Aryan, *Punjab Painting*, Patiala: Punjabi University, 1975; and R.P. Srivastava, *Art and Cultural Heritage*, p. 204.
40. A large number of these drawings and sketches, some of them very finely done, were once in the collection of Shri Ramjidas of Patiala, descendant of one of these Rajasthani families in Patiala. Most of the works bore small descriptive captions in Rajasthani *devanagari*, identifying the person portrayed.
41. This painting is now in the collection of the Sarabhai Foundation at Ahmedabad, Acc. no. KA-18.
42. The drawing is now in a private collection.

5

Sikhs in the Early Census Reports

ANURUPITA KAUR

The main focus of this paper is on how Sikhs were presented in the census reports during the first five or six decades of colonial rule in the Punjab and in the Punjab princely states. Several concerns were involved in this presentation: numbers of the Sikhs and their distribution; demographic characteristics like gender, age and literacy; castes and occupations; and the issue of religious identity. Put together, the census reports provide a dynamic image of the Sikhs, with some glimpses of sociocultural change among them. The limitations of the data embodied in the census reports also get revealed in the process.

I

The area of British Punjab did not remain uniform during the period of British rule. The total area in 1855 was 81,625 square miles. It increased to 101,829 square miles in 1868 due mainly to the addition of Delhi and Hissar Divisions. In 1881, the area was 106,632 square miles. There was no appreciable change in 1891. In 1901, however, the North West Frontier Province was created, largely with the territories of the Punjab beyond the Indus. With the creation of Delhi territory in 1911, the area of the Punjab was reduced further.[1] These changes affected the percentage of Sikhs in the total population, but not to any great extent.

The total number of Sikhs in the Punjab in 1868 was 1,144,090 in a total population of 17,611,498, constituting 6.5 per cent of the population. In 1881, the Sikhs numbered 1,716,114 in a total population of 22,712,120, amounting to 7.5 per cent of the population in the province. The percentage was 7.44 in 1891 when the Sikhs numbered 1,870,481 in a total population of 25,130,127. In 1901, the total population of the Punjab was 26,880,217 and the number of Sikhs was 2,130,987, accounting for 13.9 per cent of the total population.

PERCENTAGE OF SIKH POPULATION

Year	*Total Population*	*Sikh Population*	*Percentage*
1868	17,611,498	1,144,090	6.50
1881	22,712,120	1,716,114	7.50
1891	25,130,127	1,870,481	7.44
1901	26,880,217	2,130,987	13.90

It was observed that Sikhism seemed to have made a marked advance since 1891 possibly at the expense of the Hindus who showed an increase of only 2.4 per cent. In 1911, when there was a decline in the total population of the province, the Sikh population shot up to 2,883,729, registering an extraordinary increase of 37 per cent.[2] This sudden spurt was due largely to the change introduced for the identification of Sikhs. Consequently, the figures of 1911 are more comparable with the figures of the later census reports.

The territory of the British Punjab was divided into districts for administrative purposes, with a certain number of districts constituting a division. The data in 1868 and 1881 were arranged according to districts and divisions. In 1891, however, no statistics were compiled for divisions because they were not required in actual official work. The districts and states of the province were classified into five tracts: the hill tract, the sub-montane and central tract, the eastern plains, the western plains, and the Salt Range tract. In 1901, a scheme of natural divisions was formulated and the province was divided into four such divisions: the Himalayan, the Sub-Himalayan, the Indo-Gangetic plain east, and the north-west dry area. The district remained the primary unit for the compilation of statistics. In 1881, the British territory was covered by 32 districts grouped into 10 divisions. After the creation of the North West Frontier Province in 1901, there were 27 districts.[3]

The largest numbers of Sikhs in 1868 were living in four divisions.[4]

SIKHS IN FOUR DIVISIONS

Division	*Percentage*	*Number*
Amritsar	12.80	352,885
Lahore	22.00	318,666
Jalandhar	8.00	197,894
Ambala	9.21	152,263

The highest percentage of Sikhs at this time was in the five central districts.[5]

SIKHS IN CENTRAL DISTRICTS

District	*Percentage*	*Number*
Ferozepur	29	1,60,484
Amritsar	24	2,62,369
Ludhiana	16	95,413
Lahore	15	1,19,268
Jalandhar	14	1,20,167

On the frontier, the percentage of Sikhs was less than 1. The Delhi and Hissar Divisions also had a low percentage, with the exception of the Sirsa district which had 10.2 per cent Sikhs.[6]

In 1881, the districts of Amritsar, Ferozepur and Ludhiana had Sikhs ranging from 23 to 27 per cent of the total population, followed by the district of Lahore with 17 per cent. In Jalandhar and Sirsa the percentage of Sikhs was 12 to 13; in Ambala, Gurdaspur, Hoshiarpur and Gujranwala, it was 6 to 7. The district of Sialkot had 4 per cent Sikhs in its population. In all other districts, the Sikhs formed less than 3 per cent of the rural population. The Lahore and Amritsar Divisions accounted for 38 per cent of the Sikhs in the Punjab and for 58 per cent of the Sikhs in the British districts. Another 31 per cent of the Sikhs were in the Ambala and Jalandhar Divisions.[7]

In 1891, two districts had more than 200,000 Sikhs: Amritsar (261,452) and Ferozepur (226,361). Three districts had more than 100,000 Sikhs: Lahore (152,023), Ludhiana (141,603), and Jalandhar (110,790). Three districts had more than 50,000 Sikhs:

Ambala (93,670), Gurdaspur (85,837), and Hoshiarpur (70,709), while Sialkot had only a little less than 50,000 and Gujranwala more than 45,000. In the districts of Rawalpindi, Hissar, Gujrat, Montgomery and Jhelam the number of Sikhs was between 30,000 and 15,000. Their smallest number was in the districts of Rohtak, Gurgaon and Delhi.[8]

By 1901, the Sikh population was increasing in all those districts which had a large number of Sikhs, with the exception of Ambala.[9]

VARIATION IN PERCENTAGE OF SIKHS 1891-1901

District or State	*Number*	*Percentage of Variation (+ or –)*
Amritsar	264,325	+1.1
Ferozepur	228,355	+9.0
Ludhiana	164,919	+16.5
Lahore	159,701	+5.1
Jalandhar	125,817	+14.5
Gurdaspur	91,750	+6.9
Hoshiarpur	71,126	+.6
Ambala	58,073	–33.8
Faridkot	52,721	+11.8
Sialkot	50,942	+2.2
Kapurthala	42,101	+6.6

Significantly, the district of Jhang came to have a Sikh population of 67,719, witnessing an increase of over 1626 per cent. This was due to colonization in the lower Rachna Doab. Even in Gujranwala, the Sikh population increased by nearly 59 per cent due mainly to the same reason.[10] Thus, in all the central districts of the province Sikh population was on the increase and it was spilling over into the new canal colonies. Incidentally, there is no information in the census reports on Sikh migration as such.

Only a small proportion of Sikhs lived in town and cities. In 1881, the Sikhs were seen as 'almost wholly rustic'. In a number of districts the percentage of urban Sikhs ranged from 10 to 5: as in Amritsar, Sialkot, Jalandhar, Gujranwala, Lahore, Hoshiarpur, Gurdaspur, Ambala and Ferozepur. In Ludhiana, the percentage of urban Sikhs was less than 3. In some other districts, which had only a small Sikh population, the percentage of urban Sikhs was the highest, ranging between 75 and 50: Bannu, Kohat, Peshawar, Dera Ghazi Khan and Dera Ismail Khan. Even in Hazara, the urban Sikhs accounted for 24.5 per cent of the Sikh population. In 1891, only 6.9 per cent of the Sikhs lived in the towns and cities of the British Punjab.[11] It may be added that the growth of urban population in the province as a whole was rather slow in the late nineteenth century due to a simultaneous process of de-urbanization.

II

In 1868, the number of males above 12 years in the Sikh population was 431,819 and of females 322,278, giving the ratio of 57.26 per cent males to 42.74 per cent females. This disproportion was peculiar to the Sikhs who had the largest excess of males as also the greatest paucity of females. Female infanticide was thought to be the main reason for this disproportion between the sexes among the Sikhs. In 1881, the number of females per 1,000 males among the Sikhs was 765, while for the province as a whole, the number of females per thousand males was 843. Ibbetson suggested in 1881 that the exceptionally high disproportion between the sexes among the Sikhs was not only because of female infanticide but also due to early marriages. Female infanticide was not 'practised generally'; it was not habitual with any class, except some sections of the community, like the Bedis; an intentional neglect of the girl child, rather than actual murder, was the cause of deaths. In 1891, the number of females among the Sikhs was still much less than for any other community, the Sikh males being 783,682 and the Sikh females being 606,252. The districts in which the proportion of female children was the smallest among the Sikhs were the districts in which the Sikhs had the largest numbers: Amritsar, Lahore, Ferozepur, Ludhiana, Jalandhar and Gujranwala. In the 1850s it was thought that the chief offenders of female infanticide were the Khatri Sikhs, especially the Bedis. In the early 1860s, when an enquiry was made in Jalandhar, the Jat Sikhs were also suspected of this offence. It seemed most probable in 1891 that 'the Sikhs as a whole are more careless of their female children than persons of other faiths'.[12]

In 1901, the number of Sikh females for 1,000 Sikh males was 766. One cause for the low proportion of females given by E.D. Maclagan in 1891 was that unlike the male infant, the female infant was returned as Hindu. However, H.A. Rose found in 1901 that the number of such cases was very small and this factor could not account for the disproportion.[13] The number of females among the Sikhs was appreciably smaller than that of the males in almost all age-groups, and in all the four natural divisions.[14]

According to Rose, female infanticide was condemned in the Sikh scripture as the greatest of the four deadly sins. Sikhism had undoubtedly raised and not lowered the position of women. 'It would in truth be safer to say that female infanticide, if it exists, is practised by the Sikhs in direct contravention of their religion, for everything in Sikhism leads, or ought to lead, to its absolute avoidance.' The Sikhs, therefore, remained an 'unsolved puzzle' for Rose. The small proportion of females among them was not due to their 'religious dogmas'. 'Several causes, both social and economic, combined to render female life more precarious than the male, and these causes operated with greater force in some sections of the community than in others.'[15]

Among the various 'caste' categories of the Sikhs the number of females per 1,000 males in 1901 ranged from 703 to 879.[16]

FEMALES PER 1,000 MALES AMONG SIKH CASTES IN 1901

Caste	*Females per 1,000 Males*
Mazhabi	703
Rajput	712
Jat	751
Khatri	766
Arora	790
Bhatia	807
Chuhra	815
Mahtam	824
Labana	879

In 1868, figures were given for only three age groups among the Sikhs, for both males and females: adults (above 18), youths (12 to 18), and children (below 12).

SIKH MALES AND FEMALES IN THREE AGE GROUPS

Age group	*Males*	*Females*
Adults	432,667	293,024
Youth	219,180	170,813
Children	49,152	29,254

It was pointed out, however, that these figures were not exact, especially for the youth. Many marriageable females were returned as adults or children.[17]

In 1901, figures were given for both males and females in four age groups: below 10, 10 and under 15, 15 and under 20, and 20 and above.[18]

SIKH MALES AND FEMALES IN FOUR AGE GROUPS

Age group	*Total Number*	*Males*	*Females*
0 and under 10	499,937	284,482	215,455
10 and under 15	239,941	144,144	95,797
15 and under 20	197,501	117,988	79,513
20 and above	1,165,517	635,682	529,835
Sikh population	2,102,896	1,182,296	920,600

The details for the age distribution of the males and females among the Sikhs, and for the total population for the Punjab per 10,000 of both the sexes, were also given.[19]

No information was provided on literacy among the Sikhs in 1868. It was observed in 1881 that where the Sikhs were small in numbers, many of them were 'educated Khatris'. Only about 5.82 per cent of the Sikh males were educated. The percentage of the literates in the total male population in the province was only slightly higher, being 6.10 per cent. The largest proportion of educated Sikhs, 82 per cent in fact, were in schools run by the government. In female education, however, the Sikhs had the second highest figure for both the rural and the total population.[20]

In 1891, each person was recorded as (a) learning, that is, under instruction, (b) literate, able to read and write, and (c) illiterate. The figures showed a considerable increase in the proportion of Sikh learners and Sikh literates, from 111 to 471 in the first category and from 135 to 784 in the second for every

10,000 Sikhs. However, the proportion of literates in various ages indicated a falling-off in the rate of education. The proportion of literate Sikhs to the total literate population was 10.4 per cent, while the percentage of Sikh learners was 8.2. Possibly, the Sikh boys learning Gurmukhi were not enumerated. The Sikh element was the best educated in the classes which contained a large proportion of Sikhs, like the Jats, Tarkhans and Kalals.[21]

In 1901, literacy for English was separately tabulated. The number of Sikh literates in English was 5,141, out of whom only 23 were females. The total number of literate Sikhs was 91,313, out of which 7,252 were females. The number of literates appeared to be underestimated, especially in the case of popular scripts, which included Gurmukhi, and school-going ages. Women too were not correctly estimated in terms of literacy. Among the Sikh adults (over 20), 1 in 10 were literate, but for all ages together 1 in 15 were literate. Literacy on the whole was on the increase among the Sikhs by the end of the nineteenth century.[22]

III

In 1868, occupations were classified as professional, domestic, commercial, agricultural, industrial, and independent or non-productive. Figures in terms of religious communities were given only for agriculturists. Over 71 per cent of the Sikh population was agriculturist. Out of a total of 454,649 agriculturist Sikhs, 371,439 were proprietors and 83,210 were tenants. For every 100 proprietors, thus, there were 23 tenants. A large number of Sikhs were among the *jagirdars* of the province, numbering 56,000 in all. Apart from these three categories, there were labourers, shepherds, graziers, and herdsmen among the Sikhs. However, their total number was only 8,000. The largest number of Sikh proprietors were in the districts of Amritsar, Ferozepur, Jalandhar, Lahore, Ludhiana, Hoshiarpur, Ambala, Sialkot, Gurdaspur and Gujranwala ranging between 91,000 and 13,000, and amounting in all to 357,039. According to the census, the Sikhs did not follow industrial or commercial pursuit to the same extent as Hindus and Muslims. They were to be found in large numbers in the army, the police, and the priestly profession.[23]

The figures for occupations in 1881, according to Ibbetson, were the least satisfactory. The following categories of occupations were mentioned: administration and defence; agriculture (including land owners, tenants, joint cultivators, agricultural labourers, graziers); village menials (water carriers, workers in leather), scavengers, carpenters, blacksmiths and potters; workers in fabrics (wool workers, *pashm* workers, cotton cleaners, cotton weavers, dyers and drapers); workers in food (oilmen, milk sellers, green grocers and confectioners); industrial class (bricklayers, goldsmiths, workers in brass, and others); distributing class (grooms, domestic servants, priests, barbers, musicians and performers, beggars and *faqirs*). In 1891, occupations were divided into seven classes with further divisions: government services; pasture and agriculture; personal services; preparation and supply of material substance; commerce and transport and storage; professional, and indefinite and independent.[24] Separate figures for the Sikhs were not given for any category in 1881 and 1891.

In 1901, the census commissioner, H.A. Rose, expressed the opinion that the data on occupations was difficult to obtain in all countries and even more so in India. The enumeration was conducted by 'a half-educated agency' and the difficulty of obtaining accurate information was 'well-nigh insuperable'. Rose held the view that the great occupational castes were not abandoning their hereditary functions. Generally speaking, the Jats had advanced in wealth and education. Among the artisans, the Tarkhans were rising to the status almost of a professional caste, as they acquired qualifications as engineers. The occupations were classified into eight groups, each divided into sub-orders: government; pasture and agriculture; personal service; preparation and supply of material substance by hand; commerce and transport and storage; profession; unskilled labour; and independent. Subsidiary occupations were also recorded. The occupations recorded for women were mostly menial, personal, and household services. Preparation of food and drink, light and firing, dress and general labour, including earthwork, were the other occupations followed by women. How the Sikhs fared in all these occupations was nowhere indicated.[25]

Information on castes appeared to be more reliable, and more useful. In 1881, the castes were divided into three groups: land-owning and agricultural; religious, professional, mercantile and miscellaneous; and artisan castes. The first of these groups, which included the Baloches, Pathans, Jats and Rajputs, constituted half the population of the province and was considered to be more important than the others not only numerically but also socially, administratively, and politically.[26] Figures for the Sikh 'castes' were given.[27]

CASTEWISE SIKH POPULATION IN 1881

Caste	*Number*
Jats	1,126,861
Tarkhans	113,869
Chamars	100,310
Chuhras	45,834
Aroras	37,917
Khatris	37,521
Kambohs	29,910
Nais	21,500
Rajputs	17,761
Labanas	13,366
Kalals	8,931
Mahtams	8,366
Banias	3,334

Detailed figures for the Sikhs were given for each district of the Punjab. The Jats of the Sikh tract, who occupied the central districts, were essentially husbandsmen, and were largely agriculturists. Among the major 'castes' of the Sikh Jats were Dhillon, Virk, Sandhu, Bhullar, Mann and Her. After the Jats the most common 'caste' among the Sikh cultivators was that of the Kambohs. They were found chiefly in the Sikh districts of the Punjab, Amritsar having the largest number of Kambohs, followed closely by Jalandhar. Sikh Khatris were the strongest in the central districts where Sikhism was most prevalent, though the percentage of Khatris who joined Sikhism was less than 10. They belonged to the mercantile 'castes'. Like the Khatris, the Aroras belonged to the mercantile 'castes' and were strongest in the districts of Lahore, Gujranwala and Ferozepur. The Tarkhans in the artisan 'castes' were in the largest proportion among the Sikhs in the districts of Amritsar, Gurdaspur and Sialkot. A considerable proportion of the Sikh population on the Indus was composed of the Labanas who made ropes and worked in grass, and they were exclusively Sikh. Out of every 1,000 Sikhs 702 followed agriculture of whom 663 were Jats; 137 Sikhs belonged to the artisan castes as Tarkhans, Jhiwars, Nais, Lohars and Chhimbas; 96 of the Sikhs were menials and outcastes; 47 were Aroras and Khatris who belonged to the mercantile castes. Then there were others in smaller numbers. This was only a rough classification.[28]

Nevertheless, it was assumed for the census of 1891 that the list of castes in 1881 was nearly complete. All the large Sikh 'castes' showed increase in population.[29]

CASTEWISE INCREASE IN 1891

Caste	*Increase since 1881*
Khatris	17,700
Aroras	22,185
Chamars	25,719
Tarkhans	29,203
Chuhras	65,366
Jats	56,632

The most remarkable increase was in the number of Chuhras, indicating 'a certain amount of real conversion'. The castes were divided into classes and further divided into groups, and the percentage of each 'caste' in Sikhs to the total males of all 'castes' in Sikhs was worked out.[30] More than 64 per cent of the Sikhs were agriculturists, more than 25 per cent were artisans and village menials, and less than 8 per cent carried out commercial pursuits.[31]

In 1901 it was made clear that the main object of the enquiries made on the subject of caste was to pave the way for the Ethnographic Survey which was in progress at that time. Rose expressed the view that caste was not a social unit and attempts to classify castes in order of their social precedence had failed. He suggested that all information on castes should be regarded as 'mere notes or queries, or rough material for investigations still to be made'.[32] Sikh 'castes' were identified and figures in each were given for males and females.[33] Among the Sikh Jats, figures were given for Sidhus, Sandhus, Gills, Dhillons, Dhariwals,

Aulakhs and Bajwas. They belonged to the Majha and the Malwa areas. The Aroras were strong in the south western Punjab and the Khatris in the central districts and in Rawalpindi, Jhelum, Gujrat, Shahpur and Hazara. Important among the Khatris were Bedis, Kapurs and Malhotras. The Labanas belonged to the south western districts and the Mahtams were in the Jalandhar and Hoshiarpur districts.[34]

IV

More than thirty princely states were linked with the Punjab province for political and administrative purposes. A few of them were ruled by Sikh Chiefs and contained a substantial number of Sikhs. The area of the princely states remained the same from 1881 to 1901, covering 35,187 square miles, that is, about one-third of the area of the province. The dominions of the chiefs varied in size. Bahawalpur had an area of 15,000 square miles with a population of 600,000; Patiala had an area of 6,000 square miles with a population of 1,500,000. All the other states were far smaller in size. In 1901 the number of states was 34.[35]

The total population of the states in 1881 was 3,861,683, with the Sikhs numbering 595,110, that is, 15.41 per cent. In 1891 the total population was 4,263,280 persons, constituting one-sixth of the population of the Punjab. The Sikhs numbered 480,547, or 11.27 per cent. In 1901 the states had 4,424,398 persons, that is, less than one-fifth of the population of the Punjab. The Sikhs were 585,877, or 13.24 per cent.[36]

The Sikh element was the strongest in the states of Malerkotla, Faridkot, Patiala and Nabha. In 1881, the Sikhs formed 30 per cent of the population in these states; Malerkotla had 57 per cent Sikhs in its population.[37] In 1891, Patiala had the highest population of Sikhs, that is, 285,348, while Nabha had 63,047 Sikhs. The number of Sikhs in Faridkot was 47,164; Kapurthala had 39,493 Sikhs and Malerkotla had only 7,625 Sikhs. Patiala saw a decrease of 122,793 Sikhs in 1891, 61,390 among the Jats and 14,572 among the Chuhras. The Sikhs in Malerkotla decreased by 21,307, the greater part of this decrease (16,314) being among the Jats. No serious explanation for this change was considered possible; it was attributed to the change in the definition of a Sikh and the unevenness of its application.[38]

The number of Sikhs in 1901 was as follows:

PERCENTAGE OF VARIATION IN SIKH POPULATION IN THE PRINCELY STATES 1891-1901

State	*Total Sikhs 1901*	*Percentage of Variation (+ or -)*
Patiala	355,649	+24.6
Nabha	78,361	+24.3
Jind	29,979	+99.6
Faridkot	52,721	+11.8
Kapurthala	42,101	+ 6.6
Malerkotla	10,495	+37.6
Bahawalpur	7,985	–40.1
Total	577,291	+21.9

The increase in the number of Sikhs in the Phulkian States, amounted to a fourth in Patiala and Nabha and to 100 per cent in Jind. According to Rose, the reason for the revival of Sikhism was due to the organization of the Imperial Service Troops as the recruits were 'induced' to take the *pahul* on enlistment.[39]

In 1881, only 6.14 per cent of the Sikhs in the princely states lived in towns. The percentage rose slightly in 1891 to 6.5. The percentages for individual states were as follows:[40]

PERCENTAGE OF URBAN SIKHS IN THE STATES IN 1891

State	*Percentage of Sikhs out of total population living in towns in 1891*	*Percentage of Sikhs living in towns out of the total population of the Sikhs*
Nabha	2.2	9.9
Faridkot	2.6	6.2
Kapurthala	0.8	6.1
Patiala	1.0	5.6

The number of females per 1,000 males among Sikhs for the princely states in 1881 was 765; in the total population of the states their number was 828; in the British Punjab, it was 846; and in the province as a whole, 843.[41] In the census of 1891 the figures for males and females among the Sikhs were as follows:[42]

SIKH MALES AND FEMALES IN BRITISH TERRITORY AND PRINCELY STATES IN 1891

Area	*Total Sikh Population*	*Males*	*Females*
British territory	1,389,934	783,682	606,252
Native states	480,547	268,533	212,014
Total	1,870,481	1,052,215	818,266

In all these decades, the figures for males and females among the Sikhs in the princely states differed little from the figures for the Sikhs in the British territory. The figures for the states, however, showed a marginal increase in the number of Sikh females.

In 1901, only 1 in 44 were literate for all ages in the princely states and 1 in 30 among adults.[43] Comparison with the returns for 1891 shows that literacy among the Sikhs in the states witnessed a small increase.[44]

INCREASE OR DECREASE IN LITERACY AMONG THE SIKHS IN THE PRINCELY STATES IN 1891-1901

Area	*Learning 1891*	*Literates 1891*	*Proportion of literates 1891*	*Total literates 1901*	*Increase or Decrease*
Princely States	936	12,231	1 in 39	13,452	+1,221
Total	13,779	125,236	1 in 34	119,560	-5,676

For the population as a whole in the British territory, 1 in 10 knew English but the figure for the Sikhs was 1 in 20. The figures for the Sikh literates in English in the states were as follows:[45]

LITERACY IN ENGLISH AMONG SIKH MALES AND FEMALES IN THE PRINCELY STATES IN 1901

Territory	*Total Persons*	*Male*	*Female*
States	748	736	12
Total	7,518	7,176	342

On the whole, information on the Sikhs in the states is much less detailed than on the Sikhs in the British Punjab. However, the broad demographic trends appear to be similar. There is no information about the changing attitudes of the Sikhs in the princely states. This silence could be indicative of the slow pace of social and cultural change among the Sikhs in the states.

V

Writing in 1881, Ibbetson refers to two very different forms of Sikhism: 'the tolerant quietist doctrines of Nanak and the military propaganda of Govind Singh'. The followers of Guru Nanak were called 'Sikhs' and the followers of Guru Gobind Singh were called 'Govindi Sikhs'. But when the word Sikh was used in the late nineteenth century it referred to the latter. The vast majority of those who followed the tenets of Guru Nanak called themselves Hindus and returned themselves as such. However, the more educated among them would explain at the same time that, though they were not Singhs, they were Sikhs. Ibbetson called them Nanakpanthis or Sahajdharis as distinct from the Singhs who were popularly equated with Sikhs.[46]

The Singhs were easily distinguishable due to 'the five *ks*' they were bound to carry about their persons: uncut hair (*kesh*) with unshaven beard, short drawers (*kachh*), the iron bangle (*kara*), comb (*kangha*), and steel knife (*khanda*). Another important marker of the Singh was baptism (*pahul*). For the purposes of the census, presumably only the Singhs were treated as Sikhs. Ibbetson explicitly states in fact that 'the Sikh is to be distinguished from the Hindu by little more but the five external signs, his abstinence from tobacco, and the reverence for the Granth'.[47] Almost certainly the Sikhs of the census of 1855 and 1868 were only the Singhs.

In 1891, the enumerators were clearly instructed that only the Sikhs 'who wear long hair and do not smoke' should be entered as Sikhs. Others who called themselves Sikhs should be entered as Hindus. E.D. Maclagan observed that the line between the Hindus and the Sikhs was 'vague in the extreme'. A 'true Sikh' was a member of the Khalsa, a follower of the ordinances of Guru Gobind Singh. Such men were distinguished as 'Singhs' from the 'secondary class' of Sikhs. The 'practical test' of a Sikh, according to Maclagan, was to ascertain whether or not, calling himself a Sikh, he wore uncut hair and abstained from smoking.

Thus, for him, the Singh was clearly a Sikh; the line was vague only between the 'secondary class' of Sikhs and Hindus. In the census of 1901, the rule defining a Sikh as one who wore the hair long and refrained from smoking was retained.[48]

However, even in 1891 the rule was not strictly followed. All the Nanakpanthis who returned their religion as Sikh were not necessarily *kesh*-wearing and non-smoking Sikhs. On the other hand there were persons of the category of Guru Gobind Singhi Sikhs who were returned as Hindus. Maclagan felt convinced that the Sikh figures of 1891 on the whole included a good proportion of non-Singhs. In 1901, H.A. Rose expressed the view that the official definition of the Sikh was 'almost universally ignored'. He suggested in fact that the definition should be abandoned, firstly because it excluded a certain number of the community from the returns of the Sikhs and, secondly, because the Sikhs themselves objected to this rule in nearly all the districts with a considerable number of Sikhs. Many a non-Singh was, thus, anxious to be returned as a Sikh.[49]

In 1911, the instruction given to the enumerators was that: 'A person who says he is a Sikh must not be entered as a Hindu because he does not wear the *kesh*. All persons professing to be followers of Guru Nanak or Guru Gobind Singh and calling themselves Sikhs should be entered as Sikhs.' The distinction between Singhs and Sahajdharis was to be made in a separate column. Thus, the Sikhs were not forcibly relegated to 'a particular faith'. The question of identity was not yet resolved for the administrators: 'whether or not, all persons now returned as Sikhs are other than Hindus, still remains to be solved'. In the eyes of the administrators, the Singhs were distinguishable from Hindus (as well as Muslims and Christians); the Sahajdharis were not necessarily distinguished from Hindus.[50]

In the census reports of 1855 and 1868, no Sikh sects were mentioned. In 1881, only some 'recent sects' of the Sikhs were noted: the Kukas, the Nirankaris, and the Gulabdasis. All representing some concern for reform, only the Kukas had a considerable number of peasantry under its influence. They tried to revive some of the original doctrines of the Sikh faith. The Nirankaris were 'the purists' of Sikh religion. The Gulabdasis were said to consider pilgrimages and religious observances as a waste of time.[51]

The reports of 1891 and 1901 provide further information on these and some other 'recent sects'. The sect of the Kukas was found by one Balak Singh around 1846 'to break the power which the Brahmans had acquired over the Sikhs'. His successor, Ram Singh, preached that he was an *avtar* of Guru Gobind Singh. He wanted a 'speedy overthrow of the British power'. The Kuka outbreak occurred at Malerkotla in 1872. The Kukas called themselves Namdharis, wore the *sidha pag* and carried a necklace of woollen cords. They looked forward to 'the establishment of the Khalsa as a temporal dominion'. Their watchword was 'Sat Sri Akal'.[52] In 1901, the number of Sikhs who declared themselves openly to be Kukas was 10,331, mainly in the districts of Sialkot, Jalandhar, Gurdaspur, Amritsar and Ludhiana. 'Orthodox Sikhism' found the dispensing of *amrit* in separate vessels and the recognition of Ram Singh as the twelfth Guru 'objectionable'.[53]

The Nirankaris were a remarkable outcome of the doctrines of Guru Nanak in 'modern times'. Their number among the Sikhs in 1891 was 38,907. The founder of their sect was Bhai Dial Das, and Bhai Ratta, his successor in 1891. They held the *Adi Granth* as sacred. Marriages were performed by the circumambulation of the *Adi Granth*. A Granthi conducted the ceremony and the bride sat in public with her face uncovered. Remarriage of widows was allowed. Hindu Dharmshastras were not followed and the services of Brahmans were dispensed with. The *Adi Granth* was installed at a *darbar* on the Lei stream. The slippers of Bhai Dial Das were also kept there and looked upon with special reverence.[54]

Somewhat similar to the Nirankaris were the Bhagat-panthis who did not observe the usual Hindu ceremonies at marriage or death; the *dharmsala* and the *Adi Granth* played a role in their ceremonies of marriage, betrothal, and funeral. Passages from the *Granth* were read for a few days after the death, and *karha prasad* was distributed on the occasion of death as well as marriage. No rule of *chhut* (touch) forbade contact among castes. The sect strove after pure Sikhism and freedom from Brahmanical supremacy. The Bhagat-panthis made no pilgrimages, avoided idolatry, and performed no *shradh* for the dead. Daily worship was essential and it consisted of six recitations of the *Granth* at selected hours. The sect was returned from the Bannu district and Dera Ismail Khan *tahsil*. Aligned with the Bhagat-panthis were members of Sodhi bans who aimed at returning to the pure religion of Guru Nanak. More popular in the northwest, especially in the districts of Sialkot, Shahpur and Rawalpindi, this new movement had 2,000 followers.[55]

The Gulabdasi sect was founded by a Sikh Jat disciple of the Udasi Pritam Das. He compiled a scripture called 'Updes Bilas'. The philosophy of the Gulabdasis was thoroughly pantheistic: 'all that was visible in the Universe was God'. Their aim was gratification of the senses. There was no place for hypocrisy in their tenets. They wore white clothes and dressed like the Udasis or the Nirmalas. They were found mostly in the Lahore and Jalandhar districts. Only 299 of them returned themselves as Sikhs, and they were despised by the other Sikhs.[56]

Apart from these 'recent sects', a number of sectarian groups among the Sikhs were associated with the successors of Guru Nanak. In 1891, the number of Sikhs who returned themselves as the Sikhs of Guru Angad was 154. There were 75 others who returned their sect as Khadur Sahib; they were mainly from the Nakodar *tahsil* of the Jalandhar district.[57]

Associated with Guru Amar Das were the Niranjanis who worshipped God as Niranjan; they were found mostly in the districts of Amritsar and Jalandhar and in the Kapurthala State. They did not follow the ordinary burial customs of the Sikhs or Hindus, and did not immerse the bones of the dead in the Ganga. They had special rites for marriage and did not revere the Brahmans. They had a Gurdwara of Baba Handal at Jandiala in the Amritsar district. Another disciple of Guru Amar Das was Gangu whose great grandson, Jawahir Singh, founded a shrine at Khatkar Kalan in the Jalandhar district. His followers in Ambala returned themselves as Sikhs but his followers in Hoshiarpur returned themselves as Hindus. Another leader of this sect was Mahi Bhagat or Mahisar. Yet another sect associated with Guru Amar Das was that of Bhai Lalu.[58]

Associated with Guru Ram Das were the sects of Bhai Bhoj Singh and the Ganjbakhshi Sikhs. Far more important, however, were the Ramdasi Sikhs. The term Ramdasi applied to the followers of Guru Ram Das, and even to followers of all Gurus.

It was also used to denote a *chamar* or *julaha* who had taken the Sikh form of baptism. In 1891, a little over 40,000 Sikhs returned themselves as Ramdasis. In 1901, they were only a little more than 20,000.[59]

The Jhiwars, who looked upon Baba Kalu or Kalu Kahar as the founder of their sect, regarded him as a disciple of Guru Arjan. They looked upon the *Granth* of Guru Gobind Singh with great respect; Kalu Kahar himself was a worshipper of Krishna and a devotee of Shiva. The Jhiwar *mahant* at Panjnangal, the main shrine of the sect, was ninth in line from him. A fairly large grant of revenue-free land was attached to this shrine. There were three other shrines: one at Kiratpur, another at Panchat, and the third beyond Delhi. Apart from Jhiwars, other low-caste men were followers of this sect. In 1891, over 3,000 Sikhs returned themselves as its followers from Ambala district. Another sect associated with Guru Arjan was that of a carpenter named Lakhu, with 36 Sikhs among its followers. Yet another sect was that of Tilok Singh, a descendant from Bhai Salu who was a Sikh of Guru Arjan; 345 Sikhs returned themselves as its followers. They had a *dharmsala* in the city of Amritsar. The Sat Kartaris, associated with Guru Arjan, were like the Udasis but did not wear the *jattan* or smear themselves with ashes. Their clothes were dyed in madder. In 1891, only 84 Sikhs returned themselves as Sat Kartaris. There were 13 Sikhs who regarded themselves as the Sikhs of Guru Arjan.[60]

Associated with Guru Hargobind were the Bhais of Bagarian. And so were the Dhirmallis, with one of their chief stations at Chak Ramdas in the Shahpur district. A member of the Dhirmal family was Baba Badbhag Singh; his shrine was at Mairi, near Amb, in the Una *tahsil* of the Hoshiarpur district. The fair held there at the Holi and the Baisakhi was attended by large crowds from the Doaba, Malwa and the Majha tracts. The cult was the most widespread in the Jalandhar district.[61]

Associated with Guru Har Rai were the followers of Bhai Pheru, known also as Sangat Sahib. Counted often as Udasis, they had established a 'peripatetic *akhara*'. Another category of ascetics associated with Guru Har Rai were the Diwana Sadhs who took an excessive quantity of *bhang* and *charas*. They wore their hair uncut and necklaces of shells; on their turbans they wore a large peacock feather. They followed the *Adi Granth*. They were mainly returned from among the Jats and Chamars of the Jalandhar district, though the sect had its headquarters at Pirpind in the Malwa.[62]

Coming from the time of Guru Harkrishan were the followers of his elder brother Ram Rai, who refused to recognize Guru Hargobind and Guru Gobind Singh. They followed a scripture introduced by Ram Rai as well as the *Adi Granth*. They laid stress on being Sikhs but they did not preserve the *kes*. They were expressly disclaimed by the Khalsa Sikhs of Guru Gobind Singh. The Ram Raiyas were mainly agriculturists and labourers of the Malwa and Doaba tracts. In 1891, they numbered 27,122. Their number was reduced to 24,500 in 1901.[63]

Associated with Guru Tegh Bahadur were the Sewapanthis, the followers of Kanhaya Lal. They believed in the *Adi Granth* and abstained from meat, wine, tobacco, *bhang* and *charas*. They worked with their hands, chiefly twisting ropes and bed-cords. They were mainly Aroras and Khatris, and figured mainly in the Shahpur and Jhang districts. In the Amritsar district they were known as Adan Shahis, after the name of a disciple of Kanhaya. In 1891, only 27 Sikhs returned themselves as Sewapanthis. The number of persons who claimed to be the Sikhs of Guru Tegh Bahadur was 61.[64]

Among the adherents of Guru Gobind Singh, besides the Khalsa, were the followers of the sect of Baba Zorawar Singh in the Ambala district. A woman known as Mai Kangwali was the occupant of the *gaddi* of a sect founded by a Jat disciple of Guru Gobind Singh at Kang in the Hoshiarpur *tahsil*. The principles of this sect were close to those of Guru Nanak. The followers belonged mainly to Jalandhar and Hoshiarpur districts in 1891. The Akalis, also known as Nihangs, formed another sect associated with Guru Gobind Singh. They wore a dark blue or checked dress, with a peaked turban, surmounted with steel quoits, and retained the five Ks. Sometimes they wore a yellow turban underneath the blue one. They avoided Hindu rites in their wedding ceremonies. They consumed *bhang* rather immoderately. They met at the Akal Bunga in Amritsar, the Pir Sahib at Attock, and the shrines of Guru Gobind Singh at Patna and Abchal Nagar. Their chief home was at Kiratpur and the Gurdwara Anandpur

Sahib at Anandpur, the shrine *par excellence* of the Akalis. They took part in the 'Holi' fair there.

The Nirmalas too professed adherence to Guru Gobind Singh. They believed in the principles of Vedanta and many of the customs of the Shastras. They avoided meat and spirits. They wore the ochre-coloured dress of the Indian ascetics. Their uncut hair distinguished them from the Udasis. They were almost always celibate and lived in monasteries, and on offerings. They enjoyed a high reputation for morality and learning. In 1891, their principal *akhara* was at Hardwar and they had monasteries at Munak, Adamwal, and Alampur Kotla in the Hoshiarpur district. In the Ambala, Ferozepur and Amritsar districts, the Nirmalas returned themselves as Sikhs but in the Gurdaspur district as Hindus. The Akalis were especially bitter against the Nirmalas who, in 1891, were thought to be gradually returning to 'a pure form of orthodox Hinduism'.[65]

Apart from the categories of Sikhs enumerated in terms of their allegiance to a particular Guru, or a sect associated with a particular Guru, the descendants of the Gurus are mentioned as enjoying a respectable status among the Sikhs. The Bedis were held in great reverence by the Sikhs as having descended from Guru Nanak. Their leaders in 1891 were Baba Faqiria, Baba Mahtab Singh, and Baba Khem Singh Bedi, a descendant of Baba Sahib Singh Bedi of Una, who had a large following especially in the Jhelum, Rawalpindi and Peshawar districts. The Bedis lived mostly at Una in the Hoshiarpur district and at Dera Baba Nanak in the Gurdaspur district. The most famous of the Bedis were true Sikhs of the school of Guru Gobind Singh. The descendants of Guru Angad and Guru Amar Das, that is, the Tihun and the Bhalla families, were respected by the Sikhs. Far more influential, however, were the Sodhi descendants of Guru Ram Das. The Sikhs of Kohat and Tirah were largely followers of Sodhi Partap Singh of Lahore. The central stations of the Sodhis were in Kartarpur, Kiratpur, and Anandpur. The Sodhis of Kartarpur were largely Dhirmallis. The Sodhis of Anandpur were descended from Suraj Mal (a son of Guru Hargobind). They had nine shrines in Anandpur and made an appearance in their full glory at the time of the Holi festival. The Manji Sahibs at Anandpur and Kiratpur were worshipped.[66]

A number of persons who belonged to sects other than the Sikhs returned themselves as Sikhs. Among the worshippers of Bhairon in 1901, there were 26 Sikhs. The number of Sikhs who returned themselves as Durga Upasak or Devi Dharm was 7,493; the number of Shakat Sikhs was 482, and one belonged to the Kola-panth. The cult of the Devis was sought to be revived in the Kapurthala State around 1899 but the worship died out. Over 1,800 Sikhs returned themselves as the worshippers of Shiva from the Hoshiarpur, Jalandhar and Ambala districts. Only 8 Sikhs returned themselves as Sanyasis, mostly from Shahpur. The number of Sikhs who returned themselves in 1901 as belonging to the sect of Jogi Pir was 571; 86 Sikhs returned themselves as the followers of Gopi Chand, and 18 as the disciples of Gorakhnath. Five Sikhs in the Ambala district returned themselves as belonging to the sect of Jangams who wore matted hair, rejected the Vedas, preached the equality of all men, and were the puritan followers of Shiva. Among the sects broadly known as Vaishnava, there were 1,340 Sikhs. Among the Radhaswamis in 1901 there were 473 Sikhs. There were 62,000 Sultani Sikhs, mostly in the districts of Ferozepur, Ludhiana and Amritsar.[67]

To this great variety of Sikhs were added the Udasis who paid special reverence to the *Adi Granth*, respected Guru Gobind Singh, and attended the same shrines as the Sikhs. In 1891, they were seen as divided into four orders (*dhuans*): Phul Sahib, Balu Hasna, Almast Sahib, and Goind Sahib. There were also sections called Bhagat Bhagwan with a Gurdwara at Patna and Sangat Sahib (with an establishment at Bhai Pheru). Each subdivision had a complete organization for collecting and spending money, and was presided over by a principal *mahant*, called Sri Mahant, with subordinate *mahants* under him. With the aid of Maharaja Narendra Singh of Patiala, a follower of Sangat Sahib named Baba Manohar Das had founded the *Chhota Akhara*. The Udasis were almost always celibate, sometimes lived in monasteries, and were generally found wandering. They were strongest in the districts of Jalandhar, Ferozepur and Rohtak, and numerous in Malwa and Benares. The customs they followed were not uniform. Some wore long hair, some matted locks, and others cut their hair. Some wore *tilak* marks, while others did not. The Udasis in Ludhiana were mostly Jat in origin. They read the *Granths* of

Guru Nanak and Guru Gobind Singh, though they did not attach much importance to the *Granth* of Guru Gobind Singh. They lived in both Sikh and Hindu villages. In the family of Jaspal Bangar it was customary to marry; their endowment was large enough to support the family and the institution. The shrine at Dera Baba Nanak was in the custody of Udasi *sadhs*; their *mahant* was appointed with the consent of the Bedis. The shrine founded at Tahli Sahib by Sri Chand was also looked after by the *mahants* of the Udasi order. Apart from the Gulabdasis noticed earlier, the Suthra Shahis formed a semimonastic and semimendicant Udasi order. Their doubtful origin was attributed to Guru Arjan, Guru Hargobind, Guru Har Rai, or Guru Tegh Bahadur. They wore black marks on their foreheads and black woollen ropes twisted around their heads and necks. They burnt their dead and threw their bones into the Ganga; they used intoxicants, and smoked tobacco. They proceeded along the bazaars, clashing together a couple of short staves and shouting *dholas* or mystic Punjabi songs indifferently in honour of Guru Nanak and the goddess Devi. Their principal Gurdwara was at Lahore. They were mainly returned from the districts of Gurdaspur and Jalandhar. In 1881, there were only 52 Sikhs among the Suthra Shahis; in 1891, their number was 94. In 1901, the number of Sikhs returned as Udasis by sect was 401, and by religion 4,213. They could be divided into two main categories: those who wore topknot and refrained from smoking and thus in a sense were Sikhs, and those who did not wear topknot and used water drawn by a rope in a brass vessel and might smoke and thus were Hindus.[68]

The large number of sectarian identities among the Sikhs were seen as falling into two broad categories: the Nanakpanthi and the Khalsa. In 1891, more than 395,000 Sikhs thought of themselves as Nanakpanthis. They were roughly those who did not think it necessary to follow 'the ceremonial and social observances inculcated by Guru Gobind Singh'. The chief external difference was the disposal of hair: the Nanakpanthis did not keep their *kesh* uncut. They were also known as Sahajdharis. The form of baptism followed by the Nanakpanthis was the Hindu practice of drinking 'foot-nectar of the Guru' and even that was not very common. There was 'very little difference' between a Nanakpanthi and an ordinary lax Hindu. It was difficult to apply the term Nanakpanthi to the various categories of Sikhs. The term had several connotations: it could mean 'the followers of Guru Nanak' and hence all Sikhs. In fact, many Sikhs who cut their hair and smoked tobacco returned themselves as Sikhs in spite of instructions to the contrary given to the enumerators. Many others who kept the hair unshorn and abstained from tobacco, who did not worship idols and did not revere Brahmans to any great extent, and followed the teachings of the *Granth*, called themselves Nanakpanthi Sikhs. Still others who revered the *Granth* and also revered Brahmans, worshipped idols now and then, did not abstain from tobacco and shaved their heads, called themselves Nanakpanthi Sikhs. Some of them called themselves Nanakpanthi Hindus. There was no clear line of distinction between them. The Aroras of Kohat kept their hair uncut, did not smoke though they sold tobacco, did not as a rule take the *pahul* or observe the four remaining Ks of Guru Gobind Singh's ordinances, went to the Sikh places of worship and listened to the recitation of the *Adi Granth*, used the Sikh forms of morning and evening prayers, i.e. *Japji* and *Rahiras*.[69]

Apart from the Nirankaris noticed earlier, there were several sects among the Nanakpanthis. Included among them were the followers of Baba Buddha, a disciple of Guru Hargobind. They worshipped at Ramdas, Amritsar, Teja and Nainakot and belonged mostly to the districts of Hoshiarpur, Gurdaspur and Sialkot. Another sect was that of Baba Mula, patron of the Phulkian houses with a shrine at Sunam. Other Nanakpanthi sects were those of Baba Lakhu, Bhai Gola, Bhai Ranbar, and Baba Nand Singh. The Sanwal Shahis of the frontier believed in the Sikh scriptures and had holy places at Dera Ismail Khan, Sahiwal and Kot Shakir. However, only 11 Sikhs returned themselves as belonging to this sect in 1891.[70]

In 1901, more than 200,000 persons returned themselves as Nanakpanthis, mostly from the districts of Ludhiana, Lahore and Gujranwala. This number, significantly, was half the number of Nanakpanthis a decade earlier.[71] Many of them presumably had joined the Khalsa fold.

In 1891, more than 555,000 Sikhs thought of themselves as Guru Gobind Singhis. In terms of doctrine they were not distinguished from the followers of Guru Nanak, or those of Kabir and other Bhagats. Indeed, if the reforms of Guru Gobind Singh had not been successful the Sikhs would have been akin to the sects of the Dadupanthis or Bishnois. Guru Gobind Singh added five basic points to the Sikh religion: baptism by way of *pahul* instead of *charan pahul*, the five *kakkas*, abstaining from tobacco, eating of animal flesh decapitated by way of *jhatka*, and non-observance of the distinctions of caste or paying special reverence to Brahmans.[72] In 1901, many of the Gobind Singhi Sikhs did not return any sect. In the district of Amritsar, for example, only 20,000 Sikhs out of 264,329 were recorded as the Sikhs of Guru Gobind Singh. But the real figures were much higher. Consequently, the figures for the Gobind Singhi Sikhs as a sect fell from 550,000 in 1891 to 419,793 in 1901.[73] Many among the Khalsa had begun to think that they represented the Sikhs as the central stream.

A new line of demarcation drawn between the followers of Guru Gobind Singh was noticed in the census report of 1891. A party among them tried to combine the teachings of the Sikhs with a 'considerable latitude of thought and adoption of European methods'. The others were anxious to preserve the 'old forms as intact as possible' out of the fear that such developments would have an adverse effect on the 'character of the people and the stability of the religion'. Each school had its leaders and the opposition between them had at times been very acute.[74]

By 1901, the party that stood for change had become more influential. More than 730,000 Sikhs did not return any sect. H.A. Rose observed that this was due to a tendency among the Sikhs 'to abandon the sects and join religious associations, the Sabhas and so on'. The Singh Sabha was not returned as a sect; the omission to return any sect was the most noticeable in Amritsar itself. Instead of new sects being founded, the tendency now was to organize societies. The Deputy Commissioner of Amritsar observed that the Sri Guru Singh Sabha had stirred up the people not only in cities and towns but also in the rural areas, 'inculcating the principles of the Sikh faith and enjoining the necessity of a separate religious and political existence'. The influence of the movement was spreading in Rawalpindi too. There were three categories of Sikhs there: the followers of Sir Khem Singh Bedi, the Nirankaris, and the protagonists of the Singh Sabhas. With the advance of education, the followers of Sir Khem Singh Bedi and the Nirankaris started going to the Singh Sabhas. Still, nearly 1,400,000 Sikhs indicated their sectarian affiliation in 1901. They represented about 60 per cent of the total Sikh population.[75] They included both the Sahajdharis and the Khalsa.

In the late nineteenth century, there was a wide variety of self-identification among the Sikhs. Externally, however, they appeared to fall into two categories: the Khalsa and the Sahajdhari. The former were larger in number from the very beginning. Among both the categories appeared new ideas and practices. The number of the Khalsa was increasing more than that of the Sahajdharis. In this context, Singh Sabhas began to espouse Singh or Khalsa identity. They did not look upon their identity as sectarian. In other words, Khalsa identity for them was 'the Sikh identity' – an identity distinct from that of the 'Hindus'.

NOTES

1. *Report on the Census of the Punjab, 1868*, pp. 7, 8; *Report on the Census of the Punjab, 1901*, pp. 1, 4.
2. *Report on the Census of the Punjab, 1868*, pp. 7, 22, General Statement III A; *Report on the Census of the Punjab, 1881*, pp. 1, 141; *Report on the Census of the Punjab, 1891*, Table VI showing the religion of the people; *Report on the Census of the Punjab, 1901*, pp. 1, 122, Subsidiary Tables IA&B; *Report on the Census of the Punjab, 1911*, pp. 141, 153; *Report on the Census of the Punjab, 1911*, Part I, pp. 58, 154.
3. *Report on the Census of the Punjab, 1868*, pp. 7, 8; *Report on the Census of the Punjab, 1881*, p. 2; *Report on the Census of the Punjab, 1891*, p. 60; *Report on the Census of the Punjab, 1901*, pp. 1, 3.
4. *Report on the Census of the Punjab, 1868*, p. 23.
5. Ibid., details on percentages in all divisions and districts in the table on percentages and averages.
6. Ibid., p. 23.
7. *Report on the Census of the Punjab, 1881*, pp. 106, 138.
8. *Report on the Census of the Punjab, 1891*, Table VI, showing the religion of the people.
9. *Report on the Census of the Punjab, 1901*, Subsidiary Table IB.
10. *Report on the Census of the Punjab, 1901*, Subsidiary Table IB.
11. *Report on the Census of the Punjab, 1881*, p. 106; *Report on the Census of the Punjab, 1891*, Abstract 9.

12. *Report on the Census of the Punjab, 1868*, Appendix to General Statement no. I, showing numbers of adults and children male and female in each sect; Appendix to General Statement no. I, percentage of males and females among adults (i.e. above 12 years of age), p. 52; *Report on the Census of the Punjab, 1881*, pp. 351, 367, 370, 372, 375; *Report on the Census of the Punjab, 1891*, Table VI, showing the religion of the people, pp. 211, 217, 218.
13. *Report on the Census of the Punjab, 1901*, pp. 202, 203, 206.
14. Ibid., pp. 201, 206:

SIKHS IN THE FOUR NATURAL REGIONS IN 12 AGE GROUPS IN 1901

	Indo-Gangetic Plain		*Himalayan*		*Sub-Himalayan*		*North-West*	
Age Group	*All Religions*	*Sikh*	*All Religions*	*Sikh*	*All Religions*	*Sikh*	*All Religions*	*Sikh*
0-1	906	787	986	738	934	824	961	780
0-5	905	762	1,011	738	932	831	957	815
5-10	848	735	980	718	864	792	856	722
10-15	755	667	802	728	750	678	734	600
15-20	754	676	891	550	819	700	790	517
20-25	883	841	954	428	977	875	897	498
25-30	871	894	931	362	938	838	847	568
30-35	887	918	928	562	946	876	843	569
35-40	852	876	811	332	869	789	766	555
40-45	897	924	873	551	932	868	856	663
45-60	810	799	748	367	866	754	767	602
60& >	855	784	875	503	853	678	768	559

15. Ibid., pp. 212, 213, 216.
16. Ibid., p. 205.
17. *Report on the Census of the Punjab, 1868*, Districtwise figures in the General Statement no. 1, statistical return for the area and population in the districts of the Punjab, p. 2.
18. *Report on the Census of the Punjab, 1901*, Table VIII, Part II, District Tables.
19. Ibid., Subsidiary Table III A.
20. *Report on the Census of the Punjab, 1881*, pp. 401, 405. Table XIII gives the details on all the educated males and females among the Sikhs for the villages, districts, princely states, the British territory and the province of the Punjab.
21. *Report on the Census of the Punjab, 1891*, pp. 250, 251.
22. *Report on the Census of the Punjab, 1901*, pp. 263, 264, 269.

23. *Report on the Census of the Punjab, 1868*, pp. 25, 26, 28. General Statement no. IV, population according to occupations.
24. *Report on the Census of the Punjab, 1881*, pp. 346, 376, 380; *Report on the Census of the Punjab, 1891*, Abstract no. 88.
25. *Report on the Census of the Punjab, 1901*, pp. 358, 359, 364, 366, 371.
26. *Report on the Census of the Punjab, 1881*, p. 185.
27. Ibid., Table VII A.
28. Ibid., pp. 107, 108, 138, 230, 231, 295.
29. *Report on the Census of the Punjab, 1891*, pp. 28, 96.
30. Ibid., p. 96; Abstract no. 86.

PERCENTAGE OF SIKHS IN CASTE GROUPS IN 1891

Castes		*Percentage of each caste to the total males of all castes among Sikhs*
Agricultural		
Jat		51.00
Kamboh		2.00
Rajput, etc.		1.07
	Total	64.36
Professional & Commercial		
Arora		3.22
Khatri		2.29
	Total	7.58
Artisan & Village Menials		
Chamar		5.75
Chuhra		5.07
Jhiwar		1.18
Lohar		1.30
Nai		11.07
Tarkhan		7.21
	Total	25.60
Vagrants, Minor Artisans & Performers		1.22

31. Ibid., p. 88; Abstract no. 18.
32. *Report on the Census of the Punjab, 1901*, pp. xii, 301.
33. Ibid., p. 302; Subsidiary Table VII E.

SIKH MALES AND FEMALES IN DIFFERENT CASTES IN 1901

Caste	*Males*	*Females*	*Total*
Jat	798,128	599,510	13,97,638
Arora	39,948	31,576	71,524
Khatri	34,006	26,061	60,067
Nai	13,849	11,559	25,408
Labana	12,334	10,839	23,173
Chuhra	12,520	10,207	22,727
Rajput	11,596	8,259	19,855
Mahtam	10,515	8,668	19,183
Mazhabi	5,875	4,130	10,005
Bhatia	3,707	2,991	6,694
Karral	1,383	1,217	2,600
Gujar	1,052	818	1,870

34. Ibid., 1901, pp. 302-40.
35. *Report on the Census of the Punjab, 1881*, p. 2; *Report on the Census of the Punjab, 1891*, pp. 1, 2, 59; *Report on the Census of the Punjab, 1901*, pp. 1, 2.
36. *Report on the Census of the Punjab, 1881*, p. 2; *Report on the Census of the Punjab, 1891*, Table VI, showing the religion of the people; *Report on the Census of the Punjab, 1901*, p. 1.
37. *Report on the Census of the Punjab, 1881*, p. 106.
38. *Report on the Census of the Punjab, 1891*, p. 95.
39. *Report on the Census of the Punjab, 1901*, p. 122.
40. *Report on the Census of the Punjab, 1881*, p. 106; *Report on the Census of the Punjab, 1891*, Abstract no. 9.
41. *Report on the Census of the Punjab, 1881*, pp. 351, 367.
42. *Report on the Census of the Punjab, 1891*, Table VI, showing the religion of the people.
43. Ibid., p. 264.
44. Ibid., p. 265.
45. Ibid., p. 269.
46. *Report on the Census of the Punjab, 1881*, pp. 135, 136.
47. Ibid., pp. 136, 137.
48. *Report on the Census of the Punjab, 1891*, pp. 48, 91; *Report on the Census of the Punjab, 1901*, p. 124.
49. *Report on the Census of the Punjab, 1891*, pp. 20, 92, 93; *Report on the Census of the Punjab, 1901*, p. 124.
50. *Census Procedure for the Punjab, 1911*, Part I, pp. 59, 154.
51. *Report on the Census of the Punjab, 1881*, pp. 137, 138; *Report on the Census of the Punjab, 1891*, Table F, pp. 833, 834.

52. Ibid., pp. 168-70.
53. *Report on the Census of the Punjab, 1901*, p. 137.
54. *Report on the Census of the Punjab, 1891*, p. 157.
55. *Report on the Census of the Punjab, 1901*, pp. 125, 126.
56. *Report on the Census of the Punjab, 1891*, p. 153.
57. Ibid., p. 157.
58. Ibid., p. 158.
59. Ibid., pp. 158, 159; *Report on the Census of the Punjab, 1901*, pp. 135, 136.
60. *Report on the Census of the Punjab, 1891*, pp. 159, 160.
61. Ibid., pp. 160, 161.
62. Ibid., p. 161.
63. Ibid., p. 162; *Report on the Census of the Punjab, 1901*, pp. 135, 136.
64. *Report on the Census of the Punjab, 1891*, pp. 151, 162, 163.
65. Ibid., pp. 165, 166, 167, 168.
66. Ibid., pp. 150, 151, 156, 163, 164.
67. *Report on the Census of the Punjab, 1901*, pp. 126, 127, 129, 130, 131, 132, 133.
68. *Report on the Census of the Punjab, 1891*, pp. 151, 152, 154.
69. Ibid., pp. 148, 149, 150.
70. Ibid., pp. 155, 156, 157.
71. *Report on the Census of the Punjab, 1901*, pp. 133, 134.
72. *Report on the Census of the Punjab, 1891*, pp. 164, 165.
73. *Report on the Census of the Punjab, 1901*, p. 136.
74. *Report on the Census of the Punjab, 1891*, p. 171.
75. *Report on the Census of the Punjab, 1901*, pp. 124, 125.

6

Transition from Socio-Religious to Political Concerns: Sikh Periodicals of the Early Twentieth Century

JOGINDER SINGH

Studies in modern Sikh history have been largely confined to either the last quarter of the nineteenth century, which was the high tide of the Singh Sabha movement, or the last quarter of British rule in India when the Akalis came to the fore as a political party. Historical works on the last quarter of the nineteenth century reflect essentially the socio-religious concerns of the Sikh community.[1] Explicit political interests are seen as emerging in the third decade of the twentieth century.[2] Transformation from socioreligious to political concerns appears to have taken place in the early decades of the century. To understand the nature of this transformation I propose to analyse some periodicals published by the Sikhs specifically for a Sikh readership during this phase of transition.

The number of Sikh periodicals in circulation in the first two decades of the twentieth century was more than thirty. They were published in Punjabi, Urdu and English on weekly, fortnightly or monthly basis, and as occasional bulletins or supplements. Most of the individuals associated with these periodicals came from professional classes as teachers, lawyers, pleaders, physicians, and servicemen. Some of the proprietors and publishers were also engaged in petty business like shopkeeping, tailoring, and bookselling. However, all of them were associated directly or indirectly with the Singh Sabhas. The readership initially came from the educated section of the Sikh community which was largely confined to those towns where the influence of Singh Sabhas was considerable. With the expansion of the socio-religious associations and educational institutions, the range of the readership also became wider, covering most of the towns and many villages of the province.[3]

To begin with, these periodicals largely reflected the socioreligious programme of the Singh Sabhas.[4] New developments in the Punjab, as in the country as a whole, in the early years of the twentieth century sharpened the political consciousness of the Sikhs. They were unhappy over the indifferent attitude of the government towards the hardships of the Sikh immigrants abroad, inadequate representation of the Sikhs in the civil services and the Councils, and what they termed as the official intervention in the internal affairs of the 'Panth'. By the end of the second decade, most of the periodicals found themselves in opposition to the government.

As it may be expected, there is continuity of ideas, attitudes and concerns from the late nineteenth to the early twentieth century. The journals like the *Khalsa Samachar* and the *Khalsa Advocate* gave ample space to articles, essays and fiction dealing with Sikh traditions and theological issues.[5] They also brought out special features on the biographies of the Sikh Gurus and martyrs. This literary resurgence primarily dealt with two interrelated themes: Sikh religion and Sikh history. In Sikh religion, they emphasized the principles of *gurmaryada* and the observance of *rahit* or code of conduct, especially the five Ks. They also appealed to the Sikhs to observe due ceremonies on the occasions of birth, marriage, and death in accordance with the principles of *gurmaryada*.[6]

The periodicals emphasized the distinction between Sikhism and Hinduism, quoting Gurbani in support of their ideas. In fact, they had recourse to all kinds of sources, such as legends, *sakhis* and the works of contemporary scholars like Bhai Santokh Singh.[7] They referred to them to emphasize that the Sikh Gurus neither preached Vedic philosophy nor did they observe Brahmanical rituals and customs.[8] They asserted that the path of the Sikh

Gurus was essentially different from the one laid down in the Vedas.[9] This was partly in response to the Arya Samajist assertion that Sikhism was nothing more than a new sect of Hinduism.[10] In fact, the Sikh periodicals perceived a threat of Hinduization from the proselytizing activities of the Arya Samajists who had been insulting and humiliating Sikhism and the Sikh Gurus. No less dangerous were the Ahmadiyas and the Christian missionaries. The newspapers condemned conversions and gave statistics of converted Sikhs, or proposed to be converted. They drew attention of the Sikh leaders and local organizations to the areas where the common Sikhs had become victims of proselytization. To stem the tide, they appealed to the Panth to raise Khalsa institutions. Above all, they made a strong appeal to *sardars, zaildars, lambardars*, and *safedposhes* to adopt a liberal and sympathetic attitude towards *rahtias* and *ramdasias*. Similar appeals came from the Sikh *sangats*.[11]

Simultaneously, the periodicals, especially the tracts published by the Khalsa Tract Society, Amritsar, wrote on Sikh history.[12] Several anecdotes of the encounters of the 'Singhs' with the contingents of the Mughals and the Afghans were related to highlight the heroic tradition of the Sikhs. The 'Singhs' were honest, fearless, chivalrous and dedicated to the cause of the Panth, both in the battlefield and in their day to day life. On the other hand, the soldiers and *amirs* on the side of the contemporary rulers were corrupt, cowardly and disloyal. They remained under the dread of the 'Singhs' and avoided a straight fight.[13] Bhai Vir Singh's works depicted 'the wholesale persecution of the Sikhs and indiscriminate massacres launched against them by the later Mughals'.[14]

Another recurrent theme was the martyrdom of the Sikh Gurus which focused on the ideological conflict between the Gurus and the contemporary rulers. The former were the upholders of righteousness, whereas the latter personified tyranny and fanaticism.[15] The martyrdom of Guru Arjan was also explained in terms of the tension between the existing orthodoxy and the nascent religion. Explaining the causes and circumstances of the martyrdom of Guru Arjan, the editor of the *Khalsa Advocate*, for instance, stated that 'at bottom of all this lay, in fact, the hatred that the Diwan (Chandu) being an orthodox Hindu, bore against the new doctrine of Sikhism preached by the Gurus; a doctrine that aimed at the refutation of weaknesses and superstitious aspects of Hinduism'.[16]

This period saw the proliferation of literature on Sikh religion and Sikh history. Concern with socioreligious symbols and institutions was clearly evident in the books and periodicals published in the wake of the Singh Sabha movement. The Khalsa Tract Society alone under the patronage of Bhai Vir Singh produced tracts numbering more than six lakhs. The writings of Gyani Gyan Singh, Bhai Kahn Singh, Bhagat Lakshman Singh, Principal Teja Singh and Bhai Jodh Singh also aimed at serving the cause of the Panth.[17] In 1909, M.A. Macauliffe also produced his monumental work on *The Sikh Religion*, largely presenting the new Sikh viewpoint.

The periodicals understood the relevance of modern education in the wake of new challenges. They noted that the education imparted in the institutions of the Christian missionaries and the Arya Samajists could alienate the Sikh youth from their socio-cultural heritage. Therefore, they pleaded with the Sikh organizations to establish their own educational institutions which could educate the Sikh youth in the Sikh traditions. Such an orientation was extremely essential to meet the challenge from the Arya Samajists and the Christian missionaries. In this context, the *Khalsa Samachar* warned Sikh parents that their children would go astray from the Sikh way of life and become non-Sikhs if they were sent to non-Sikh educational institutions. To prove its contention, it quoted statistics regarding the conversion of the Sikh youth either to Arya Samaj or Christianity. This newspaper made an appeal to the Sikh leaders to establish Khalsa institutions in which the curricula should include celebration of birth and death anniversaries of the Sikh Gurus and martyrs as well as the study of Sikh history and theology.[18]

Education of women was considered equally important. The columnists of the newspapers thought that their very task of educating the Sikhs could be defeated without educating women. The primary aim was to impart religious education to the Sikh youth, as nothing could be more useful for the propagation of Sikhism than educating women who were instrumental in introducing the Sikh youth to religious traditions at an early age.

The women were regarded as an important channel of transmitting ethical and moral values. There were certain skills which needed to be taught to the Sikh women, the skills of home science. Schemes were conceived to introduce separate classes for girls in the middle and high schools to impart training in cooking, nursing and tailoring.[19]

Language was considered to be a vehicle of progress for the community and the country. The newspapers took up the cause of Punjabi language and Gurmukhi script. The founders of the newspapers thought that the Gurus had adopted Punjabi language for the progress of the Panth, and for the same reason, Gurmukhi was invented by Guru Angad.[20] In 1909, the editor of a newspaper stated that Punjabi was the language of Punjabis, irrespective of their caste or creed.[21] Regarding its script, it was propagated that the Gurmukhi script was more suitable than the Devanagari. Punjabi literature in Gurmukhi script was the repository of Sikh cultural heritage. This was one of the primary causes of the importance which the Sikhs gave to Punjabi language and Gurmukhi script. They asked the other Punjabis to adopt them.[22]

For the development of Punjabi language, the periodicals pleaded with the government to make it the medium of instruction, at least at the primary level. For the convenience of laymen, they asked the government to conduct the proceedings of the civil and military courts in Punjabi. For the same reason, the government should permit people to address their letters in Punjabi; the third class compartments of the trains in the Punjab should carry signs in Punjabi.[23] At the same time, the protagonists of Punjabi published a variety of articles, essays, and stories of eminent scholars and new writers. They dealt not only with the socio-religious or historical issues but also with contemporary problems in the field of science, education, technology, and politics, though marginally.

Mismanagement of Gurdwaras associated with Sikh Gurus and martyrs attracted the attention of Sikh periodicals. The Gurdwaras had been under the control either of *mahants* and *pujaris* or the *sarbrahs* appointed by the government.[24] The controllers of the shrines had begun to misuse the funds and convert landed property of Gurdwaras into their personal possession. The *mahants* and their *chelas* were living 'a life of luxury and dissipation verging on depravity'.[25] The periodicals began to expose the evil practices of the *mahants* and their un-Sikh predilections. They protested against this flagrant disregard of the injunctions laid down by the Sikh Gurus. The *Khalsa Advocate* reminded the *mahants* that the Gurdwaras and their endowments belonged to the Panth and that they had no right to use them for their personal ends.[26] When the *mahants* and *pujaris* did not mend their ways, and even assaulted the Sikh *sangats* in the precincts of Gurdwaras, the periodicals such as the *Khalsa Samachar* and the *Khalsa Advocate* began to ask for their removal.[27] They also pleaded with the government that the Panth should have the right to manage its shrines. Voicing this concern, the *Khalsa Advocate* stated that if the Panth was not given the powers to supervise the shrines, it would reduce the sanctity of Gurdwaras and give protection to 'these blackguards and cheats who can cloak their mischief under the garb of granthiship'.[28]

Until this time, the tone of most of the periodicals had been either clearly 'loyalist' or at least 'moderate'. A section of the editors, publishers, and proprietors had been directly or indirectly associated with the Singh Sabhas and shared the 'loyalist' stance of the Chief Khalsa Diwan. The *Khalsa Advocate* professed to work for 'God, Guru and Government'. The *Sikh Sepoy* undertook to serve three Cs: 'Crown, Country and Community'. It contained recruitment news, poems on loyalty, and essays about the Sikh heroes and their bravery.[29] However, serving the interests of the community was their *raison d'être* which they would not compromise despite their loyalist stance. They criticized, and even protested against the government policy and attitude which they thought were against the Panth. The *Khalsa Advocate*, termed as 'moderate' in the official circles, had to be warned three times for printing objectionable matter.[30]

The demolition of a wall of Gurdwara Rakabganj at Delhi and the ban on carrying *kirpan* brought the government in direct opposition to what was regarded as the 'legitimate' interests of the Sikhs.[31] Even the moderate periodicals like the *Khalsa Samachar* and the *Sikh Sepoy* described such actions as official intervention in the internal affairs of the Panth, contrary to the claims of the government to a policy of religious neutrality.[32] It was asserted that the Panth should have the right to manage its own affairs and have the freedom to observe Sikh rituals and sacraments.[33] In fact, these periodicals thought of launching a *morcha* (battlefront) if the government did not reconstruct the boundary wall of Gurdwara Rakabganj on its original plinth.[34] Many periodicals began to criticize the loyalist politics of the Chief Khalsa Diwan. They also believed that unless the Sikhs had a new political organization, the community's interests would not be protected. The foremost among these periodicals were the *Sikh Review*, the *Khalsa Sewak* and the *Punjab Darpan*. This implied rejection of the loyalist politics of the Chief Khalsa Diwan, with a clear anti-British stance.

Politicization of the Sikh periodicals was also related to their concern for the problems of the Sikhs living abroad. Due to the agrarian crisis, many Punjabi peasants had sold or mortgaged their small holdings and left for countries like Canada and USA. At the end of the nineteenth century, their number was in thousands.[35] Reports began to pour in about their hardships as a result partly of restrictions imposed by the American and Canadian governments on their entry into these countries. As most of the immigrants were Sikhs, the periodicals took note of the problems of their brethren.[36] They pleaded with the Indian Government that the Sikhs were loyal subjects of the king. Therefore, it was the moral obligation of the British Government to solve their problems and to keep them happy and satisfied.[37] They appealed to the Viceroy to intervene in this matter and ask the Canadian Government to permit their entry.[38] At the same time, they appealed to the local Sikh organizations to hold public meetings and pass resolutions (*gurmatas*), expressing sympathy with the problems of the Sikhs abroad, and to send those resolutions to the 'Hind Sarkar'.[39] To apprise the government of the gravity of their problems, resolutions passed by the Singh Sabhas and Diwans in and outside the province were reproduced in the columns of newspapers like the *Khalsa Samachar* and the *Khalsa Sewak*.[40] The deliberations of the joint conferences of Hindus, Muslims and Sikhs on the problems of immigration of Hindustanis were also reported.[41]

The second decade of the twentieth century saw the growing concern of the periodicals with the inadequate representation of the Sikhs in the civil services. Earlier, they had acquiesced in the official argument that there was paucity of qualified Sikhs.[42] But this argument lost its validity with the increase in the number of educated Sikhs. The *Khalsa Advocate* pointed out that there was 'paucity of the Sikh youth in nearly all the departments'. There was not 'a single Sikh in the Indian Civil Service'. There were very few Sikh Munsifs and Extra Assistant Commissioners. There was also a paucity of Sikhs in the Superior Traffic Branch; in the Superior Police Department, their number was very small. 'In short, as compared with the people of other religions, the number of the Sikhs is always insignificant.'[43] However, the situation did not improve. The *Khalsa Advocate* made an enquiry into the number of Sikhs working in some of the major government departments like Excise and Taxation, Post and Telegraph, Judiciary, and Education, and came to the conclusion that, except in the Military Department, the Sikhs were almost non-existent in nearly all the departments of the government.[44]

The political and constitutional developments in the province also attracted the attention of the Sikhs.[45] The *Khalsa Samachar* and the *Khalsa Sewak* asked for separate representation for the Sikhs on government and semi-government bodies like the educational institutions, municipal committees, district boards, and provincial and imperial councils.[46] Before the Sikhs could ask for constitutional safeguards they had to assert that they had a separate political identity while even their distinct socio-religious identity was being questioned. They were treated as a section of the Hindus.[47] The periodicals began to publish a series of articles, speeches and addresses of the Sikh leaders, resolutions and appeals of the Sikh organizations, and editorials focusing on the theme of a separate Sikh political entity.[48] The journals also objected to the practice of recording the Sikhs as Hindus in the official records.[49] The government conceded their demand and the Sikhs began to be recorded separately in official and semi-official papers.

Since communal electorate had been introduced and Muslims had already got separate electorate under the Act of 1909, the *Khalsa Samachar* requested for a similar concession for the Sikhs.[50] In the elections to the Provincial Legislative Council under the Act of 1909, the Sikh candidates were completely muscled out by their rivals from other communities. The Lieutenant Governor of the Punjab had to complete the Sikh quota by nominations.[51]

Recalling this experience of the elections nearly a decade later, and advocating separate electorate for the Sikhs, the editor of the *Khalsa Advocate* stated:

> Every body knows that an able lawyer like Hon'ble Sardar Gajjan Singh could not succeed in election not because those in competition with him were more capable but because Sardar Bahadur was a Sikh. ... The experience of the last election alone is a great advocate for a separate electorate for the Sikhs.[52]

The political alliance between the Indian National Congress and the Muslim League, concluded at Lucknow in 1916, impelled the Sikh leaders to strive harder for separate representation. The claim of the Indian National Congress that it represented all the Indians, irrespective of their racial and religious affiliation, was questioned by the *Khalsa Advocate*, the *Sikh Sepoy* and the *Punjab Darpan*. The leaders began to feel that the Congress had been formed to protect the interests of the Hindus.[53] For the Sikhs, the Lucknow Pact was an agreement between two big brothers over share in the emerging power-structure in the country. The *Punjab Darpan* and the *Sikh Sepoy* interpreted this as an alliance of Punjabi Hindus and Muslims against the Sikhs.[54]

The implications of the Lucknow Pact became more serious in the face of the demand for Home Rule by the nationalists. The *Sikh Sepoy* and the *Punjab Darpan* saw this demand as a danger to the political existence of the minority communities.[55] Consequently, all the Sikh journals demanded 'weightage' for the Sikhs on all the representative bodies so that they could vote a bill or resolution in the interests of the community whenever the situation warranted. They also asked for one-third representation in the Provincial Legislative Council.[56] Their claim was based on two things. First, the Sikh community held a special position in the province, and second, they had been rendering 'unique' service to the British rulers, especially during the First World War.[57] The periodicals reinforced their argument by pointing out that the Sikhs were the predecessors of the British in the Punjab; that out of 218 families of note, 106 were Sikh; that the reform scheme was an outcome of the services rendered by the Sikhs in the War; and that the military contribution of the Sikhs was larger than that of the other communities.[58]

The official response to Sikh demands appeared to be favourable. The Punjab Government supported these demands and made recommendations to the Viceroy. The authors of the *Montague-Chelmsford Report* consequently recognized the Sikhs as a distinct and important people in the Punjab. The report also recognized their services to the rulers. However, the Franchise Committee did not accept their demands entirely and conceded only 'separate electoral role and separate constituencies for the Sikhs with 54 non-official seats'.[59]

Some of the periodicals like the *Panch*, the *Punjab Darpan* and the *Sikh Sepoy* challenged the underlying criteria of the Franchise Committee and questioned that if the Muslims could be given weightage in U.P. and Madras, why should it not be given to the Sikhs in the Punjab? The *Panch* protested against the numerical subordination of the Sikhs to other communities in the Punjab Legislative Council. They felt that they would not survive as a political entity unless they were given separate political rights.[60] Eventually, in the wake of the reforms of 1919, the Sikh journals came to realize that to safeguard their political existence and rights, the Sikhs needed a political organization of their own.[61] In fact, even before the War, the *Khalsa Advocate*, the *Khalsa Samachar* and the *Sikh Review* had maintained that in a competitive political system, a distinct political organization of the community was a necessity. The *Khalsa Sewak* noted that the British Government conceded demands only under pressure and that the other communities succeeded in getting their demands accepted because they could exercise pressure on the government through their respective political organizations.[62]

By now, most of the moderate Sikh periodicals had become disillusioned with the ineffective and pro-government political role of the Chief Khalsa Diwan. Since its inception in 1902, the Diwan had been extending moral and material help to the government, particularly during World War I.[63] It had also stood by the rulers at the time of the anti-British agrarian agitation of 1907 and the Ghadar movement of 1914-15. It had condemned all Sikh political activists who were opposed to the Raj.[64] The editor of the *Khalsa Sewak* said in exasperation that it was sheer illusion to hope for *panthic sewa* (service) from the leaders created by the British.[65] This exasperation culminated in the demand for a new representative body of the Sikhs which could create a situation favourable for the emergence of a new leadership.[66]

The process of founding a new political organization was initiated by the moderate Sikhs themselves. They observed that if the Hindus and the Muslims were opposing the separate rights of the Sikhs in the Punjab Legislative Council and also in the Viceroy's Council, it was simply because of the absence of a Sikh political organization. In response to this situation, the Sikh barristers of Lahore 'evinced a keen interest' in founding a political association. Active among them were Sant Singh, Devinder Singh, and Tirath Singh.[67] Another active leader was Sardul Singh Caveeshar who had recently shifted from Delhi to Lahore and started the *New Herald* in English. The local Sikh leaders had formed District Sikh Leagues in Lahore, Gujranwala, Sialkot and Lyallpur. The leaders of far-off towns like Jhelum and Peshawar were also active. Encouraged by these developments the Sikh leaders of Lahore resolved to form a central organization which could co-ordinate political activities of the district leagues. The Central Sikh League was founded in Bradlaugh Hall, Lahore, on 30 March 1919, the day of protest against the Rowlatt Bills.[68]

The formation of the Central Sikh League was a momentous political event as it provided an alternative platform to a large number of those Sikh activists who did not share the political perceptions and strategies of the Chief Khalsa Diwan. Among them were retired civil and military personnel, lawyers, medical doctors, and journalists. Sardar Bahadur Gajjan Singh, Member Legislative Council and Public Prosecutor became the President of the Central Sikh League, with Gyani Gurbax Singh Barrister as Secretary. Subsequently, the moderate leadership of the League was supplanted by 'extremists'. Important among them were Baba Kharak Singh, Sardar Mangal Singh, Master Sunder Singh Lyallpuri, Sardul Singh Caveeshar and Hira Singh Dard.[69] They launched the *Akali*, the most radical of Sikh newspapers.

Thus, Sikh journalism of the first two decades of the twentieth century reflects the growing political resurgence and a collective consciousness of the Panth among the Sikhs. It also reflects the continuation of the community's aspiration to maintain its religious symbols, and to manage its own socioreligious institutions. Since the existing set-up denied this right, there were repeated calls for *morchas*, reflecting the growing alienation of the Sikhs from the government. The journals also took up the problems of the Sikhs concerning their economic condition and their share in civil services and representative bodies. In view of the ascendancy of the other communities in the Provincial Legislative Council and the ineffectiveness of the Chief Khalsa Diwan, it became imperative for the Sikhs to form a new political organization which could promote their political interests. By the end of the second decade, Sikh resurgence had clearly acquired a political form, overshadowing the concern for socioreligious reform. The formation of the Central Sikh League, with its radical political agenda, ushered a new era in Sikh politics.

NOTES

1. Joginder Singh, 'The Sikh Resurgence 1849-1947' M. Phil. dissertation, Amritsar: Guru Nanak Dev University, 1980. See also, Gurdarshan Singh, 'Character and Impact of the Singh Sabha Movement on the History of the Punjab', Ph.D. thesis, Punjabi University, Patiala 1973; Harbans Singh, 'Origin of Singh Sabha Movement', *Panjab Past and Present: Essays in Honour of Dr. Ganda Singh*, ed. N.G. Barrier and Harbans Singh, Patiala: Punjabi University, 1976, pp. 273-83; Teja Singh, 'The Singh Sabha Movement', *Panjab Past and Present*, vol. IV, 1973, pp. 31-45.
2. Sukhmani Bal, 'Politics of the Central Sikh League', M. Phil. dissertation, Delhi: Jawaharlal Nehru University, 1982. See also, K.C. Gulati, *The Akalis Past and Present*, Delhi: Ashajanak Publications, 1979; Baldev Raj Nayar, *Minority Politics in the Punjab*, New Jersey: Princeton University Press, 1966.
3. For detail, see the Appendix.
4. The Singh Sabha movement had a very modest beginning in 1873 with the foundation of the Singh Sabha Association at Amritsar. But, by 1900 the number of the Singh Sabhas shot up to one hundred and twenty, covering most of the towns and villages of the province. The coordinating and guiding bodies like the Diwans and the Chief Khalsa Diwan also came into being. The movement aimed at the readjustment and reorientation of the community in the new set-up. Two broad areas were selected for its programme: first, to inculcate love for Sikhism and the propagation of its principles through editing and publishing of historical and religious literature; second, the propagation of current knowledge, to be accomplished by educational development and by starting newspapers and magazines. This programme was to be carried

out through the medium of the Punjabi language. For detail, Joginder Singh, 'The Sikh Resurgence 1849-1947', pp. 96-127.

5. The *Khalsa Samachar* was devoted entirely to the cause of the Khalsa Panth. It undertook to propagate Sikh religion, education and Punjabi language in Gurmukhi script. However, the periodical had hardly worked for a few years when the Chief Khalsa Diwan noted that the propagation of Sikh religion through Punjabi journals did not reach the English-educated Sikhs. Moreover, the Diwan felt that the Panth was under attack from the journals of other communities. To meet this challenge the *Khalsa Advocate* was founded in 1903. For detail, Mahan Singh Giani, *Bhai Sahib Bhai Vir Singh Da Gurmukh Jivan* (Pbi), Amritsar: *Khalsa Samachar*, 1977, pp. 74-5; *Third Annual Report of the Chief Khalsa Diwan*, Amritsar, 1903, pp. 27-8.
6. *Khalsa Samachar*, 25 November 1908, p. 6; 4 March 1909, p. 4; 6 May 1909, p. 5.
7. Bhai Santokh Singh (1787-1843) wrote several works, the most important being *Gurpartap Surya*. Kahn Singh Nabha, *Gurusabad Ratnakar Mahan Kosh* (Pbi), Patiala: Punjab Languages Department, 1986 (rpt.), pp. 182-3.
8. Baba Bishan Singh, *Aise Ko Taisa* (Pbi), Lahore: Sri Gurbax Press, 1911, pp. 23-8.
9. Jodh Singh, *Guru Sahib Ate Ved*, Amritsar: Wazir Hind Press, 1912, pp. 29-30.
10. Bawa Narain Singh, *Sikh Hindu Hain* (Pbi), Amritsar: Public Service Printing Press, pp. 4, 6-30. See also, Avtar Singh, *Chehrah Dekhan Da Shisha* (Pbi), Amritsar: Gurmat Press, 1911, p. 40.
11. For detail, *Khalsa Samachar*, 6 January 1909, pp. 4-6; 28 April 1909, p. 3; 10 June 1909, pp. 3-6; 5 August 1909, pp. 3-4; 23 September 1909, pp. 3-4; 7 October 1909, pp. 4-5; 27 October 1910, pp. 1-5; 15 May 1913, p. 3; 4 September 1913, pp. 4-5; 16 October 1916, p. 6.
12. Some of the historical tracts published by this Society were: *Bhai Tara Singh Shahid, Miran Kotia Mahtab Singh Di Bahaduri, Waddha Ghalu Ghara*. 'Khalsa Tract Society Amritsar Walon Chhappe Ithasik Tract', *Bhai Vir Singh Di Ithasik Rachna* (Pbi), Patiala: Punjabi University, 1974, pp. 221-50.
13. Ibid., p. 233.
14. Ganda Singh, 'Scholars of History', *Bhai Vir Singh Shatabadi Granth*, ed. Harbans Singh, Delhi: 1972, pp. 286-9.
15. For detail, Kirpal Singh, *Bhai Vir Singh Di Ithasik Rachna* (Pbi), pp. 221-50.
16. *Khalsa Advocate*, 26 May 1917, p. 3.
17. For detail, Ganda Singh, *Bhai Jodh Singh: Abhinandan Granth* (Pbi), Patiala, 1962; Ganda Singh (ed.), *Punjab: Bhai Jodh Singh Abhinandan Granth* (Pbi), Ludhiana, 1962; Ranjit Singh (ed.), *Principal Teja Singh Abhinandan Granth* (Pbi), Patiala, 1956.

18. *Khalsa Samachar*, 1 August 1909, pp. 3-5; 30 October 1908, pp. 2-7; 30 September 1904, pp. 3-4; 5 May 1913, p. 3; 16 October 1916, pp. 1-4.
19. Ibid., 25 November 1908, p. 6; 9 December 1908, p. 7; 22 April 1909, pp. 1-8.
20. The first page of the first issue of the *Khalsa Samachar*, 7 November 1899. Giani Mahan Singh, *Bhai Vir Singh Da Gurmukh Jiwan*, Amritsar, 1977, pp. 74-5.
21. Ibid., 12 October 1911, pp. 4-5.
22. Ibid., pp. 4-5.
23. Ibid., 22 April 1909, p. 3; 6 January 1909, p. 3.
24. Joginder Singh, 'The Sikh Resurgence 1849-1947', p. 85.
25. Mohinder Singh, *The Akali Movement*, Delhi: Macmillan, 1978, pp. 4-5.
26. *Khalsa Advocate*, 9 June 1913, p. 5.
27. Ibid., 9 June 1917, p. 3.
28. Ibid., p. 3.
29. For detail, N.G. Barrier, *The Sikhs and Their Literature*, Delhi: Manohar, 1970, pp. 75-87.
30. Ibid., pp. 75-88.
31. The policemen and the honorary magistrates arrested and punished the persons wearing *kirpans* with fines and imprisonment. In some cases, the Sikh soldiers were dismissed on account of their refusal to stop wearing the *kirpan: Sikh Sepoy*, 4 July 1919, p. 3.

    In the first decade of the twentieth century, the officials generally refused permission to establish *jhatka* slaughter houses and to sell *jhatka* meat in the locality of the town where such houses did not exist before. The Sikhs pleaded with the officials that use of *jhatka* meat had been their custom. Their demand was partly met by the officials only after the Sikhs launched an agitation in the second decade of the twentieth century. For detail, *Khalsa Samachar*, 14 August 1913, p. 2.
32. *Sikh Sepoy*, 7 March 1919, p. 3.
33. *Punjab Darpan*, 24 January 1917, p. 1.
34. For detail, *Khalsa Samachar*, 6 January 1919, p. 3; 12 June 1913, p. 3; 11 August 1913, p. 2; 30 October 1913, p. 2; *Punjab Darpan*, 24 January 1917, p. 1; *Sikh Sepoy*, 7 March 1917, p. 3; 24 January 1919, p. 2.
35. Only 45 Indians had entered Canada in 1905. Then the number swelled; 387 reached there in 1906; 2,124 in the following year, and 2,623 in 1908. Thereafter the entry of Indians into Canada was practically banned by the Dominion Government. Since many of these Indian immigrants crossed over to the United States, their actual number in Canada at the end of 1908 was around 3,500. Fresh emigrants now sought entry directly into the USA. The officially recorded number of

these Indian emigrants who entered the USA between 1899 and 1913 was 6,656, Harish K. Puri, *Ghadar Movement: Ideology, Organisation & Strategy*, Amritsar: Guru Nanak Dev University, 1983, pp. 15-16. See also, M.L. Darling, *The Punjab Peasant in Prosperity and Debt*, London: Oxford University Press, 1925, pp. 32-3. Fauja Singh, 'The Effects of Land Transfers on Rural Economy During the Later Half of the 19th Century', *Punjab History Conference Proceedings*, Patiala: Punjabi University, 1979, pp. 258-69.

36. *Khalsa Sewak*, 27 August 1913, p. 1.
37. *Khalsa Samachar*, 12 June 1913, p. 4.
38. Ibid., 25 September 1913, p. 7; 30 October 1913, p. 2.
39. *Khalsa Sewak*, 27 August 1913, p. 1.
40. For detail, *Khalsa Samachar*, 1 July 1913, pp. 4-5; September 1913, pp. 2-4.
41. Ibid., 21 August 1913, pp. 4-5.
42. Ibid., 4 August 1909, p. 2.
43. *Khalsa Advocate*, 6 March 1915, p. 2.
44. *Khalsa Advocate*, 15 September 1917, p. 30:

Department	*Posts held by Sikhs*	*Total*	*Percentage*
Excise Inspectors	3	34	8.8
Supdts. of post office	2	28	7.1
Extra Judicial Assistt. Commissioners	1	25	4.0
Subordinate Judges	Nil	27	Nil
Extra Assistt. Commissioners	9	130	6.9
Extra Deputy and Extra Assistt Commissioners	1	12	8.3
Munsifs of 1st, 2nd and 3rd Grades	4 (each)	90	17.7
Education Dept.	1	3	33.3

45. In the last quarter of the nineteenth century, the local self-governing institutions had been introduced. The municipal committees in towns and the district boards for rural areas were functioning on the electoral principle. In 1892, the British introduced separate electorates so that members of a constituency could only vote for their co-religionists in the municipal elections. The Punjab Legislative Council was established in 1897. It consisted of nine members nominated by the Lieutenant Governor. Moreover, the introduction of Minto-Morley Reforms of 1909 conceded separate electorate and weightage to the Muslims in

the provinces in which they were a minority as well as at the centre. *The Land of Five Rivers: Punjab Administration Report, 1921-23*, Lahore: 1923, pp. 90-3. See also, N.G. Barrier, 'Muslim Politics in the Punjab 1870-1890', *Panjab Past and Present*, vol. V, 1971, p. 91. Khushwant Singh, *A History of the Sikhs*, vol. II, Delhi: Oxford University Press, 1979, p. 219.

46. *Khalsa Samachar*, 6 May 1909, p. 4.
47. In the Census Reports of 1881 and 1891, the Sikhs were recorded along with the Hindus.
48. *Khalsa Samachar*, 2 September 1908, p. 8. *Punjabi Bhain*, April to December 1910.
49. *Khalsa Samachar*, 2 September 1908, p. 2.
50. Ibid., 2 November 1913, p. 4.
51. Khushwant Singh, *A History of the Sikhs*, vol. II, p. 219.
52. *Khalsa Advocate*, 15 September 1917, pp. 2-3.
53. *Sikh Sepoy*, December 1918, p. 3.
54. Ibid., 12 December 1918, p. 3.
55. *Punjab Darpan*, 9 February 1918, p. 1.
56. Ibid., 27 March 1918, p. 2.
57. *Sikh Sepoy*, 5 December 1918, p. 2.
58. Ibid., 19 December 1918, p. 3.
59. Ibid., 23 January 1919, p. 3; 23 January 1920, p. 3.
60. *Panch*, 14 February 1920, p. 5.
61. *Punjab Darpan*, 6 January 1918.
62. For detail, *Khalsa Sewak*, 20 August 1913, pp. 1-3.
63. For instance, when the Punjab Government took over the management of the Khalsa College, Amritsar in 1908, the Diwan found no fault with it. Similarly, in the case of land purchase of Gurdwara Rakabganj, Delhi and the demolition of its wall, the Diwan leaders deputed one of its members to look into the matter. This inquiry could find no fault and gave a clean chit to the official action and tried to pacify the sentiments of the agitated Sikhs. *Khalsa Samachar*, 28 May 1914, p. 6.
64. Joginder Singh, 'The Sikh Resurgence 1849-1947', pp. 133-4. *Proceedings of the Chief Khalsa Diwan*, Amritsar, 1916, p. 25.
65. *Khalsa Sewak*, 2 July 1913, p. 11.
66. Sardul Singh Caveeshar, editor and publisher of the *Sikh Review*, was one of the protagonists for a new representative body of the Sikhs. In his periodical, editorial notes and articles he criticized the functioning of the Chief Khalsa Diwan. It was alleged that the Diwan leaders manipulated to maintain the *status quo*, and that they did not allow the emergence of a new leadership. It was also alleged that the delegates of the Sikh Educational Conference could neither take an 'active part' in the deliberations nor move resolutions or even register their differences with the Diwan's policy. Moreover, it was also held that the

Diwan was not a representative body of the Sikhs. Sardul Singh Caveeshar, 'Progress of the Sikhs', *Sikh Review*, vol. 14, no. 14, 1915, pp. 3-4; vol. IV, no. 20, 1916.

67. *Punjab Darpan*, 29 October 1919, p. 1. *Khalsa Samachar*, 28 November 1918, p. 3. See also, Teja Singh, *Essays in Sikhism*, Lahore, 1941, p. 143.
68. *The Sikhs and Sikhism*, 1 July 1918, p. 10; 3 April 1918, p. 6.
69. Sukhmani Bal, 'Politics of the Central Sikh League, 1919-1929', *Punjab History Conference Proceedings*, 1982, p. 325.

APPENDIX

Political resurgence of the Sikhs during the first two decades of the twentieth century is reflected in the following Sikh periodicals which were published contemporaneously and were directly or indirectly associated with the socioreligious and educational institutions of the Sikhs.

Journal	*Place of publication*	*Years of publication*	*Periodicity*	*Proprietor Editor*	*Issues Analysed*
Akali (Pbi)	Lahore	1920	Weekly	Sunder Singh Lyallpuri	1920: 28 October, 6 & 25 November.
Bir (Pbi)	Amritsar	1910	Monthly	Mahtab Singh	1914: 3 April.
Khalsa Advocate (Eng)	Lahore	1903	Monthly	Bhai Jodh Singh	1915: 6 March, 20 November. 1917: 6 January, 26 May, 2, 16, 23 & 30 June; 7 & 28 July; 1, 15 & 29 September; and 6 October. 1918: 9 & 18 February.
Khalsa Samachar (Pbi)	Amritsar	1899	Monthly	Bhai Vir Singh	1908: 9, 23 & 30 December. 1909: 14, 21 & 28 January; 11 February; 4, 11, 18 & 25 March; 1, 8, 22 & 29 April; 6, 20 & 27 May; 3, 10, 17 & 24 June; 1, 8, 15, 22 & 29 July; 5, 12, 19 & 26 August; 2, 16, 23 & 30 October; 4, 11, 18 & 25 November; 9, 10, 23 & 30 December.

					1913: 15 May; 5, 12 & 19 June; 10, 17, 24 & 31 July; 7, 14 & 21 August; 4, 11 & 25 September; 16, 23 & 30 October; 20 & 27 November; 4 & 25 December. 1914: 1, 8, 15, 22 & 29 January; 5, 12 & 26 February; 5 & 26 March; 23 & 28 May. 1916: 19 & 26 October. 1917: 8 & 15 March; 29 November. 1918: 31 January; 18 April; 29 August; 18 April; 29 August. 1919: 13 March.
Khalsa Sewak(Pbi)	Amritsar	1903	Weekly	Jiwan Singh	1913: 18 & 25 June; 9, 16 & 23 July; 20 & 27 August; 3 & 10 September; 1, 8, 15 & 17 October.
Panch (Pbi)	Lahore	1909	Weekly	Ram Singh	1920: 14 & 21 February.
Punjabi Bhain (Pbi)	Ferozepur	1908	Monthly	Vir Singh and Takhat Singh (1919)	1910: April, June, August; September, October, November & December. 1911: January, April, May, June December. 1912: March, April, May, June, July, August, September, October, November & December.

(Contd.)

APPENDIX (Contd.)

Journal	*Place of publication*	*Years of publication*	*Periodicity*	*Proprietor Editor*	*Issues Analysed*
					1913: January, February, March, April, May, June, September, October, November & December. 1914: January & February. 1916: June, September & October. 1917: January, February, March, April, May, June, July, August, September, October, November & December. 1918: February, March, April, May, June, August, September, November & December. 1919: January, February & March.
Punjab Darpan (Pbi)	Amritsar		Weekly	Sucha Singh	1916: 13 December. 1917: 24 January. 1918: 16 January & 26 February. 1919: 20 February, 27 March & 25 June.
Sikh Sepoy (Pbi)	Ferozepur	1917	Weekly	Bhai Tek Singh and Bhai Takhat Singh	1918: 28 November; 5, 12, 19 & 26 December. 1919: 3, 10, 17 & 31 January; 7, 21 & 28 February; 4, 14, 21 & 28 March;

					4, 11 & 18 April; 2, 9, 16, 23 & 30 May; 20 & 27 June; 4, 11, 18 & 25 July; 1, 9, 15, 22 & 29 August; 5, 12, 19 & 26 September; 3, 10 & 17 October; 21 & 28 November; 12, 19 & 26 December. 1920: 2, 9, 23 & 30 January; 6, 13, 20 & 27 February; 5, 12 & 26 March; 9 & 23 April; 7, 14 & 28 May; 4 June; 23 July; 6 August; 10 September; 1 & 8 October; 5, 12 & 19 November; 3, 10, 24 & 31 December.
Sikh Review (Eng)	Delhi	1913	–	Sardul Singh Caveeshar	1914: vol. II, no. 6, 7, 9. 1915: vol. III, no. 14. 1916: vol. IV, no. 23.

7

Mission Abroad: Sant Teja Singh in the Western World

DARSHAN S. TATLA

Despite the establishment and proliferation of saintly traditions among the Sikhs abroad, few Sikh *sants* have managed to match the contribution of Teja Singh in nurturing and defending overseas Sikhs' faith and interests. As an advocate of racial justice for Canadian Sikhs, Teja Singh played a crucial role in articulating their grievances while establishing several institutions to nurture their faith. Though he is well known as the founder of the first Sikh Gurdwara in Britain, his overseas activities have remained largely undocumented. This paper describes and assesses his pioneering role among the Sikhs overseas.

I

By and large, the contribution of Sikh *sants* remains a neglected field of Punjab historical and social studies. Apart from much slandering of Sant Bhindranwale's role in the tragedy of 1984,[1] there are few analytical or historical studies of various *sants* of the Sikh Panth, despite the fact that in the twentieth century Sikh *sants* became a predominant force within the community: Randhir Singh, Fateh Singh, Harchand Singh Longowal, Atar Singh Reruwale, Atar Singh Mastuana, Ishar Singh Rarewal, Nand Singh Nanaksar, Chanan Singh, Wazir Singh Harkhowal, among others. In most cases, only some hagiographic accounts are available, usually written by a devout follower of a particular *sant*.[2]

Teja Singh was obviously a product of Western style education which affected largely the urban Sikh population, but he came under the influence of a rural Sikh *sant*, Atar Singh, and spent much of his life following his mission. Atar Singh in turn was one of several Sikh *sants* who roamed rural Punjab, presenting a close parallel with the Singh Sabha movement among the urban Sikhs. Two other enduring traditions of Nirankari and Namdhari movements were also established by *sants* prior to the Singh Sabha era. It may be reasonable to assume that the twentieth century Sikh *sant* traditions were largely popular among rural peasantry from which had sprung most of the Sikh *sants* in the previous century.[3]

Teja Singh (1877-1967) was born in a Mehta Khatri family at Balowali (now in Pakistan) on 14 May 1877. His parents belonged to a petty trading class. Though *sahajdhari* Sikhs, they named their child Niranjan Singh. His grandfather, Nanak Chand, was a shopkeeper in this ancient village; his grandmother, Chand Kaur, came from a lineage of Sikh ancestors, one of them being a scribe of the holy scripture. Niranjan's mother Sadda Kaur was nurtured as a staunch Sikh, while his father Ralla Singh was an educated person with a diploma in public health. The household was rather small with just two children, Niranjan and his sister, Narain Devi.

With a diploma titled H.M.H. from Lahore Medical College, Ralla Singh held a government post. Due to frequent transfers, his young son's education followed his postings in different towns. Halfway in his middle school education at Fazilka Municipal Board School, his father was transferred to Lahore central jail; Niranjan joined the D.A.V. School there. Before completing his middle school education, he was married to Bishan Kaur. He then went to Gujranwala Mission School. After High School examination, he obtained the B.A. degree in 1896, gaining distinction in chemistry. In 1900 he obtained the LL.B. degree and was licensed by the Punjab Chief Court to practise as a lawyer. Diligent and keen on higher education, Niranjan Singh added an M.A. degree to his qualifications in 1901.

Niranjan Singh started his legal practice in Gujranwala in partnership with an advocate, Lala Kishan Lal. Within a month, however, he felt disillusioned with his profession. Having passed the Northern Indian Salt Revenue Official Grade Examination, he accepted the post of Assistant Superintendent in the Salt Department at Sambar; he was later shifted to Rajanpur in Agra Division. But his restless mind was still looking for a more satisfying profession. He wrote a letter to Sardar Sundar Singh Majithia, asking for a suitable post for someone who had M.A. and LL.B. degree to his credit. Majithia immediately offered him the post of Vice-Principal of Khalsa College, Amritsar. Teja Singh's English boss, Assistant Commissioner F.M. Buckley, granted him leave without pay, making it easy for him to leave the government post.

Teja Singh took over as Vice-Principal of Khalsa College, Amritsar, in 1904. Soon he became its Acting Principal when the English Principal left for Britain for a year. At religious gatherings and congregations in Amritsar, Niranjan Singh met many Sikh and other denominational *sants*. Through one such *sant*, Sham Singh, he eventually attended a congregation of Atar Singh who became a beacon for all his later life.

Sant Atar Singh (1865-1927) had enlisted as a soldier in a Sikh regiment to be released after a brief period. Due to his intense religious convictions, he adopted the life of a roving missionary and began touring the countryside, visiting newly established Sikh schools and colleges. In one such itinerary, he visited Khalsa College, Amritsar, and had a meeting with Niranjan Singh. Immediately they were drawn together and a life-long rapport grew between the two. In 1906, Niranjan Singh was baptized by Atar Sigh and given a new name Teja Singh. With this transformation started his career of lifelong service as a roving Singh missionary.

II

As an ex-soldier-turned-*sant*, Atar Singh valued education and visualised a future for Sikhs through Western educated leaders and intellectuals.[4] He persuaded Teja Singh to go abroad for higher education. Besides moral support, he gave him Rs. 125 for the journey and asked him to observe four rules: (a) keep the five Ks,[5] (b) establish Gurdwaras abroad, (c) prefer spiritual life to worldly goods, (d) and not to meddle or argue unnecessarily with others.[6] Teja Singh was accompanied by his wife and two young children on his overseas voyage, which was quite an uncommon practice among emigrating Sikhs at the time. Three other Sikhs joined him for foreign education; Amar Singh, Dharma Anant Singh, and Hari Singh Basra. On 6 August 1906, they boarded a ship from Bombay and landed at Marseilles. They boarded a train to Bologne and crossed the English Channel to reach Folkestone on 24 August. Their first stop was East London where they rented rooms for temporary accommodation.

Teja Singh was enrolled for a science degree at the University of London, simultaneously attending lectures for a teacher training course. His companions enrolled in other courses. Hari Singh Basra joined Edinburgh University for M.A., Dharma Anant Singh enrolled for electricity training course in a London college, and Amar Singh went to Manchester for a textile and clothing course. All of them resolved to keep their hair intact despite all difficulties.

In his autobiography, Teja Singh narrates that another Sikh student taunted him, saying that 'Sikh students with turbans' could not study at the Cambridge University as cap and gown were the custom there. Whether or not this was meant as a mere provocation by a fellow student, it prompted Teja Singh to apply to Cambridge. He met a tutor surnamed Jackson at Downing College who heard Teja Singh's strange story and offered him a place on Science Tripos, reminding him to wear the black gown with his turban: 'this was the first occasion when a Sikh was seen around Cambridge with his turban'.[7] More Sikh students joined Cambridge, leading to the formation of the Khalsa Jatha of British Isles under Teja Singh's inspiration. The news was duly published in the *Khalsa Samachar*, edited by Bhai Vir Singh at Amritsar.[8]

The lure of America constantly nagged Teja Singh. He applied to Columbia University's Teachers Education course and was pleasantly surprised with the response of admission and a scholarship of $150. He decided to join Columbia without completing his Cambridge course. First, he wrote to Sant Atar Singh, seeking permission for the American voyage and mentioning that in America he might help his Sikh brethren whose plight was attracting some notice in the Punjab newspapers. While the Sant consented, Sundar Singh Majithia cautioned him against meddling with the political affairs of the Sikhs overseas.

In 1908, Teja Singh enrolled at Columbia University for a teachers' training course. Sailing from Portsmouth, he reached New York in seven days and observed the 'strange city' with houses over twenty storeys high; the 'turban almost fell as one looked up'. He found Columbia 'pleasantly situated' on the Hudson river. He took residence in the university hostel and called his wife and children from Cambridge. He took up 'education for young children', 'school administration', and a course in literature on the 'prominent poets under Queen Victoria's reign'. During a lecture on Kipling's humour, Teja Singh had a discussion with a visiting professor from Dalhousie University, Canada, who suggested to Teja Singh to deliver a lecture on contemporary India. Teja Singh delivered two lectures; the second lecture was on Guru Nanak. It was well attended, and noted by the local and national press.[9] As a result, some Americans expressed interest in Teja Singh's eastern philosophy and asked him to form a local group for meetings. The news of this lecture spread to some Canadian Sikhs via Tarknath Das – an educated Bengali exile who had extensive contacts with the British Columbia Sikhs.[10] Balwant Singh, a *granthi* at Vancouver Gurdwara, was actively searching for an educated Sikh to assist the Sikhs in their representation to the Canadian Government. Within three weeks, Balwant Singh contacted Teja Singh and requested him to come over.

On receiving the fare from Balwant Singh, Teja Singh travelled by train through Montreal, Ottawa and Winnipeg to Vancouver. Describing his journey from New York to Vancouver he praises America's excellent railway service which included 'provision for clean bedding for one dollar'. In Vancouver, Teja Singh was duly impressed by the Gurdwara, a wooden structure of two storeys, with a spatial hall measuring 35 by 60 feet. On the following Sunday, many Sikhs called on the new visitor, including Bhag Singh, an ex-soldier, and Wariam Singh, a Sikh from Shanghai, who was well known for hymn-singing. They worked some 8 miles away at Millside factory as baptized Sikhs and had contributed substantially to the building of the Gurdwara. On

Sundays, be it rain or storm, the two would sing hymns beating *dholak* (drum) through bazaars, attracting considerable curiosity from the white people.

Teja Singh took the opportunity to visit some Sikh workers' residential camps and was duly impressed by their collective living, cooking and sharing of *langar*. Near the Gurdwara, Badan Singh Mahiwal was well known for organizing workers' free *langar*. Teja Singh also visited some factories of Port Moody and extolled Millside workers who strictly observed the *rahit* and recited *nitnem* as *taksali* (staunch) Sikhs. Gaining such positive impression of the British Columbia Sikhs, Teja Singh returned to New York via Seattle, Portland, San Francisco and Chicago after four weeks.

In New York, American disciples were waiting for him. Among them was C. Crawford who had adopted Sikh meditation in earnest. Teja Singh named him Himmat Das and met him almost everyday. One morning, Crawford narrated the story of an impending misfortune about his shares in Jackson Ville gold mine. His partner wanted to knock him out and he desperately needed $50,000 to keep his partnership. In return for raising cash, he was willing to donate a quarter of million dollars' worth of shares for the Sikh community. Teja Singh remarked jokingly that his wealth stood at just 5 cents. Crawford took his cap off and 'placed it at his feet'. Teja Singh assured him that he would enquire from his newly found Canadian Sikhs if they could help. Crawford deposited 25 pounds for Teja Singh's railway fare to Vancouver and placed a promissory note of 2,50,000 shares in the gold mine in return for raising $50,000 cash. On the following day, Teja Singh boarded the Canadian Pacific Railways for Vancouver. On the train, a Canadian passenger told Teja Singh how his Sikh brothers in British Columbia were in dire trouble; there were plans to send them to Honduras where there was unemployment, and the work conditions and wages were poor. They would not be able to earn the return fare, and there was yellow fever. Teja Singh arrived at the local Gurdwara in Vancouver and every one was surprised at his sudden appearance. After saying prayer in the main hall he met Wariam Singh, Bhag Singh, Badan Singh Mahiwal, Badan Singh Kahri and Balwant Singh, the *granthi*, who apprised him of the misfortunes of the

British Columbia Sikhs and how the media were maligning them as 'idle and dirty'.[11] They emphasized that the reality was quite different. The chief difficulty was their inability to convey their viewpoint to the white people. They told him how the community, within the last three or four years, had built a Gurdwara at the cost of $15,000. There was hardly any unemployment amongst Sikh workers who earned around $1.5 or $2 per day. Many Sikh workers lived together in camps, cooked together, and they were God-fearing and clean people. Teja Singh was also told how a government commissioner from Ottawa had taken Satnagar Singh and Sham Singh Dogra to British Honduras with a proposal to settle Sikh immigrants there. Hearing their woes Teja Singh could only reiterate that the Guru would protect them and justice would prevail. He told them that his immediate mission was about a financial deal offered by Crawford and suggested that a mining company should be registered by some leading Sikhs and some land acquired for the community's collective use.

The group approved of the plan, and Teja Singh's training in legal matters came in handy. On the day following, he contacted a legal firm, drafted articles and rules for the company and registered it as Guru Nanak Mining Company within a week.[12] Then he took stock of the media's propaganda against the Sikhs. He hired a large hall and delivered two forceful lectures, defending the Sikhs and their viewpoint. He spoke like a man who believed that he had a sacred mission to perform. The *Daily Province* published a full front page article on the 'mystery and power of Teja Singh', regarded by his people as 'Demi-God'.[13] As a result of this publicity, Sikhs gained a few Canadian sympathizers. Some white Canadians became interested in Sikhism, and some of them became friendly with local Sikhs. The local media also mellowed somewhat. Knapp, who was a real estate dealer, was deputed to acquire suitable land by the sea, measuring about 250 acres. He came up with an offer of land at Eagle Harbour. This was duly inspected and after approval bought for $25,000, with $10,000 paid in advance. A 10-acre plot was also bought and earmarked for a Gurdwara with provision for a sacred pool. $15,000 were sent to Crawford and shares were acquired in his company.

After concluding these deals, Teja Singh called a conference to counter the media propaganda against the Sikh workers. For this gathering, he invited not only the Sikh workers but also many prominent white people. Citing figures about Sikhs' employment, wages and their general prosperity, Teja Singh delivered public lectures, questioning the media's portrayal of Sikhs as poor and unclean. He informed his audience that Sikhs had just bought a large tract of land, acquired shares in a mining company, and in the last few years built an elegant Gurdwara at the cost of $15,000. He also laid emphasis on Sikhism as a young and dynamic faith with a noble mission. He further warned that forcing the Sikhs to British Honduras would be a gross act of injustice. This lecture received considerable publicity and eventually gained some sympathy among the white people.

Satnagar Singh and Sham Singh returned from the British Honduras, and Teja Singh requested them to report their findings to the congregation in the Gurdwara on the following Sunday. Many Sikhs were aware of a scheme to send them to the British Honduras. Over a thousand of them turned up in the Gurdwara to hear the fact-finding mission's report. The gist of what Satnagar Singh and Sham Singh told the congregation was: 'British Honduras was a poor country where the already settled Hindustanis were suffering because of poor wages, lack of facilities and a common disease of yellow fever.' A consensus emerged immediately in the congregation to refuse the government's proposal, and these deliberations were reported by the local paper on the following day. The government's move stood effectively pre-empted and rejected. By now Teja Singh was fully involved in the British Columbia Sikh affairs. He abandoned the idea of education and asked his family from New York to join him. He arranged a short tour to meet his family at the US border with Canada and arranged their transfer on to a Canadian railway to Vancouver.

Teja Singh received a letter from the authorities, complaining about the pre-emptory discussion of the Sikhs about the British Honduras proposal without hearing a detailed report. Teja Singh replied that Sikhs were willing to discuss the commissioner's report, and suggested possible dates on the following Sundays. The commissioner arrived at the Gurdwara, but on the advice of Hopkinson, a covert police officer, and Wright, a priest, he had arguments regarding the appropriate form for discussion with the gathered Sikhs, and left amidst confusion without reading his report. The Federal Government then sent for Brigadier General Swayne, Governor of British Honduras, who had experience of India and could speak Hindustani. On his visit to Vancouver, he sent a message to persuade the Sikhs regarding their good prospects in British Honduras, but drew a negative response. In his report to Ottawa, the governor blamed Teja Singh for his overblown reaction and language, but conceded that he was substantially right about Sikhs' unwillingness to settle in the colony. He also underlined that if forced the reaction of the Sikhs in the British Indian army could be adverse.[14] With the governor's statement, the Canadian Government shelved the proposal and the Canadian Sikhs' worry concerning British Honduras was laid to rest.[15]

With a major issue amicably settled, Teja Singh undertook his missionary work in earnest. Forming a *jatha* of five devout Sikhs, consisting of Balwant Singh, Wariam (Sundar) Singh, Hari Singh and Wariam Singh, a programme was chalked out to visit the Sikh workers' camps across the Pacific Coast. They wanted to persuade the Sikhs to become baptized by taking *amrit*. After sailing on a ship to Victoria, Balwant Singh guided the *jatha* to a nearby camp. Although most workers were drunk, the *jatha* was cordially received, given food and lodging. In the morning, the *jatha* sang hymns and meditation was arranged. On Teja Singh's passionate appeal, almost twenty were baptized on the same morning. They also agreed to offer one month's wages for building a Gurdwara at Victoria. A committee was formed for the project with Teja Singh as its leader, and within months land was purchased through Robert William Clark, an estate agent, whose wife had become interested in Sikhism. On her initiative, Teja Singh delivered a lecture at the Victoria Hall and Mrs Clark published his pamphlets on the Sikh faith.

From Victoria, the *jatha* arrived in Seattle after obtaining the required passports and travel permits. Teja Singh gave a lecture at Washington University, attended by many Hindustani students, including Swami Satdev. The *jatha* then left for Portland where many saw mills employed Sikh workers. Usually these Sikh workers lived like a 'commune', sharing food and living in one large communal hall. Here they had also kept a copy of a small-sized *Guru Granth* for worship. Many agreed to be baptized. The *jatha* then met Giani Partap Singh, working on a railway line, who was later appointed Jathedar of Keshgarh Sahib. The *jatha* managed to baptize a number of Sikhs. On their way back to Vancouver, they came to know of Doaba Sikh farm workers. Only a few of them agreed to be baptized. As they reached the Vancouver station, a Sikh named Harnam Singh thrashed Balwant Singh and Teja Singh for some reason. Balwant Singh wanted to hit back, but eventually both forgave the offending man. On the following Sunday, Balwant Singh read a report on their mission to various Sikh workers' camps at the Gurdwara.

The Canadian Sikhs had already formed the Khalsa Diwan Society in Vancouver in October 1907. Teja Singh formalized this through registration on 13 March 1909. Within weeks of the *jatha's* return to Vancouver, a letter came from Plesantan Sikhs in California to baptize them. Teja Singh led the *jatha* to Portland and reached Plesantan where Sikh workers felt very excited by their arrival and many were baptized.

III

Feeling that his mission among the Canadian Sikhs was over, Teja Singh took a trip to London, accompanied by his young son Hari Singh. Renting a room in Hampstead Heath, he sent letters to well known Sikhs in England and Scotland as also to many London students with a proposal for a Gurdwara in London. Before he could hold a meeting, he received an urgent call and fare from Bhag Singh, asking him to return to Vancouver immediately. Teja Singh took out a berth on Mauritanian to New York, then a train to Chicago. There he met Rev. Jenkins Lloyd Jones in the main city cathedral who invited Teja Singh to a world religions conference being organized in Germany. Teja Singh also met Henry Ford, proprietor of the Ford cars in the Utah State. He presented his card to Ford's secretary and was allowed to meet him. Teja Singh enquired from Henry Ford about his wealth and asked whether it had brought him real satisfaction. He advised him to donate part of his wealth for good causes and blessed him with a *simarna* (rosary) for mental peace.

In Vancouver, Teja Singh discovered that he was implicated in some irregularities in Guru Nanak Mining Company by the auditor's report. Raja Singh, secretary of the trust, also levelled charges through the chairman. A meeting was summoned to scrutinize the accounts in the presence of the trustees and the auditor, and a detailed account sheet was prepared in English and Punjabi. The meeting ended with a heated exchange between Bhag Singh and Raja Singh. Due to difference of opinion among the trustees, a decision was taken to dispose of the properties. Consequently, Jackson Ville gold mine shares were sold and $19,000 recovered from Crawford. The land at Eagle Harbour was sold despite Teja Singh's advice that its value would appreciate in future.

Teja Singh arrived in London after a short stop in Chicago where Rev. Jones confirmed dates for the Berlin Conference and invited him as a delegate. He went to the conference from London. On the way he met L. Vasvani, a prominent Brahmo Samaj activist and some Buddhist delegates at Cologne. After a tour of the Rhine Valley, the delegates were taken to Berlin. Teja Singh's lecture on Sikhism impressed many participants. Returning from the conference, he called a meeting of Sikhs in London. He planned to offer baptism at the meeting, but he could find only four baptized Sikhs for the initiating rites. Also, Teja Singh was short of money. Both the problems found resolution 'through providence's kindness' when Tara Singh from the Malaya States Guides, who had arrived in London and called on his wife in his absence, offered 20 pounds cash and became the fifth *amritdhari* Sikh for the baptizing *jatha*. As the Sikhs gathered on the fixed day, Teja Singh made a strong appeal for establishing a Gurdwara in London by buying freehold property. Others felt that it would be an arduous task to raise 2,500 pounds. Teja Singh attributed such negative attitude to half-believing Sikhs' worldly wisdom. In any case, the 'Khalsa was deprived of the honour of having a permanent religious shrine in London'. At the baptism ceremony, Dharma Anant Singh and Narain Singh were baptized; the latter was nominated as secretary of a committee formed for the proposed Gurdwara. Narain Singh promised to collect donations from India and, after making an appeal through the *Khalsa Samachar* and at the Sikh Educational Conference, he raised about Rs. 30,000.[16] The biggest benefactor was the Maharaja of Patiala, Bhupinder Singh, who promised Rs. 1,25,000 and offered 1,000 pounds immediately.[17] At another meeting of the Gurdwara committee, a 60 years leasehold property near Shepherd Bush was bought and a Gurdwara was established in this house.

Teja Singh now remembered his original purpose of obtaining higher education. He dashed to Cambridge and met Jackson at Downing College in the hope that the college would allow him to take one more term to complete the requirements for a degree. But Jackson rejected him, saying that the university had 'a full report of your work among Canadian Hindus especially of your role in lobbying against the British Honduras option', and that the senate had 'decided not to award you any degree even if all requirements were fulfilled'. Teja Singh decided to return to America, borrowing forty pounds from Muhammad Qasim, an old friend.[18] Accompanied by Tara Singh on the ship to New York, he met the president of Columbia Teachers' College and requested him to allow him to complete his unfinished course. Here again, the president refused, saying that he was not a student and that a report from Vancouver had reached the college; he could not be admitted for the degree.

Teja Singh now thought of his admission to Harvard. But he had only 15 dollars left with him. Still, he took a flight to Boston, rented a house for the family and enquired at the university office. The university offered him admission, asking for 150 dollars as fees payable in two instalments, the first 90 dollars immediately and the rest in the second term. Teja Singh bought some cloth from the market and his wife set to make cushion covers. Selling it in the market for 9 dollars, Teja Singh paid the house rent and bought more cloth for 5 dollars. This household economy enabled them to survive while some financial support came via his New York connections. He was given 25 dollars for a lecture, while a woman admirer posted him 50 dollars. He got through the first term. Payment of the second instalment proved difficult. A letter from the university arrived, banning him from further lectures until the fees were paid. Teja Singh asked his wife if she had entertained any 'greedy' ideas about his future after education. She had, dreaming of a plum job on their return to the Punjab. Now 'they both offered a prayer and asked for forgiveness' promising that his career 'will be for the service of the community and the *sant*'. They returned home, hoping to ask a white woman for loan of sixty dollars. They had just entered the house when someone knocked at the door. It was his English literature teacher, Bliso Perry, who had heard about his financial difficulty and offered him 60 dollars, saying that 'when you can afford it, help another student'.[19] Teja Singh managed to obtain M.A. degree from Harvard in March 1911.

Preparing to leave for the Punjab, Teja Singh asked his wife to leave ahead for the Far East with a mission to preach. She left for California with the younger son Hari Singh. She was asked by Jawala Singh to stay at his Holtsville farmland, as it was unwise for a woman to travel alone. With his elder son, Teja Singh boarded the train from Boston by pawning the gold watch given to him by his Maharashtrain friend, D.G. Panse. After paying for the ticket, they had 50 cents to sustain themselves during travel for the next six days. They 'survived on bread and water alone'. Stepping down at Stockton, they joined the family on Jawala Singh's ranch.

Jawala Singh and Wasakha Singh led a traditional Sikh life in their California homes. At the farm, *langar* was prepared and shared by all. After the evening prayer on Teja Singh's suggestion, a proposal to build a Gurdwara was considered. Next morning, Teja Singh drafted a letter, calling upon all Sikh workers for a gathering at the farm. At this meeting, a committee was set up for the proposed Gurdwara at Stockton, besides baptizing some 25 people, including a reluctant Tara Singh, who had become clean shaven. Wasakha Singh, Jawala Singh, Tara Singh, Bawa Singh and Teja Singh were members of the committee and the latter three then went to collect funds from the other Sikh workers. Within days, a farm with an existing building and a wind operated water pump was bought for $3,400. Eventually, some $20,000 were raised for the building. The Gurdwara was to be formally opened on 27 May 1912 in Stockton to become a resting place for the roaming Sikh workers in the Californian valleys.

Jawala Singh offered employment to some workers on his Holtsville farm and many Indian students worked there during holidays. In consultation with Teja Singh, Tarknath Das and Har Dayal paid several visits to the farm in 1912. There was a serious talk of raising funds for the education of Indians. Jawala Singh offered some money for Guru Gobind Singh scholarships for Indian students at the University of California, Berkeley.[20] A committee comprising of the above three and Dr Arthus Pope of the university selected the first batch of scholars, which included Darisi Chenchiah from Nelore (Mardas), Nand Singh Sihra (Bombay), and Gobind Behari Lal (Delhi), a cousin of Har Dayal's wife. Even Teja Singh briefly enrolled at the university for a Doctor of Literature degree but soon abandoned it.

By this time the issue of families' re-union had become most pressing. Only Teja Singh and Sundar Singh had their families with them while others desperately wanted to bring their families to Canada. Teja Singh was a part of the lobby at Berkeley when Balwant Singh and Bhag Singh arrived with their families at the San Francisco port along with Wariam Singh. Despite strenuous lobbying by Californian Sikhs, they were deported to Shanghai.

Teja Singh conferred with the leading Sikhs of Vancouver, and soon a large meeting was held in the Gurdwara and funds were raised for the representation of the Sikhs' case to the Federal Government. It was agreed that the best course was to take a petition to Ottawa. The delegation to Ottawa consisted of Teja Singh, Sundar Singh, Raja Singh and Rev. L.W. Hall who prepared a comprehensive memorandum with many statistics to argue its case with the Federal Government. The Sikh delegation met the Interior Minister, Robert Rogers, of the newly elected Conservative Government in November 1911.[21] A carefully worded memorandum was presented to him:

> We the delegates of the United India League and Khalsa Diwan Society, Vancouver, B.C. instructed by them make the following representations to your honourable government for all Hindustanis domiciled in Canada or who may be domiciled. ...
>
> Our first claim for consideration at the hands of your honourable government is that we are British subjects, of proven loyalty. More than 90 per cent of these Hindustanis in Canada are Sikhs. With the name Sikh is linked up fidelity and heroic loyalty to the Empire. The Sikhs have always been ready in the past to give willing service to the Empire. A large number of these men now in Canada have seen active service and many among them have medals for special bravery. The questions

involved are not local, as being purely Canadian they are in their very nature Empire questions, and hence must be dealt with from this broad standpoint.

While the minister turned down the delegation's major proposal to withdraw the 'continuous passage' legislation,[22] he showed some sympathy regarding restrictions on the families and children of the Sikhs. The delegation was disappointed in its aim of getting the legislation reversed, or getting concrete concessions for men stranded without families.

Teja Singh was able to establish the second Canadian Gurdwara at Victoria, the provincial capital, which was a major achievement of the community. The land had already been purchased in 1909; Teja Singh got the design prepared, with estimates of cost. Many Sikh workers donated part of their wages for several months and a contractor started work on the site. When Teja Singh's *jatha* returned from California after three months, the Gurdwara building was ready. He made an elaborate plan for its inauguration by organizing a huge procession of Sikhs through the capital. For the opening day, almost four thousand Sikhs lined up, forming a regimental order of four persons in a row, all dressed up in their colourful costumes, some retired soldiers in full regimental gears. A six-wheeler horse drawn carriage with the *Guru Granth Sahib* was in front. Teja Singh joined the carriage with an unsheathed sword and it took five hours for the procession to pass through the city. Canadian spectators were impressed by the gala scene and the event attracted wide coverage in the local media. In the evening, Teja Singh read the accounts relating to the newly constructed Gurdwara which had cost $25,000. As he announced the shortfall, the assembled Sikhs offered more money to make up the deficit.

The bitter contest over the immigration of families of Bhag Singh and Balwant Singh had changed the atmosphere at the Gurdwara and within the community. They had started from Hong Kong on the understanding that the Minister had agreed to let the families in. Although Teja Singh had told the congregation that the Minister's assurances were ambiguous, many Sikhs assumed that he had failed them. The mission cost $1,599. As Bhag Singh and Balwant Singh arrived with their families on the ship, their wives and children were deported and then released on $2,000 bail pending an appeal to the Minister. The issue was seen as a blatant discrimination to split the families. But the Sikhs had even fewer sympathizers this time.[23]

Teja Singh noted that there were sharp differences on how to tackle the worsening situation. The United India League led by Tarknath Das and Guru Dutt Kumar offered radical solutions in terms of liberation of India, and they were joined by some Sikh workers led by Balwant Singh, the *granthi*, who had a bitter experience at the hands of immigration officials. However, there was hope of getting concession through deputations and representations and the Khalsa Diwan Society thought it wise to send a deputation to London and to India. It consisted of Balwant Singh, Narain Singh and Nand Singh Sihra. Teja Singh prepared the necessary papers for talks. He gave these to Nand Singh Sihra with the advice that no word should be changed, seeking an 'assurance in the presence of *Guru Granth*'.[24]

The changed environment within the community, new managers of Gurdwaras, and perhaps a dwindling circle of admirers who sheltered and supported Teja Singh and his family must have contributed to his decision to leave for the Punjab. In his autobiography he confounds this rational motive by stating that this move was prompted by his younger son, Hari Singh, who had a vision of Sant Atar Singh insisting that the family should leave Canada as soon as possible. Soon an appeal was made for the family's sea fare. From this collection, Teja Singh bought four intermediate class cabin seats on Canadian Pacific Company's ship Monteagle, leaving for Yokohama, Japan. After a prayer at the Gurdwara, the family sailed, accompanied by another Sikh passenger, Tarlok (Ishar) Singh.

After clearing all outstanding financial dealings with Canadian Sikhs, Teja Singh had just 40 dollars to spare as the family left Vancouver in December 1912. They were expecting to contact a *jatha* in Yokohama to assist the family's onward travel. But the *jatha* had disbanded, leaving no money for travel. Teja Singh booked a train for Kobe where the Monteagle was to stop for 24 hours before leaving for Shanghai. The family reached the port at the last minute. The ship stewards thought they were re-joining the ship after a visit to the city and allowed them aboard. As the ticket collector arrived later, Teja Singh was summoned by the captain. Teja Singh assured full payment before disembarking and asked the captain to wire the Gurdwara managers in Shanghai.[25] When they disembarked at Shanghai, the family was greeted by two *granthis* who had brought enough cash to pay for the family's fare. To the crew's surprise, several hundred Sikhs stood at the port to greet the family.[26] Teja Singh preached in Shanghai for two weeks. He was given cash and silk cloth used later as *chanani* (ceremonial cloth) for the *Guru Granth* at Mastuana Gurdwara.

Teja Singh left Shanghai after a warm farewell and reached Hong Kong where he delivered sermons. After a week, the family left for Singapore and onwards to Teiping by train. At Teiping he was greeted with enthusiasm by the Sikhs from the Malaya State Guides. Then the family travelled to Ipu and onwards to Penang. His fellow passengers included Gurdit Singh, the veteran of Komagata Maru. Finally, they arrived at Calcutta. When their train reached Ambala, they stepped down to visit Sant Atar Singh, and to offer him presents from the overseas Sikhs.

IV

After his return to the Punjab in 1913, education and religion remained the major concerns of Teja Singh. The Akal College at Mastuana was now established as an important institution, with Teja Singh as its founder-principal. He collected donations for the college from the ruling chiefs of the Malwa and the Sikh *sangats* of Burma. He came to be associated with the school established by Babu Teja Singh, known for his advocacy of radical reform in Sikhism, for the education of girls at Bhasaur.[27] During the Gurdwara Reform movement, Teja Singh remained associated with the Shiromani Gurdwara Prabandhak Committee. For some time, he acted as *jathedar* of the Akal Takht. He came to be associated with Maharaja Ripudaman Singh of Nabha, which was not appreciated by Maharaja Bhupinder Singh of Patiala.[28] However, Teja Singh's interest in politics remained subordinate to his interest in religion and education. In the 1950s he toured East Africa and South East Asia, giving lectures on Sikhism; he participated in the World Conference of Religions in Japan in 1956.[29] At this time he revisited North America where he was honoured by the Sikhs for the work he had done for the community in the early twentieth century.[30] Before his death in 1965, Teja Singh had founded a school at Barhu in Himachal Pradesh as a model school for Sikh education, and written a biography of Sant Atar Singh.[31]

The career of Teja Singh illustrates some aspects of Sikh renaissance at the beginning of the twentieth century. A product of the newly established Western education in the Punjab, Teja Singh was among several Sikh reformers who played a prominent part in fermenting a new consciousness among the Sikhs. As a highly educated intellectual, he was a participant in and witness to many crucial developments. With a firm belief he saw himself as a missionary for the propagation of Sikhism. During his mission abroad he was able to establish two Gurdwaras in America and one in UK, which was a remarkable achievement in those days. His work among the Sikhs of Vancouver showed him as a sophisticated interpreter of the Sikh viewpoint; he rallied Sikhs around their common cause, and effectively countered the media stereotype of Sikhs as ignorant, rural peasants. With enterprising skills, he was able to project a good image of the Sikhs in the media, and he forced the Canadian politicians and officials to take South Asian concerns seriously. His sojourn abroad unveils a unique picture of the mental and spiritual world of the overseas Sikhs in the first decade of the twentieth century.

NOTES

1. On the life of Jarnail Singh Bhindranwale there are several publications, roughly divided into negative accounts by Hindu journalists and laudatory by Sikhs. See the listings in Darshan Singh Tatla and Ian Talbot, *Punjab*, Oxford: Cilo, 1997.
2. Sant Visakha Singh, *Malwa Itihas*, 4 vols., Kishangarh: published by the author, 1970.
3. The introduction of written media led to the launching of community newspapers and the English press necessitated a re-interpretation of the past heritage of the Punjabis. This began to take the form of religious revivalism. An urgent issue was the challenge thrown up by Christian missionaries who converted some lower class Punjabis to their faith. The

Punjabi elite responded by establishing schools and colleges leading to religious fervour. Punjabi Hindus were much swayed by Swami Dayanand who established the Arya Samaj, while Muslims established their Anjumans. In each community, many reformers emerged to propagate their respective faiths. Baba Ram Singh led the Namdhari sect into a virtual rebellion against the British rule, and he was deported. Singh Sabhas were established in Amritsar and Lahore before the 1890s. Parallel to the Singh Sabha movement, which was more or less an urban phenomenon, there arose many saintly lineages in the rural Punjab. Preaching to the Sikh peasantry, the most prominent *sants* of this period included Atar Singh Reruwale, Atar Singh Mastuana, Nand Singh Kaleran (which later proliferated into many other branches), Ishar Singh Rarewale and others.

4. For the life of Atar Singh, see Teja Singh, *Jivan Kahani, Raj Yogi Sant Atar Singh Ji Maharaj de vrosae sewak Sant Teja Singh ji di apni kalm ton likhi hoi*, 2 vols., Barhu Sahib: Kalgidhar Trust, 2000.
5. Kesh, Kangha, Kara, Kachh, and Kirpan were prescribed for a baptized Sikh.
6. If Sant Atar Singh told Teja Singh that as an educated person he should not unnecessarily get into arguments with others it makes sense. But the Punjabi version literally translates as 'lecture if you wish but do not if you do not wish'.
7. Teja Singh's residence was at 33 Montague Road, Cambridge.
8. For the news on Khalsa Jatha of British Isles and its constitution, *Khalsa Samachar*, 27 October 1910, vol. 10, no. 46, p. 7.
9. Teja Singh mentions a crowd of ten thousand listeners, which seems highly inflated.
10. On Tarknath Das' Sikh connections, see James Campbell Ker, *Political Trouble in India, 1907-1917*, Calcutta, 1973 (rpt.; 1st pub. in 1917).
11. Doreen Indra, 'The portrayal of South Asians in the Vancouver Press, 1905-1976', *Ethnic and Racial Studies*, vol. 2, pt. 2 (1979), pp. 164-87.
12. *Khalsa Samachar*, 7 July 1910, p. 6. Guru Nanak Mining and Trust Co. Ltd. resolution by Bhag Singh, Bhan, Ratan, Hakam and Hari. Teja Singh was still the trustee of the company.
13. *The Daily Province* (Vancouver), 12 December 1908, p. 1.
14. In an interview to the *The World* (Vancouver), 14 December 1908, Swayne stated: 'Should the Sikhs waver in their loyalty, it would require 100,000 white troops to cope successfully with the situation'.
15. Nihal Singh termed it as 'The triumph of the Indians in Canada', in *Modern Review,* August 1909, pp. 99-108.
16. *Khalsa Samachar* (December 1909, p. 4) reported on Teja Singh's discourse on the full-moon Katak celebrations in London. It also reported that Narain Singh and Gurbakhsh Singh were appointed

secretaries of the Gurdwara for the next year. *Khalsa Samachar* (6/10/1910, vol. 11, no. 43, p. 6) reported *amrit parchar* in London. Tara Singh *granthi* from Malaya States Guides appealed to Narain Singh for vigorous movement towards baptism. Dharma Anant Singh, who had accompanied Teja Singh to London, eventually wrote a number of books on Sikh mysticism and contributed to Bhai Kahn Singh's monumental *Mahan Kosh*.

17. *Khalsa Samachar* (3/8/1911, p. 2) carried an editorial on the London Gurdwara, appreciating the Patiala Maharajah's offer of Rs. 1,25,000 as donation. *Khalsa Samachar* (3/8/1911, p. 2) has news item from Teja Singh who described how the Maharaja of Patiala inaugurated the London Gurdwara on 2 August and took a seat by *Guru Granth*. *Khalsa Samachar* also carried an appeal for funds from Narain Singh; in another issue there is a moving poem on the building for Sikh *dharmsala* in London.
18. Qasim became an engineer and remained a life long friend of Teja Singh. He was later called to prepare a design of Cheema Gurdwara being built in the memory of Atar Singh. Qasim came down to Cheema and completed this project, while Teja Singh went out to seek donations for the building.
19. Teja Singh, *Jivan Kahani*. The teacher said, 'Mr Singh, I have been a student in Germany. Students face many problems in overseas countries. I have heard only today about the letter from the university regarding your non-payment of fees'. He also gave 50 dollars cheque for university library deposit returnable after the completion of the course.
20. *Khalsa Samachar* (vol. 3, no. 20, p. 7) reported that Jawala Singh from Moorland, California, had provided three Guru Gobind Singh scholarships to encourage higher education for Hindustani students. *Khalsa Samachar* (vol. 14, no. 8, 15/10/1912, pp. 5-6) also carried a news item about a Sikh procession from Holt to Stockton which was led by *Guru Granth* mounted on a four-horse drawn buggy.
21. Memorandum of Khalsa Diwan Society and Indian United League, 1911. *Khalsa Samachar*, 20 October 1910, vol. 11, no. 45, p. 7. Hari Singh (M.A. Edinburgh) and Raja Singh met Canada's minister Sir William Wilfred Laurier in Vancouver who asked them to make a list of their problems in the form of a memorandum. Report by Bhag Singh *granthi*.
22. Norman Buchignani, Doreen M. Indra and Ram Srivastava, *Continuous Journey: A Social History of South Asians in Canada*, Toronto: McLelland and Stewart, 1985. These years were very hard for Punjabis in Canada. Of the 6,000 pioneers, only 2,342 were enumerated in the Census of 1911. While 490 were settled in Vancouver, 85 were in Victoria. Most of the rest were scattered throughout the Fraser Valley. Less than 50 were outside British Colombia. Many had migrated to

the United States across the border. Many had returned to the Punjab, while those left behind were facing increasing hostility from the white population. Reports on the problems of the Canadian Sikhs find increasing space in *Khalsa Samachar* in 1912-13. See *Khalsa Samachar*, vol. 14, no. 25, p. 7; no. 26, p. 2; no. 34, pp. 4-5; no. 38, p. 3; no. 39, pp. 4-5 (report of Lahore gathering by Canadian delegation); no. 44, pp. 3, 5; no. 45, p. 3; no. 47, p. 2 (Canadian Sikhs' delegation to Punjab).

There is information about a pamphlet in Punjabi on 'Mistreatment of Hindustanis in Canada', in *Khalsa Samachar*, 3 February 1910, vol. 11, no. 10, p. 7. Bhag Singh, secretary of Vancouver Gurdwara, reported that glasses of the Gurdwara were broken by some Americans on 4 October night. The police arrived late and Bhag Singh lamented, 'although they call us black men but law ought to treat everyone equally. Our view is that because they treat us as foreigners and slaves, our nation is facing serious issues and problems all over the places. And we are handicapped by our lack of education, cooperation and thoughts.' *Khalsa Samachar*, 10 January 1910, vol. 11, no. 8, p. 4. Balwant Singh from Vancouver came as a delegate to the Sikh Educational Conference in the Punjab. A letter from Hari Singh informed that the Khalsa Diwan paid for his fare and he was on a preaching mission.

23. Johnston states that even the Women's National Council claiming to represent 400 local women and the Ministerial Association of Vancouver opposed the admission of Indian women. It was the much hated Hopkinson who recommended to the Minister that the families should be allowed in with the understanding that no further entry would be permitted.
24. The deputation left for England on 17 March 1913. Hopkinson preceded them to brief British officials regarding the 'real' motive of the delegation. The Secretary of State refused to meet them on the ground that they did not represent the Government of Canada. The delegation could only secure an informal interview with Sir John Anderson, Under Secretary of State for the Colonies. In India the delegates were warned by O'Dwyer about making political propaganda and as they went to see the Viceroy, the Lieutenant Governor of the Punjab had already sent a note about the delegation's likely 'seditionist' motives. See O'Dwyer's *India as I knew it*, and Buchignani, Indra and Srivastava, *Continuous Journey.*
25. *Khalsa Samachar* (vol. 14, no. 30, p. 5) carried a report of Professor Teja Singh's activities in Shanghai. *Khalsa Samachar* (vol. 14, no. 31, p. 6), for news from Stockton.
26. Teja Singh mentions 35,000 Sikhs, a rather unbelievable figure.
27. Babu Teja Singh had developed differences with Teja Singh and the

latter had to resign from the college. The differences arose mainly over the scriptures compiled by Babu Teja Singh.

28. Teja Singh, *Jivan Kahani*, pp. 135-54, 157.
29. The full text of his lecture to the Congress is given in *Jivan Kahani*, pp. 221-35.
30. Dr Khem Singh Gill, a former Vice-Chancellor of the Punjab Agricultural University, and President of Akal Academy, has established a new school at Barhu.
31. Teja Singh, *Jivan Kahani*, pt. 2, p. 328.

8

The Nabha Affair: Akali Interest in a Sikh Princely State

MOHINDER SINGH

The 'abdication' of Maharaja Ripudaman Singh of Nabha and the involvement of the Shiromani Gurdwara Prabandhak Committee (SGPC) in the affair is one of the most controvertial issues. While there is no denying that the Maharaja had close affiliation with the Akalis and other nationalists of the time, the common belief that he was deprived of his throne mainly because of his having championed the Akali movement is only partially true.

A study of the early career and activities of the Maharaja reveals that he had come to acquire an independent and nationalistic outlook as a young prince.[1] While still in his early twenties he gave ample evidence of his feelings for the national aspirations. As a member of the Viceroy's Legislative Council (1907-8), he openly aligned himself with the non-official members like Gopal Krishna Gokhale and Rash Behari Ghose and became an acknowledged representative of the national viewpoint. He was also responsible for the introduction of the Anand Marriage Bill in the Council which aimed at legalizing the Sikh marriage ceremony. In February 1907, he took up the cause of a Sikh *granthi* of the 14th Sikhs who had been unjustly dismissed because, while sitting in attendance on the holy *Granth*, he did not salute an English officer. A few days later he wanted to ask a question about the injury done to the religious feelings of the Sikhs by Trumpp's translation of the *Adi Granth*.[2] Similarly in affairs of national importance he always sided with the nationalists and championed the cause of Indians. Speaking in the Council on the question of the relations between the Indians and the Europeans he had the courage to say that 'the European officers do not often show due courtesy and politeness either in writing to or in conversation with Indian gentlemen. This ignorance of Indian manners, customs, religions, languages and etiquette, which they do not trouble to study and consider not worth their while to learn, is a growing evil'.[3] He advocated the association of Indians with higher administration of the country. During the discussion on the Seditious Meetings Bill he did not lend his support to the government.

Furthermore, Ripudaman Singh's succession to the *gaddi* of Nabha was marked by a serious conflict with the government. He raised strong objection to the practice of placing Indian princes on their *gaddi* by an Agent of the British Government. The Maharaja believed that his succession, which was flawless in law as well as in usage, was a matter of right and valid without any British sanction or ceremony. Thus when the Political Agent for the Phulkian States, C.H. Atkins, wrote to the Maharaja on 22 March 1912 that he was 'to place the necklace round Young Highness's neck, to fasten the *sarpech* on Your Highness's turban and to bind the sword on Your Highness's person', the Maharaja wrote back that all this was unacceptable to him.[4] In his coronation speech he told the Political Agent that he had agreed to the installation ceremony under protest and reserved to himself the right to appeal to the Secretary of State for India.

Brought up to cherish independence, the Maharaja took special pleasure in challenging the authority of the British officers, whenever he could. When Sir Louis Dane, Lt. Governor of the Punjab, wished to pay a visit to the Maharaja, he curtly replied that it was not possible for him 'to receive a visit from His Honour'.[5] He also earned the displeasure of the government because of his close association with the political leaders of his day. During the foundation ceremony of the Benares Hindu University, when all the Indian princes left the meeting in protest against the speech of Mahatma Gandhi, the lone Indian prince who had the courage to watch the deliberations till their close was Ripudaman Singh. Again, at a Tilak Memorial meeting held at Mussouri, the Maharaja not only presided over it but also expressed his sincere regard for the great leader and contributed to the Memorial Fund. After the Nankana tragedy, when the Akali Dal gave a call to observe 5 April 1921 as the 'Nankana Sahib Day', the Maharaja responded by foregoing food for the day, donning a black turban and sleeping on the ground.

Conscious of his own rights and privileges as a prince he resented the unwarranted interference of the Government of India in the internal affairs of his state. This, he thought, was violation of the treaty rights conferred upon the state. In February 1918, when the Viceroy desired to bring to his notice any cases in which the princes considered that there had been 'a failure to fulfil pledges given by the British Govt', the Nabha Darbar furnished a long list of instances of such violations enlisting *inter-alia* the defects in the procedure on occasions of the reception of the ruler, entertaining claims from Nabha subjects, harbouring and encouraging state servants and deserters, and taking unauthorized possession of land.[6]

The Maharaja incurred serious displeasure of the British officials and their pent-up wrath found an opportunity of expression in the Patiala-Nabha dispute. While the two princes were busy in sorting out their differences through the efforts of Sir Ali Imam, the government appointed Justice Stuart to hold an enquiry. His independent nature and the halo of his personality were an eyesore to the British. This is evident from an important line in the Resolution of the Governor-General in Council: 'Ever since the Maharaja of Nabha succeeded his father, the Government of India have had abundant proof that the whole policy of the State has been dominated by his personality'.[7] In his findings Justice Stuart held both the princes guilty of one offence or the other. However, while the Maharaja of Patiala was given indemnity, Maharaja Ripudaman Singh was made to abdicate in favour of his minor son on 9 July 1923, and was removed to Dehradun. As to the nature of his 'abdication' it is not within the scope of this paper to go into detail.[8] What is important to discuss is the question whether or not the Maharaja was made to abdicate because of his sympathies with the Akalis and whether or not the Akalis were, legally and technically speaking, competent to take up the question of his restoration.

There is no doubt that the Maharaja had incurred the

displeasure of the British Government because of his tenacious will and his unyielding and abrasive style of expression.[9] His long and continued association with the nationalists, even when he had ceased to be a member of the Viceroy's Council, was not relished by the government. The intrigues and machinations of his unfaithful officials and his politically shrewd opponent, the Maharaja of Patiala reinforced the image created by his own activities. A ruler of his type could have only a precarious lien to the throne. His association with the Akalis hastened his severance with the administration of his state, but his dissociation from them could not have stopped it.

II

About the legitimacy of the SGPC taking up the Nabha issue, opinions differed from the very beginning. Some of the members of the SGPC felt that the deposition of the Maharaja of Nabha was a 'political issue' and as such the SGPC, which had been formed simply to look after the affairs of the Sikh Gurdwaras, was not competent to take up the question of the restoration of the Maharaja. If the community felt that in deposing the Maharaja the government had injured the Sikh feelings, the question could then have been taken up by the Central Sikh League or some other political body. But the 'extremist' Akalis did not bother about the technical and legal niceties and took up the question of the restoration of the Maharaja of Nabha in their hands on the plea that this action of the government 'was a side-attack to suppress the Akali movement'. To begin with, it was decided to mobilise public opinion in support of the Maharaja through press and platform. But the SGPC and the Akali Dal ultimately took the plunge, by issuing a statement on 9 July 1923, saying that the hereditary ruler of Nabha was 'unjustly and forcibly detached from the administration of his state by the Govt. of India'.[10] The communique also made serious allegations of arbitrary conduct and high-handedness against the Political Agent. July 29 was fixed as a day of prayer for the restoration of the Maharaja, and September 9 as a day for barefoot protest march in the principal streets of all the important towns of the Punjab. The *sangats* on such occasions were urged to pass resolutions condemning the action of the government and the Political Agent and sending messages of sympathy telegraphically to whatever place the Maharaja might have been removed.[11]

On 2 August 1923, the SGPC sent a long telegram to the Viceroy briefing him as to how the officials of the Nabha State and the Agent to the Phulkian States, had forced the Maharaja to sign the abdication letter. On 5 and 6 August the SGPC passed more resolutions in which the government was accused of deliberately taking advantage of the Patiala-Nabha dispute to wrest the administration of Nabha State from the Maharaja. Another resolution authorised the Executive Committee of the SGPC to take up the question of the restoration of the Maharaja by all peaceful and legitimate means. The resolution said that this action against a Sikh state of great historical and religious traditions and an orthodox and self-respecting Sikh prince was 'calculated to give a severe blow to the Panthic orthodoxy, organisation and well-being'. The resolution also condemned the actions of the Nabha officials for their treacherous role in the deposition of the Maharaja.[12]

Having sensed the Akali feelings over the question of the deposition of the Maharaja and the possibility of an agitation being launched by the SGPC, the Nabha administration forearmed itself by issuing certain ordinances, prohibiting political meetings in the Nabha territory to discuss the issue of restoration.[13] The Akali defiance of these orders by holding several *diwans* to discuss the prohibited affair resulted in a big agitation. Among the many *diwans* organized to condemn the government's action and to pray for the restoration of the Maharaja, one began at Jaito on 25 August 1923. A great procession was taken out on the first day. On 27 August one of the resolutions passed was that 'the Diwan expressed feelings of contempt at the oppressive means which the government had used in deposing the Maharaja of Nabha'. Another resolution regretted the arrest of Bhai Sant Singh of Patiala and other Akalis. The third resolution moved by Sardara Singh Akali of Patiala expressed feelings of regret on taking the royal palaces under guard. The fourth resolution moved by Rai Singh of Amritsar condemned the actions of disloyal and unfaithful Ahlkars of the Maharaja. Two other resolutions condemned the arrest of Rai Singh and criticized the bad behaviour of Tara Singh Sub-Inspector of Police.[14]

The Nabha Administrator arrested the organizers, Akali Inder Singh and others, on the charge of delivering 'political speeches'. This action offered the Akalis a challenge and the *diwan*, which was originally fixed for three days, was prolonged. The Report submitted by the Nazim of Phul, who witnessed all these proceedings and was reporting them to the Nabha authorities, is very revealing in this context:

> The Diwan might have dispersed had not Inder Singh been arrested. Now they have determined to remain here until the departure of state forces. I have also come to know that they have got some promises of help from the SGPC. If it is so, the agitation will not be put down easily.[15]

So far the *diwan* held at Jaito was a local affair, but this action of the Administrator offended the Sikh feelings and the SGPC came to the fore. More and more Akalis started pouring into Jaito, including some members of the SGPC. The Nabha authorities retaliated by making more arrests and declaring the SGPC and the Akali Dal 'unlawful associations'.[16] On the night of 13 September 1923, all the sixty members of the Interim Committee were arrested from different places and put on trial for 'treason' against the King-Emperor.[17]

When these arrests were going on, the Akalis assembled at Jaito began an *Akhand Path*. The arrest of an Akali who was reading the holy *Granth* on 14 September 1923, greatly agitated the Sikhs. They felt that this was an unprecedented sacrilege and an interference in their religion.[18] Though the *Path* was interrupted but not stopped, this action produced a great commotion in the Sikh community and the news of desecration spread like wild fire.[19] Jaito, a small town in the Nabha State, became the scene of a virulent *morcha*. Batches of Akalis began to march to jails from the Akal Takht in order to vindicate their right to pray for the rehabilitation of the Maharaja and to redeem the sacrilege committed by the police in interrupting the continuous reading of the Holy Book.

From 15 September 1923, Akali *jathas* of 25 each daily walked on foot to Jaito after taking a pledge of nonviolence in thought and deed at the Akal Takht at Amritsar. The aim of these *jathas* was to resume the interrupted *Akhand Path* at Gangsar, and to suffer in meek and humble spirit all hardships and tortures inflicted on them by the officials for establishing the Sikh birthright of free congregation and free worship in all Sikh Gurdwaras.[20]

The Nabha authorities did not allow the *jathas* to proceed to the Gurdwara. The Akalis were arrested and after being kept in custody in very unhygienic conditions and without food, were severely beaten and removed to Bawal Kanti, some 300 km away from Nabha, where they were left penniless to fend for themselves as best as they could. This treatment was meted out to no less than 5,000 Akalis in a period of seven months.

Finding that the struggle was getting prolonged without making any impression, the SGPC decided to send bigger *jathas* to Jaito. On 9 February 1924, a *shahidi jatha* of 500 Akalis started from Amritsar on its way to Jaito. It was given warm welcome by all the villagers it met on the way. On 20 February, the *jatha* reached Bargari, about 16 km away from Jaito. It left for Jaito on 21 February at about 12 noon. Dr Kitchlew, Principal Gidwani and S. Zimand of the *New York Times* also accompanied the *jatha*. According to many observers and eyewitnesses, including some impartial persons like Zimand, the *jatha* was moving in perfect order with large crowds of people on its right and left, and five Nishan Sahibs in front and *Guru Granth* in the centre.[21]

When the *jatha* was about 150 yds away from the Gurdwara Tibbi Sahib, Wilson Johnston, the Administrator of Nabha, ordered it to stop. He warned that if the *jatha* did not comply with his instructions, he would order firing.[22] The *jatha*, which had taken a solemn vow at the Akal Takht to resume the disrupted *Akhand Path* and to face calmly and non-violently any hardships which might befall them in the achievement of this purpose, continued to move and took a turn to the right in the direction of Tibbi Sahib. Noticing the intention of the *jatha*, the Administrator gave the signal to open fire. According to S. Zimand, the firing started at 2.25 p.m. The firing was in regular volleys and there were no desultory shots. The first round of firing lasted for full two minutes, i.e. from 2.45 to 2.47 p.m. The second round started at 2.55 p.m. and it lasted for full three minutes.[23] This, according to another contemporary, was a scene unique in the history of the world for calm restraint, cool courage, and a remarkable capacity for suffering in a righteous cause displayed by the Sikh victims of official fury.[24] The *jatha*, which from the very beginning knew the risk involved in their march, was not deterred and continued its onward march under the shower of bullets. Many of them fell dead or wounded; but lifting them up the rest of the members went straight to Tibbi Sahib. Bullets poured upon them from all directions. According to Zimand the dead and wounded were left uncared for. It was at this juncture that Kitchlew and Gidwani decided to motor to Jaito in order that they might take care of the wounded.[25] According to the SGPC version of the incident, 'the Sikhs were checked by the army men from removing the dead and the wounded and thus many of the wounded died for lack of attendance and water'.[26] According to some other eyewitnesses, the 'dead and wounded from amongst the *sangat* were seen scattered in the corn-fields. Medical staff travelling with the Jatha and the store of medicine, etc., were taken in custody.'[27] According to the statement of Gulab Singh, 'Dr Kehar Singh, in-charge of the medical arrangements of the *jatha*, was also arrested.'[28] Cavalry was employed to beat the rest of the *jatha*. After beating them to senselessness and tying them with strong ropes the Akalis were huddled into bullock carts to be transported to the barbed wire enclosures, from where they were subsequently taken to the fort.

Opinions differ regarding the number of casualties. The exact number of the dead and the wounded could not be ascertained as the scene of tragedy was made inaccessible to independent observers and press reporters, like Kitchlew, Gidwani and Zimand. The SGPC reports claim that there were over three hundred casualties including 70 to 150 dead.[29] The official report put the number at 19 dead and 28 wounded.[30]

The moral significance of the Jaito firing was far greater than that of the Nankana massacre, because the perpetrator of this tragedy was not an irresponsible Mahant but a so-called civilized government, headed by a European officer, with tall professions about justice and law and order, and well informed about the objectives and methods of its victims. The sacrifice on the part of the *jatha* becomes all the more impressive as it was not caught unawares, unlike the *jatha* of Bhai Lachhman Singh at Nankana.

The Akalis knew from the very beginning that the supreme sacrifice might be required of them, and knowing this they had voluntarily and cheerfully gone to face the situation.

The Nabha authorities tried to justify their action first by issuing some statements in which it was alleged that the firing was first started by the Akali mob which was armed with *lathis, chhavis*, spears and fire arms, and that there was a danger of an attack on the Nabha State by the mob.[31] When there was a strong protest from all quarters against this barbarous action of the Nabha authorities and a demand for an independent commission of enquiry, the government tried to whitewash the action of its officials by appointing a Subordinate Magistrate of Nabha to enquire into the incident of the Jaito firing. In a long report that he submitted to the government, he states that the *jatha* on its march 'was visited by a large crowd, which openly declared its intention of using force'. Among the many charges against the Akalis the one given in the report is that the firing was first started by an 'unknown' Akali of the Nabha State. Imamudin of Dabri Khanan received a shot under his left thigh. Another bullet, says the report, 'passed through the turban of Hazure Sawan Singh'. The report justified the official action: 'the mob was prepared to achieve its end by all possible means; and were so constituted that a prudent man under the circumstances had no option but to open fire to repel their menacing advance in military formations'.[32]

Jawaharlal Nehru, who went to Jaito along with K. Santhanam and Gidwani, to find out what was happening there, was arrested and kept in Nabha Jail. He gives an interesting account of the arbitrary nature of justice and the executive's domination over the judiciary: 'I realised that it is difficult for this court to act independently or to dissociate itself from the executive which has taken the initiative in starting the case against us. Indeed I learnt with some surprise that even applications made by us to the court were being referred to the Administrator of the State for orders.'[33] How could in the present Enquiry an Indian Magistrate, who was a subordinate of the European Administrator of Nabha, go against the will of the executive? How difficult it would have been for him to act independently? He had to justify the action of the Administrator firstly because he was his subordinate and secondly, as was the case with most of the Indian subordinates in those days, he was more enthusiastic and loyal to the British officials than the officials themselves. And the present magistrate, in keeping with the traditions of his class, tried to exonerate the Nabha Administrator of the brutal charge of playing with the lives of many an innocent people and shifted the responsibility to the Akali shoulders. The arguments given by him are not only baseless and fabricated but also unconvincing. A careful study of the strategy and planning made by the Nabha administration in dealing with the Akalis leaves no doubt about its intentions to punish the Akalis.[34] The passage leading to the Gurdwara and the fort had been narrowed by a barbed wire barrier on one side, and a long row of about 200 chained bullock-carts filled with thorny bushes and masses of barbed wire on the other. A number of Pathan policemen from Jhelum and Attock districts, known for their brutal and merciless beatings at Guru-ka-Bagh, were seated on the top of the bullock-carts. Trenches had been dug by the Nabha State Infantry near the Tibbi Sahib Gurdwara under the command of Major Bell Kingsley while the Faridkot Sappers and Miners stood ready a little beyond the Gurdwara. Colonel Minchin had his camp in the middle with two detachments of cavalry.

The charges against the Akalis become meaningless in the light of the above arrangements. Yet, for the sake of argument, they can be taken up for discussion. The first charge that 'the Jatha was armed with *lathis*, *chhavis*, spears and fire arms' is totally wrong in the light of the evidence given by S. Zimand, who in his letter to Mahatma Gandhi says, 'I want therefore to repeat again that I observed carefully the Jatha and the crowds following the Jatha from February 20th, 7 p.m., till February 21st, 2 p.m. when they entered Nabha territory and that to the best of my knowledge the Jatha and the crowd following the Jatha *were not armed* and behaved in a peaceful and orderly manner.'[35] This evidence is further confirmed by responsible persons like Kitchlew and Gidwani in addition to many an eyewitness. It is possible that some of the crowd might have been carrying *lathis* with them because *lathi* is a handy weapon that every villager generally carries and when the *jatha* marched through their fields, they joined it with whatever they had in their hands. Again it is possible that some of the Akalis were wearing *kirpans* but this cannot be taken to mean that they were carrying arms. *Kirpans* are still carried by the baptized Sikhs. But these are not called fire arms.[36]

The second charge that the Akalis opened fire first is contradicted by the Magistrate himself when he writes: 'To the question, who began the firing, I consider that whichever party began the firing does not matter.' This suggests that the firing was not started by the Jatha. In any case, it is clear from the testimony of Zimand and others that the Akalis had no firearms with them. If there were even the slightest possibility of the *jatha* having opened fire, the magistrate would not have spared them. The allegation in the Punjab Government communique of 3 March 1924 that shots were fired at eight British officers is interesting because no one was injured as a result of this firing by the Akalis. The argument that the mob was violent and the firing had become a necessity is questionable because a bigger mob at Nankana had remained perfectly non-violent. The *jatha* or the crowd would not have done any harm to any one if they were permitted to go their own way without any interference on the part of the authorities. The authorities made a prestige point not to allow the *jatha* to fulfil its vow of completing the interrupted *Akhand Path*.

The Nabha authorities are to be blamed, first, for not having issued any warning before firing and then for resorting to regular volleys and indiscriminate firing. If the intention was only to disperse the mob, *lathi*-charge could have been resorted to and if at all there was an extreme need for firing, this could have been done in a discriminate manner killing only a few and terrorising others. From all accounts it seems that the firing resorted to by the Nabha authorities was uncalled for.

Next to the Nankana massacre, the Jaito firing caused the greatest sensation in the country. Public meetings were held at Delhi, Calcutta, Bombay, Madras and Karachi and addressed by popular leaders like Maulana Mohammad Ali and Shaukat Ali, C.R. Dass, Pandit Moti Lal Nehru and Pandit Madan Mohan Malaviya. Mahatma Gandhi and Lala Lajpat Rai expressed their sympathy with the Akali cause. The Congress expressed its dissatisfaction with the official enquiry, and set up its own enquiry committee and a report was published by its Secretary.[37] On

25 February 1924 Pandit Madan Mohan Malaviya moved in the Legislative Assembly the adjournment of the House to discuss the Jaito affair. But the motion was not allowed by the Home Member. Sikh members, Jodh Singh and Narain Singh, made an unsuccessful attempt to discuss the issue in the Punjab Legislative Council.[38] The Akali agitation at Jaito received the support of the Central Sikh League and other Sikh organizations.[39]

The nationalist and Sikh leaders failed to bring about any amicable settlement, and the SGPC continued to send *shahidi jathas*. To avoid repetition of the miseries that befell the first *shahidi jatha* and to give the government time to think over the problem and come to settlement, some of the nationalist leaders, particularly Mahatma Gandhi, advised the SGPC to stop sending more *jathas* to Jaito. In his letter of 28 February 1924 to the Secretary of the SGPC, Mahatma Gandhi wrote: 'But I would ask the Akali Sikhs not to send any more Jathas without further deliberations and consultation with those leaders outside the Sikh community who have hitherto been giving their advice.' The Mahatma further exhorted the Akalis: 'It would be well to stop and watch the developments arising out of the tragedy.'[40] Lala Lajpat Rai, who was with Mahatma Gandhi at this time, addressed a letter to the SGPC asking them to postpone sending further *jathas* to Jaito so that national leaders might have time to consider the whole matter and then advise the Akalis as to their future course. The SGPC, while thanking the Mahatma for his sympathy with the movement and assuring him that perfect non-violence was the sheet anchor of the Akali hopes, expressed its inability to stop sending more *jathas* to Jaito till the object of completing the *Path* was achieved.

The national and Sikh leaders started advising the Akalis to give up the agitation over the restoration of the Maharaja of Nabha. The SGPC assumed a lukewarm attitude, neither dropping it altogether nor making it a life-and-death question any longer. A section of the Sikhs had already started feeling that in taking up the Nabha issue, which was a political issue, the SGPC had no *locus standi* and was backing a wrong horse. The Maharaja of Nabha also realized that the Akalis were unable to get back the throne for him. On 31 July he made the statement: 'I am not responsible for the present agitation about Nabha affairs and have no sympathy with it.'[41] The prolonged agitation, with another front having been opened at Bhai Pheru, was putting great strain on the resources of the SGPC in men and money. Most of the leaders having been sent behind the bars, the movement had quite weakened outside and it was becoming increasingly difficult to get volunteers to continue the agitation. The increasing influence of the extremists and the growing popularity of the Babbar Akalis in the rural areas compelled the SGPC leaders to come to an understanding with the government and to get whatever they could, lest the situation should get out of control. The government also became tired of the long struggle and was in a reconciliatory mood. It was under these circumstances that the national leaders like Pandit Malaviya made serious efforts for a compromise. While the Nabha Administrator was willing to allow the Akalis to fulfil their vow of 101 *Akhand Paths*, he expressed his fears that a long period of ten months that was needed to complete them was excessive and the duty he owed to the subjects of the state made it 'impossible for him to allow an invasion of the state territory by outside people for a period of ten months'.[42] The Administrator insisted that the *Akhand Paths* should be finished in a very short period, say seven days. Pandit Malaviya emphasized that the unconditional admission of the *jatha* into the Gurdwara would enable the Akalis to fulfil their pledge to restart the *Akhand Path*. The government could carry on its negotiations with the SGPC. These parleys were unsuccessful but on 9 July 1925 the Sikh Gurdwaras Act was passed in the Punjab Legislative Council.[43] Most of the Akalis arrested in connection with Jaito and other *morchas* were set at liberty. On 27 July 1925, many *jathas* reached Jaito after being released from the Nabha *Birs* and its jails. The deadlock finally ended with the Akalis completing their 101 *Akhand Paths* on 6 August 1925.

III

While the Gurdwaras Act settled the question of the disrupted *Akhand Path*, the issue of the restoration of Maharaja Ripudaman Singh of Nabha to his throne, for which the agitation had been started, was by now almost forgotten or given up. It was this attitude of the Akalis that was criticized by a section of the Sikhs.

As already noticed, some members of the SGPC from the very beginning and the Sikh Legislators had felt that the removal of the Maharaja from Nabha was, technically speaking, a political issue and the SGPC, or the Akali Dal, which were formed to look after the affairs of the Sikh Gurdwaras, were not competent to take up the question of his restoration. Some of the Akali leaders inside the Lahore Fort had begun to feel that the movement was becoming weaker day by day and it was unable to get any support from the masses because the restoration of the Maharaja of Nabha was not a religious issue. When they were asked by the national leaders like Mahatma Gandhi and Pandit Malaviya how the 'abdication of Maharaja Ripudaman Singh was a religious issue', the Akali leaders were 'unable to satisfy them'. Sardar Amar Singh Jhabal resigned the membership of the SGPC, saying that in taking up the Nabha question the Committee had made a very serious mistake. Another Akali leader, Master Sunder Singh Lyallpuri, suggested that this question should be handed over to the political organization of the Sikhs, the Central Sikh League, and that if it was not done, he threatened, he would launch a campaign against it. Even Mahatma Gandhi advised the Akalis that the performance of the disrupted *Akhand Path*, which was a purely religious question, should be separated from the question of the restoration of the Maharaja of Nabha, which was political in nature. 'The agitation which the Akalis want to carry on in connection with the restoration will be on an independent footing and will be purely a separate movement.'[44]

There were serious differences of opinion among the SGPC members inside the Lahore Fort Jail about the Nabha affair. Out of 37 members there were only six who wanted nothing less than the restoration of the Maharaja as the basis of settlement with the government. An equal number of members wanted to drop the Nabha question altogether. About a dozen other members wanted to keep the agitation alive as a matter of expediency simply because they felt that its suspension or stoppage would weaken the agitation and would be interpreted as a moral defeat of the Akalis. These members were willing to give up the question as soon as the remaining issues were settled with the government. All the members of the SGPC inside the jail felt that they should be able to mould their attitude towards the Nabha issue in accordance with the changed circumstances. Even an extremist leader like Master Tara Singh supported this stand. It was the Nabha question which caused the first major split among the Akali leaders because after the passage of the Act most of the Akalis came out of the jails as they felt they had got in the form of the Gurdwaras Act all that they had been agitating for. Others thought that giving up the Nabha question was a betrayal and remained behind the bars.[45]

The long agitation did not help the Maharaja. In fact it stiffened the attitude of the government towards him. Thinking that Dehradun was too close to keep him away from Akali politics, the British authorities removed him to the far off Kodaikanal in the south early in 1928. After being unable to get back his throne with the help of his Akali supporters, the Maharaja charged them with having betrayed his cause. He pointed out that when Teja Singh Samundri, Bawa Harkishan Singh and Master Tara Singh had come to him he was not willing to let them take up his cause but they said: 'Either you will be restored to your throne or the whole Sikh nation will die for your cause but will not give up the issue.'[46] The Maharaja did not want the Akalis to accept the Gurdwaras Act because by securing the measure they would of necessity have to give up the question of his restoration and he would be deprived of whatever little was left with him. In the end the Maharaja wanted to know as to why the Akalis were dropping the question of his restoration. It was in a similar state of helplessness that he had signed the abdication letter. He knew that the Akalis were being forced to give up his cause.

True, the Akalis can be held guilty of having first raised the hopes of the Maharaja for restoration to the sky and then causing him disillusionment and disappointment by giving up the issue as a matter of expediency. However, the Maharaja himself was more to be blamed. Impressed with the Akali victories against the government in the Keys Affair and at Guru-ka-Bagh, he overestimated their potential and prompted them through some of his agents to take up his cause. When he realized that the Akali agitation was worsening his claims, he shifted his stand and dissociated himself from the Akalis. His indecision was mainly responsible for his sufferings. He wished the Akalis to take up his cause but at the same time he did not want to offend the British authorities. If he wanted the Akalis to take up the issue earnestly, he should have come out openly against the government. When the SGPC representatives, K.M. Panikkar, Sardar Arjan Singh and Sardar Raja Singh reached the Maharaja's residence at Dehradun, it was with great difficulty that they managed an interview with the Maharaja. When they asked him for a written statement, he tried to put them off with one excuse or another. When they pressed for it the Maharaja complained of having been badly treated by the Akalis and said: 'Then why not leave the Nabha Question.'[47] The Maharaja had, in the words of Mahatma Gandhi, 'made it practically impossible for his well-wishers to carry on an effective agitation for his restoration'. The Mahatma felt that if the Maharaja issued a public statement 'that all the writings were practically extorted from him and that he is quite willing and anxious that all the facts against him should be published', if he was prepared to face all the consequences of the agitation, i.e. deprivation of titles, annuitys, etc., and if all his allegations regarding duress could be proved, 'it is possible to carry on an effective and even successful agitation'.[48] But the Maharaja did not come up with such a statement. Had he made a declaration of this kind, his question could have been taken up even by the national leaders, and an effective agitation on all-India level could have been launched for his restoration.

With regard to their stand on the Nabha issue the British officials and the Administrator of Nabha had no valid grounds. A large number of daily reports from the *Khangi Karobari* (Minister in-charge of Household Affairs) of Nabha stationed at Jaito, as also the reports of the Nazim of Phul who had all along been a witness to these happenings at Jaito, fully expose the government. Conscious of its moral defeat and the loss of prestige in the Keys Affair and at Guru-ka-Bagh, the British Government was anxious to forestall any Akali designs of winning one more popular battle against the authorities. The Nazim of Phul admitted that the Jaito agitation was nothing more than a point of prestige between the government and the Akalis. The Akalis were prepared to leave Jaito as soon as the place had been cleared of the military and the police. The above official carefully records in his weekly report submitted to the Administrator of Nabha: 'Now it is a matter of prestige; if the police leaves the station before, Akalis will think themselves successful. If the Akalis leave the station prior to the police they will be ashamed of their obstinacy and will not dare return.'[49]

It was this war of prestige which the government wanted to win, thinking that the suppression of the Akalis would restore its lost prestige in the eyes of the people. While going through the proceedings of the daily *diwans* at Jaito and the speeches delivered vis-à-vis the daily and weekly reports of the government officials, one finds at least some justification in the Akali claims that the government policy with regard to the Nabha affair was a side-attack to suppress the Akali movement. In the Report of Enquiry published by the government as well as the Judgement in the Jaito Firing Case, the Akalis have been accused of having delivered 'political speeches'. On this plea, the government went ahead with declaring the SGPC and the Akai Dal 'unlawful associations', banning the entry of the Akalis, or any other national or Sikh leaders, or even the entry of the press reporters and representatives into Nabha. The proceedings of the *diwan* at Jaito reveal that the Akalis who were conducting the *diwan* were the least politically conscious and could say nothing more than expressing their sympathy with the deposed Maharaja. On 1 September 1923, the Nazim of Phul reported to the Nabha Administrator: 'Since last three days they (the Akalis) are delivering no political speeches at all.' Even if we accept that the Akalis were not allowed to hold the *diwan* because they wanted to express sympathies with the Maharaja, which according to the government was a political question, one wonders why similar *diwans* organized by the opponents of the Maharaja were fully encouraged and patronized by the government. If discussing the virtues of the Maharaja could be termed as political, how could his condemnation by his opponents be seen as being free from politics?

While the Akali obstinacy dragged them into the struggle, the government's obstinacy prolonged it to a period of over two years, causing a great strain on its resources and giving one more blow to its prestige. Had the government acted wisely and understood the Akali character rightly, the trouble could have been easily averted. The Akalis would have left Jaito after completing the *Akhand Path* had not the government offered them a challenge by disrupting it and arresting them *en masse*.

The Nazim of Phul could read the character of the Akalis better than an alien Administrator. He rightly warned the government: 'The more they are suppressed the more they will be helped by the Panth.'[50] But the government did not pay any heed to his advice, anxious as it was to score a victory that broke its previous record of suppression.

NOTES

1. Born on 4 March 1883, Ripudaman Singh succeeded to the *gaddi* of Nabha on 24 January 1912.
2. A German missionary, Ernest Trumpp, was officially employed to prepare an English translation of the *Adi Granth*. His work, according to M.A. Macauliffe, 'was highly inaccurate and unidiomatic and furthermore gave mortal offence to the Sikhs by the odium theologicum introduced into it': *The Sikh Religion*, Oxford, 1909, vol. I, p. vii.
3. Legislative Council Proceedings, March 1908.
4. Letter dated 22 March 1912, from the Political Agent, Phulkian States to the Maharaja of Nabha, File no. 18 (Chief Minister, Nabha) PGRO.
5. Letter dated 11 January 1913, from Maharaja Ripudaman Singh of Nabha to C.H. Atkins, Political Agent, Phulkian States, *Nabha Affairs* (1912-17), p. 1.
6. Confidential letter (no. 205 CA), dated 12 April 1918, from the Political Agent to the Foreign Minister, Nabha, *Some Confidential Papers of the Akali Movement*, ed. Ganda Singh, Amritsar: SGPC, 1965, pp. 8-9.
7. File no. 298 (Chief Minister, Nabha), PGRO.
8. The Maharaja in his letter dated 14 December 1923 addressed to the Viceroy emphasizes more than once how he was intimidated by his self-seeking officials and the Political Agent: 'I was driven into the presence of the Agent by clever schemers and it was he who *demanded abdication* from me threatening worse and dire consequences in case of my non-compliance'. File no. 18 (PGRO).

   A careful perusal of the large number of letters of the British officials in the Punjab to the Viceroy will leave an impartial student of history in no doubt about the nature of the Maharaja's abdication. It was under the great pressure and clever manoeuvres of the Agent for the Phulkian States that the Maharaja signed the letter of abdication. In his D.O. letter no. 794-C of July 1923, Minchin informed the Viceroy, 'Mr. O'Grady tells me that he had great difficulty in inducing H.H. to sign the letter' (*Nabha Affairs*, NAI). Soon after the signing of the document the Maharaja realized his mistake and sent his fastest car to get the document back. But it was too late.

9. Conscious of his independent nature, the Maharaja states: 'the root-cause of my troubles is the want of blind obedience'. File no. 18, (PGRO).
10. Press Communique, dated 9 July 1923, issued by the SPGC.
11. Press Communiques nos. 5, 7 and 12, dated 9, 17 and 22 August 1923, respectively, issued by the SGPC.
12. SGPC Resolutions dated 5 and 6 August 1923.
13. Press Communique, dated 13 October 1923, issued by the Punjab Govt. from Lahore, File no. 28 (PGRO).
14. File no. 70 (PGRO).
15. Ibid., report dated 30 August 1923.
16. Punjab Govt. orders no. 23772-73, dated 12 Oct. 23, File no. 28 (PGRO).
17. Giani Nahar Singh's article in *Bhai Jodh Singh Abhinandan Granth*, part II, p. 227.
18. There are many divergent opinions about the *Path* being interrupted. The Akalis allege that armed soldiers in uniform literally dragged the man reading the *Granth*. The official reports assert that the reading was taken up by a Sikh sepoy who was seated near the *granthi*. Sardar Gurdial Singh, Assistant Administrator, Nabha State, in his statement published in the *Pioneer* of Allahabad, refuted the Akali charge of interruption in the *Path*. According to him the *Path* was finished to the end under his orders and the final Bhog ceremony was performed in his presence and the Prasad was offered out of the state funds. According to Giani Nahar Singh, the *Path* was taken up by another man of the Nabha State. R.R. Sahni, another contemporary and eyewitness of a greater part of the struggle, also corroborates this view.

    Evidence given by Mir Muhammad Ali, Supdt. of Police, Nabha, in the case *Crown* vs *S.S. Mehtab Singh* and others, and the Nazim of Phul mention one Bhai Atma Singh who took over the *Path* from Inder Singh.
19. On 29 September 1923, the SGPC passed a comprehensive resolution in five parts condemning the action of the Nabha State authorities in interrupting the *Path*. The resolution held the Government of India responsible for this unbearable insult to the scripture. The resolution further declared the SGPC's determination to maintain the dignity of their places of worship. The resolution also censured the government for having declared the SGPC and the Akali Dal 'unlawful associations'. In the end, the resolution affirmed the SGPC's faith in complete non-violence in word and deed.
20. SGPC Communique no. 94, n.d.
21. *Some Confidential Papers of the Akali Movement*, p. 74
22. According to the Judgement in the Jaito Firing Case, a notice was served on the *jatha* by the Nabha authorities prohibiting their entry into the state territories: File no. 221, p. 47 (PGRO).

23. S. Zimand's letter to Mahatma Gandhi, dated 9 April 1924, quoted in the *Quarterly Register*, April 1924.
24. Ruchi Ram Sahni, *Struggle for Reform in Sikh Shrines*, Amritsar: 1965, p. 225.
25. S. Zimand, quoted in *Quarterly Register*, April 1924.
26. SGPC, *Truth About Nabha: Struggle for freedom of Religious Worship at Jaito*, p. 8.
27. Statement of Mohinder Singh, Harbans Singh and Bhagat Ram Singh, quoted in the *Quarterly Register*, April 1924.
28. Statement of Gulab Singh, quoted in ibid., p. 104.
29. *Truth About Nabha*, p. 9.
30. Report of the Enquiry conducted by Balwant Singh, issued by the Govt. of India, 8 March 1924 (PGRO).
31. File no. 210 (PGRO).
32. Enquiry Committee Report, *Quarterly Register*, April 1924.
33. Statement of Jawaharlal Nehru, File no. 168 (PGRO).
34. 'A Plan of Jaito Massacre' given in the beginning of the *Truth About Nabha*. The Report of Enquiry by S. Balwant Singh also confirms that the plan was to punish the Akalis.
35. S. Zimand's letter to Mahatma Gandhi, quoted in the *Quarterly Register*, April 1924.
36. The statement of Dr Saifuddin Kitchlew, given to the Congress Akali Sahayak Bureau, is very relevant in this context: 'We had absolutely satisfied ourselves that the Jatha and the Sangat had no fire-arms or Chhavis (except *kirpans*) or any other instruments other than ordinary *lathis*'.
37. The Report concludes: (1) That the Jatha remained perfectly non-violent to the end (2) that the crowd was unarmed except for the *lathis*, was never aggressive and it certainly had no fire-arms (3) there was no justification whatever for the action of the Administrator and the firing, even if it had been opened only as a precautionary measure, was carried on for an unnecessary length of time.
38. Punjab Legislative Council Proceedings, Feb. 1924.
39. The Central Sikh League passed a Resolution in a meeting held at Lahore on 4 April 1924, expressing 'its sentiments of contempt that the government had not so far moved forward to undo the injustice done to a venerable prince'. *Akali*, dated 7 April 1926.
40. Mahatma Gandhi's open letter to the SGPC, dated 28 February 1924, quoted in the *Quarterly Register,* April 1924, pp. 112-13.
41. *Some Confidential Papers of the Akali Movement*, p. 74. From the report of the Political Agent to the Viceroy it appears that this statement was forcibly obtained by the Agent from the Maharaja. *Nabha Affairs* (N.A. Foreign Pol).
42. File no. 195 (PGRO).

43. The Governor of the Punjab stated in his speech that the Administrator of Nabha would permit bands of pilgrims to proceed for religious worship to the Gangsar Gurdwara under the following rules:

    1. That they abstain from holding political Diwans or spreading political propaganda during their sojourn within the state boundaries.
    2. That they confine themselves to the use of the Gurdwara itself and such reasonable space around it as may be set apart for their accommodation.
    3. That they will be self-supporting during their visit, the village and Mandi of Jaito being excluded from the area set apart for their accommodation.
    4. That any such band will arrive at Jaito by rail or by a road decided upon by the Administrator and that suitable arrangements shall have been made to ensure that any such band of pilgrims will be unaccompanied by any Sangat or following.
    5. And that the date of arrival of any such band at Jaito is communicated to the Administrator in order to enable him to make suitable arrangements in connection with the same.

    Extract from the speech of the Governor delivered in the Punjab Legislative Council on 9 July 1925 at Simla.
44. *Some Confidential Papers of the Akali Movement*, pp. 53, 237-8.
45. For further detail, ibid., pp. 244-5.
46. Ibid., pp. 172-4.
47. Ibid., pp. 113-14.
48. Mahatma Gandhi's letter dated 4 March 1924 to the SGPC, quoted in the *Confidential Papers*, p. 55.
49. Weekly Report dated 1 Sept. 1923, from the Nazim of Phul to the Administrator of Nabha, File no. 70 (PGRO).
50. Ibid.

9

The Patiala Enquiry: Paramount Power Protects its Sikh Protégé

KULDEEP KAUR GREWAL

The period after 1857 saw a major shift in the British policy towards the princely states. Though Viceroy Canning assured that there would be no more annexations of the princely states, he established at the same time a further principle, which was to assume an even greater significance for the future relationship between the British and the states. As Canning himself clarified, the proposed measure would not debar the Government of India from stepping in 'to set right such serious abuses in a Native government as may threaten any part of the country', 'nor from assuming temporary charge of a Native State'.[1] Subsequent Viceroys kept giving reminders to the princes to keep their administrations in order. Lord Mayo (1869-72) said crisply: 'If we support you in your power we expect in return good government'.[2] According to Lee-Warner, the Paramount Power was not bound by treaties while deciding cases of misgovernment. 'When there is gross misrule, the right, or the duty, of interference arises, notwithstanding any pledges of unconcern or "absolute rule" which treaties may contain.'[3]

Thus, in their relations with the Indian rulers, the British as the Paramount Power considered it their right as well as duty to interfere in cases of gross misrule in the princely states. Some general principles were drawn by C.L. Tupper on the basis of precedents. There were various penalties for crimes or atrocities or other forms of misconduct, such as murder, complicity in murder, outrages on women, mutilations, dissent against the Paramount Power, contumacy, disobedience, and breach of engagement. Though the government had the widest discretion regarding the cases to be taken up, penalties were imposed according to the nature of the case: like deposition, fine, or deprivation of power, honours or salute. Deposition of a ruler on account of general misrule was an act of state, beyond the cognizance of the courts of law.[4]

Of the cases taken up by Tupper, only in the case of Baroda were commissions of enquiry constituted in 1873-5. The first commission consisted of four members: the British Chief Commissioner of Mysore, the Prime Minister of Jaipur, and two members nominated by the Bombay Government. The commission gave a period of grace to the ruler to improve his administration. The second commission was appointed after an attempt on the life of the British agent. This commission had three European officers, two Indian chiefs and an Indian minister. It was a political and not a judicial tribunal. The decision was to rest with the Government of India. The ruler was deposed after the verdict of the second commission.[5]

Two other rulers were deposed for misgovernment during the late nineteenth century: the chief of Suket in 1893 and that of Kalat also in 1893. In nearly twenty other cases, action was taken on the basis of the reports of the British officers. The punishments ranged from reprimands to deprivation of all, or only criminal authority, and joint administration of the ruler with an Indian or a British official.[6] During the period of Curzon, when the intervention in the internal affairs of the states reached its zenith, about fifteen princes were either forced to abdicate or temporarily deprived of their powers.[7]

The Montford Report mentions the question of depriving the ruler of a state of his rights, dignities, and powers, or of debarring from succession of a member of his family:

> If such cases occur in the future we think that they should be always referred to a commission to be appointed by the Viceroy to advise him. It should consist of five members, including ordinarily a high court judge and two Ruling Princes. The names of the commissioners should

be intimated in advance to the defendant before they were appointed; and the proceedings of the commission should be made public only if the defendant so desires.[8]

During an informal conference of political officers called by Lord Irwin at Simla in July 1927, L.W. Reynolds, the Agent to the Governor-General (AGG) for Rajputana, expressed the view that it was virtually impossible to make effective use of the Commission of Enquiry:

> Before recourse is had to this remedy, the state of misrule must be so bad as to leave in no doubt what the verdict of the Commission, if appointed, will be. For obviously a verdict favourable to the defendant Prince would be disastrous. Consequently the probability is that the State concerned will be reduced to the verge of ruin, and the subjects to great misery before the remedy is applied.[9]

In fact, a Commission of Enquiry was rarely appointed. In the case of Udaipur in 1921 and that of Hyderabad in 1926, the princes concerned did not request for an enquiry. The offers of commissions to the ruler of Indore in 1926 and to that of Bharatpur in 1927 were declined. In the case of Nabha in 1923, the request for a commission was refused.[10]

In the case of Patiala in 1930, it was deliberately decided by the Paramount Power not to appoint a commission and by the Maharaja of Patiala not to ask for it. Several popular writers have taken notice of this enquiry, generally treating it as a farce or a scandal.[11] The most recent writer to discuss the Patiala enquiry is K. Natwar Singh. He has devoted a whole chapter to this subject. He attributes the genesis of the enquiry to the publication of a book entitled the *Indictment of Patiala*. He quotes from the correspondence between the Viceroy and the Secretary of State for India, and shows clearly that the Maharaja was taken into confidence by the Viceroy who was keen to shield him for political reasons. The Maharaja was a premier prince of the Punjab; he was critical of the Indian National Congress; two Indian rulers had already been deposed in the 1920s. Moreover, the Maharaja had good public relations and competent lawyers. The Indian States' People's Conference boycotted the enquiry. K. Natwar Singh makes it absolutely clear that the enquiry was meant to rescue Maharaja Bhupinder Singh rather than to punish him – an interesting comment on the way in which the paramountcy worked.[12] Natwar Singh's discussion is based on archival materials, but he does not give full references to them.

II

The *Indictment of Patiala*, the report of the Patiala Enquiry Committee appointed by the Indian States' People's Conference (ISPC),[13] was published at Poona in February 1930. This committee had been formed after the General Secretary of the Conference received a copy of a memorial submitted by ten 'citizens' of Patiala to the Viceroy, levelling several charges against Maharaja Bhupinder Singh. Printed copies of this memorial were distributed among the delegates to the Bombay Session of the ISPC held in May 1929. The report held the Maharaja guilty of most of the charges levelled against him in the memorial and underscored that a *prima facie* case existed against the Maharaja for an official enquiry.[14] The Patiala Enquiry Committee found the Maharaja of Patiala guilty on twelve counts:

1. Murder of Lal Singh, a cousin of the father-in-law of the Maharaja. The charge was that the Maharaja had got Lal Singh murdered in order to keep his wife in his palace as one of his wives.
2. Setting up and maintaining a bomb factory in the fort of Bahadur Garh in the Patiala State.
3. Disappearance of Bachittar Kaur, her daughter and son. Bakhshish Singh, the husband of Bachittar Kaur, had accused the Maharaja of getting his wife and daughter murdered.
4. The Maharaja forcibly keeping the wife of Amar Singh, and not releasing her.
5. Illegal arrest and confinement of Harchand Singh Jaiji without trial, and confiscation of his properties worth twenty lakhs.
6. Concoction of false cases against individuals who were the objects of the Maharaja's wrath.

7. Inhuman tortures, illegal arrests and imprisonments, and high-handed confiscations of property.
8. Ruinous consequences of the Maharaja's *shikar*.
9. Tyranny of *begar*.
10. Non-return of war loan.
11. Increments in revenue assessment, imposition of new taxes, and other financial matters.
12. Misappropriation of funds raised for public purposes.[15]

On 25 February 1930, placards were exhibited by small boys when the Chamber of Princes was meeting in Delhi, mentioning the *Indictment*.[16] Women organizations like the National Council of Women in India, Indian Women's Association, and Gujarati Hindu Stri Mandal passed resolutions, criticizing the continued inactivity of the government and requesting the Viceroy for enquiry. There was a petition from the representatives of the subjects of Patiala and resolutions were passed at a meeting of the residents of Delhi.[17]

This made the government sit up and take notice. Lord Irwin was aware of the financial situation of the state. He had written to W. Wedgewood-Benn, the Secretary of State for India, on 9 January 1930 about the Maharaja of Patiala: 'He is in rather grave financial difficulties, and I shall have to put a pistol at his head in the course of the next two or three weeks about them and tell him that, unless he is prepared to accept advice with the object of getting his finances into order, I should not find it easy to concur in his continuance as Chancellor.'[18]

In the new situation, the initial reaction of the government was to consider action against the *Indictment* and the posters under the Princes Protection Act.[19] These materials did 'exercise hatred, contempt and disaffection' against the ruler. But the government's action was likely to be followed by an appeal to the High Court, which could be damaging to the Maharaja and court hearings could lead to complications. It was left to the Maharaja to decide.[20]

On the morning of 15 March 1930, a *jatha* of Akali Sikhs arrived in Delhi to see the Viceroy in connection with the allegations. They could not meet the Viceroy, but they were asked by C.C. Watson, the Political Secretary, to put their grievances in writing and assured them of redressal.[21]

Alarmed by these incidents, the Maharaja approached J.A.O. Fitzpatrick, the AGG, to ensure the government's sympathy and protection. The response of the AGG was reassuring: he attached no weight to this picked deputation of a handful of State Akali agitators and Congress malcontents. In his letter to the Government of India, he named three factors responsible for the attack on the Maharaja: first, the Maharaja was the Chancellor of the Chamber of Princes, and princes were regarded as being hostile to the national movement; second, the extremist Akalis were against the Maharaja because he did not support them; third, the movement was financed by the former Maharaja of Nabha to satisfy his personal grudge against Patiala. Talking of the agencies, the AGG mentioned the name of Diwan Singh Maftoon who, he said, was in the pay of the ex-Maharaja of Nabha. Sardul Singh Caveeshar belonged to the Punjab Riasti Praja Mandal, a revolutionary society closely associated with Naujawan Bharat Sabha and Kirti Kisan movement. The Maharaja wanted the agitators to be discouraged and the *Indictment* to be proscribed. The AGG pointed out that certain issues of the *Sacha Dhandora*, containing attacks on the Maharaja, had been proscribed earlier and those very attacks were repeated and amplified in the *Indictment*.[22]

The AGG was aware of the attempts made earlier to get an enquiry instituted against the Maharaja of Patiala. At this time, a letter had been received from Chudagar on behalf of the Indian States' People's Conference, enquiring whether the Government of India had received the petition of the Patiala state subjects demanding an enquiry into allegations against the Maharaja, and adding that if no action had been taken it was open to him to present a public petition to the Parliament.[23]

These communications were sent to the AGG who replied to the Government of India that it was politically inadvisable to institute any detailed enquiry into the Patiala affairs. However, he gave his comments on the various allegations based on informal enquiries made through the Patiala Home Minister, Nawab Liaqat Hayat Khan. H. Wilberforce-Bell, the Deputy Secretary (Political) was aware that some of the allegations could be true but he also thought that no action was required. The papers were sent to the

India Office.[24] The Government of India was inclined to shield the Maharaja of Patiala for political reasons.

The detailed evidence provided in the *Indictment* appeared now to call for an enquiry into the affairs of Patiala. It was thought that the authority of the Maharaja could be restricted, temporarily at first and if necessary, permanently. The majority of the cases were linked to his personality. Even the case of police action could not be dissociated from the autocratic rule of the Maharaja. The case of Lal Singh's murder had been taken up by the Patiala High Court. Still Wilberforce-Bell thought it possible that the Maharaja had been aware of the plan even if the murder was instigated by Daya Kishan Kaul, or Nanak Singh, to gain favour with the Maharaja. The Viceroy had received a petition from Bakhshish Singh in June 1929 regarding the disappearance of his wife Bachittar Kaur, their daughter and son and allegations of murder of the first two and detention of the third by the Maharaja. These too were forwarded to the AGG who was assured by the Home Minister, Patiala, that the charges were unfounded. Wilberforce-Bell was of the opinion that there was some truth in it as the Patiala Darbar could not tell the whereabouts of the daughter and that an enquiry would be legitimate.

Regarding the wife of Amar Singh, the Maharaja had admitted the charge in 1917 and pleaded his youth in extenuation of the circumstances. A copy of the letter was with the Political Department in which L.M. Crump, Political Agent of Phulkian States, had advised Amar Singh to accept Rs. 20,000 and withdraw claims over his wife. But Amar Singh did not do so. It was said that the whole case had been made worse by the arrest of Amar Singh on a charge of theft in 1914 when he was sentenced to imprisonment. The Lieutenant-Governor of the Punjab had confirmed that Amar Singh's wife was abducted before he was punished. Nothing was actually done about it then. Regarding the arrest and confinement of Sardar Harchand Singh without trial, and the confiscation of his property, the officials at Delhi had no knowledge and felt that the case could be made the subject of enquiry. Regarding the concoction of false cases against certain individuals by the Patiala Darbar, it was felt that evidence was not sufficient for the item to be made the basis for an enquiry. In the case of inhuman torture, illegal arrests, etc., of the Akalis, it was admitted that strong measures might have been taken but there was no information that these were inhuman. Wilberforce-Bell thought that the evidence in the *Indictment* on this count was not sufficient to warrant a special enquiry. Regarding *shikar*, the Maharaja had recently revised the game rules. Justification for an enquiry into *begar* would depend upon whether or not the charges could be substantiated. However, the item was not sufficiently important for enquiry. The matter of war loans could be enquired into by the newly appointed Finance Minister, Frederick Gauntlett. The increased revenue demand, mentioned by the Punjab States' People's petition in 1929, could also be examined by the Finance Minister. It was not unlikely that in the present position of the state's finances, methods to raise money had been resorted to which could 'legitimately be termed oppressive and prejudicial to good government'. The charge of misappropriation of funds raised for public purposes could be true and could be the subject of enquiry. The principal charges were related to women who took the Maharaja's fancy, and high-handedness with respect to those who opposed him in his desires and whose presence was inconvenient. Wilberforce-Bell's comments on each of the counts clearly show that the British officials were aware of the actual happenings in the state and that these were not mere allegations. The serious financial position was an additional reason for proceeding to extremes, if necessary.[25]

An enquiry was necessary because the *Indictment* had gone beyond such items as *begar* or *shikar*, public works at inadequate rates, revenue exactions and ill-treatment of Akali *jathas*. Probably these were some of the common features of the administration of the states. The *Indictment* differed from previous memorials and petitions against the Maharaja and his administration because the allegations were supported by proof, and witnesses were prepared to be cross-examined. Some of the charges were of too grave a character to be disposed of in a perfunctory manner and some were already the subject of an enquiry. The Secretary of the Political Department, Watson, agreed with Wilberforce-Bell, and noted that the misgovernment and oppression had their roots in the Maharaja's predilection for women.[26]

Lancelot Graham of the Legislative Department was consulted regarding the procedure to be adopted for the enquiry. In his view, it was impossible to proscribe the *Indictment* in the first place. The matter could not be hushed up as copies of the *Indictment* had been distributed all over India, and also sent to England for distribution among members of British Parliament. It was unfortunate that the scandal related to the Chancellor of the Chamber of Princes. Had the charges not received wide publicity, Watson would have recommended a private enquiry in view of the Maharaja's past services in the War and during the Akali troubles. According to the Legislative Department, the first six counts were more important, even though counts 7,8,10 and 11 indicated a condition of gross misgovernment in the state.[27]

The Political Secretary told the Maharaja on 24 March that only two courses were open: (a) that the Maharaja should prosecute the publishers of the *Indictment* under the Princes Protection Act; (b) that he should ask the government to hold an enquiry. The Viceroy had a meeting with the Maharaja on 25 March along with the Political Secretary who gave the impression that a judicial rather than a political officer should conduct the enquiry. The Maharaja pointed out its drawbacks. The Viceroy suggested a middle course – that a judicial officer and a political officer should both be associated with the enquiry. The Maharaja did not like this as it looked like a Committee. However, this was kept as a basis for discussion. The Maharaja wanted to know whether the purpose of the enquiry was to vindicate his honour, to attack his administration or to satisfy public opinion. The Viceroy said that his primary desire would be to secure the vindication of the Maharaja's honour but the vindication of the truth was also important and he could not put himself or the Government of India in the position of appearing to wish to hush up grave charges. Between truth and honour, he would choose the truth. The Maharaja said that he had nothing to fear. After the Political Secretary had left, the Maharaja made a personal appeal to the Viceroy saying that if an enquiry was to take place he could not possibly remain a Ruling Prince. Furthermore, it would mean that 'the whole Order was on the brink of destruction' and the Ruling Princes could be 'exposed to such public humiliation on the allegations of men of no account who were admittedly their enemies'.[28] The Maharaja's argument was essentially political.

The Viceroy wrote to the Secretary of State on 26 March that the problem of Patiala was causing him great concern. The *Indictment* could not be quietly overlooked. The statements were grave and witnesses were willing to come forward. Moreover, the material was advanced as *prima facie*. The government could not refuse to enquire. The Maharaja of Patiala would not prosecute. 'We cannot afford to sponsor an administration which has thus laid itself open to attack that it dare not meet.' The Viceroy said that he would have 'a very frank' talk with Patiala in a day or two.[29]

The Maharaja met Fitzpatrick on 31 March and spoke openly of the ingratitude of the government in sacrificing him after all his loyal services only in order to conciliate the irreconcilable extremist politicians who were after him because of his resolution on Independence in the Chamber of Princes and his speech at the Basant Darbar at Patiala in which he had criticized the Congress. The AGG sympathized with the Maharaja for being attacked for acts alleged to have been committed many years ago. The Maharaja told Fitzpatrick that he would agree to an enquiry held by the AGG. Fitzpatrick was also of the view 'that the considered finding of a Political Officer should suffice to satisfy the Viceroy and through him the British Parliament and public, however vehemently British India might repudiate it'.[30] Watson reassured Fitzpatrick on 5 April that in recognition of Bhupinder Singh's well known loyalty and services, the government was 'ready to go to the extreme limit in helping him in his present difficult and unpleasant position'.[31]

III

The Viceroy had made up his mind on the form of enquiry. On 2 April he wrote to the Secretary of State for India why it was necessary to conduct an enquiry against the Maharaja. The preferential course was to order the AGG to make a full enquiry. In case the charge of murder or abetment to murder was proved, it might be necessary to ask the Maharaja to abdicate, or accept a formal Commission of Enquiry under the Resolution of 1920. But the Viceroy did not think 'this result was at all likely'. He added that this form of preliminary enquiry was usual and would not prejudice the Maharaja.[32] The Secretary of State agreed with the proposal. He had two comments to make: the Paramount Power had the right to institute an enquiry and this prerogative should not be 'made to appear to depend on the ruler's consent', and if the enquiry satisfied the Government of India, 'the *Indictment* should be proscribed without the prosecution of authors by Maharaja of Patiala'.[33] The Secretary of State was even more helpful than the Viceroy.

On 20 April, a meeting was held between the Viceroy and the Maharaja at Simla. The Viceroy informed the Maharaja that an enquiry by the AGG would suffice. This was the normal preliminary procedure. The Maharaja wanted to know the terms of reference. The Viceroy replied that the AGG would enquire into and report upon all the allegations made against the Maharaja and his administration in the *Indictment*. All witnesses who wished to depose could do so. A counsel would be allowed, and the press would be excluded. As far as the government was concerned it would be the only enquiry. The initiative of asking for enquiry was to lie with the Maharaja as he had already published a communiqué through his Home Minister, saying that he was considering his course of action.[34] The terms were the same as for the Patiala-Nabha Enquiry, with the exception that a counsel was allowed.[35]

As mutually agreed, the Maharaja asked for a 'full and independent' enquiry and Lord Irwin wrote to the Maharaja on 10 May that he had decided to order the AGG to hold an enquiry into the charges. He 'will have full powers to fix times of hearings, to adjourn hearings, to adjust and arrange methods of procedure to settle the course which the enquiry shall take, to call for and to receive or reject evidence, documentary or other, to hear counsel and such persons on behalf of the parties as he may think fit, and generally to guide the whole of the proceedings'. The Viceroy appreciated the Maharaja's demand for a 'full and independent' enquiry.[36]

A communiqué directed Fitzpatrick to conduct an enquiry. He fixed 9 June for starting the enquiry at Dalhousie. He notified the Maharaja, all the four signatories to the *Indictment*, Bhagwan Singh Longowalia and the General Secretary of the Indian States' People's Conference. He asked for the release of two signatories,

Amritlal Seth and A.V. Thakkar. In case the signatories and the Mandal decided to boycott the enquiry, he would proceed *exparte*. All the witnesses whose statements had been recorded would be notified of the time and place of enquiry. He proposed to record the statements of convicts either in Dalhousie or in Patiala jail. The Secretary of the Punjab Riyasti Praja Mandal objected to the venue, but the Viceroy replied that his apprehensions had no real basis.[37]

The All India States' People's Conference and the Punjab Riyasti Praja Mandal decided not to take part in the proceedings. Fitzpatrick decided that he would record the statements of witnesses in Patiala jail after the conclusion of the Dalhousie proceedings. He would thereafter return to Simla to hear the Counsel's address and write his report. Fitzpatrick hoped to be in Simla by 27 June to hear Tej Bahadur Sapru's final address as Patiala's Counsel. He hoped to complete the report in another fortnight. Patiala was represented by a galaxy of lawyers: Tej Bahadur Sapru, C.P. Ramaswamy Iyer, Ms Nehru and half a dozen juniors.[38]

Meanwhile, the Punjab Government received a large number of visitors from almost the whole of the Punjab to represent that the enquiry should be dropped, particularly in view of the fact that the other party was not bringing any proof forward. The British administrators had the inkling that these representations were orchestrated.[39] Raja Harchand Singh, Rais of Bhadaur, and Sardar Jai Singh, Naib Sardar Sahib Deorhi Mualla of Patiala were the persons entrusted by the Patiala Darbar with the task of gathering support for the Maharaja. They worked during May, June and July in 17 districts of the Punjab which were relatively thickly populated by the Sikhs. They gave the exclusive charge of the districts of Ferozepur, Hissar and Montgomery to Pritam Singh Sidhu, City Magistrate of Patiala, and to Sardar Tara Singh, Kotwal of Patiala. They sent written memorials and representations signed by notable Sikhs to the AGG and the Punjab Governor. Individual memorials were sent from the *tahsils* of Ferozepur, Moga, Zira, Fazilka and Muktsar. Deputations were sent to the Punjab Governor at Simla by the Bhaichara Association of the Phulkian States, from the district of Hissar as well as from Muktsar and Fazilka *tahsils*. Three leading Sikh gentlemen of Ferozepur and Rawalpindi individually interviewed the Governor of the Punjab, while some leading persons of different areas interviewed their respective Deputy Commissioners and Superintendents of Police and presented memorials. The persons involved in the propaganda work were Biswedars, Zaildars, Jagirdars, Raises, members of district boards, members of legislative council, and magistrates. Regarding the people's reaction to the enquiry, those of Ferozepur district displayed the greatest sympathy, followed by Hissar. On the other hand the people of Montgomery district, especially the Sikh immigrants from Ludhiana district, 'did not show an iota of sympathy' and did not give their signatures for the memorials. This attitude was attributed to the propaganda by the other party.[40]

The Secretary of State was questioned in the Parliament regarding the procedure of the enquiry, appointment of Fitzpatrick, the enquiry not conforming to the procedure laid down in the Montford report, and being held in camera. Bhagwan Singh Longowalia, Secretary of Punjab Riyasti Praja Mandal, also wrote to the Viceroy that the Mandal protested strongly against the appointment of Fitzpatrick. They had expected Commissioners who would bring an 'independent and judicial mind' to deal with the case. It was unprecedented in the history of such enquiries that a commissioner should be appointed at the direction of the interested party. In any case, Fitzpatrick had been closely associated with the Maharaja and had 'intimate and friendly' relations with him. He had been approached by the injured parties many times before and he had always favoured the Maharaja. Bhagwan Singh requested the transfer of the prisoners from the Patiala jail to British jails before their testimony was recorded. There had been harassment of those who had earlier given evidence before the Patiala Enquiry Committee.[41]

After witnessing the Patiala proceedings for a day, Amritlal Seth issued a statement to the press on 30 June. He had gone to Patiala, he said, to study the situation created by the appointment of the Fitzpatrick enquiry. Fitzpatrick showed unusual hurry in conducting the proceedings which, he thought, was strange and suspicious. The AGG was sitting in judgement on several things about which he had given decisions on earlier occasions. Witnesses were cross-examined by the Counsels unprotected and unrepresented. Vernacular evidence was translated into English by Patiala ministers. Compromises were offered by the Counsels. The impression he got was that Fitzpatrick was not so much enquiring into the grievances as he was redressing them. In Harchand Singh Jaiji's case only a brief note was made. Nanak Singh was allowed to escape from the prison. Fitzpatrick and the Patiala Counsels were putting up in the Maharaja's palaces and the enquiry was held in one of the palace rooms. With all these goings on 'it looked as if the whole thing was a Patiala show, if not a family affair of the Maharaja'. He declared that a supplement to the *Indictment* would be published on the basis of a large quantity of fresh materials.[42]

Patiala resented this attack on its Counsels and the impartiality of Fitzpatrick. Permission for rejoinder was sought from the AGG, which was given. A statement refuting the charges was issued by Liaqat Hayat Khan, the Home Minister, in the *Times of India* of 3 July. For the first four charges, the AGG had given no opinions earlier because the events had taken place before his appointment as AGG. Count 5 was heard by him but no decision was taken. Only two convicts were examined at Patiala, Amar Singh and Harchand Singh Jaiji. Harchand Singh had already tendered his apology to the Maharaja on 27 June and the order was given to set him free and to release his property. There was no overlapping during cross-examination by the Counsels. Fitzpatrick knew Punjabi and did not need the services of an interpreter. In the case of Amar Singh, the word 'compromise' was not used.[43]

Throughout May telegrams were sent to the Viceroy to protest against the enquiry from all over the country. The Deccan Sabha and Daxini Sansthan Hitavardhak Sabha appealed for an impartial enquiry. Newspapers like the *Servant of India*, *Indian Social Reformer*, *New India*, *Tribune*, *Leader*, and the *Amrit Bazar Patrika* criticized the appointment of Fitzpatrick. To counteract this criticism, the Patiala Darbar mobilized support in its favour. Letters were written to the Viceroy from all over the Punjab expressing faith in the Maharaja.[44] While Fitzpatrick was building a defence from inside, the Maharaja was mending the fences from outside.

IV

Fitzpatrick submitted his report to the Political Secretary to the Government of India on 11 July 1930. The report stated the terms of reference and the scope of the enquiry. The terms of reference were contained in the official communiqué issued on 9 May. Fitzpatrick gave details of the notices he had sent to various parties to attend the enquiry, and gave reasons for the boycott of the enquiry by the Indian States' People's Conference, the main reason being the appointment of Fitzpatrick. He said that after his interview with a deputation of the Punjab Riyasti Praja Mandal at Simla on 14 June, its members had expressed their satisfaction with his appointment. The matter was disposed of by the Secretary of State in the Parliament, as also by the Viceroy. The other grounds of objection were that the enquiry was in camera and the prisoners in the Patiala custody. On the first point Fitzpatrick said that it was 'a normal and natural procedure', followed even by the authors of the *Indictment*. On the second, he said that Amar Singh was the only prisoner. Refuting the various charges levied by the Conference he said that they lacked confidence 'not in the personnel or procedure of the present enquiry but in themselves and their cause'. The enquiry was not conducted in a hurry. When the enquiry opened at Dalhousie on 9 June, he sat from six to nine hours till 24 June. He heard evidence at Patiala on the 26th. From 28 June to 3 July he heard the Counsel's arguments at Simla. He recorded the statements of 145 witnesses and examined around 430 documentary exhibits. He gave the genesis of *Indictment* and attributed its publication to a conspiracy against the princes. He contended that the anti-Patiala agitation could be traced to Stuart's enquiry into the dispute between Nabha and Patiala. This systematic campaign was conducted by the ex-Maharaja of Nabha to secure his own re-instatement by re-opening his case. The Akali leaders were in league with him. After this preliminary argumentation, Fitzpatrick comes to the foregone conclusion: to clearly absolve the Maharaja of each of the twelve charges.[45]

Wilberforce-Bell felt that the Maharaja could not be absolved of all responsibility in the case of the murder of Lal Singh. On all the other counts, however, he agreed with the AGG. He admitted a serious deficiency in the financial administration of the State, as was evident from the non-return of the loans. The deterioration, he said, was probably due primarily to the Maharaja's personal extravagance. He commented that Daya Kishan Kaul, the Prime Minister, came out of the enquiry in a very bad light. He was clearly unfit for the position; his general control of the judiciary and of the finance were open to severe strictures. Wilberforce-Bell also felt that the authors of the *Indictment* had achieved their object to some degree.[46]

The Viceroy congratulated the Maharaja that the 'result of the enquiry, has been to exonerate your personal honour from the charges made against it'. The Maharaja could make arrangements to proceed to London to attend the Round Table Conference.[47] In his reply, the Maharaja said that he was grateful to the Viceroy for his congratulations on the 'vindication of my honour'.[48]

On 4 August, the Viceroy informed the AGG that he was pleased to accept the findings, except on a few counts where the state was told to make improvements in its administration. The AGG wrote to the Viceroy on 29 August that he had taken cognizance of the directions given by the Viceroy, and had conveyed his orders to the Maharaja. He enclosed with his letter a copy of a very confidential letter he had received from the Maharaja on 22 August, detailing the steps taken to reform the police and judiciary of the state. The Maharaja had dismissed Hazura Singh Dhillon, Judge of the High Court, whose conduct came in for the AGG's criticism in connection with the illegal detention of certain Akalis (count 6). He had also removed Arjan Singh from the High Court. The High Court now reconstituted consisted of Diwan Bahadur Pindi Das, Sukhdev Singh and Man Singh.[49]

The Viceroy informed the Secretary of State regarding the findings of the Fitzpatrick report, expressing his agreement with the findings and proposing a press communiqué. In view of the possible concoction against Diwan Singh Maftoon, he would ask the AGG to make improvement of the state's judiciary his immediate concern, and also to see that the financial obligations to the state's subjects referred to in count 10 were discharged at the earliest possible opportunity. Proscription of the *Indictment* would have invited attention to the report, which could not be made public. He would communicate privately, and through the AGG, the results of enquiry to the Maharaja as soon as possible so that he could make arrangements for going to the Round Table Conference.[50]

On 2 August, the Secretary of State wrote to the Viceroy that he was 'glad to learn that enquiry had resulted so favourably for Patiala'. He wanted to know if the Viceroy had any intention of making a further enquiry.[51] The Viceroy replied that 'it is not my intention to entertain such evidence if adduced or to re-open the enquiry, which was of a definitive nature', and that 'you will appreciate the desirability of closing the matter and of leaving no ground for uncertainty upon the point'.[52] The Secretary of State accepted the view that further evidence regarding the charges investigated by Fitzpatrick should not be entertained. The Secretary of State wanted to be informed about the steps the Viceroy would take to mark the recognition of the association of the ex-Maharaja of Nabha in the preparation of the *Indictment* and also the action considered against the Punjab Riyasti Praja Mandal or the Indian States' People's Conference.[53]

The Viceroy was worried about Patiala's finances. He wrote to the Secretary of State that Gauntlett, the Finance Minister of Patiala, was finding it 'rather an uphill task to pull Patiala's finances together'. The Viceroy was keen that the Maharaja should not exceed the budget allotted to him for his trip to England, which was around Rs. 16 lakhs. He was also concerned that members of his staff might give extravagant orders without the Maharaja even knowing of them. He wanted the Secretary of State to give the Maharaja advice in the right direction and keep him within bounds.[54]

The propaganda against the Maharaja did not stop after the enquiry. A pamphlet entitled 'The Grievance of an Indian Prince' was widely distributed in England. Its author, S. Vedamurti, was associated with the *Indictment* and was appointed by the Indian States' People's Conference to conduct publicity in England. The publication was a clever attack on the Maharaja of Patiala, purporting to be written in his interest. Vedamurti hoped by his publicity to force a public trial of the Maharaja by constitutional means.[55] The Maharaja also had to face opposition when he was about to sail for London. Fitzpatrick wrote to Watson that members of the Punjab Riyasti Praja Mandal were trying to organize hostile demonstrations in Bombay on the Maharaja's return from Europe. The Bombay Government was requested to take preventive measures.[56] Though elaborate arrangements were made by Bhagwan Singh Longowalia and other Praja Mandal members to take out a black flag procession at the time of the arrival of the Maharaja, Liaqat Hayat Khan, the Prime Minister, discussed the matter personally with Longowalia and persuaded him to call off the demonstration. Strict measures were taken by the Bombay police to check the agitators.[57] The opposition to the Maharaja continued outside the state, mainly in Amritsar, but it was firmly handled by the Punjab Government.[58]

V

The British Government knew that some of the charges brought against the Maharaja were grave and the financial condition of the state was bad. But there was no inclination to institute an enquiry. It was only after the publication of the *Indictment*, which had clearly made out a *prima facie* case against him, that an enquiry became a political necessity. After considering various courses, the Viceroy decided to appoint the AGG as the commissioner of enquiry. His views on the charges, and his personal sympathy with the Maharaja, were well known. The Maharaja's exoneration was built into the appointment of Fitzpatrick as the enquiry officer. His task was made easier by the boycott of the enquiry by the Indian States' People's Conference. The financial situation of the state remained a cause of concern to the British Government, and agitation against the Maharaja also continued. This is a telling comment on the working of paramountcy. A prince who was loyal to the British was rescued from a grave situation through an enquiry that was merely a farce. The crucial consideration for the Paramount Power in its relations with the Indian princes was political.

NOTES

1. S.R. Ashton, *British Policy towards the Indian States, 1905-1939*, New Delhi: Select Book Service Syndicate, 1985, p. 18.
2. Ibid., p. 18.

3. William Lee-Warner, *The Native States of India*, London: Macmillan and Co., 1910, p. 302.
4. C.L. Tupper, *Indian Political Practice*, Delhi: B.R. Publishing House, 1974 (rpt., 1st pub. 1895), vol. I, pp. 72, 93-4.
5. Ibid., pp. 49-56.
6. Ibid., pp. 44-73, 80-2.
7. Ashton, *British Policy*, p. 24.
8. *Report on Indian Constitutional Reforms*, Calcutta: Superintendent Government Printing, 1918, p. 196.
9. Ashton, *British Policy*, p. 90.
10. Ibid., pp. 101-2.
11. John Gunther, *Inside Asia*, London: Hamish Hamilton, 1939. John Lord, *The Maharajas*, London: Hutchison, 1971. C.C. Trench, *Viceroy's Agent*, London: Jonathan Cape, 1987.
12. K. Natwar-Singh, *The Magnificent Maharaja: The Life and Times of Maharaja Bhupinder Singh of Patiala, 1891-1938*, New Delhi: HarperCollins, 1998, pp. 172-93.
13. The All India States' People's Conference came into existence at Bombay in December 1927. The main slogan of the Conference was that people of the states had a right to be heard and that princes should not be accepted as their only spokesmen. Among their other demands were fixation of privy purses of the rulers, grant of civil rights and liberties to the states' people, reforms in the administrative system of the states, and responsible government. Ramesh Walia, *Praja Mandal Movement in the East Punjab States*, Patiala: Punjabi University, 1972, pp. 10-13.
14. *Indictment of Patiala: Being a Report of the Patiala Enquiry Committee appointed by the Indian States' People's Conference*, Bombay, 1930, pp. 1-2.
15. Ibid., pp. 3-4.
16. Crown Representative Records (CRR), Punjab States, Accession no. 13, File no. 115-P(Secret),1930, Part I, National Archives of India (NAI), New Delhi, p. 10.
17. CRR, Punjab States, Accession no.14, File no. 115-P (Secret), 1930, part III, NAI, pp. 2, 4, 6-17; 10, 14, 33.
18. Irwin to W. Wedgewood-Benn, 9 January1930, Halifax Collection, Accession no. 3885, NAI, pp. 9-10.
19. Princes Protection Act of 1922 allowed the British Government to launch criminal proceedings against publishers of offending literature without prior warning and the penalties were heavy. Ian Copland, *The British Raj and the Indian Princes: Paramountcy in Western India,1857-1930*, Bombay: Orient Longman, 1982, p. 249.
20. CRR, Punjab States, Accession no. 13, File no. 115-P (Secret), 1930, part I, pp. 9-17.
21. Ibid., p. 18.
22. Ibid., pp. 25-8.

23. Ibid., p. 29.
24. Ibid., p. 30.
25. Ibid., pp. 41-53.
26. Ibid., pp. 54, 59.
27. Ibid., pp. 60-1, 70.
28. Ibid., pp. 77-81.
29. Irwin to W. Wedgewood-Benn, 26 March 1930, Halifax Collection, Accession no. 3885, NAI, pp. 66-7.
30. J.A.O. Fitzpatrick, AGG, Punjab States to C.C. Watson, Secretary, Political Department, 31 March 1930, CRR, Punjab States, Accession no. 13, File no. 115-P (Secret), 1930, part I, pp. 82-5.
31. Watson to Fitzpatrick, 5 April 1930, ibid., p. 100.
32. Irwin to W. Wedgewood-Benn, 2 April 1930, Halifax Collection, Accession no. 3895, NAI, pp. 57a, 58.
33. W. Wedgewood-Benn to Irwin, 10 April 1930, Halifax Collection, Accession no. 3890, NAI, p. 57.
34. CRR, Punjab States, Accession no. 13, File no. 115-P (Secret), 1930, part I, pp. 117-22.
35. Ibid., p. 145.
36. Ibid., p. 29.
37. Ibid., pp. 18-19, 154-5, 162-4, 172.
38. Ibid., pp. 175-6, 210.
39. Ibid., p. 190.
40. Patiala State Records, Prime Minister's Office, File no. 1314, Basta no. 41, Punjab State Archives, Patiala, pp. 1-100.
41. CRR, Punjab States, Accession no. 13, File no. 115-P (Secret), 1930, part I, pp. 251-5, 157-60.
42. 'Truth about Fitzpatrick Patiala Enquiry', Foreign and Political, Secret, File no. 368-P, nos. 1-3, 1932, NAI, pp. 11-14.
43. CRR, Punjab States, Accession no. 13, File no. 115-P (Secret), 1930, part I, pp. 235-43.
44. Ibid., Accession no. 14, File no. 115-P (Secret), 1930, part III, NAI, pp. 38, 42, 89, 116-40, 153, 159, 162, 181, 187, 190-4, 197-206, 221-34, 236, 241.
45. Ibid., Accession no. 7, File no. 115-P (Secret), 1930, Part II, pp. 1-60.
46. Ibid., pp. 1-7.
47. Irwin to Maharaja, 4 August 1930, ibid., p. 10.
48. Maharaja to Irwin, 9 August 1930, Halifax Collection, Accession no. 3905, NAI, p. 677.
49. CRR, Punjab States, Accession no. 7, File no. 115-P (Secret), 1930, part II, pp. 65-9.
50. Irwin to W. Wedgewood-Benn, 28 July 1930, Halifax Collection, Accession no. 3890, NAI, pp. 220-3.

51. W. Wedgewood-Benn to Irwin, 2 August 1930, ibid., pp. 153-4.
52. Irwin to W. Wedgewood-Benn, 5 August 1930, ibid., p. 230.
53. W. Wedgewood-Benn to Irwin, 12 September 1930, CRR, Punjab States, Accession no. 7, File no. 115-P (Secret), 1930, part II, p. 70.
54. Irwin to W. Wedgewood-Benn, 5 September 1930, Halifax Collection, Accession no. 3885, NAI, p. 248.
55. CRR, Punjab States, Accession no. 7, File no. 115-P (Secret), 1930, p. 15.
56. Ibid., Accession no. 10, File no. 18(14)-H, Foreign and Political, 1930, p. 5.
57. Home Political, File no. 79, 1931, NAI, p. 16.
58. Punjab States Agency, Political, File no. P-408, 1933, NAI, p. 18.

10

Sikh Spatial Dispersal (1881-2001)

GOPAL KRISHAN

The Sikhs are perceived to be ubiquitous, dynamic, enterprising and ready to avail themselves of any opportunity, anywhere. They are perhaps the most mobile and versatile people in the whole of India.[1] To what extent is this true? What is the pattern of their distribution? How did their spatial dispersal take place over time? The present paper is an inquiry into these questions on the basis of the data made available by the decennial rounds of the Census of India from 1881 to 2001, and the estimates of 'Sikh Population' in different countries of the world on the internet. The former set of data for 13 census years is available up to the level of provinces/states and districts in India. The data on the Sikh diaspora pertains to the time around 2001 and covers all the countries where their number is considerable.

The Census of India in 2001 recorded a Sikh population of 19.2 million. They accounted for 1.87 per cent of the total population of the country. The number of Sikhs outside India is estimated between 1.6 and 2.0 million, giving the mean figure of 1.8 million. The Sikh population the world over can be placed at 21 million at the beginning of the present century.

I

The first regular Census of India in 1881 recorded a Sikh population of 1.85 million, less than the Sikh population of 2.38 million in Amritsar district alone in 2001 (Table 1). They made barely 0.86 per cent of the total population of the country at that time (Table 1). No less than 93 per cent of them resided in the Punjab province and the princely states. Their main concentration was in the tract between the Ravi and the Ghaggar rivers – 'the area where Sikhism was born and where it grew'.[2] Put in another way, the bulk of the Sikhs were settled within the triangle formed by Lahore, Kangra and Patiala.[3] The remaining Sikh population was distributed mostly in Sind, Jammu & Kashmir, and the North-West Frontier Province. The rest of the Indian subcontinent did not have even ten thousand Sikhs put together.

The 1.91 million Sikh population recorded at the 1891 census marked an increase of hardly 2.4 per cent over that of 1881. India's population increased by 9.3 per cent during this decade. A stricter definition of the Sikh adopted at the 1891 census led to a depleted growth rate of the Sikh population. Only those who wore long hair and who refrained from smoking, in compliance with the tenets of Sikhism, were enumerated as Sikhs. A large number of *sahajdhari* Sikhs, who sheared their hair and most of whom were domicile in Sind, the North West Frontier Province

TABLE 1: INDIA: SIKH POPULATION, 1881-2001

Census year	*Sikh population*	*Percentage share in India's population*
1881	1,853,426	0.86
1891	1,907,833	0.81
1901	2,195,339	0.92
1911	3,014,466	1.20
1921	3,238,803	1.29
1931	4,335,771	1.55
1941	5,691,447	1.79
1951	6,219,314	1.72
1961	7,845,915	1.79
1971	10,378,747	1.89
1981	13,078,146	1.91
1991	16,259,744	1.93
2001	19,215,730	1.87

Source: Census of India, Relevant Volumes of the Successive Decennial Census for the period 1881 to 2001.

and Baluchistan, were recorded as Hindus rather than Sikhs. No wonder, 98 per cent of the Sikhs were found confined to the Punjab province and the princely states.

The next decade of 1891-1901 was somewhat different. The Sikh population marked a high growth rate of 15.1 per cent, increasing their number from 1.91 million to 2.2 million. This rate was significantly higher than the rate of natural increase of just 2 per cent. The factor of voluntary conversion to Sikhism had come into play. One of the developments of the late nineteenth century was a proliferation of old and new sects within Sikhism.[4] The proselytization activities of the Singh Sabhas and other Sikh organizations were showing their effect. The Sikh denial of caste and their willingness to accept converts was a great inducement for the lower castes to change their religion for gaining a higher social status. This was true particularly of those who worked for the Sikh peasantry as labourers or service providers. Even earlier in history, the Jats had entered the new Sikh religion in large numbers because of its egalitarian character which rejected the theory of caste.[5] There was some conversion from high caste Hindus as well. This is explained by partly the inherent appeal of Sikhism as a comparatively ritual-free religion and partly the consideration given to the Sikhs by the British for army service. Since conversion took place mostly within the Punjab province and its princely states, 97 per cent of the Sikh population was residing in this territory.

Meanwhile, a process of internal migration of the Sikhs, as also of Hindus and Muslims, had already started taking place. This was associated with the raising of nine canal colonies in the *doabs* (interfluves) of Bari, Rachna and Chaj. The Sidhani canal colony was the first to be completed (1885-8), followed by Sohagapara (1886-8), Chunian (1896-8 and 1904-6), Lower Chenab (1892-1905 and 1926-30), Lower Jhelum (1902-6), Lower Bari Doab (1914-24), Upper Chenab (1915-19), Upper Jhelum (1916-21) and Nili Bar (1926-40). About 6 million acres of barren and uncultivated wastelands were converted into highly productive agricultural tracts.[6] This was one of the phenomenal developments in the annals of British rule in India.[7]

The availability of newly developed agricultural land in these colonies set in motion a process of massive redistribution of population in the Punjab from its densely populated districts of Jalandhar, Hoshiarpur, Ludhiana and Amritsar in the east to the newly raised agricultural frontier in the west and south-west. The demographic scene of the Punjab was redefined and a new land–people equilibrium got established. An a result, the number of Sikhs in the tract between the Ravi and the Jhelum rivers increased dramatically. It also gave rise to a prosperous Sikh peasantry (oriented) to commercial farming in wheat, rice, cotton and sugar cane on relatively large irrigated landholdings.[8] These Sikh agriculturists, and their progeny, played an important role in revolutionizing agriculture in the Punjab, as also in Haryana, Rajasthan and Uttar Pradesh, after their exodus from canal colonies and subsequent resettlement in these parts of India on the eve of the partition of the Indian subcontinent in 1947.[9]

The first decade of the twentieth century stands out prominently for the highest rate of growth of Sikh population, 37.3 per cent, when the rate of natural increase was just around 6 per cent (Table 2). Two factors contributed to this phenomenal growth rate. The first was the relaxation in the definition of a Sikh at the 1911 census. Anybody declaring himself a Sikh, including

TABLE 2: INDIA: COMPARATIVE GROWTH RATES OF THE SIKH AND TOTAL POPULATION, 1881-2001

Decade	*Percent growth rate of*	
	Sikh population	*Total population of India*
1881-91	2.40	9.30
1891-1901	15.07	1.45
1901-11	37.31	5.75
1911-21	7.44	-0.31
1921-31	33.87	11.00
1931-41	31.27	14.22
1941-51	9.27	13.31
1951-61	26.16	21.64
1961-71	32.28	24.80
1971-81	26.00	24.66
1981-91	24.33	23.86
1991-2001	18.18	21.34

Source: Census of India, Relevant Volumes of the Successive Decennial Census for the period 1881 to 2001.

thousands of *sahajdharis*, was recorded as such. Secondly, the process of conversion to Sikhism had also gained momentum, especially among the lower castes. The Hindus lost 158,806 Chuhras and 169,103 Chamars during this decade.[10] In 1911, the Sikh population in India was recorded as 3.02 million. Though migration to canal colonies within the Punjab was picking up its pace, the movement of the Sikhs outside the province was meagre. No less than 96 per cent of the Sikhs still remained confined to their native territory.

During the decade of 1911-21, while India's population suffered a decrease due to excessive mortality caused by the influenza epidemic of 1918, the Sikh population recorded an increase by 7.4 per cent. The demographic loss caused by influenza, and additionally by casualities of the Sikh soldiers during World War I, was more than compensated by the continuing conversion. The internal migration to canal colonies also continued unabated. Of the 3.24 million Sikhs in India in 1921, as many as 96 per cent were still recorded within the confines of the Punjab.

As such, the four decades (1881-1921) witnessed a massive increase in the number of Sikhs. They recorded a growth rate of 75 per cent while India's population increased hardly by 22 per cent during these forty years. Conversion to Sikhism made all this difference. Another outstanding feature of this period was the massive redistribution of the Sikh population within the Punjab. Tendency to migrate out of their native territory was yet to gain momentum.

During the following two decades of 1921-41, the Sikh population again recorded a growth rate of about 75 per cent while India's population as a whole increased by only 27 per cent. Apart from the factor of a continuous rise in the rate of natural increase due to falling mortality, conversion to Sikhism explains this phenomenon. A salient feature of this phase was the slowing down of Sikh migration within the Punjab, and a growing tendency to migrate outside. Big cities such as Calcutta, Jamshedpur, Delhi and Bombay, held great attraction for them. This development was associated with a gradual rise in the pace of industrialization, urbanization, transportation and internal migration in India in general after 1921. There was also some agricultural migration of the Sikhs to the Gang Canal Colony opened in 1927 in the Ganganagar district of Rajasthan (Table 3).

The migration of Sikhs associated with their recruitment in the army, especially during the Second World War, stands as a class in itself. The Sikhs had a strong military tradition, and were heavily recruited in the imperial army.[11] In 1944, when the Indian army was over two million strong, the Sikhs accounted for 10 per cent of the total, nearly 7 times their proportion in the population at large.[12] Service in the army took the Sikhs to different areas, exposed them to external influences, and made them aware of the opportunities outside their native land. All this provided a stimulus to their mobility. No wonder, the proportion of the Sikhs living in the Punjab and its princely states as against the total number of Sikhs in India declined from 96 to 90 per cent in 1921-41.

II

The Sikh population increased by only 9.3 per cent in 1941-51. This is ascribed mainly to the high incidence of mortality due to the communal riots at the time of the partition of India in 1947. This calamitous event was a landmark in the history of re-distribution of Sikh population. About 2.5 million Sikhs poured out of Pakistan into India.[13] Most of them settled in the Indian Punjab. As a result, they gained an absolute majority in the area constituting the present Punjab. This was an event of great significance in the political geography of India.

The scarcity of land in the then Punjab for allotment to displaced persons from (West) Pakistan impelled the government to settle many of them, including the Sikhs, in other parts of India. A sizeable number of agriculturist Sikhs were rehabilitated in Karnal and Hissar districts of Haryana, the terai (foothill) zone and western districts of Uttar Pradesh, and the Ganganagar, Alwar and Bharatpur districts of Rajasthan. The availability of agri-cultural land vacated by Muslims migrating to Pakistan, and reclamation of agricultural land through clearing of vegetation and provision of irrigation, facilitated this process. A number of non-agriculturist Sikh refugees moved to big cities like Delhi, Kanpur, Bombay and Calcutta. Thus, partition had a three-fold

TABLE 3: DISTRIBUTION OF THE SIKHS IN BRITISH INDIA: 1881-1941

	1881	*1901*	*1921*	*1941*
British territories				
Ajmer - Merwara	182	264	219	867
Andaman & Nicobar Islands	–	370	390	744
Assam	14	505	988	3,764
Baluchistan	–	2,947	7,645	11,918
Bengal	549	328	2,363	16,281
Bihar and Orissa	–	–	1,475	13,445
Bombay	127,100	1,122	8,319	39,022
Burma	–	6,596	4,843	–
Central Provinces and Berar	622	477	1,529	14,996
Coorg	–	–	–	–
Delhi	–	Part of Punjab	2,764	16,157
Madras	–	92	5	418
North West Frontier Province	3,644	28,091	28,040	57,939
Punjab	1,121,004	1,517,019	2,294,207	2,757,401
United Province of Agra and Oudh	–	15,319	14,234	232,445
Feudatory States				
Assam States	–	–	21	381
Baluchistan States	–	25	96	126
Baroda State	–	38	70	566
Bengal States	–	12	17	28
Bihar & Orissa States	–	–	83	177
Bombay States	30	451	787	689
Central India Agency	1,445	2,004	827	2,731
Central Provinces States	2	95	152	689
Gwalior State	–	–	661	2,342
Hyderabad State	3,644	4,335	2,745	5,330
Jammu & Kashmir	–	25,828	39,507	65,903
Madras State Agency	–	12	134	309
Mysore	41	–		
NW FP Agencies	–	–	4,458	4,472
Punjab States	595,110	585,877	813,089	1,360,424
Rajputana Agency	9	2,054	8,703	81,896
Sikkim	–	–	–	–
United Provinces States	–	14	32	731
INDIA	1,853,426	2,195,339	3,238,803	5,691,447

Note: – denotes data not available.

Source: Census of India, Relevant Volumes of the Census for 1881, 1901, 1921 and 1941.

effect upon the distribution of Sikhs: they were evacuated from the newly born (West) Pakistan; they acquired an absolute majority in the territory reorganized as the present Punjab in 1966; and they scattered considerably to other parts of India for agriculture, mostly in the neighbouring states and for non-agricultural enterprises to big cities, virtually all over the country.[14] Nonetheless, almost 85 per cent of the Sikhs were living within the limits of the Punjab in 1951.

The Sikh population increased by nearly 25 per cent in 1951-61. This growth rate corresponded with the rate of their natural increase. Conversion to Sikhism had practically ceased after independence. As against their increase by only 17 per cent in the Punjab, the Sikhs recorded a growth rate of 80 per cent in other parts of India. This represented a considerable outflow of Sikhs from the Punjab, mainly from the rural areas of the Uppar Bari and Bist Jalandhar Doabs. Other factors included the high rate of natural increase, relatively small and declining size of land-holdings, and the growing menace of water-logging, all of which intensified population pressure on land. The desire of the Sikhs to move out for better economic opportunities cannot be ignored in explaining this mobility. Outmigration amounted to about one-third of the natural increase of the Sikh population in the present Punjab, as reorganized in 1966.

In 1961-71, the Sikh population increased by 32.3 per cent, a rate which was the highest for any post-independence decade. The rate of natural increase was around 25 per cent. There was no influx of the Sikhs from outside India. Whether this considerable excess of the actual growth rate over the natural increase rate was due to adoption of Sikhism by many in the Punjab after its formation in 1966 or it arose out of some discrepancy in the adjustment of data to the boundaries of the reorganized Punjab is difficult to say. The migration of the Sikhs to Uttar Pradesh, Rajasthan, and Haryana as also to the cities like Delhi, Bombay and Hyderabad continued. As a result, the percentage of Sikh population in the Punjab came down from 86 in 1961 to 79 in 1971 (Table 4).

The three decades of 1971-81, 1981-91 and 1991-2001 were noted for a fall in the rate of increase in Sikh population, successively from 26 to 24.3 and further down to 18.2 per cent.

TABLE 4: INDIA: SIKH POPULATION BY STATES AND UNION TERRITORIES, 1951-91 (ARRANGED IN DESCENDING ORDER OF NUMBERS IN 1991)

State/Union Territory	*1951*	*1971*	*1991*
Punjab	5,553,918*	8,159,972	12,767,697
Haryana	–	631,048	956,836
Uttar Pradesh	197,612	369,672	675,775
Rajasthan	148,229	341,182	649,174
Delhi	137,096	291,123	455,657
Jammu & Kashmir	...	105,873	...
Maharashtra	41,436	101,762	161,184
Madhya Pradesh	39,914	98,973	161,111
Chandigarh	–	65,472	130,288
Bihar	37,947	61,520	78,212
West Bengal	30,623	35,084	55,392
Himachal Pradesh	5,019	44,914	52,050
Gujarat	7,027	18,233	33,040
Andhra Pradesh	5,169	12,591	21,910
Orissa	4,163	10,204	17,296
Assam	3,949	12,347	16,492
Karnataka	3,951	6,830	10,100
Tamil Nadu	2,386	4,355	5,449
Meghalaya	–	1,262	2,612
Kerala	308	1,284	2,224
Andaman & Nicobar Islands	126	865	1,350
Manipur	50	1,028	1,301
Arunachal Pradesh	–	1,255	1,205
Goa	–	855	1,087
Tripura	35	318	740
Nagaland	158	687	732
Sikkim	18	–	375
Mizoram	–	–	299
Daman & Diu	–	–	101
Dadra & Nagar Haveli	–	3	20
Pondicherry	–	51	29
Lakshadweep	–	4	1

Notes: * Including Haryana and Chandigarh.
... Census not held due to difficult political situation.
– State/union territory yet to take form.

Soures: Census of India, 1961, Table C-VII, Religion, pp. 481-5;
Census of India, 1971, Table C-Statement I, Religion, pp. 2-5;
Census of India, 1991, Table C-9, Religion, pp. 4-11.

These rates were close to the rate of natural increase, which had been declining due to increased adoption of family planning. At the same time, the Sikh emigration to other countries and out-migration to other parts of India was also picking up. This tendency was accentuated, particularly during the 1990's. To what extent this can be linked to the communal frenzy against the Sikhs in 1984 is a moot point. The decade was marked by the lowest growth rate of the population since 1951. In 2001, the Punjab's share in India's Sikh population came down to 76 per cent due to the continuing dispersal of Sikhs from their native state to other parts of India. They were now migrating more to the western states of the country, signifying a departure from the earlier migration to the eastern states.

On the whole, the Sikh population in India multiplied 3.1 times during 1951-2001, from 6.2 million to 19.2 million, whereas India's population became 2.8 fold from 361 million to 1027 million. The relatively greater loss of the Sikh population through emigration was more than compensated by their comparatively higher rate of natural increase, especially during 1951-71.

The data pertaining to Sikh population by states/union territories and for all the 593 districts in India in 2001 lays bare the distributional pattern as it has evolved over time (Table 5). The Mahe district of the Pondicherry union territory is the only one in the country which does not have any Sikh population (Table 6). In 13 districts, all in the Punjab, the Sikhs have an absolute majority, with Moga at the top (85.8 per cent). The remaining four districts of the state, namely Gurdaspur, Hoshiarpur, Jalandhar and Nawanshahr, have a Hindu majority. As noted earlier, the Punjab had 76 per cent of the Sikh population in India. The adjacent districts in Jammu & Kashmir, Himachal Pradesh, Haryana and Rajasthan claimed another 8 per cent. The rest of India was left with only 16 per cent of the Sikh population. A high degree of concentration coupled with wide (dispersal) describes the distribution pattern of the Sikhs in India.

Next to the Punjab, Haryana is home to the largest number of Sikhs, followed by Rajasthan and Uttar Pradesh, sharing 6.1, 4.3 and 3.5 per cent of the Sikh population in India. Among the union territories, Delhi has 2.9 per cent and Chandigarh 0.8 per cent. All these states and union territories are located close to the

TABLE 5: INDIA: SIKH POPULATION BY STATES AND UNION TERRITORIES, 2001 (ARRANGED IN DESCENDING ORDER OF NUMBERS)

State/Union Territory	*Sikh population*	*Percentage share in India's Sikh population*
Punjab	14,592,387	75.94
Haryana	1,170,662	6.09
Rajasthan	818,420	4.26
Uttar Pradesh	678,059	3.53
Delhi	555,602	2.89
Maharashtra	215,337	1.12
Uttaranchal	212,025	1.10
Jammu & Kashmir	207,154	1.08
Madhya Pradesh	150,772	0.79
Chandigarh	145,175	0.76
Jharkhand	83,358	0.43
Himachal Pradesh	72,355	0.38
Chhattisgarh	69,621	0.36
West Bengal	66,391	0.35
Gujarat	45,587	0.24
Andhra Pradesh	30,998	0.16
Assam	22,519	0.11
Bihar	20,780	0.01
Orissa	17,492	–
Karnataka	15,326	–
Tamil Nadu	9,545	–
Meghalaya	3,110	–
Kerala	2,762	–
Arunachal Pradesh	1,865	–
Manipur	1,653	–
Andaman & Nicobar Islands	1,587	–
Tripura	1,182	–
Sikkim	1,176	–
Nagaland	1,152	–
Goa	970	–
Mizoram	326	–
Daman & Diu	145	–
Dadra & Nagar Haveli	123	–
Pondicherry	108	–
Lakshadweep	6	–

Note: – denotes negligible.

Source: Census of India 2001, The First Report on Religion Data, p. xxxiv.

TABLE 6: INDIA, GROUPING OF DISTRICTS BY PERCENTAGE OF SIKH POPULATION, 2001

Percentage of Sikh population	*Number of districts*	*Locational pattern*
50 and above	13	All in Punjab
25 to 50	5	Punjab (4), Haryana (1)
10 to 25	8	Haryana (3), Rajasthan (2), Chandigarh (1), Delhi (1), Uttar Pradesh (1)
5 to 15	6	Haryana (4), Jammu & Kashmir (1), Himachal Pradesh (1)
1 to 5	37	Several states and union territories
Less than 1	523	Several states and union territories
Zero	1	Mahe district of Pondicherry union territory
Total	593	

Source: Census of India, 2001, The First Report on Religion Data.

Punjab. Among the relatively distant states, Maharashtra shares 1.2 per cent. Almost the same share is noted in the case of the neighbouring state of Jammu & Kashmir. The Sikh population in Haryana, Uttar Pradesh and Rajasthan is largely rural and agricultural while in the case of the union territories of Delhi and Chandigarh it is predominantly urban.

The Sikhs are in considerable numbers in the state capitals and in industrial and cantonment cities. Illustrations include Mumbai, Kolkata, Bhopal, Hyderabad and Ahmedabad among the capital cities; Jamshedpur, Faridabad and Raipur among the industrial; and Pune, Indore and Jabalpur among the cantonment. Cities located in the western Indian states such as Maharashtra, Gujarat and Rajasthan, are emerging as prominent places of Sikh immigration. Earlier such an attraction was more typical of the cities in states towards the east, such as Uttar Pradesh, Bihar and West Bengal.

However, the entry of Sikh population in the southern states of

India has been neglible. The four states of Kerala, Tamil Nadu, Karnataka and Andhra Pradesh together have a Sikh population of only about 59,000 or 0.3 per cent of the total. The same holds good for the eight north-eastern states which together have a Sikh population of just around 25,000.

III

The Sikhs migrated not only to various parts of India but also to a number of foreign countries, attracted by the opportunities abroad and impelled by not-so-satisfactory economic conditions at home. They had a significant presence in the army of British India, which accounted for their mobility and exposure to a wider world. A small number of them began emigrating during the closing decades of the nineteenth century. Settling first in Burma (Myanmar), Malaya States (Malaysia and Singapore), and Hong Kong, the Sikhs reached as far as Canada in 1904. All these countries were part of the British empire. Similarly, some of them moved to East African countries. Another wave was directed to Australia, New Zealand and Fiji Islands. The United Kingdom was also a destination for a few of them. The relevance of the colonial context in this migration is evident.

Most of these emigrants belonged to agricultural and artisan families, and hailed from the densely populated districts of Jalandhar, Hoshiarpur, Amritsar and Ludhiana. Initially they earned a living as security guards in the former Malaya States, as businessmen in Hong Kong, lumberers in Canada, farm hands in the United States, railroad construction workers in East Africa and factory workers in the United Kingdom.

At present, the United Kingdom has the largest number of the Sikhs outside India, around 500,000 (Table 7). Initially, it was the only country to allow Indians to enter freely for a livelihood till the Commonwealth Immigration Act came into effect in 1962.[15] It experienced a large inflow of the Sikhs as construction and factory workers after World War II. A subsequent entry was in the form of repatriates from East Africa toward the close of the 1960s and the early 1970s when Uganda, Kenya and Tanzania got independence from the British. A simultaneous immigration for business, professions and education was also taking place.

TABLE 7: THE SIKH EMIGRANTS, *c.* 2001

Country/region of emigration	*Estimated number of the Sikhs*
United Kingdom	500,000
Canada	410,000
United States	350,000
Malaysia	75,000
Middle East (UAE, Saudi Arabia and Kuwait)	50,000
Thailand	25,000
Kenya	25,000
Australia	2,000
Singapore	15,000
Germany	15,000
Nepal	12,000
New Zealand	6,000
Scandinavian Countries (Sweden, Norway, Finland and Denmark)	5,000
Myanmar	5,000
Indonesia	5,000
Hong Kong	5,000
Fiji Islands	5,000
France	2,500
Netherlands and Belgium	1,500
Italy	1,000
Greece	1,000
Mexico	1,000

Source: Website 'Sikh Population'.

Today most of the Sikhs are concentrated in Southall, East End and other parts of London, Birmingham Conurbation, Bradford, Lamington Spa and Glasgow.

Canada has the second largest number of Sikhs, around 410,000. It was through British Columbia in the first decade of the twentieth century that they had made their first entry. Taking advantage of the liberalized emigration policy of Canada since 1967 and faced with a difficult political situation in the Punjab during the 1980s, the Sikh emigration to Canada has surged in a big way. Moreover, Canada has also been one of the major recipients of Sikh repatriates from East Africa. Most of the Sikhs in Canada live in and around Vancouver, Toronto, Montreal,

Edmonton and Calgary, engaged in a variety of economic activities including industrial labour, retailing and professions.[16]

It was from British Columbia that the Sikhs moved into California, United States, and found work in the construction of the Western Pacific Railway and as farm hands in the early decades of the twentieth century. They were small in number, around 5,000 till the mid-1960s. With liberalization of the immigration policy in 1965, the inflow of Sikhs gained momentum. Today the United States is the most coveted destination, and the number of Sikhs in that country is estimated at 350,000. They are concentrated mainly in New York, New Jersey, Illinois and California states, engaged in a variety of economic activities, including professions, technical jobs, retailing and taxi driving. The Gurdwaras also happen to be their social and political centres.[17] As an institution, the Gurdwara (Sikh place of worship) is a great facilitating factor to Sikh emigration anywhere.

Emigration of Sikhs to the South-East Asian countries belongs to the initial phase of their spread out of India. Burma (Myanmar) became a part of British India in 1886 – a factor which facilitated migration of Indians, including the Sikhs, to that territory. The Sikhs started emigrating to Malaya States and Hong Kong almost at the same time. They came initially as soldiers on guard duties but were recruited later mostly in police. Besides, a good number of them got employed as watchmen in banks, factories and offices while some others joined trade. The descendants of these Sikhs are now to be found in all walks of life as teachers, lawyers and lecturers. Some of them, residing in rural areas peripheral to cities, are dairy farmers. With opportunities getting reduced, many a Sikh emigrated from here to Thailand, Singapore, Indonesia and Hong Kong, which received Sikh repatriates from Vietnam, Laos and Cambodia as well. Today, the number of Sikhs is estimated at 75,000 in Malaysia, 25,000 in Thailand, 15,000 in Singapore and 5,000 each in Hong Kong and Indonesia.

East Africa has been one of the early areas of Sikh immigration. Kenya, Uganda and Tanzania were former British colonies, and the Sikhs came here initially as contractors and labourers to construct the Kenya-Uganda Railway in the later decades of the nineteenth century.[18] Gradually they and their descendants entered into other economic activities, such as trade, industry, teaching, and general services. They were repatriated in large numbers during the 1960s and 1970s but no less than 25,000 Sikhs are estimated as still living in Kenya, most of them in Nairobi.

Today, Canada, United States, Australia and New Zealand are the four countries relatively liberal to immigration. This facility is being availed of by Sikhs in significant numbers. Australia has a Sikh population of about 25,000 and New Zealand of 6,000. Most of them are in professions and education.

Sikh emigration, as of other Indians, to the Middle East followed the oil boom in the early 1970s. The United Arab Emirates, Saudi Arabia and Kuwait are estimated as having a Sikh diaspora of around 50,000. They also received a large number of Sikhs settled earlier in Iran but repatriated after the Islamic Revolution of 1979. Technical jobs, general labour and retailing are the main vocations of the Sikhs there.

Continental Europe has also been a popular destination for Sikhs during the closing years of twentieth century. Germany has as many as 15,000 Sikhs, Scandinavian countries 5,000, and France 2,500, among others. European countries granted political asylum to some of the Sikhs who sought it because of the difficult situation back home during the 1980s.

A colonial backdrop to the Sikh emigration is evident. The United Kingdom and the former British colonies scattered in different parts of the world were the traditional destination for the Sikhs. Today, the Untied States, Canada, Australia and New Zealand, all former British colonies but all in the new world, are the most popular destinations. The economic opportunities these countries offer, and their relatively liberal immigration policies, are the main attraction. The Middle East is no less rewarding economically but restrictions it puts on the style of life in many ways relegates it to second option as a destination for professionals.

IV

To the basic question posed by this paper, the response is as follows: in 2001, about three-fourths of the Sikh population of 19.2 million in India (are) confined to their home state; around three-fourths of the Sikh diaspora, estimated at 1.8 million, are concentrated in the United Kingdom, Canada and the United States. While only the district of Mahe in India is without any Sikh population, 13 districts, all located in the Punjab, account for two-thirds of the Sikh population in the country. On the whole, the distributional pattern of the Sikh population can be described as 'high concentration coupled with wide scattering'.

At the first regular Census of India in 1881, the Sikh population was found concentrated mainly between the Ravi and the Ghaggar rivers, the tract which coincides with the territory of the present Punjab, with the notable exclusion of the Lahore district, now in Pakistan. The opening of the canal colonies between the Beas and the Jhelum caused massive movement of the Sikhs, as also of Hindus and Muslims, from the crowded districts of the central Punjab to these newly reclaimed agricultural frontiers. This resulted in a considerable redistribution of the Sikhs within the Punjab. As these colonies got filled up gradually, the Sikhs started migrating in considerable numbers to places outside their home state. However, even by 1941, about 90 per cent of the Sikhs were in the Punjab and the princely states.

Consequent upon the partition of the subcontinent in 1947, the distributional pattern of the Sikhs underwent a phenomenal change. They were evicted *en masse* from Pakistan, including from the canal colonies. A large majority of them settled in the territory constituting the present Punjab. Eventually it got carved out as the only Sikh majority state of India.

The process of Sikh migration continued unabated after independence in 1947. In the initial years, they moved to newly reclaimed agricultural lands in Uttar Pradesh, Rajasthan and Haryana or were rehabilitated on lands evacuated by the Muslims in these states. At the same time, they migrated to capital, industrial and cantonment cities in different parts of India. Now the urban places located in Maharashtra, Gujarat and Rajasthan are the major recipient of Sikh migrants. Earlier the states towards the east had held a greater attraction for them.

At the same time, Sikh emigration to other countries of the world has been a regular feature. It had made a beginning in the closing years of the nineteenth century, moved steadily during the colonial period, picked up pace after independence, and surged during the last decade of the twentieth century. Earlier this emigration was oriented primarily towards the former Britain colonies and the United Kingdom; of late it is the former British dominions of Canada, the United States and Australia which hold the main attraction for the Sikh emigrants. The Sikh population accounted for less than 2 per cent of India's population in 2001 but for no less than 7 per cent of the Indians abroad, estimated at 25 million.

NOTES

1. E.B.J. Rose, *Colour and citizenship: A Report on British Race Relations*, London: Oxford University Press, 1969, p. 52.
2. G.S. Gosal and A.B. Mukerji, 'The Religious Composition of India's Population – A Spatial Analysis', *Tijdschrift voor Economische en Sociale Geografic*, vol. 16, 1970, p. 97.
3. Ethne K. Marenco. *The Transformation of Sikh Society*, New Delhi: Heritage Publishers, 1976, p. 107.
4. Ibid., p. 155.
5. W.H. McLeod, *The Evolution of Sikh Community*, New Delhi: Oxford University Press, 1975, p. 11.
6. Ian Talbot and S. Thandi (eds.), *People on the Move, Punjabi Colonial and Post Colonial Migration*, Oxford: Oxford University Press, 2004, p. 1.
7. Darbara Singh, 'Historical Geography of the Colonial Punjab 1849 – 1947', Ph.D. thesis, Chandigarh: Panjab University, 2004, pp. 151-82.
8. Malcolm Darling, *The Punjab Peasant in Prosperity and Debt*, London: Oxford University Press, 1947, pp. 111-13.
9. Gopal Krishan, 'Demography of the Punjab', *Journal of Punjab Studies*, 2004, vol. 11, no. 1, p. 83.
10. Marenco, *The Transformation of Sikh Society*, p. 256.
11. Kingsley Davis, *The Population of India and Pakistan*, Princeton: Princeton University Press, 1963, p. 2.
12. Raleigh Parkin, *India Today*, New York: John Day, 1945, pp. 89-90.
13. Khushwant Singh, *The Sikhs*, London: George Allen & Unwin Ltd., 1953, p. 120.
14. Gopal Krishan, 'Distribution of the Sikhs outside the Punjab (India)', *Indian Geographical Journal*, vol. 46, nos. 1&2, 1971, p. 37.
15. Rashmi Desai, *Indian Immigration in Britain*, London: Oxford University Press, 1963, p. 2.

16. Shubha Singh, *Overseas Indians: The Global Family*, New Delhi: Shipra Publications, 2005, p. 114.
17. C.H. Loehlin, 'The Sikhs in California', in Harbans Singh and N. Gerald Barrier (eds.), *Punjab Past and Present: Essays in Honour of Dr. Ganda Singh*, Patiala: Punjabi University, 1996 (2nd edn.), p. 300.
18. Harprasad Chattopadhaya, *Indians in Africa, A Socio-Economic Study,* Calcutta: Bookland Private Limited, 1970, pp. 335-41.

11

Punjab Agrarian Economy: Role of Remittances by the Sikhs Overseas

SHINDER SINGH THANDI

The aim of this paper is primarily to illustrate that under specific historical conditions remittances can play an important role in the development and strengthening of capitalist relations in agriculture. The information provided in a tabulated form was collected in the course of fieldwork in the region over a period of four months in the summer of 1977 when several villages were studied, and three were scrutinized in considerable depth and detail. The villages under study were relatively prosperous in terms of agricultural income as reflected in high yields, irrigation intensity and infrastructure developments. All had virtually completely adopted the green revolution technology. All the selected villages had experienced high rates of overseas migration, especially since the post-independence period.

I

The Punjab, usually referred to as the land of peasant proprietors, has unquestionably been regarded as one of the most prosperous agricultural regions of the Indian Union. Advocates of the green revolution are quick to point out the outstanding, though unevenly distributed, success achieved through their strategy in the Punjab.[1] Major comments made in this paper refer generally to the central regions of the Punjab, but more specifically to the Jalandhar district. The Jalandhar *doab* is one of the most densely populated areas of the Punjab, but is at the same time one of the most prosperous. A combination of regular rainfall, rich alluvial soils and extensive irrigation by canals and wells made it one of the richest areas of north India all through the Mughal, Sikh, British and post-colonial periods.

Important changes in agrarian conditions in the Punjab began to appear with the creation of a land market under British rule. The land revenue demand for the Punjab was finalized at a value of 'half the net produce' payable in cash; it was fixed for 30 years at a time which decreased its value in real terms over the years. The effects of the British land policy on the Punjab are well documented.[2] We may outline only those which had an irreversible impact on agrarian conditions.

Before the end of the nineteenth century, British administrators became increasingly concerned about the rising indebtedness of the Punjab peasantry and the rapid transfer of land from the historically dominant agricultural castes. These developments represented an acute political danger to the colonial regime for two important reasons. First, most of the Punjab army was recruited from these agricultural castes and hence the potential containment of the army was at stake, and second, because of the rising indebtedness, a political crisis similar to the Deccan Riots of 1875 was anticipated.[3]

In response to the ensuing political crisis, the colonial government passed the Land Alienation Act in 1900. This Act, with subsequent legislation in 1913, reinforced the local character of the land market and re-established the superiority of the traditional agricultural castes in the ownership of landed property. These Acts, however, did not in any way halt the alienation of land; they merely altered the direction of the land transfer. Large Sikh Jat landowners in the central and eastern districts began to amass landholding at the expense of the weaker or 'extravagant' peasant classes. Thus the period of the late nineteenth and the early twentieth century, saw the emergence and dominance of the rural areas by agricultural moneylenders and traders. The increasing concentration in landholding was in part helped by the rising value of land which itself was specifically a consequence of the fall in the real value of land revenue demand all through the early part of the twentieth century. Indeed, by the mid-1930s, rich peasants had begun to dominate the rural economy, a feature which was quite consistent with developments in other parts of India.[4]

To give an indication of the extent of this emerging socio-economic differentiation by 1939, 82 per cent of the peasants (i.e. those owning less than 10 acres of land) owned only 24 per cent of the total cultivated area, whereas the remaining 18 per cent held 76 per cent of the land.[5] Land under tenancy (mostly tenants-at-will) amounted to almost 50 per cent and there emerged a sizeable class of agricultural landless labourers, to be 12.4 per cent of the rural population in the census of 1931.

Productive forces during the colonial period were certainly not stagnant. The establishment of the canal colonies greatly increased the net cultivated area and cropping intensities. With the growing involvement of Punjab cotton and wheat in world markets, various high-yielding varieties were introduced to increase yields and hence production. The extension of these high-yielding varieties, in particular American cotton and I-R 8 wheat, however, remained limited to only small areas of the province.[6]

After independence, and partition, in 1947 the Indian Punjab remained in relative stagnation. A clear break with the past came in the mid-1960s: yields doubled within a few years as a consequence of the widespread adoption of high-yielding varieties, initially of wheat but also of cotton, maize and lately of rice, and the heavy use of chemical fertilizers and capital inputs. As a result, irrigation and cropping intensities underwent a marked improvement. The increase in capital inputs into agriculture, aided by liberal advance of institutional credit, was of critical importance; the extent of this increased mechanization as reflected in Jalandhar district is indicated in Table 1.

Of the total working population in the state in 1971, 42.6 per cent could be categorized as peasant cultivators and 20.1 per cent as agricultural labourers. In Jalandhar the comparable figures were 33 per cent and 18 per cent respectively. The Jalandhar district also had one of the highest urbanization rates as 30 per cent of the district could be considered as urbanized – a figure exceeding that for the Punjab as a whole. To give some indication of the 'relative agricultural prosperity' in the region, the gross area of crops irrigated as a proportion of the total cropped area

TABLE 1: AGRICULTURAL MACHINERY AND IMPLEMENTS IN JALANDHAR, TAHSILWISE, 1972

Tahsil	*Ploughs*			*Cane Crushers*			*Tractors*	*Oil eng. Pump sets*	*Elec. Pump tube-well*
	Wooden	*Iron*	*Total*	*Power*	*Bullocks*	*Total*			
Jalandhar	7,144	17,158	24,302	178	2,171	2,349	1,736	5,749	4,015
Nakodar	13,680	16,616	30,296	122	3,168	3,290	1,023	8,505	1,217
Phillaur	6,462	14,181	20,643	626	3,693	4,319	1,091	4,805	2,249
Nawanshahr	10,798	21,790	32,588	389	5,094	5,483	1,167	6,261	1,568
Total 1972	38,084	69,745	1,07,829	1,315	14,126	15,441	5,017	25,320	9,049
Total 1966	68,573	45,341	1,13,914	299	19,292	19,591	813	1,854	4,306

Source: *District Statistical Abstract* (Jalandhar, 1973-4), p. 150.

was already as high as 83 per cent in 1971-2 and rose to 89 per cent in 1976-7.

II

The role of remittance, whether from towns to countryside or from international migration, in influencing capitalist development, especially in their effect on transforming the agrarian structure, is far from clear. Broadly speaking, there are two opposing theoretical tendencies.

The neoclassical school, following W.A. Lewis, looks upon capitalist development in terms of a shift from a low productivity agricultural population to a high productivity manufacturing sector. Put crudely, it is argued that since only the poorest migrate, their wages, reflected in their remittances, redistribute income in their favour, narrowing rural income differentials. Often international migration is seen as a way out, for as Griffin has argued 'the series of allegations against migration ... are almost entirely false. The migration of ordinary working people to higher paid jobs abroad, whenever feasible, is in principle a major avenue of escape from poverty and oppression'.[7]

Griffin continuing on the theme of intra-national rural-urban migration, states:

> Internal migration is likely to improve the distribution of income in rural areas ... and accelerate capital formation and technical change on small peasant farms. Migration, in effect, allows the peasantry to overcome the imperfections of the rural credit market by creating opportunities to amass finance capital in the cities for subsequent use in agriculture. ... Migration [is also] a way for some members of the peasantry to accumulate 'human capital'.[8]

The second theoretical orientation is associated with the centre-periphery or dependency theorists,[9] who argue that migration and hence remittance lead to even greater inequalities in the rural areas of emigration. It is asserted that migration blocks balanced development and leads to increased dependency, presumably through increased consumption of Western consumer durables, although this latter argument is not always coherently or explicitly stated. A 1978 survey article by Rempel and Lobdell on the effects of remittances on the rural areas came to the following conclusion:

> Although such remittances serve as a useful income redistribution function, they can also be seen as the means of maintaining the traditional system in the rural areas. The need for any one village to adopt to a changing environment is reduced precisely because of remittances. Therefore, it is not merely a matter of a failure to use the remittances for development purposes, they may be used for the opposite purpose of delaying change required for rural development.[10]

The literature on the impact of remittances on the Punjab also reflects the two diverging views presented above. Both Helweg[11] and La Brack[12] have spoken favourably about their impact, the latter referring to migrants as the 'new patrons'. Kessinger[13] and Ballard,[14] however, have tended to undervalue their contribution. Ballard, for instance, having considered the comparative impact of remittances on Jalandhar and Mirpur villages argues: 'What has been most crucial has been the local entrepreneurial activity in agriculture, industry and commerce and the growth of a flourishing symbiosis between these sectors. Migrant remittances may have added gilt to the gingerbread but they have not produced the gingerbread itself.'[15]

The main objective here is to demonstrate that under the specific historical conditions prevalent in Punjab agriculture, remittances, by providing off-farm income and changing the structure of the land and lease markets, played a vital role in economic development. In the villages that were studied, remittances proved to be a crucial accelerating factor in the process of differentiation of the peasantry and, therefore, contributed significantly to strengthening the development of capitalism in agriculture.

That productive uses of remittances were made rests on two important assumptions: the first relates to the nature and intensity of migration – most of it was overseas and hence the absolute value of remittances would be far greater; second, and perhaps more important, given the class characteristics of these migrants, productive use was perceived to be the only outlet for their accumulated surpluses. It needs to be borne in mind that the majority of these overseas migrants were peasant proprietors, initially coming from the middle peasant category but more lately from the rich peasant one.[16] Thus, given these specific conditions, remittances have the potential to accelerate the process of development of peasant capitalism which had already started with the advent of the green revolution in the 1960s.

III

The Jalandhar district, along with the neighbouring areas of Hoshiarpur and Ludhiana, has a long tradition of migration. This district, as well as the villages studied, provided migrants to the canal colonies in the 1880s, to other industrial cities in India, for example, Jamshedpur and overseas to Australia, Malaysia, Fiji and Canada in the first half of the twentieth century.[17] The period of mass migration from the Punjab is usually considered to be the 1950s and 1960s. An early study by Rose stated that migrants from the Punjab constituted four-fifths of the total Indian immigrants into Britain up to 1968.[18] Rose's estimates suggest that by 1968, when the Commonwealth Immigration Act came into force, there would be at least 200,000 migrants from the Punjab. As pointed out earlier, most of these migrants were landed Sikh Jats initially coming from the middle peasant category. More recent estimates by La Brack put the number of Sikhs in the UK between 300,000-500,000.[19]

Determinants of international migration are rather complex, but many researchers have suggested that most migratory movements arise from the existence of prior links between sending and receiving countries and are based on such variables as colonization, political influence, trade, investment or other cultural ties. The foregoing factors also constitute important explanation for Punjabi overseas migration. Although there are a number of major socioeconomic causes that can readily be listed, an important causal factor is the traditional Sikh ties with the British – their loyalty to the British during the Indian Mutiny, their 'martial' qualities which made them the backbone of the British Army, and their allegedly being the 'pampered minority' of the Raj. These colonial links increased the international mobility of the Punjabis, and still remain an important variable in explanations of the dispersion and emergence of the Punjabi diaspora. It was inevitable, therefore, that when there was increase in demand for unskilled wage labour in Britain, the Sikhs would respond to it by migrating.

The period of mass migration came to an abrupt end in 1968 with the passing of the Commonwealth Immigration Act. Since then immigration from the Indian subcontinent has been strictly restricted. A majority of the migrants in the 1970s have comprised elderly dependents and male spouses of rich peasant origin. It needs to be remembered that this migration occurred and is indeed still occurring to other areas of settlement of the Sikh diaspora from a very localized region. And even then from a cluster of villages of the district at a rate estimated to be around 100,000 per annum.

There is, unfortunately, very little published data on the extent of remittance inflow into the Punjab but an estimate in 1977 by the Punjab Finance Minister put the official foreign remittance inflow at around £ 20 million per annum. Government officials, however, guesstimate the amount to be at least four times as great during the late 1960s and the early 1970s. During this crucial phase, a very large percentage of the total remittance came through unofficial 'black market' channels in which £ 1 sterling was reportedly being exchanged for around Rs. 30 when the official exchange rate was around Rs. 16-17. Helweg and La Brack have attempted to estimate remittance inflows and the latter has suggested that about half a billion found its way into the Punjab out of $ 2 billion coming from abroad.[20]

The 'unofficial' remittance flow from Britain had somewhat begun to diminish from the mid-1970s, especially after the Indian Government started to inaugurate favourable terms and facilities for non-resident Indians (NRIs) to open up convertible sterling accounts. This was quickly manifested in the mushrooming of Indian banks in Britain during this period. However, it needs to be reiterated that the rural areas being examined are unlikely to have suffered significantly from this decrease because of the new compensatory 'inflow' from Punjabi migrant workers benefiting from the construction boom in the Gulf States.

Observations made during fieldwork suggested that the way in which remittances were utilized was highly dependent on the initial size of holdings of the peasant migrant family household. For example:

1. Poor peasants (owning up to 5 acres), forming a very small number of the total migrant families, mainly utilized remittances for purchasing more agricultural land and on installation of a tube well or a pumping engine.
2. Middle peasants (owning up to 10 acres), forming the greatest number in the initial period, again put purchases of agricultural land as their first priority, followed by installing irrigation technology, purchasing tractors and other agricultural implements and more lately, house construction in both the village and the main neighbouring city.
3. Rich peasants (owning up to 25 acres), migrated only in rare instances initially. It was not until the middle peasants began to compete with them for the limited village agrarian resource, did they consider the migration option seriously. In the earlier period they apparently had been quite content with their dominant position in the village socio-economic hierarchy. The uppermost priority of these peasant households tended to be purchases of agricultural machinery, mainly tractors, investment in small-scale industry, petrol stations, shares in transport companies, etc. Many were recipients of rental income from shops, particularly so in the largest village, Jandiala.

Thus the priority list for utilizing remittances by the peasant migrant households can be summarised as follows: (a) purchases of agricultural land; (b) productivity-raising investment in land, e.g. tractors, tube wells and wheat threshers, etc.; (c) house construction (this activity became very popular in the 1970s, no doubt reflecting both decreased land mobility and a means of raising social status. The land market remained more or less 'frozen' as very little land was offered on the market either in their villages or in the neighbouring ones); and (d) miscellaneous–shops, small-scale industry, shares in transport companies, cold stores, hotels, cinemas and warehouses.

Most of the remittances, therefore, were absorbed within the local agrarian economy. There are very few early examples of urban industry-oriented investments by migrants, although this was anticipated by government officials to be their next direction.

For example, in 1977, within four months of its opening, the Indian Investment Centre in Chandigarh received 100 applications from NRIs to set up a varied number of small and medium-scale industrial units with proposals to invest Rs. 1 lakh to 50 lakh. However, every effort by the non-resident prospective entrepreneurs to set up industrial units was met with bureaucratic delays of at least six months, often leading to frustration and resentment.[21] Some of the remittances, although forming a very small proportion of the total, have also been utilized in the development of infrastructure, e.g. 'pukka roads', schools, colleges and hospitals. Very often these medical centres, schools, colleges and places of worship were opened up after vociferous community or village fund-raising campaigns from the various Sikh areas of settlement in Britain. Collectively, these 'philanthropic' investments should be seen as being quite important in aiding the general circulation and movement of commodities which is crucial for the further strengthening of commodity relations and the eventual dominance of the capitalist mode of production.

It is recognized that any attempt to assess the 'productive' and 'unproductive' uses of remitted income is problematic. The assessment partly depends upon the level of analysis under consideration. For example, improvements in the quality of housing, expenditures on imported luxury consumer goods or on lavish marriage ceremonies do raise the prestige and social status of migrant households, enabling them greater access to village agrarian resources and improving the marriage prospects of their children. Thus for the migrant household concerned such 'investment' will yield considerable productivity gains even though these expenditures may be considered by 'outsider' researchers to have been wasteful. The external benefits of such 'consumptive' expenditures are an important source for improving the efficiency of the human resource base. In our survey villages, increased house-building activity did stimulate the local construction industry and generate much needed employment opportunities. Where the funds were used for philanthropic purposes, for example, to improve schools, colleges or hospitals or other community facilities, the repercussions of overseas migrant labour are of benefit to the entire village. On the edge of the village of Sang Dhesian, for instance, a migrant-income-funded hospital provides health care facilities and a college similarly funded, and intermediate educational facilities for girls from several neighbouring villages.[22]

An additional problem in trying to identify what is 'productive' or 'unproductive' expenditure is the lack of consideration given to the local or regional multiplier effects of the remitted income, especially in terms of employment generation. Furthermore, it is possible that remittances enable the release of alternative capital for productive uses. As far as migrant households are concerned remittance monies merely represent *one component of total household income* and thus it becomes impossible to identify the exact use to which the remitted income is put.

Bearing in mind the constraints highlighted above, it is not being argued here that all of the remittances were used for 'productive' purposes, but only that, given the migrants' class origins, pressure on them to consume was far less. There is no doubt that some remittances did get spent on elaborate marriage ceremonies and/or on purchases of luxury consumer durables. It was not surprising to find, for example, that most migrant households had acquired electric fans, radios and mopeds, and it can be argued that these expenditures facilitate the magnetisations and circulation of commodities generally.

Nor is it being implied that other regions will generally experience similar modes of remittance utilization. There is plentiful anecdotal evidence for the Punjab and for the other states in India to support alternative forms of remittance utilization. For example, it has been argued by Chayanov[23] for Russia and by Kessinger[24] for the Punjab that outside earnings can typically be used by peasants to counteract the possible differentiation effects of uneven agrarian performance. In retrospect Kessinger certainly appears to have underestimated the potential role played by remittances in his survey village which, incidentally, also lies in the same *tahsil* as our villages. However, evidence gathered from our fieldwork strongly indicates that remittances and their form of utilization enhanced the process of capitalist differentiation of the peasantry in the Punjab.

As an alternative mode of remittance utilization take the case of village Baladiya. The village lies in a drought-plagued barren region north of Bombay. It is estimated that at least 2,000 of its

4,500 population are overseas, mainly in UK. The majority of the Indian public sector and commercial banks have established branches there, with total deposits exceeding £ 10 million. A large percentage of the remittances have ended up being used on 'unproductive' luxury consumer goods.[25]

A more typical picture for many of the migrant villages is depicted by the conditions in Dayalpur, located just off the main road between Nawanshahr and Phillaur. This village boasts the following: TV antennae on every roof, colour television, VCRs, cassette players, refrigerators and imported telephones in most houses. Out of the village population of 1,600, around 700, mostly Sikh Jats, are overseas. Around 80 per cent of the mail handled by the village post office is overseas-related. The village is proud of its 150-line electronic telephone exchange and a 25-bed, well-equipped, migrant-funded hospital. However, all is not well in this village. Loneliness and boredom '*inhabits the village that is just not in keeping with its affluence. In one of those savage ironies of fate, as money has poured into Dayalpur, life had ebbed away*' (emphasis added). The author's sobering conclusion reads:

> Dayalpur may have found a foolproof method to send its men abroad, but it has no way of giving meaning to the life of its citizens who walk around in a haze of alcohol or opium generated stupor. For Dayaplur, the price of a foreign-earned prosperity may finally be a heavy one.[26]

It is also possible to conceive of a situation similar to the one illustrated by the neighbouring district of Ludhiana, where vast surpluses of capital accumulated through profitable use of the green revolution technology by rich peasants may be used for unproductive purposes like moneylending at usurious interest rates, to strengthen pre-capitalist relations of production.[27] It may suffice to say that such 'unproductive' uses were not found to be of any great significance in the villages that were studied.

To get a clear example of 'productive' remittance utilization, we can consider the characteristics of tractor-owning families in our selected villages. As can be seen from Table 2, there is a significant correlation between the number of migrant families and the total number of tractor-owning families in all the villages studied. The majority of the tractors were, furthermore, paid for

TABLE 2: CHARACTERISTICS OF TRACTOR-OWNING HOUSEHOLDS IN SELECTED VILLAGES (1977)

	Jandiala	*Rurka*	*Sang Dhesian*	*Dhahan*	*Moranwali*	*Total*
Total no. of tractor-owning families	27	24	8	8	13	80
No. of migrant families	22	17	6	6	13	64
No. of non-migrant families	5	7	2	2	0	16
Mode of payment						
Cash	24	19	4	7	13	67
Loan	3	5	4	1	0	13
Tractors coming from abroad	4	3	0	1	2	10

Source: Personal interviews with migrant families.

in cash. A significant number of these tractors even came from abroad as 'gifts'. According to Helweg the Massey Ferguson Tractor Company delivered 1,038 tractors to the Punjab between 31 August and 24 October 1970, paid for in sterling by Indians in England.[28] The overall effects of overseas remittances may be summarized as follows: they led to the creation of an agrarian structure which was conducive to further capital accumulation and transformation.

IV

An attempt is made in this section to pinpoint some of the emerging capitalist relations and to identify and separate the effects of remittances from the more general effects of the development of productive forces and changing production relations associated with the green revolution technology. One general conclusion that emerges is that remittances had the effect of increasing both land values and concentration of holding in landed property. General trends in land values and land transfers in the three villages under study are set out in Table 3.[29]

TABLE 3: TOTAL LAND TRANSFERS AND AVERAGE PRICE PER ACRE, 1950-76

Year	*Jandiala*			*Rurka*			*Sang Dhesian*		
	Acres Transferred	*Average Price per Acre (Rs.)*	*Index no. 1950-1 1951=100*	*Acres Transferred*	*Average Price per Acre (Rs.)*	*Index no.*	*Acres Transferred*	*Average Price per Acre (Rs.)*	*Index no.*
1950-1	39	3,316	100	16	2,850	100	2	5,343	100
1951-2	32	3,208		9	2,412		3	3,633	–
1952-3	24	4,590	148	2	7,042	268	–	–	–
1953-4	5	4,332	133	–	–	–	–	–	–
1954-5	1	4,000	123	–	–	–	–	–	–
1955-6	7	5,086	156	7	3,029	115	–	–	–
1956-7	50	2,662	82	19	4,747	180	–	–	–
1957-8	42	3,008	92	65	3,477	132	2	5,830	130
1958-9	73	2,734	84	52	3,693	140	2	5,600	125
1959-60	79	2,734	84	19	2,292	87	–	–	–
1960-1	39	2,483	76	71	2,081	113	–	–	–
1961-2	29	3,496	107	27	4,605	175	26	2,572	57
1962-3	94	3,733	114	50	4,795	182	5	7,060	157
1963-4	20	3,655	112	51	5,375	204	–	–	–
1964-5	45	6,438	197	86	6,183	235	4	7,825	174
1965-6	38	7,142	219	47	9,270	352	10	12,350	275
1966-7	46	8,282	257	45	14,435	549	5	8,757	195
1967-8	19	13,489	414	28	12,750	485	2	17,700	394
1968-9	14	7,446	228	27	20,129	765	1	16,750	373

1969-70	22	18,500	567	14	38,885	1,364	1	36,500	813
1970-1	34	34,849	1,068	1	29,500	1,121	3	35,833	798
1971-2	38	28,850	885	51	15,171	577	5	17,000	379
1972-3	21	34,812	1,067	33	26,358	1,002	19	22,221	445
1973-4	73	13,812	423	37	14,068	538	2	39,950	890
1974-5	20	14,517	445	19	21,842	830	4	22,750	507
1975-6	62	17,101	524	27	19,288	733	1	42,099	938

Notes: During the period 1950-76, the percentages of total village areas transferred were: Jandiala – 28.4 per cent, Rurka – 26.2 per cent, Sang Dhesian – 20.1 per cent. The above data only shows land transfer within the villages. It excludes land purchase in neighbouring/other villages.

Source: Village Notebooks (Lal Kitabs).

Given the tendency to acquire as much land as possible, especially in the period of the greatest remittance flow, that is, during the late 1960s and the early 1970s, and given the natural rigidity of the land market, land values increased sharply in both nominal and real terms. These dramatic inflationary trends in land values shown in Table 3 do not appear to be replicated elsewhere in the Punjab, even in the model Intensive Area Development Programme district, Ludhiana. As a consequence of these land market transactions a considerable number of migrant families joined the ranks of the new rich peasant class through acquiring more land. This newly acquired upward social mobility (from middle to rich peasant status) is clearly visible from our sample village Dhahan in Table 4.

The trend in upward social mobility was in fact observable in all of the villages that were under investigation. As a consequence the percentage of total cultivated land under migrant households increased considerably; nearly 70 per cent of the total cultivated area in the villages under scrutiny was under migrant control by 1977.

Who then were the dispossessed? First, rising land values made it worthwhile for many poorer peasant and artisan households to sell their meagre plots of land in these villages. Instances were cited of many such households buying double the amount of land elsewhere, either in other villages of the district or in the neighbouring states. Second, some households, including those

TABLE 4: SOCIAL MOBILITY OF MIGRANT HOUSEHOLDS IN DHAHAN (1977)

	No. of Migrant Holdings	*Area owned (acres)*	*No. of Migrant Holdings after Purchases*	*Area Owned After Purchase (acres)*
Landless	1	0	0	0
Poor Peasants	2	7	0	0
Middle Peasants	13	92.5	3	20
Rich Peasants	6	74	18	250
Landlords	3	92	4	125
Total	25	265.5	25	395

Source: Personal interviews with migrant households.

from the upper strata, sold off their land and migrated to the cities; in other words, they became 'voluntarily proletarianised' or chose to become permanent urban dwellers.

Given that data on the actual volume of remittance into these villages are very scanty and that these were also green revolution villages, can it be implied that the cause of rise in land values and increased concentration in land-ownership was due to the effects of remittances and not just the impact of relative prosperity ushered in by the green revolution strategy? It needs to be remembered that despite the increasing concentration in land-ownership and other agricultural assets, the majority of the peasant holdings are still of less than 10 acres as can be seen from the landholding data of the selected villages in Table 5. Tables 6 and 7 give some indication of the profitability levels associated with the full adoption of the green revolution package. Given these conditions, despite rising net returns per acre, it is very unlikely that such land transfers could have taken place or could be capable of being financed except through the availability of extra off-farm income, that is, remittances. In other words, the surplus funds needed to finance the rising value of land could not have been accumulated from the surplus generated via agricultural production alone.

Considering Tables 3, 6 and 7 together, during the crucial years from 1969 to 1972, when land values were at their peak

TABLE 5: PERCENTAGE DISTRIBUTION OF OWNERSHIP HOLDINGS OF TOTAL MEMBERS OF THE PRIMARY AGRICULTURAL CO-OPERATIVE CREDIT SOCIETIES (1977)

Size of Holdings	*Jandiala*		*Rurka*		*Sang Dhesian*	
	% *Holdings*	% *Acres*	% *Holdings*	% *Acres*	% *Holdings*	% *Acres*
Landless	37.1	–	24.1	–	19.3	–
0-2.5	28.8	19.1	36.7	19.7	37.2	18.2
2.51-5	23.2	36	20.6	24.1	17.2	21.7
5.01-10	7.6	22.9	13.9	34.7	23.4	47.0
10.01-25	3.1	18.9	4.7	21.5	2.8	13.2
25+	0.2	3.1	–	–	–	–

Source: Land Registry of Village Co-Op. Credit Societies.

TABLE 6: NET RETURNS PER QUINTAL OF HYV WHEAT (PUNJAB) (IN RS. PER QUINTAL)

Year	*Total Cost*	*Procurement Price*	*Profit Margin*
1969-70	62.90	76	20.8
1970-1	61.04	76	23.8
1971-2	59.71	76	27.3
1973-4	74.34	105	41.2

Source: A. Mitra, *Terms of Trade and Class Relations*, London: Frank Cass, 1976.

TABLE 7: WHEAT-YIELDS PER ACRE AND GROSS VALUE OUTPUT (PUNJAB)

Year	*Quintals per Acre*	*Index no.*	*Gross Value Output*	*Index no.*
1960-1	5.03	100	190.28	100
1965-6	5.00	94	313.00	165
1969-70	9.08	182	752.55	369
1971-2	9.74	194	764.78	402
1972-3	9.04	180	692.28	364
1973-4	8.27	178	1,032.36	543
1974-5	9.69	193	1,050.40	532
1975-6	9.60	191	1,014.43	533

Note: Harvest prices instead of procurement prices are used; the former are closer to market prices being obtained by the peasants.

Source: Calculated from Table 3.7, *Statistical Abstract, Punjab*, Chandigarh: 1976.

and remittances were at their highest, gross value output remained almost stagnant. This stagnation primarily reflected the fact that during these years procurement prices for wheat remained almost stagnant, fixed at Rs. 76 per quintal. These crucial years, then, clearly demonstrate the greatest divergence between land prices and gross value output. A strong feasible explanation lies in the injection of vast amounts of off-farm income into the village agrarian economy. Some scholars have argued that in the Punjab, the agricultural co-operatives, given their historically successful operations, have played an important role in providing institutional credit for land purchases and implements, but the published data do not support such a contention because loans given for the purposes of land purchases were negligible.[30]

Thus the accumulation of land (and other productive farm assets such as tractors and complementary machinery) in the hands of the rich peasants has gone a long way in firmly rooting capitalist relations in agriculture. It is generally argued that during this process of transition to capitalism, land will increasingly become concentrated in fewer and fewer hands until there is a clear emergence of two antagonistic classes – the capitalists and the agricultural proletarian. However, as will be argued below, given the complexity of the Punjab social formation, concentration of landholding need not be a necessary precondition for the development of capitalism in Punjab agriculture.

V

The 'classical' trajectory of capitalist concentration in agriculture is perhaps the most controversial and misunderstood aspect of the Marxist-Leninist theory of capitalist development as applied to agriculture. Kautsky in his 'The Agrarian Question – A Review of the Tendencies in Modern Agriculture and Agrarian Policy', arguably provides the first extensive discussion of the process of economic concentration in agriculture under capitalism. The classical case of *concentration* and *centralization* in industry, however, was initially outlined by Marx towards the end of the nineteenth century. It is perhaps worth recalling that by *concentration* Marx was referring to the tendency of larger capital to expand more rapidly through faster accumulation, while by *centralization,* he meant the amalgamation or bringing together of atomistic capitals under unified control, that is, under a single operator.

A major controversy amongst the Marxists of the late nineteenth and early twentieth centuries and contemporary Marxists arose over the question of whether the 'laws' of *concentration* and *centralization* of capital applied in the same way in capitalist agriculture as they did in manufacturing.[31] The main impediments to the operation of this 'law' of capital are primarily related to the specific features of land as a means or factor of production relative to other factors. In the first instance, land is fixed spatially

– it is usually very difficult to increase the acreage under cultivation in the short or even the medium term. Second, and perhaps more important, land is restricted by virtue of being in private ownership. Part VI, and particularly Chapter 47, of Marx's third volume of *Das Kapital* clearly illustrates the barriers constituted by restricted private property (hence absolute ground rent) to capitalist production in agriculture. In other words, in countries with large peasant populations and highly concentrated landholding, the usual case in most developing countries today, the payment of pre-capitalist 'hunger rents' by a mass of petty peasants and tenants acts as an insurmountable barrier to capitalist penetration in agriculture. The root cause of the existence of high pre-capitalist rents is precisely the monopoly of landed property and the consequent landlessness or the near propertylessness of a high proportion of the working population and their struggle for livelihood within agriculture in the absence of alternative job opportunities.

However, perhaps as a safeguard against being too carried away by the above argument, it needs to be emphasized that historically capitalism has always succeeded in overcoming this barrier constituted by pre-capitalist ground rent. The obstacle was overcome in the past when capitalist investment embodying technically improved production methods was undertaken and when more and more branches came under the control of capitalist production with the consequent result of an improvement in productive forces. At the general level, it will be accepted that the tendency towards concentration and centralization also operates in capitalist agriculture. What is required is a more concrete and comprehensive analysis of the concrete situation of the Punjab peasantry. Only then will it be possible to identify specifically how the existence of private landed property modifies or affects the operation of the tendency towards concentration and centralization of capital.[32] The Marxist theory of absolute ground rent, it is argued, enables us to specify theoretically the manner in which capitalist development in agriculture differs from industry and at the same time allows us to understand why the process of *concentration* is likely to be different or operate in a modified form.

The first and foremost reason why the tendency will operate in a more modified form is due to the existence of monopolised landed property. Under these circumstances the expansion of the scale of production or accumulation becomes very difficult. Since all of the land is already occupied, the only way of enlarging the surface area of the farm is by centralizing several plots. In the Punjab, especially in the villages under study, land transfers remained restricted primarily because the acquisition of land by migrant families would have led to an even greater fragmentation in landholding and consequently inefficient utilization of agrarian capital. It is precisely because of this reason that we see a continuous outward movement by rich peasants into areas such as the Terai region of western Uttar Pradesh and into Rajasthan where acquisition of continuous surface area did not act as a constraint on accumulation. Ladejinsky, describing the plight of the nascent 'gentleman farmer' capitalist stated:

> The medical doctor from Jullundur who turned part-time farmer is sitting pretty. The 15 acres purchased four years ago have tripled in value ... his only vexation is whether or not he will succeed in buying another 10 acres he has his eyes on ... and what a disappointed man be will be if they escape him.[33]

There is, therefore, acute land hunger in the Punjab. For the purpose of acquiring a piece of land, endless litigation goes on from generation to generation and from court to court. In this process, many of the petty producers are economically ruined, families are estranged and murders committed. Any peasant who mortgages his land or sells any portion of it, falls in the estimation of his fellow cultivators and loses his social status. Sometimes it becomes difficult for him to marry off his children and only in extreme circumstances will a mortgage or sale take place. Commenting on the rigidity of the land market as elaborated upon by Kautsky, Lenin remarked that:

> acquiring the small plots is a difficult matter partly because the small plots are occupied by agricultural labourers (whom the big farmer needs) and partly by small peasants who are the masters of the art of maintaining their hold by reducing consumption to an unbelievable minimum.[34]

A further limit on agrarian capitalism as outlined by Kautsky was the shortage of workers in the countryside. Due to the migration of rural workers, the big landowners are compelled to apportion land to labourers to create a small peasantry and to provide labour power for the landlord. Kautsky further argued that when small producers were disappearing very fast the big landowners would attempt to strengthen or revive them by the sale or lease of land. Although it would be futile to argue that such conditions prevail in the specificity of the Punjab situation, recent events in Punjab do, however, illustrate the modified way in which the existence of a specific type of labour force inhibits the wholesale domination of capitalist production through productive investments. For a variety of complex socio-economic reasons, the two important ones being the migration of traditional agricultural and skilled rural labour overseas, including migration to the Gulf States, and the general enhancement of the socio-economic status of the *dalit* agricultural labourers especially in terms of their increased ability to organize and bargain for higher wages and acquire non-agricultural employment, there has been an influx of *purabia* agricultural labour from the eastern states. The overall effect of this inward labour migration has been to depress real wages received by agricultural labour households to such an extent that productive investments in agriculture can be temporarily postponed.[35]

The third limit on the further growth of agrarian capitalism is imposed by the independent development of usury. Lenin emphasized the critical role of usury as an example of a difficult barrier which stands in the way of capitalist development. Considering whether usury acted as a factor and a motive force of differentiation or whether it retarded differentiation, he concluded that 'the independent development of merchant's and usurer's capital in our countryside retards the differentiation of the peasantry',[36] and thereby fetters agrarian capitalism. There is some evidence for the Punjab which appears to suggest agrarian capitalism halting in mid-track with parasitic and unproductive capital once again threatening to dominate and become a fetter on agricultural production. There were genuine fears that if this 'regressive' tendency amongst capitalist farmers continued, production relations similar to those existing prior to the green revolution era would reappear but at a higher technical level of production.[37] Such, therefore, are the barriers to the process of concentration and centralization of capital in agriculture. As pointed out earlier, for the Punjab at least, rigidity of the land market constitutes the principal barrier.

So far in this discussion we have ignored the role of the state. The state, as is well documented for several Third World regions, also plays an important role in reviving or maintaining small-scale production. Given that often the national economy is unable to generate sufficient employment in the urban centres, the state attempts to create a viable small peasantry, especially through providing: (a) low interest institutional credit; (b) subsidized inputs through agricultural cooperative credit societies; (c) providing knowledge of agricultural techniques especially through agricultural universities; and finally (d) through supporting an agricultural price policy which offers favourable returns for cultivators.

Of course, the above arguments are open to criticism. For example, it is often argued that only the rich peasants benefit from institutional credit and subsidized inputs, that agricultural universities act as powerful lobbies for rich peasant demands and that despite the state setting high procurement prices, poor peasants fail to benefit because of the increased cost and credit intensity of cultivation and the unfavourable terms of trade obtained by them. There is ample evidence to suggest that class differentiation has been accelerated by the relative worsening of the distribution of farm income and assets amongst differing peasant classes. However, despite the uneven distribution of gains, the viability of petty family production has undoubtedly been strengthened primarily because of the state policies.

How has the modified tendency towards concentration operated in the context of the Punjab? The hypothesis being advanced here is that the differentiation or what is the same thing, capitalist concentration in terms of surface area, is a sufficient condition for the development of capitalism in agriculture but not a necessary one. To establish concentration, we need to speak of the scale on which production is carried out not, as is often the case, of the surface area of the farms. To quote Lenin, 'the fact that large landed property is one of the conditions of large scale production, does not in the least signify that it is a sufficient condition'.[38] Kautsky and later Lenin, therefore, repeatedly warned of the dangers of taking simply the physical area of the farms as an accurate index of their scale of production.

Given the difficulties involved in accumulation through expansion of the physical area of farms, the only other form of accumulation in agriculture, namely the intensive application of capital to a given area, acquires special significance. It becomes possible to raise output (and surplus per unit of area) by applying both more constant and variable capital, that is, through 'capital intensification'. Evidence based on numerous micro-level studies on labour and capital absorption in the Punjab has shown the extent to which middle and rich peasant households make intensive applications of both constant and variable capital. According to H.K. Manmohan Singh:

> The data on investment show that the households operating 10-15 acres are the most dynamic category. More than half of investment on improvement of land (56%) is made by this group. This group also makes the highest proportionate investment on purchase of land, which is indicative of increasing concentration of landownership with upper middle and large farmers. Of total investment, 40% is on implements.[39]

Thus, it follows that any study of capitalist concentration in agriculture must place emphasis on all the economic indices and not just on the concentration of land area alone. If, as in the case of the Punjab, the region was undergoing a process of rapid capitalist penetration, this will ultimately be reflected in the increasing concentration of the operated area. It is precisely in this context that migration and remittances begin to play an important role in strengthening the process of capitalist production.

VI

I will now try to outline more elaborately the way in which migration and remittances were able to play such an important role in the Punjab. Given that there is tremendous competition for land and that there are ceilings on land-ownership but none on lease holdings, one would expect to see the emergence of large-scale production with a mixture of owned and leased-in land. Such large-scale production is indeed emerging, especially with increased mechanisation of all operations, in many parts of

India, but primarily so in the high agricultural growth areas like the Punjab, Haryana and western U.P.[40] In the villages that were selected for fieldwork this phenomenon is more profound and manifest, especially because of the impact of overseas migration and remittances.

For a variety of economic reasons, traditional tenants have been pushed down into the ranks of the agricultural proletariat. Where petty tenants have not been evicted by landlords, economic pressures have forced them out of cultivation, particularly in view of the increased cost and credit intensity of the agricultural technology based on privately controlled irrigation (pumps and tube wells) and purchased inputs (fertilizers and pesticides) in the context of a highly imperfect credit market. As Bardhan has clearly demonstrated (using Farm Management Survey data for Ferozepur),[41] nearly 25 per cent of primarily tenant farms belonged to this category. Furthermore, according to the National Sample Survey (NSS) data for the Punjab (including Haryana) in 1970-1, though only 9 per cent of the rural households did not *own* any land, as many as 54 per cent did not *operate* any land; the corresponding figures for 1960-1 were 12 per cent and 39 per cent respectively. Indeed, of all the Indian states, the Punjab and Haryana have seen the sharpest rise in non-cultivating households between 1960-1 and 1970-1. The ultimate result is, of course, reflected in a very significant increase in agricultural labourers as a proportion of rural workers accounting for 20.11 per cent in 1971. Moreover, as Bardhan has shown, there has been an unambiguous increase in inequality in the distribution of the operated area over the period 1960-1 and 1970-1. Table 8 outlines the prevailing tenurial condition in the three selected villages.

Data on the evolution of land tenure in these villages show a substantial increase in the area under self-cultivation after 1960-1. Self-cultivation continues to be the dominant form of tenure. This is of course to be expected, especially after the mid-1960s, because of the increasing profitability associated with the green revolution. The above data on tenancy relations admittedly do not reflect an unambiguous impact of remittances and migration. It seems, however, that the impact differed between the larger and smaller villages. The larger villages like Jandiala and Rurka

TABLE 8: LAND TENURE IN SELECTED VILLAGES OF PUNJAB

Year	*Village*	*Total Cultivated*	*Self-Cultivated*	*Batai*	*Hala*	*Relatives*
1971-2	Jandiala	2,999	2,418	315	201	65
		(100)	(80.6)	(10.5)	(6.7)	(2.1)
1976-7	Rurka	2,775	2,145	175	375	80
		(100)	(77.3)	(6.3)	(13.5)	(2.9)
1972-3	Sang	412	204	110	71	27
	Dhesian	(100)	(49.5)	(26.7)	(17.2)	(6.6)

Note: Figures in brackets are percentages.
Source: Village Jamabandis (1977).

show a high proportion of the area under self-cultivation. It is quite reasonable to argue that the impact of migration and remittance on tenurial conditions in Sang Dhesian (and Dhahan) may be more indicative of the real situation. This can be qualified by one important factor which shows up the limitations of the data presented in Table 8. It is well known that the *jamabandis* kept by *patwaris* show only *registered tenants*. As a consequence of the various Security of Land Tenure Acts it is now generally believed that the village lease markets operate on an *oral basis*. The *patwari's* figures would fail to catch these 'disguised' tenancies which are quite widely prevalent particularly in these villages.

As the agro-economic data for Dhahan in Table 9 show, given that the village experienced a high level of overseas migration by landed peasants (hence a large number of elderly dependents), one would expect to see the widespread prevalence of *batai* (share-cropping) and *hala* (fixed-rent tenancy) tenurial arrangement. It is precisely in these conditions of ample availability of land for leasing that rich peasants were able to establish themselves as the dominant tenants. For the migrant household, as the data from Dhahan confirm, the type of tenancy under which land was leased out depended very much on the family's particular migration pattern. If the migrant family still had dependents in the village, it was advantageous for them to lease-out land on *batai*. If, however, all the family members were living abroad, leasing out on *hala* appeared to be the most favoured alternative.

TABLE 9: AGRO-ECONOMIC ACTIVITIES OF MIGRANT FAMILIES IN VILLAGE DHAHAN

Name of Migrant Family	*No. of Migrant*	*Total Land Owned (acres)*	*Leased out (acres)*	*Leased in (acres)*	*Type of Tenure*	*Land Purchased since 1950 (acres)*	*Investment Irrigation and Agricultural Machinery*	*Wage Labour hired (permanent)*	*Other Investments H = Housing*	*Other Comments*
Kemar Singh	2	12	–	–	–	5.5	1 tube well, 1 pumping engine, 1 tractor, 1 wheat thresher	1 (Bihar)	H = 20,000	
Jagere Singh	1	12	–	9	*batai*	7	2 tube wells, 1 1 tractor, 1 wheat thresher	1 (Bihar)	H = 40,000*	Share had a return of 4,000 pa.
Ujagar Singh	2	32	32	–	*batai*	–	1 wheat thresher	–	–	A non-cultivating household. This elderly man lives alone in the village; all the sons are abroad.
Gurbax Singh	2	20	20	–	3 *hala* 7 *batai*	7	1 tube well	–	H = 40,000	Non-cultivating household. Only 2 elderly men and 1 son living in the village.
Hari Singh	2	24	–	–	–	20	1 tube well, 1 pumping engine, 1 wheat thresher	1 (Bihar)	H = 20,000	

(Contd.)

TABLE 9 (Contd.)

Name of Migrant Family	*No. of Migrant*	*Total Land Owned (acres)*	*Leased out (acres)*	*Leased in (acres)*	*Type of Tenure*	*Land Purchased since 1950 (acres)*	*Investment Irrigation and Agricultural Machinery*	*Wage Labour hired (permanent)*	*Other Investments H = Housing*	*Other Comments*
Pritam Singh	1	11	–	–	–	4	1 tube well, 1 pumping engine, 1 wheat thresher	–	H = 40,000	
Kishan Singh	3	17	–	–	–	10	1 tube well, 1 wheat thresher	–	H = 50,000	
Chanchal Singh	2	12	–	–	–	7	1 wheat thresher, 2 pumping engines	–	H = 20,000	He himself & his sons are abroad. Land is being cultivated by his brothers.
Kartar Singh Gara	1	12	12	–	*batai*	–	1 tube well	–	H = 10,000	
Ujagar Singh	3	14	–	–	–	4	1 tractor (from abroad), 1 tube well, 1 wheat thresher, 1 bore	–	H = 25,000	Elderly couple live alone in the village.
Bhagat Singh	1	12	–	–	–	2	1 pumping engine, 1 tube well, 1 wheat thresher	–	H = 15,000	
Joginder Singh	1	10	10	–	4 *hala* 6 *batai*	4	1 tube well, 1 pumping engine, 1 wheat thresher	–	H = 70,000	

Budh Singh & Teja Singh	2	12	8	–	8 *hala*	4 4	1 tube well	–	–	All abroad.
Bhullan Singh	2	17	17	–	mortgaged *batai*	10	1 tube well	–	–	Only elderly lady living in the village.
Kishan Singh	1	10	10	–	*batai*	2	2 pumping engines	–	H = 10,000	
Naranjan/ Hukma Singh	2	8	8	–	*batai*	–	1 bore	–	–	Non-cultivating household – joint holding of the two brothers who are abroad – their land being looked after by their nephew.
Gurmail Singh	3	33	–	–	–	24	1 tractor, 2 tube wells, 1 pumping engine, 2-3 bores, 1 wheat thresher	3	H = 10,000	Joint household – richest house of the village.
Isher Singh	2	14	14	–	*hala*	5	1 pumping engine	–	H = 25,000	
Sohan Singh	1	14	14	–	*hala*	–	1 tube well, 1 engine, 1 wheat thresher	–	H = 15,000	

(Contd.)

TABLE 9 (Contd.)

Name of Migrant Family	*No. of Migrant*	*Total Land Owned (acres)*	*Leased out (acres)*	*Leased in (acres)*	*Type of Tenure*	*Land Purchased since 1950 (acres)*	*Investment Irrigation and Agricultural Machinery*	*Wage Labour hired (permanent)*	*Other Investments H = Housing*	*Other Comments*
Sem Singh Gill	1	30	–	–	–	–	1 tractor, 1 tube well, 1 engine, 1 wheat thresher	1 (Bihar)	H = 10,000	
Karam Singh	1	30	–	–	5 on mortgage	–	1 pumping engine, 1 tractor, 1 tube well, 1 wheat thresher	–	H = 30,000	Joint holding but brothers on the verge of separating.
Prakash Singh	1	12	12	–	*hala*	12	1 tractor (later sold), 2 pump engines	–	H = 25,000	
Gurdev Singh	1	16	–	–	–	–	1 tube well, 1 pumping engine	–	H = 10,000	
Piara Singh	1	5	–	–	–	2	1 pumping engine, 1 wheat thresher	–	H = 30,000	
Pakhar Singh	1	7	7	–	*hala*	–		–	–	

Note: *Share in Onkar Bus Company.

The *hala* rental would then be collected either by a relative still resident in the village or by a relative from another village, or the migrant himself may make periodic returns to the village to collect it.

The thrust of the argument here is that migration and remittances enable large-scale production and intensive farm cultivation through 'unlocking' of lease market. The main beneficiaries of this unlocking have been the rich peasants who remained behind and it is this class of rich peasants, adequately backed by overseas remittances themselves, who have emerged as full-fledged capitalist farmers. At the same time it is precisely this class which began to hire permanent labour, particularly from the eastern states.

Thus a paradoxical situation arises: while a majority of the migrant peasant households have accumulated land and other agricultural assets, only a minority is able to reap full benefits from these investments. The real beneficiaries of these developments are the upper crusts of the village peasantry who are left behind, the majority having overseas migration connections. Given that the law favours the tenant, it is possible to cite numerous instances of migrant families rushing back to the Punjab to secure their legal ownership rights. The emerging property structure and property relations have created problems which are particularly acute for the wholly migrated nuclear families; they are in many cases forced to mortgage their land. These ongoing processes only go to alienate the migrants even further from the socio-economic environment prevalent in the villages, casting doubt on their eventual return.

VII

In conclusion, overseas migration has undoubtedly facilitated the emergence of a class of dominant tenants, who are already socially, politically and economically powerful by reason of belonging to the dominant class in the rural areas. Their bargaining power, especially in areas like our overseas migration villages where there is an unusual amount of land entering the lease market, is strengthened even further. The lessor gives preference to larger farmers not only because of minimal risk of default on rental payments but also because of their supposed superior advantage in the credit and product markets and hence the assurance overall of high value of output per acre and a higher rental. The phenomenon discussed above is not peculiar to the Punjab alone and indeed has emerged as a major characteristic of lease relations in Indian agriculture, particularly in areas of high agricultural growth. Under our specific conditions, migration and remittances fuelled this process of polarization in rural areas and capitalist concentration in agriculture. Concentration of the operational area, facilitated by migration and remittances, leads to a special and higher form of large-scale capitalist farming in which several large estates (accumulated by migrant families) are combined to form a single economic unit managed by a single rich peasant household.

Concentration in agriculture as experienced in the 'classical' case was a long-term process but the mere fact that this concentration (purely in terms of surface area) is not proceeding rapidly in Punjab, does not in any way invalidate the process. Capitalist accumulation in the Punjab has taken place as a result of the *intensification of capital* in a given area and over time, and as the process continues, it is likely to manifest itself in the increasing concentration of non-landed assets, for example, in equipment and productive capital like tractors, in output and employment on a minority of large holdings. What we have argued above is that the increasing concentration in area, that is, the accumulation resulting from capitalist development, which is of course the classical case of capitalist concentration in agriculture, is a *sufficient* indicator for the emergence of a capitalist concentration tendency, *but* is by no means a *necessary* one. What we have witnessed in the Punjab was a process of capital intensification, the application of more constant capital (fertilizers, irrigation, high-yielding seeds, etc.) and variable capital (labour) to a given area. Migration and remittances fuelled this process both in terms of increasing economic concentration, especially in terms of productive capital and in the institution of newly emerging property relations.

NOTES

1. See for instance G.K. Chadha, *The State and Rural Economic Transformation: The Case of Punjab, 1950-1985*, New Delhi: Sage, 1986. For an environmentalist 'failure' of the green revolution strategy, Vandana Shiva, 'The Green Revolution in the Punjab', *The Ecologist*, vol. 21, part 2, 1991; D.S. Kang, 'Environmental Problems of the Green Revolution with a focus on Punjab, India', in *International Dimensions of the Environmental Crisis*, ed. Richard Barrett, Boulder: Westview press, 1982.
2. For different aspects of British policy in the Punjab, T.G. Kessinger, *Vilyatpur 1848-1968: Social and Economic Change in a North Indian Village*, Berkeley: University of California Press, 1974; Shigemochi Hirashima, *The Structure of Disparity in Developing Agriculture*, Tokyo: Institute of Developing Economies, 1978, chs. 1-4; Imran Ali, *Punjab under Imperialism*, Princeton: Princeton University Press, 1988, esp. chs. 5 and 6; also Richard G. Fox, *Lions of the Punjab: Culture in the Making*, Berkeley: University of California press: 1985, esp. ch. 3.
3. The question of indebtedness among the Punjab peasantry during the colonial period has been extensively discussed. See, for example, the classic work of Malcolm Lyall Darling, *The Punjab Peasant in Prosperity and Debt*, London: Oxford University Press, 1925. N. Gerald Barrier has written a number of books and articles relating to the issue of land alienation legislation and its effects. See especially *The Punjab Land Alienation Bill of 1900*, Duke University, Monograph, no. 3, 1966.
4. See the essays by N. Charlesworth and D. Washbrook in C. Dewey and A.G. Hopkins (eds.), *The Imperial Impact: Studies in the Economic History of Africa and India*, London: Athlone Press for the Institute of Commonwealth Studies, 1978.
5. For details of degree of concentration in land-ownership, see H. Calvert, *The Wealth and Welfare of the Punjab*, Lahore: Civil and Military Gazette Press, 1922; also, Dewey and Hopkins, *The Imperial Impact.*
6. For an extended discussion of the 'globalisation' of the Punjab economy, Imran Ali, *Punjab under Imperialism*; Fox, *Lions of the Punjab.*
7. Keith Griffin, 'On the Emigration of the Peasantry', *World Development*, vol. 4 (1976), p. 353.
8. Ibid., p. 359.
9. See for example M. Nikolinakos, 'Notes Toward a General Theory of Migration in Late Capitalism', *Race and Class*, vol. XVII, part 1, 1975; A. Ward, 'European Capitalism's Reserve Army', *Monthly Review*, vol. 27, part 6, 1975.
10. H. Remple and R.A. Lobdell, 'The Role of Urban to Rural Remittances in Rural Development', *Journal of Development Studies*, 1978, pp. 336-7.

11. A.W. Helweg, *Sikhs in England*, Oxford University Press, 1986.
12. Bruce La Brack, 'The New Patrons: Sikhs Overseas', in *The Sikh Diaspora: Migration and the Experience beyond Punjab*, ed. N. Gerald Barrier and Verne A. Dusenberry, Delhi: Chanakya Publications, 1989.
13. Kessinger, *Vilyatpur.*
14. Roger Ballard has written a number of articles on the effects of international migration on the village economies of Mirpur (Pakistan) and the Punjabi villages of Jalandhar. See especially 'The Context and Consequences of Migration: Jullundur and Mirpur Compared', *New Community*, vol. 11, part 4, 1983.
15. Ibid., p. 122.
16. One general criticism of the literature available is that it has tended to ignore the specific class origins of the migrants. A greater number of the migrants are often regarded as coming from the poorest strata of village (i.e. landless labourers and poor peasant households), and all the remittances they send back are assumed to be used up either to pay off their debts or on consumptive expenditures.
17. This international migration has led to the emergence of a thriving Punjabi diaspora spread across the globe. See, for example, Barrier and Dusenberry, *The Sikh Diaspora.*
18. E.J.B. Rose et al., *Colour and Citizenship: A Report on British Race Relations*, Oxford University Press, 1969.
19. La Brack, 'The New Patrons'.
20. Ibid.
21. Quoted in 'Overseas Indian Eager to Invest', *Economic Times*, New Delhi, 13 August 1977. In recent years both the Indian and Punjab Governments have woken up to the potential 'development agent' role of NRIs and have consequently instituted a number of incentive schemes to woo NRI investments.
22. At the time of writing, a number of prominent migrant families from a cluster of villages around Dhahan were busy collecting funds for a major hospital project based on the edge of the village to be financed entirely out of migrant-remitted income.
23. A.V. Chayanov, *The Theory of Peasant Economy*, Homewood (Illinois), 1966.
24. Kessinger, *Vilyatpur.*
25. This village boasts of the ownership of four Mercedes and scores of Indian-made cars and Western style country houses with attached garages. Sometimes the cars stay locked up in the garage until the migrant returns. For the girls of Baladiya, their great ambition is to be chosen as a bride by a man earning good money abroad. The demand for educated girls continues to grow and the more ambitious mothers send their daughters to private schools to learn English. For detail see

S. Venkat Narayan, 'Poor Millionaires', *Sunday Times*, London, 18 January 1975.

26. For more detail, Ramesh Vinayak, 'The Price of Prosperity', *India Today*, New Delhi, 15 July 1992, p. 23.
27. See 'Arrested Green Revolution', *Economic and Political Weekly*, (hereafter *EPW*), Bombay, 21-28 June 1975.
28. For a case study of the impact of remittances on a Punjabi village, see Helweg, *Sikhs in England*.
29. These crude average land transfers and value figures need to be treated with great caution. Land values are influenced greatly by the size of the plot being transferred, the number of total transactions in any particular year, the quality of the land being transferred (i.e. whether it is irrigated, unirrigated or uncultivable because of soil salinity) and proximity to the main village or market site.
30. Data published by the Registrar of Punjab Co-Operative Credit Societies in 1974-5 shows that loans advanced for the purpose of purchase of land constituted only 3.89 per cent (Rs. 62.28 lakh) of the total loans advanced, whereas loans for purchase of tractors and installation of tube-wells constituted 25.31 per cent and 45.05 per cent, respectively.
31. According to V.I. Lenin, 'There cannot be any doubt that in agriculture the process of the development of capitalism is immeasurably more complex and assumes incomparably more diverse forms': *Complete Collected Works*, 45 vols., Moscow: Progress Publishers, 1980, vol. 45, p. 111.
32. Lenin, in his *Collected Works* (vol. 4) was at pains to point out the many diverse forms in which capitalism in agriculture manifests itself. For example, Lenin, quoting Kautsky argued:

    There is not the slightest doubt ... we are prepared to accept this *a priori* ... that agriculture does not develop according to the same pattern as industry ... it is subject to special laws. *The task is to investigate whether capital is bringing agriculture under its domination and how it is dominating it, how it transforms it, how it invalidates old forms of production and forms of property and creates the need for new forms.* (p. 112, emphasis added)

33. W. Ladejinsky, 'Green Revolution in Punjab: A Field Trip', *EPW*, June 1969, A-75.
34. Lenin, *Collected Works*, vol. 4, p. 134.
35. The Jat landowners have found the cheap *purabia* labour as a convenient way of dispensing with the services of the traditional village agricultural labourers. The landlord-labour relations have increasingly deteriorated, especially as a result of the sharpened economic and political contradictions in the countryside. For an account of the effects of migratory

labour, see S.S. Gill, 'Migratory Labour in Punjab Agriculture', *PSE Economic Analyst*, 3 and 4: 1 and 2, 1986, pp. 110-23.

36. V.I. Lenin, *The Development of Capitalism in Russia*, Moscow: Progress Publishers, 1977, p. 188.
37. 'Arrested Green Revolution'. A more rigorous analysis of such pre-capitalist relations is provided by the semi-feudal school (of Indian agriculture) whose contributors among others, include A. Bhaduri, Pradhan Prasad, N.K. Chandra, and R. Sau. For an overview of the 'mode of production' debates, Utsa Patnaik, *Peasant Class Differentiation: A Study in Method with Reference to Haryana*, Delhi: Oxford University Press, 1987.
38. Lenin, *Collected Works*, vol. 4, p. 131.
39. H.K. Manmohan Singh, 'Population Pressure and Labour Absorbability in Agriculture and Related Activities: Analysis and Suggestions Based on Field Studies Conducted in Punjab', *EPW*, 17 March 1979.
40. A number of research articles have observed this growing phenomenon of the dominant tenant class approximating the rich peasant: M.V. Nadkarni, 'Tenants from the Dominant Class: A Developing Contradiction in Land Reforms', *EPW*, Review of Agriculture, December 1976; K.N. Raj, 'Ownership and Distribution of Land, *Indian Economic Review*, April 1970; P. Bardhan, 'Trends in Land Relations: A Note', *EPW*, Annual no. 1970; Idem 'Variations in Extent and Form of Agricultural Tenancy – II: Analysis of Indian Data across Regions and over Time', *EPW*, 18 September 1976; M.L. Dantwala and C.H. Shah, 'Pre-reform and Post-reform Agrarian Structure', *Indian Journal of Agricultural Economics*, July-Sept. 1971; V.S. Vyas, 'Tenancy in a Dynamic Setting', *EPW*, Review of Agriculture, June 1970; V.M. Raj, 'Village Lease Markets for Agricultural Land: Some-Approaches for Analysis', *EPW*, Review of Agriculture, June 1974; H. Bhardwaj, 'Tenurial Conditions and Mode of Exploitation: A Study of Some Villages in Orissa', *EPW*, Annual no., 1975.
41. Bardhan, 'Variations in Agricultural Tenancy – II'.

12

Sikh Identity and the Issue of Khalistan

J.S. GREWAL

Attempts have been made to give a coherent and multicausal explanation of what has been termed as the Punjab problem. Atul Kohli, for example, has referred to the tendency to blame Indira Gandhi either because she was an indecisive leader or a Machiavellian leader, or a power-hungry leader who over-centralized the Indian polity. Kohli thinks that the last explanation best fitted the evidence, but it remains inadequate. There has been a similar tendency to blame the Sikhs either because of the marriage of religion and politics in Sikhism, or because of the factionalism within the Akali Party, or because the Sikh community was bent upon imposing its will on the Hindus. Kohli took the middle factor in his fuller explanation, but none of these propositions explains the intensity of the crisis.

Concentration on socioeconomic changes pointed to the growing differentiation among the Sikhs, resulting in antipathies. These changes were relevant for understanding the attempts 'to create political unity in a class-divided ethnic community'. But they were not decisive variables either. The origins of Punjab's complex and tragic civil disorder could be traced essentially to the political conflict between Indira Gandhi and the Akali Dal. A number of factors made the situation especially explosive. Two of these factors were not new but nonetheless relevant and important: the relatively even division of the population between the Sikhs and the Hindus; the close linkage of religion with politics, which made it difficult for the Akalis to search for political support outside the Sikh community. Four other factors are mentioned by Kohli as having contributed to the growing turmoil. One of these was 'the weakness of the Akali Dal as a party'; another was some egregious political blunders by Indira Gandhi, like her support to Sant Jarnail Singh Bhindranwale and the military assault on the Golden Temple; the third was the political impact of wealth in the context of economic differentiation among the Sikhs; and lastly, the presence of educated but unemployed Sikh youth in large numbers.[1]

After giving a condensed account of the events, Kohli comes to the conclusion that the driving force behind the conflict was a power struggle between Indira's Congress and the Akali Dal. 'Both Sikh nationalism and the increasing militancy are better understood as products rather than the source of the power struggle.' It was equally clear to Kohli that the leadership passed into the hands of Bhindranwale because of the failure to achieve a negotiated settlement in 1982-4. A settlement would have meant a political victory for the Akalis, with adverse electoral consequences for the Congress in the Punjab and Haryana, and possibly elsewhere in the country. A more self-assured or a more enlightened leader could have followed a different track. Not that the Akalis were any better; they also demonstrated the same kind of unprincipled electoral opportunism. But the final responsibility of resolving the conflict was Indira Gandhi's. In any case, both the Congress and the Akalis lost initiative and made room for 'a theocratic fundamentalist movement' with all its consequences: the Operation Blue Star, the assassination of Indira Gandhi and the politically directed massacre of large numbers of Sikhs in Delhi.[2]

However, there has been a general tendency to present the problem in terms of Sikh 'communalism' or 'fundamentalism' in opposition to nationalism and secularism. Even when sophisticated arguments are given, which bring in the implications of 'modernization', economic change, imbalanced development, social differentiation and unemployment, the close connection between religion and politics is presented as being the heart of the problem. Given one's commitment to nationalism and secularism, this becomes virtually a foregone conclusion. Wittingly or unwittingly, therefore, one tended to support those who upheld or professed to uphold nationalism and secularism. On the ground, this turned out to be the ruling party. From the very start, therefore, the dice got loaded against the opponents of the government. In nine cases out of ten, the explanations offered were in terms of communalism and fundamentalism in opposition to nationalism and secularism. But, as Atul Kohli points out, governments or national leaders can be partisan, can be mistaken or do something wrong.

Indeed, there were critics of the establishment. The tragedy of the Punjab was not the making of the Punjab alone, said one such critic, and went on to add that the entire nation was a party to it. He underlined certain facts which were generally unpalatable. The non-reading of the Anandpur Sahib Resolution, coupled with persuasive misinformation and disinformation spread by the Centre, created the chimeric image of the Sikh fanatic. The Congress never faced the Akali demands squarely. The Anandpur Sahib Resolution was called secessionist, the case of river waters was withdrawn from the Supreme Court, and the issue of Chandigarh was linked with Abohar and Fazilka. The Congress insisted on communalizing the demands of the Akalis by raising the bogey of Sikh separatism. At the same time, the Congress was able to place a communalizing catalyst in the shape of Sant Bhindranwale.[3]

The concept of communalism does not appeal to some scholars any more. The dyad of communalism/nationalism is a poor formulation to understand the Indian realities on the ground. The concept of communalism is a category arising out of a particular kind of political agenda. Just as the new nationalism – secular, democratic and, in time, socialist – was defined largely in opposition to growing politics of communalism, so communalism – or the politics of 'religious community' or 'communities' which gave rise to much tension, suspicion and strife – was defined in opposition to what was now conceived of as nationalism.[4] Furthermore, the problem of recognizing and accommodating the necessary autonomies and rights of defined social 'collectivities' or 'segments', call them ethnic, regional, linguistic or religious, was one of the major items of the contemporary politics of states and international organizations.[5]

Another scholar finds dichotomous conceptualizations analytically useless when applied to religious or ethnically heterogeneous societies. When an either/or conceptualization becomes the basis for policy analysis, the policy makers wedded to dichotomous analytical categories tend towards repressive solutions. But there is no reason to believe that ethnic sub-political systems cannot exist side by side with secular systems and compete 'constructively within the same geographical area'.[6]

On the concept of secularism too, we are told: 'The academic debate that has gone on for some time, about whether or not secularism is an Indian concept, applicable to Indian conditions, seems to me to be somewhat misplaced. For the alternatives are clear: the struggle for a genuine pluralism, which would engender respect for divergent beliefs and the rights of individuals and minorities, on the one hand; narrowness, intolerance and murder, on the other.'[7] The conception of the modern state is seen as an obstacle in the way of 'a context sensitive' approach because it does not recognize within its jurisdiction any form of community except the single, determinate, demographically innumerable form of the nation. 'It must therefore subjugate, if necessary by the use of violence, all such aspirations of community identity. These other aspirations, in turn, can give to themselves a valid historical justification only by claiming an alternative nationhood with rights to an alternative state.' Unless the conception of the state changes, ethnic identities cannot be accommodated: they can only revolt.[8]

In the world of politics and scholarship, the term generally used for Sikh politics is 'communal' or 'fundamentalist'. However, the constitutional movement for greater autonomy for the states in India and the militant movement for a sovereign Sikh state outside the Indian Union, both get related to the consciousness of a distinct Sikh identity. Therefore, Sikh identity in itself does not inevitably lead to a movement for autonomy or Khalistan. In fact, the earliest assertion of Sikh identity in the twentieth century did not see any contradiction between a distinct Sikh identity and Indian nationalism.

II

Both the Akalis and the protagonists of Khalistan invoked Sikh identity as essentially relevant for their political programmes. It figured prominently in their political discourses and praxis. What they shared was primarily the Khalsa or Singh identity. This identity was visible in their external appearance. They wore *kesh* and turban, kept a flowing beard and uncut hair, carried a *kirpan*, and wore *kara* and *kachh*. These four symbols begin with the letter 'k'. The fifth 'k' is *kangha* or the comb tucked in the *kesh* for keeping the hair clean and orderly. These five Ks form the most important items in the Khalsa conception of *rahit*. The strictest prohibition is on the use of tobacco in any form. Sant Jarnail Singh favoured the idea of bearing modern weapons in addition to a long sword. For prohibition, he added drugs and alcohol to tobacco. On the first point, he was closer to the Khalsa of the eighteenth century. On the second, he was more in conformity with the *Adi Granth*. Whereas the followers of Sant Jarnail Singh insist on *amritdhari* identity, involving the observance of the five Ks after the baptism of the double-edged sword (*pahul* or *amrit*), the Akalis prefer this identity but do not seriously object to what may be called the Singh identity as less exacting than the *amritdhari* identity. Besides carrying the epithet 'Singh' in one's name, by far the most important items of this identity are keeping the hair uncut, wearing turban, and refraining from the use of tobacco. Ordinarily, the Singhs of this description would wear *kara* and less frequently also *kachh*. Theoretical preference for *amritdhari* identity is thus common to both the Akalis and the Damdami Taksal, but they differ in actual practice. Since the *keshdharis* have been far larger than the *amritdharis*, the Akalis have worked with a much broader base.

Apart from external appearance, the Akalis and the Damdami Taksal observe distinct rites of passage – ceremonies connected with birth, marriage and death. On these, as on several other occasions, the *Adi Granth* is of crucial importance. No such ceremony can be performed without it. This is because the *Adi Granth* is not only the exclusive scripture of the Sikhs in the eyes of the Akalis and the followers of Sant Jarnail Singh but is also the embodiment of the Guru. Therefore, *Guru Granth Sahib* is its proper title. This title and this attitude spring from the doctrine of the continuity of Guruship. Guru Nanak, the founder of the Sikh faith and the Sikh Panth, was followed by nine successors. Just as he chose Angad to be the Guru, and Guru Angad chose Amar Das, and so on, Guru Gobind Singh chose the *Adi Granth* to be the Guru. What ended with the death of Guru Gobind Singh was personal Guruship but not Guruship itself. The reverence and regard which the Sikhs of the ten Gurus gave them are due now to *Guru Granth Sahib* as well. This doctrine of *Guru-Granth,* it must be added, is more than 250 years old, and the equation of Gurbani with the Guru can be traced back to the sixteenth century. Since the Gurus have spoken through the *Granth*, *Guru Granth Sahib* has been the source of Sikh ideas and ethics. As the exclusive scripture of the Sikhs, it is the only valid source now. But to this source are added the known injunctions and practices of the ten Gurus. Both the Akalis and the followers of Sant Jarnail Singh agree that the *Adi Granth* inculcates monotheism or worship of One God and rejects gods, goddesses, incarnations, and idols. Sikh doctrines and Sikh worship too, therefore, are distinctive.

The Sikh institution *par excellence*, both for the Akalis and for the followers of Sant Jarnail Singh, is the Gurdwara. There was a time when the Sikh sacred space was known as *dharmsal*. It was the place where congregational worship was held, sacred food (*prashad*) was distributed, and community meal (*langar*) prepared and eaten. This was also the place where matters of common interest to the local community could be discussed. The *dharmsal* where the Guru was personally present was regarded for that reason as the premier institution, like Kartarpur (Dera Baba Nanak), Khadur Sahib, Goindwal, Amritsar, Kiratpur and Anandpur. Also, the idea became current that the Guru was present in the *sangat*, which added a new dimension to the sanctity of the *dharmsal*. This idea became all the more important when there was no personal Guru any more. This development reached its culmination with the doctrine of *Guru-Granth*; its presence in the *dharmsal* approximated its sanctity to that of the premier *dharmsals* of the days of the Gurus. Gradually, the name *dharmsal* was dropped in favour of Gurdwara, literally the door of the Guru, because of the presence there of both the *sangat* and the

Granth. The change in the name given to the Sikh sacred space was an index of its increased sanctity in the eyes of the Sikhs. This transition had become conspicuous before the end of the nineteenth century. Not only the Akalis and the followers of Sant Jarnail Singh but also the Sikhs of all other descriptions look upon the Gurdwara as an indispensable institution. Its function is related to the sociocultural as well as the religious life of the local communities everywhere. For the Akalis and the followers of Sant Jarnail Singh, the Gurdwara is also the place for political discourse and action. This is not a mere empirical fact. It gets related to the doctrine of *miri-piri* according to which the spiritual and temporal concerns of the Sikh Panth are one indivisible whole. In this specific form the doctrine is attributed to Guru Hargobind in the early seventeenth century, though the idea can be traced to Guru Nanak who had renounced renunciation.

Given the sanctity and the importance of the Gurdwara, it is easy to appreciate the importance of the SGPC for the Akalis. As its name suggests, the Shiromani Gurdwara Prabandhak Committee was initially formed in 1920 for management of the Gurdwaras which were historic in the sense of their association with the Sikh Gurus and Sikh martyrs. But these Gurdwaras were indirectly controlled by colonial administrators and directly managed by approved individuals or committees who were not necessarily Singhs. The Sikh leaders who constituted the SGPC as a voluntary body did so on the assumption that the historic Gurdwaras belonged to the Panth as the successor of the Gurus. The idea of Guru-Panth had come into currency in the early eighteenth century to take the tangible form of *gurmatas* by the Sarbat Khalsa, generally adopted at the Akal Takht, and of united action by the Dal Khalsa under the command of a single leader. With the establishment of Sikh rule in the late eighteenth century, this doctrine became less popular and the doctrine of *Guru-Granth* came to occupy the foreground. After the loss of political power finally in 1849, the idea of Guru-Panth gradually began to be revived. The demand that the historic Gurdwaras should be controlled and managed by the true representatives of the Sikh Panth had begun to be aired much before we come upon the Gurdwara Reform movement of the 1920s. The epithet used for members of the *jathas* which were meant to take physical control of Gurdwaras to be placed under the management of the SGPC was 'Akali'. The Akalis and the SGPC in a sense were born together. The Sikh Gurdwaras Act of 1925 gave constitutional recognition to a Central Board which was given the name of Shiromani Gurdwara Prabandhak Committee by its members to identify it with the body founded in 1920. The Akalis became a political party after 1925. Between themselves, and each by itself, the Akalis and the SGPC, have represented the temporal and religious concerns of the Sikh Panth for over eight decades now. The erstwhile followers of Sant Jarnail Singh questioned the authority of the SGPC by holding meetings of the Sarbat Khalsa, invoking implicitly the doctrine of Guru-Panth. They failed because, among other things, this doctrine forms the basis of the SGPC as a statutory body. It embodies and contains the doctrine of Guru-Panth at one and the same time.

Both the Akalis and the Damdami Taksal maintain that the Sikh Panth was meant to be egalitarian. In other words, it was based on the idea of equality. Conversely, the degree of equality to be actually observed in the Sikh social order distinguishes the Sikhs from others and, thus, becomes a mark of their identity. In any case, equality among the Sikhs is most conspicuous in their Gurdwaras. No Sikh, male or female, is debarred from participation in the worship, from contributing to the sacred food or receiving it, and from serving and eating in the *langar*. Equality among males in public life is also quite striking. In social life, equality is more visible in terms of 'intercaste' relations than in terms of gender relations, more in terms of commensality than in connubium. The Sikh Panth is open for admission to all human beings, irrespective of their creed, nationality, or sex. The relatively egalitarian character of the Sikh Panth was far more striking in the past than it is in the contemporary context. The ideal of equality in the Sikh Panth presented a contrast to the idea of inequality built into the caste system and maintained in theory as well.

The scholars who have studied the subject of Sikh identity most seriously are agreed that it is legitimate to talk of a distinct Sikh identity in the twentieth century, particularly after the Gurdwara Reform movement. They are also agreed that the emergence of this identity was due to the work of the Singh

Sabha movement. However, there are politicians, journalists and publicists (perhaps some academic persons too) who still go on questioning this identity, particularly in relation to the Hindus. The debate about whether or not Sikhs were Hindu was actually over for the Sikhs before the First World War. The arguments generally used by those who wanted to prove that the Sikhs were Hindu can be summarized thus. To start with, Guru Nanak was a 'Hindu'. The social background of his followers and the followers of his successors was 'Hindu'. The Sikhs and Hindus intermarried and ate together. The Sikhs observed caste distinctions in matrimony and commensality, like the other Hindus. They believed in the Vedas, if not also in the other Hindu scriptures, in addition to their own *granths*. The *Dasam Granth* composed by Guru Gobind Singh contained long compositions in praise of the Goddess and the incarnations of Vishnu and Shiva, particularly the human incarnations of Vishnu, that is, Rama and Krishna. The *Adi Granth* was a popular version of Vedantic philosophy. The Khalsa, instituted by Guru Gobind Singh for protecting the Hindus, was a temporary measure. At any rate, the external appearance of the Khalsa did not mean and did not justify a separate identity. If all these arguments sound familiar, it is largely because they have often been repeated in the twentieth century and they are repeated even today in the same or in a modified form.

There is quite a general impression that the leaders of the Singh Sabha movement started insisting all of a sudden that the Sikhs were not Hindu. The book entitled *Ham Hindu Nahin* [We are not Hindus] is often referred to in this connection.[9] This impression is erroneous. Speaking historically, it would be more correct to say that some Hindus began to claim that Sikhs were 'Hindu'. *Sikh Hindu Hain* [The Sikhs are Hindu] was the title actually of two books which appeared in the context of this debate. A relevant question to ask, therefore, is why in the late nineteenth century for the first time some people started arguing that the Sikhs were 'Hindu'. What was meant by the term 'Hindu'? There was a time when the term Hindu referred vaguely to the people of this country. This, for instance, is the usage in Alberuni's *Kitab al-Hind*. With the coming of the Turks, the term Hindu tended to be used increasingly for 'Indians' who were not Muslim.

It was used in two other senses during the medieval period: first, for the socioreligious system represented and upheld by the Brahmans; and second, for the upper caste non-Muslims. These connotations were not suddenly discarded in the nineteenth century, but the religious connotation steadily gained greater currency. The presence of the Christian missionaries and the movements for socioreligious reform under colonial rule had much to do with this development. Even in the late nineteenth century several different meanings were attached to the term 'Hindu'. One question began to be posed rather sharply: whether or not Buddhists, Jains, Sikhs, Kabirpanthis and Vallabhacharyas, and also of course the 'untouchable' and 'tribal' groups and castes who literally lived on the physical/geographical fringes of settled Hindu society, were to be included among the Hindus.[10] Some of the Hindus and Sikhs of the Punjab, already before the end of the nineteenth century, had given their answer that the Sikhs were 'Hindus'.

Bhai Kahn Singh Nabha's *Ham Hindu Nahin*, which has turned out to be a classic statement of Sikh identity, was initially written in Hindi – indicating the audience for which it was primarily meant. He is quite explicit on the point that he wrote in response to the claims being made that Sikhs were Hindu. As a literary artifice though, he reproduces the arguments put forth by the 'Hindu' participant in the debate. This work has been analysed in some detail. Bhai Kahn Singh's arguments are quite comprehensive in scope, relating to scripture, religious doctrines, the mode of worship, the code of conduct, the rite of initiation, the rites of passage, the character of the Sikh Panth, and the consciousness of a separate identity. It is interesting to note that most of the time Bhai Kahn Singh invokes Sikh writings of the pre-colonial centuries in support of his arguments, covering a wide range and a strikingly large volume of Sikh literature. What is remarkable about his book is that, though his preference for the Khalsa or Singh identity is quite clear, he regards the *sahajdharis* (who did not take *pahul* and, therefore, did not necessarily keep their hair uncut or bear the epithet Singh) as an integral part of the Sikh Panth. The implication is extremely important. A distinct Sikh identity did not start with the Khalsa:

it had already emerged during the sixteenth and seventeenth centuries. Anyone who looks upon Sikh identity as a product of the colonial period has to contend with Bhai Kahn Singh Nabha, and with much more.

Harjot Oberoi is one among those who maintain that the distinct Sikh identity in which the *sahajdharis* were pushed out or pushed to the periphery and the *keshdharis* came to occupy the centre stage was created by the Singh Sabha movement. But even he concedes that the early eighteenth century Khalsa background was helpful to the Tat Khalsa. There are other scholars who look upon the Khalsa of Guru Gobind Singh as clearly distinct from other Indians. In fact there is a long historiographical tradition in which the Khalsa figure as a community distinct from both Hindus and Muslims. In the eighteenth century Sikh literature itself the Khalsa are presented as different from both Hindus and Muslims. They represent 'the third *panth*'. There is hardly any doubt that the Khalsa identity was the most dominant identity among the Sikhs of the early nineteenth century. The colonial rulers were quick to recognize this fact. The change introduced by the Singh Sabha leaders has to be understood in terms of differences of degree, coherence, magnitude and insistence on conformity. All this was made possible by the new means of communication, including education and the press.

The Khalsa identity was far more pronounced than the identity of the Sikhs in the earlier Sikh tradition. But in what sense were the Sikhs Hindus? If we apply the connotation of 'Hindu' as a non-Muslim Indian to the Sikhs of the sixteenth and seventeenth centuries, they were certainly Hindus. However, if we take the 'Hindus' to mean upper caste non-Muslim Indians, the Sikhs were not 'Hindus'. The Sikh Panth included not only Khatris, Brahmans and Rajputs but also Jats, Tarkhans, low caste labourers and outcastes. If we take 'Hindus' to represent the socio-religious systems upheld by the Brahmans, the Sikhs were not 'Hindu'. It is significant to note that the seventeenth-century *janamsakhis* look at the *panth* of Guru Nanak not only as a new *panth* but also as a *panth* which was distinct like the *panth* of the Vaishnavas, the *panth* of the *jogis*, and the *panth* of the Muslims. The Nanak-panthis had their distinctive places and modes of worship. Even their mode of salutation was distinctive. The consciousness of distinct identity is much more pronounced in the compositions of Bhai Gurdas who wrote mostly in the early seventeenth century. The Sikh consciousness of a distinct identity sprang from empirical realities: scripture, doctrines, institutions, sacred spaces and sacred places, their own sense of brotherhood, and the recognition by outsiders that they were different. In any case, not being different in every way from others in the seventeenth century did not mean that one was a Hindu in the religious sense of the term. The context in the *janamsakhis* in which Guru Nanak says that he is a 'Hindu' makes his meaning abundantly clear: he was not a Muslim. We have noticed already that the Sikhs could be regarded as Hindus in the sense that they were non-Muslim Indians. As such, they stood bracketed with millions of other Indians.

Interestingly, Bhai Kahn Singh Nabha has no objection to the Sikhs being called Hindu if the term meant simply Indian, without bringing in any religious dimension. The crucial question about the Hindu-Sikh debate is why at that particular juncture so much importance came to be attached to religious identity. A part of the answer is provided by Bhai Kahn Singh. He is keen to establish that the Sikhs were a distinct *qaum* (earlier, *panth*), like Hindus and Muslims. To recognize this was to recognize that the Sikhs were a political community, a nationality. This recognition should lead to their worldly progress. To be an appendage of another *qaum* was to remain at a perpetual disadvantage. To say this was not unpatriotic. The Sikhs were prepared to struggle for the common interests of all Indians, shoulder to shoulder with the other 'nations' like Hindus and Muslims. Overarching all of them was the Indian nation. In a sense, Bhai Kahn Singh subscribed to the idea of communitarian nationalism. In this he was not alone. By many others at the opening of the present century, and even later, 'the nation of Indians was visualized as a composite body, consisting of several communities, each with its own history and culture and its own special contribution to make to the common nationality. India, and the emerging Indian nation, was conceived as a collection of communities: Hindu + Muslim + Christian + Parsi + Sikhs, and so on.' The issue of religious identity was closely linked with politics. If it is a problem, it is at least a century old.

III

Turning to the Akalis and their politics, we find that they co-operated with the Congress to get the province partitioned in 1947. This freed them from what they called 'Muslim domination'. But in itself the partition did not solve their problems. They had to pursue their old concerns in the Indian Union. These were essentially three: adequate share in political power, promotion of Punjabi language in Gurmukhi script, and protection of their religious identity. All these concerns were actually three aspects of a single concern – the position of the Sikh Panth in free India.

The partition brought about an important demographic change in the East Punjab. The Hindus formed more than 60 per cent of the total population of the state and their leaders were anxious to retain this majority status. The Sikhs formed about 35 per cent of the total population, a much higher percentage than what they had in the British Punjab. Furthermore, they were concentrated in six districts in which their population was actually more than half: Amritsar, Gurdaspur, Jalandhar, Hoshiarpur, Ludhiana and Ferozepur. Then there were the princely states in which the Sikhs had a majority on the margin. This demographic change eventually came to have an important bearing on their politics. Used to weightage in the British Punjab, the Akali leaders thought of weightage first in free India as well. However, the idea of weight age to religious minorities was categorically discarded by the Constituent Assembly. The Akalis demanded proportionate representation on the basis of joint electorates, with the right to contest general unreserved seats. This too was rejected by the Constituent Assembly. The Akali members of the Assembly were so resentful that they refused to sign the Constitution to be adopted on 26 January 1950.

The Akali members of the Punjab Legislative Assembly joined the Congress party in March 1948 and three months later Giani Kartar Singh was included in the Cabinet in place of the Congress Sikh member Ishar Singh Majhail. Within a year Gopi Chand Bhargava was replaced by Bhim Sen Sachar as the Chief Minister of the Punjab. In consultation with Giani Kartar Singh, Sachar evolved in 1949 a language formula which is known as the Sachar Formula. A Punjabi zone was created under this scheme by adding the Ropar and Kharar *tahsils* of the Ambala district to the six Sikh majority districts. Punjabi was to be the medium of education at the primary level in all the schools of this zone. Hindi was to be introduced in the last year of primary education. In the Hindi zone, the position of Punjabi was to be reversed. The Akalis had some reservations about details but they welcomed the formula as a reasonable solution of the language problem. Unfortunately, this scheme was not acceptable to the Arya Samaj leaders of the Punjabi zone: they refused to implement it. In fact the reaction among the 'Hindu' leaders was so strong that Sachar lost his Chief Ministership and Bhargava was back in office by October 1949. The Akali members felt themselves to be ineffective in the new ministry. Before long, the Working Committee of the Akali Dal decided to revoke the merger of the Akalis with the Congress on the grounds that the Congress leaders had belied all their hopes of constructive sympathy and support.

In 1952 the Akalis fought the elections on a new issue: the Punjabi-speaking state. The idea of reorganization on the basis of language was not new. It had been an important item on the agenda of the Congress. After 1947, however, the Congress leaders were no longer enthusiastic about it. In 1948 the Dar Commission recommended that no linguistic state be created without the consent of a substantial minority included in its area. Its report was accepted by a committee consisting of Nehru, Patel and Sitarammaya who made a recommendation of their own that in north India no provincial boundaries should be changed irrespective of the merit of any such proposal. In the British Punjab, reorganization had been suggested from time to time to accommodate the interests of religious communities. But languages and scripts too had come to be associated with them: Urdu and Persian script with Muslims, Hindi and Devanagari script with Hindus, and Punjabi and Gurmukhi script with Sikhs. Therefore, the question of language appeared to carry political implications as well. In 1950 Hukam Singh tried to clarify that the demand for a Punjabi-speaking state was democratic and secular. The Working Committee of the Akali Dal passed a resolution in favour of a state on the basis of Punjabi language and culture. Some of the Hindu leaders of the Punjab reacted to the demand by telling their followers to return Hindi as their mother tongue for the Census of 1951. They had canvassed for Hindi before 1947 also, but now their idea was to thwart the formation of a Punjabi-speaking state by demonstrating that there was a substantial Hindi-speaking minority in the proposed Punjabi-speaking state. The movement for a Punjabi-speaking state continued for more than a decade and a large number of Punjabi-speaking Hindus returned Hindi as their mother tongue in the Census of 1961 as well.

With their defeat in the elections of 1952, the Akali aspiration to be 'free and equal partners in the destiny of the country' became stronger. Before the year ended, Potti Sriramula died during a fast for the creation of Andhra Pradesh, and the Prime Minister announced the separation of Andhra from Madras as a Telugu-speaking state. As the movement for linguistic states gained momentum, the formation of States Reorganization Commission was announced before the end of 1953. The Akali leaders prepared their case on the basis of pre-1947 data. According to them there was an area of 90,000 sq km in which nearly 12 million persons spoke Punjabi. The Sikhs formed much less than a half of the total population of this area. Nevertheless, the proposal was countered by the protagonists of Maha Punjab who advocated the merger of Himachal Pradesh and a few districts of Uttar Pradesh as well as Patiala and East Punjab States Union (PEPSU) with the East Punjab. Without going into any detail of either the mounting tension between the two parties or the arguments which they used, we may note that the Commission came to the conclusion that the majority of the people were opposed to the creation of a Punjabi-speaking state, and recommended the merger of Himachal Pradesh as well as PEPSU with the East Punjab. The Akalis rejected the Commission's report on the day following its release on 9 October 1955.

Hukam Singh evolved a formula which met the essential demands of the Akalis without the creation of a Punjabi-speaking state. This came to be known as the Regional Formula. PEPSU alone was to be merged with the East Punjab, and the whole area was to be divided into two 'regions'. One of these was to be the Punjabi region in which the medium of school education was to be Punjabi. The other region was to give the same status to

Hindi. Both the regions were to have regional committees for legislation on fourteen important subjects. The Regional Formula came closest to accommodating the political and cultural interests of the Akalis who accepted the scheme. The Working Committee of the Akali Dal also decided to have no political programme of its own and to concentrate on the religious, educational, cultural, social and economic interests of the Sikh Panth.

The reorganized Punjab state was inaugurated on 1 November 1956 when Partap Singh Kairon was the Chief Minister. The Akali legislators joined the Congress party. The Hindi Raksha Samiti agitated against the scheme and Kairon remained reluctant to allow the regional committees to legislate. In fact he tried to keep the former Akali leaders out of the Legislative Assembly and to dislodge the Akalis from the SGPC. Given Kairon's attitude and outlook the Regional Formula had little chance of success. Within a few years, the Akalis felt obliged to revive the movement for a Punjabi-speaking state.

The agitation launched by Master Tara Singh in 1960 proved to be a failure. By 1962 his place was taken by Sant Fateh Singh who presented the demand as clearly a linguistic demand. Both the leaders demonstrated their patriotism during India's war with China. During the war with Pakistan in 1965 Sant Fateh Singh was all out to support the government. Nehru had died in 1964 and Kairon had been assassinated early in 1965. There were new actors on the scene. After the ceasefire in September 1965 the Union Home Minister announced that the issue of the Punjabi-speaking state would be examined all afresh. Lal Bahadur Shastri appointed a Parliamentary Committee under the Chairmanship of Hukam Singh, who was now the Speaker of the Lok Sabha. To advise the Parliamentary Committee, a Cabinet Sub-Committee was also constituted. It consisted of Indira Gandhi, Y.B. Chavan and Mahavir Tyagi. Indira Gandhi became the Prime Minister in January 1966 after the death of Lal Bahadur Shastri. The Punjabi-speaking state was inaugurated on 1 November 1966.

However, the Akali agitation did not end with the reorganization of the Punjab in 1966. Sant Fateh Singh went on fast unto death within seven weeks of the inauguration of the new state. It is important to know why. Contrary to the general impression, the new state was not created in accordance with the recommendations of the Parliamentary Committee constituted by Lal Bahadur Shastri. Indira Gandhi was unhappy with this committee, especially because of the views of its Chairman. In her *My Truth* she makes it abundantly clear why she was not in favour of creating a Punjabi-speaking state: she did not wish to deviate from a well considered policy of the Congress, and she did not wish to let down the 'Hindu supporters' of the Congress in the Punjab. Both these concerns arose from electoral considerations. She did not wait for the recommendations of the Parliamentary Committee. A resolution of the Congress in March 1966 accepted the principle of reorganization of the Punjab. A commission was appointed, known as the Shah Commission. The terms of reference given to the Commission stipulated that the Census of 1961 was to be used for data on language, with the *tahsil* as the basic unit. Consequently, genuinely Punjabi-speaking villages and Chandigarh were left out of the Punjab. Furthermore, the Union Government took over the power and irrigation projects and became the arbiter of river waters in case the two new states failed to come to an agreement. Sant Fateh Singh protested against all these decisions even before the new state was inaugurated. In December 1966 he went on fast on the issue of Chandigarh. The issue is still unresolved, like the issues of river waters and the Punjabi-speaking territories.

To these issues was added another: the relations of the state with the Centre. The idea of autonomy had begun to be aired before the reorganization of the Punjab in 1966. In May 1965 'Justice' Gurnam Singh, leader of the opposition in the Punjab Assembly, moved a resolution at a conference in Ludhiana in favour of a self-determined status for Sikhs within the Indian Union. It was interpreted by the language press in the Punjab as a demand for a sovereign Sikh state. In July 1965 Master Tara Singh, who was no longer influential, gave an elaborate argument in support of the idea of 'a Sikh Homeland', an autonomous state within the Indian Union. Opposing the Punjab Reorganization Bill in the Parliament, Kapur Singh referred to Nehru's statement of July 1946: 'I see no wrong in an area and a setup in the North wherein the Sikhs can also experience a glow of freedom'. Kapur Singh argued in favour of a Sikh Homeland with a special internal constitution and a special relationship with the Centre irrespective of the number of Sikhs in this Homeland. Furthermore, the experience of the Akalis as the ruling party in the new Punjab between March 1967 and June 1971 convinced them that they could not exercise power adequately, or for long, under the constitution which placed the states at a great political and economic disadvantage in relation to the ruling party at the Centre. Within three years the Punjab was twice placed under the President's rule, a euphemism for the rule of the ruling party. The Akalis lost the elections in 1972. A year later came the Anandpur Sahib Resolution. Its basic thrust was on a genuinely federal system with only defence, foreign affairs, communications, and currency as the prerogatives of the Centre. Couched partly in the language of the supporters of a Sikh Homeland, it was interpreted by the opponents of the Akalis as 'secessionist'. The Akalis returned to power in 1977 and in a crowded conference held at Ludhiana in 1978, they reiterated their stand without any ambiguity in favour of a truly federal system.

The most important issues for the Akalis had, thus, emerged on the reorganization of the Punjab in 1966 and before their return to power in 1977: Chandigarh and other Punjabi-speaking territories, Centre-State relations, and river waters. On two of these, Indira Gandhi had already taken decisions. On the issue of Chandigarh Sant Fateh Singh had announced his decision to go on fast on 26 January 1970 and to immolate himself on 1 February if Chandigarh was not given to the Punjab. Indira Gandhi awarded Chandigarh to the Punjab. The award was meant to be implemented five years later, in 1975. At the same time she awarded part of Fazilka *tahsil* to Haryana with a corridor on the Punjab border with Rajasthan to link the awarded territory with the state of Haryana.

Indira Gandhi's decision on river waters came in 1976, after the Akalis had put up what was probably the strongest opposition in the country to the Emergency imposed by her in 1975. The non-riparian Rajasthan was given 8.00 maf of water. Of the remaining 7.20 maf, she gave 0.20 to Delhi and divided the rest in two equal shares for Haryana and the Punjab. Thus, the Punjab was to get 3.5 maf of water, which was less than what the state was actually using. The Akalis took up this matter with Morarji Desai as the Prime Minister. He could tell the Rajasthani leaders that their state was not a part of the Indus basin but he was not prepared to change the award. However, he had no objection to the Punjab going to the Supreme Court for adjudication. The matter was lying with the Supreme Court when the Akalis lost the elections in 1980.

In July 1981 Sant Harchand Singh Longowal, who had conducted successful agitation against the Emergency as the President of the Akali Dal, presided over a World Sikh Conference which directed the Akali Dal to plan *dharmyudh* for pursuing the Anandpur Sahib Resolution. An agitation was launched in September and memoranda of demands were sent to Indira Gandhi. She met the Akali leaders on 16 October 1981 primarily to identify issues which could then be taken up by the Foreign Minister P.V. Narasimha Rao. A meeting with him later appeared to be 'a waste of time' to the Akali leaders. They met the Prime Minister again on 26 November. The suit of the Punjab regarding the river waters was pending in the Supreme Court. Indira Gandhi was not in favour of revising her earlier decision but she gave assurances of much larger supplies of water and energy to the Punjab in the future on the basis of more scientific exploitation of resources. Within five weeks, however, she gave a unilateral decision, adding 0.72 maf of water to the Punjab's share from an estimated surplus of 1.32 maf. Significantly, she gave 0.60 maf out of this surplus to Rajasthan, making it clear to the Akalis that their talk of Rajasthan not being a riparian state had no meaning. What is more, all the three Chief Ministers concerned accepted this decision, and the Chief Minister of the Punjab was obliged to withdraw its case from the Supreme Court. It was also decided to complete the Sutlej-Yamuna Link (SYL) canal for Haryana in two years. On their third and last meeting with the Prime Minister on 5 April 1982 the Akali leaders got the impression that she had already made up her mind to let the issues wait. But they were wrong. She was keen on the construction of the SYL canal.

The *nahar roko* (stop the canal) *morcha* of the Akalis against the construction of the SYL canal failed to evoke much response. Another call a month later failed to mobilize the peasantry. The Akalis decided at last to launch a *dharmyudh morcha* on 4 August to get all their demands accepted. Soon afterwards, Sant Jarnail Singh was allowed to join the *dharmyudh morcha*. The *morcha* picked up. It became increasingly difficult for the government to find room for the agitating volunteers in the existing jails. By the middle of October Indira Gandhi had decided to release the Akali volunteers on the Diwali day. Swaran Singh hammered out a mutually acceptable formula on the important issues of Chandigarh, river waters and the Centre-State relations. A Cabinet Sub-Committee consisting of Pranab Mukherjee, R. Venkataraman, P.V. Narasimha Rao and P.C. Sethi accepted the formula and Swaran Singh told the Akali leaders that the government had approved of it. But the statement placed before the Parliament turned out to be materially different from what had been agreed upon. The Prime Minister had changed her mind. The Akalis decided to hold a demonstration in Delhi at the time of the Asiad. Amrinder Singh negotiated another mutually acceptable agreement. But this was sabotaged by Bhajan Lal, Chief Minister of Haryana, with the assurance that he would not let the Akalis pass through his state. He proved to be truer than his word. No Sikh was allowed to pass through Haryana without being humiliated.

Not to have gained anything through negotiations was a setback for the Akalis, and it appeared to justify the idea of militancy propagated by Sant Jarnail Singh. In any case, his popularity increased in 1982-3. And so did militancy. He appeared to be running a parallel government. The Akalis pursued their *morcha* against all odds as a political necessity. Sant Longowal asked the Akali legislators to resign their seats with effect from 21 February 1983. He also gave a call to ex-servicemen for a meeting at Amritsar. Nearly 5,000 responded. In April 1983 the Akalis organized their *rasta roko* (block the roads) campaign. Twenty-six persons were killed in the violence that erupted in spite of their peaceful intention. In June, they organized their *rail roko* (stop the trains) campaign and the government decided not to run any trains. Yet there was some violence. The *kam roko* (stop work) campaign of August 1983 proved to be a great success. And so was the *bandh* they organized in February 1984 to demonstrate their strength and their trust in non-violent agitation. Within a week, a meeting of five Akali leaders, five cabinet ministers, five secretaries and fifteen leaders of the opposition parties was held at Delhi. The meeting came close to a successful settlement but anti-Sikh violence was orchestrated in Haryana, and the Akali leaders returned to the Punjab. Before the end of the month, the Akalis burnt the pages of the Constitution containing Article 25(2)(b) at Delhi and Chandigarh. They were arrested, but the government also announced its willingness to amend the Article. Early in March, Indira Gandhi appointed the Sarkaria Commission to go into Centre-State relations but her decision being unilateral the Akalis did not withdraw the *morcha*. They were prepared to work out a reasonable settlement in the last week of May but nothing short of the demands of the Anandpur Sahib Resolution was acceptable to Sant Jarnail Singh who had moved into the Akal Takht in December 1983.

At the time of the Operation Blue Star, Lt-General Sunderji was told by the government that there were two groups in the Golden Temple complex, one that of Sant Jarnail Singh and the other that of Sant Longowal. He was also instructed to ensure that there was no fighting between the two groups. The 'extremists' were to be flushed out without any damage to the Golden Temple and the least possible damage to the Akal Takht. These instructions indicate that Sant Longowal and his followers were not to be treated as 'extremists'. Some writers have wondered why they 'surrendered', or why they did not resist. Quite simply, they were neither rebels nor up in arms against the state. The government knew this better than anyone else. The Akali leaders were arrested and detained. When they were released, they strongly condemned the action of the government. Nevertheless, Sant Longowal signed an accord with the Prime Minister, picking up the old threads of Chandigarh, river waters and Centre-State relations, and adding some new issues. But he was assassinated before the elections were held. The Akalis fought the elections, won, and formed the government. The Accord failed and so did the Akalis in containing militancy. They did not contest the general elections of 1992 but they fought by-elections with considerable success against all sorts of disadvantages. In the Parliamentary elections of May 1996 they won eight out of thirteen seats, under the leadership of Parkash Singh Badal. Advocacy of militancy, or independence, on the part of an Akali leader was looked upon as deviation and not as the norm. The political objective of the Akalis has been greater autonomy for the Punjab, and for other states. Their approach has been either constitutional or agitational, but not militant. They are quite distinct from the militants who stood for secession. They won the general elections of 1997. Ironically, however, they did not talk about any of the major issues raised before 1984.

Nevertheless, there has been a general tendency to look upon the Akalis as secessionist. This may be due partly to sheer ignorance and partly to deliberate intention to malign them as political opponents. This may also be due to the distant background of the 1940s when the Akalis, conditionally or unconditionally, put forward the idea of a Sikh state. The concentration of the majority of the Sikhs in a contiguous area lends much greater plausibility to the aspiration of sovereignty. Their compromising gestures towards militants in the recent past may be yet another reason for bracketing them with the secessionists. Many of the Akali leaders had shown willingness or even keenness to participate in the mortuary rites (*bhogs*) of some known or alleged militants. More important perhaps were their dealings with Sant Jarnail Singh. One of the Akali demands, for instance, was his release in 1981. In 1982 he was allowed to merge his *morcha* with the Akali *dharmyudh*. No one could stop him from staying in one of the 'hostels' of the SGPC, where the government also could reach him if it wanted to, but towards the end of 1983 he was allowed to stay in the Akal Takht, which could not be done without the tacit consent of the SGPC. But this tacit consent sprang from helplessness more than anything else. Sant Jarnail Singh on his part did not care much for Sant Longowal who had demonstrated his opposition to the methods of Sant Bhindranwale even before he moved into the Akal Takht. In 1984 there was an open hostility between them.

Why the Akalis did not always keep a politically respectable distance from Sant Jarnail Singh is a relevant question. According to Mark Tully and Satish Jacob, Giani Zail Singh enabled Sanjay Gandhi to discover the Sant for breaking the Akali Dal after its electoral success in 1977. They also looked for a cause which could be both religious and political. For this they identified the Nirankaris. The Dal Khalsa, floated by them some time later, was also anti-Nirankari. After the death of twelve Sikhs at the hands of the Nirankaris on the Baisakhi day of 1978 at Amritsar, anti-Nirankari agitations were encouraged not by the Akalis but by the Congress party. The Dal Khalsa as well as Sant Jarnail Singh contested elections for the SGPC in 1979 against the Akali candidates. In 1980 Sant Jarnail Singh campaigned for Congress candidates, including R.L. Bhatia. He is believed to have shared a platform with Indira Gandhi. In any case, she admitted that he had supported a Congress candidate. After the murder of Baba Gurbachan Singh, the Nirankari Guru, in April 1980, Giani Zail Singh told the Parliament that Sant Jarnail Singh had nothing to do with the murder. After the murder of Lala Jagat Narain in September 1981, the Chief Minister of the Punjab wanted to get Sant Jarnail Singh arrested as a suspect. He was in a Haryana village at that time. Giani Zail Singh rang up Bhajan Lal to tell him not to let the Sant be arrested. When the Punjab government did arrest him in October, Giani Zail Singh told the Parliament that there was no evidence of his involvement in the murder. He was released. 'The government has done more for me in one week,' remarked Bhindranwale, 'than I could have achieved in years.' After the murder of Santokh Singh at Delhi in December 1981, his memorial service was attended by Sant Jarnail Singh as well as Giani Zail Singh and Rajiv Gandhi. The Akalis may not have known all this, but they knew that Sant Jarnail Singh was being supported and protected by the Congress to undermine the Akalis. They, in turn, were tempted to use the Sant against the Congress if and when they could.

When the Akali leaders met Indira Gandhi in October 1981 for the first time, they told her that Sant Jarnail Singh was being backed by the Congress. If some of the Akali leaders maintained their contact with him till the end, so did some of the Congress leaders. The Sant had fallen out with the Congress by the end of 1981 but the Congress did not fall out with him. Indira Gandhi continued to consult Giani Zail Singh when he became the President of India. It was possibly due to his influence that Sant Jarnail Singh was not arrested after the murder of a DIG in April 1983 in the precincts of the Golden Temple. When the government of Darbara Singh was suspended and the President's rule was imposed in the Punjab due to the cold-blooded murder of some Hindu passengers in the first week of October 1983, a senior colleague of Darbara Singh claimed that President Zail Singh was in daily contact with the Sant. The implication was that Darbara Singh's downfall had been brought about through the Sant's instrumentality. Indira Gandhi maintained contact with Sant Jarnail Singh through R.L. Bhatia who remained in regular contact with Bhai Amrik Singh till April 1984. Even if the idea of the President and the Prime Minister of India was to use Sant Jarnail Singh for their purposes, the knowledge of his connection with them added much to his prestige and influence. The Akalis had to contend with him, his prestige, and his influence.

IV

The term Khalistan was used by a medical doctor, V.S. Bhatti of Ludhiana, as the title of a pamphlet in 1940, published soon after the Lahore Resolution of the All India Muslim League, popularly known as the 'Pakistan Resolution'.[11] Dr Bhatti's Khalistan was meant to be a counterblast to the idea of Pakistan assumed to be embodied in the Lahore Resolution. Covering much of the area between the Chenab and the Jamuna, the Khalistan of Dr Bhatti was meant to serve as a buffer state between India and Pakistan. With the Maharaja of Patiala as its head, Khalistan was to be a 'theocratic' state, consisting of several federating units. A corridor was to link it with the Arabian Sea. Master Tara Singh, who was President of the Shiromani Akali Dal at this time, denounced the pamphlet for making the confusion already created by the Muslim League more confounding. Two conferences were organized by Baba Gurdit Singh of Komagata Maru, a known supporter of the Indian National Congress, to popularize the idea of Khalistan. However, Maulana Abul Kalam Azad expressed his disapproval of Khalistan by stating that some Akalis were using the Congress platform to propagate the idea of Sikh Raj for scuttling the idea of Pakistan.

The term 'Khalistan' was never appropriated by the Akalis. However, in their opposition to the idea of Pakistan in the 1940s, they did come out with counterproposals. With the prospect of freedom coming closer, their concern for the future became greater. In March-April 1942 Stafford Cripps conceded in principle that it was not obligatory for a province to join the Indian federation. This concession appeared to carry the implication that the Punjab could become an autonomous political unit outside the Indian state. The Akali leaders did not like to be subordinated permanently to Muslim majority. The Sikh All-Parties Committee submitted to Cripps the proposal of a province with different boundaries and different proportions of the three major communities of the Punjab. The name given to the province of their conception was 'Azad Punjab'. This gave the impression as if it was meant to be an independent state. Keen to sell the idea to Hindus and Sikhs, the Akali leaders explained subsequently that this province was meant to be a part of the Indian federation.[12] The term *azad* was meant to suggest that each community of this province would be free of the fear of domination by another community. The Muslims and Hindus of this province would account for the bulk of its population: 40 per cent each. The Sikhs would form the remaining 20 per cent. Rooted in a genuine fear of creation of Pakistan, which would place the Sikhs under the domination of a hostile community for ever, the Azad Punjab scheme was essentially a defensive strategy adopted in response to the recognition of the idea of Pakistan by the British Government through the Cripps proposals and by the Congress through its resolution of 2 April 1942. In their opposition to the idea of Pakistan, the Sikh leaders did not hesitate to share platforms with the leaders of the Hindu Mahasabha who stood for India as a single political unit. Unlike Khalistan, the Azad Punjab was to be a part of India; it was also to have a democratic constitution. All that the Sikhs could hope to gain was possibly an effective collaborative role in the affairs of the Azad Punjab.

The Azad Punjab remained on the political agenda of the Akali leaders for about two years. After the 'C.R. Formula', and the Gandhi-Jinnah talks on its basis, the Azad Punjab scheme was theoretically modified in two ways. Its name was dropped to bring in the idea of a Sikh state; and this state was meant to be sovereign. However, in terms of the religious composition of the people in this state there was no change. Furthermore, its creation was conditional upon the creation of Pakistan. During the second half of 1944 the idea of this conditional sovereign Sikh state was advocated not only by the Akalis but also by many other Sikh leaders. This viewpoint was spelt out in a memorandum submitted to the Sapru Reconciliation Committee early in 1945 by Sikh leaders who represented nearly the entire community. The memorandum underlined the fact that, accounting for four million persons in British India, the Sikhs were numerically next only to Hindus and Muslims. But their political, economic and historical importance was much greater than their numbers suggested. Their contribution to the defence and economy of the country was unique. The Punjab was their 'holy' land as well as their homeland. Nonetheless, the constitutional reforms of 1935 had reduced them to 'a state of political subjugation'. The Hindus as well as Muslims had disowned their mother tongue in favour of Hindi and Urdu. Discrimination against the Sikhs was exercised even in matters of religion. The Sikhs were opposed to 'any partition of India on a communal basis'. However, if the Pakistan scheme was accepted they would 'insist on the creation of separate Sikh State'. The basic demand of the memorandum was a strong, united India, and weightage for the Sikhs in a reorganized Punjab.

The Sikh leaders in general and the Akali leaders in particular tried to promote their idea of a Sikh state in 1945. At the time of the Simla Conference in June-July, Master Tara Singh met Lord Wavell and emphasized that the Sikhs were strongly opposed to the creation of Pakistan. At the same time he expressed the view that if Pakistan was to be created then Jinnah should agree to the creation of a separate state for the Sikhs. The Akalis fought the elections of 1945-6 in cooperation with but independently of the Congress. Opposition to Pakistan, and not a Sikh state, was the foremost item on their agenda. The landslide in favour of the Muslim League more than neutralized their own unprecedented success in the elections. From a mere possibility, Pakistan advanced now to the stage of probability. Two days before the arrival of the Cabinet Mission in March 1946, the Shiromani Akali Dal passed a resolution in favour of 'the creation of a Sikh State'. When Master Tara Singh met the Cabinet Mission he underlined the fact that the Sikhs were opposed to any division of India, but if a division was decided upon, a separate state should be created for the Sikhs with the right to federate with Hindustan or Pakistan. Giani Kartar Singh was more categorical and asked for a separate Sikh state irrespective of whether or not Pakistan was created. The pleas and arguments of the Sikh leaders however cut no ice with the Cabinet Mission. Its recommendations went not only in favour of the idea of Pakistan but also against any reorganization of the Punjab. The idea of a Sikh state was thus wholly set aside. In theory, the Akalis had the option to seek concessions from Jinnah as the condition of their consent to opt for Pakistan. In practice, they favoured the idea of getting the Punjab divided with the support of the Congress. During the last year of colonial rule, the Akalis worked in close cooperation with the Congress, and no Sikh leader talked of a Sikh state.

Understandably, the most elaborate argument in support of a sovereign Sikh state was published before the recommendations of the Cabinet Mission were made public. In April 1946, Gurbachan Singh of Sikh National College, Lahore, and Lal Singh Gyani of Sikh Missionary College, Amritsar, published *The Idea of the Sikh State* on the premise that the Congress would not resist the demand for Pakistan and India would be divided in the near future into Hindustan and Pakistan as two independent countries. Freedom for Hindus and Muslims would mean 'slavery' for the Sikhs who too constituted a 'nation'.[13] As a nation, the Sikhs had the right to 'self-determination', admitted to be the 'right of nations all over the world'. As stated in the then recent resolution of the Shiromani Akali Dal, no constitutional safeguards and weightage were adequate for ensuring the growth of the Sikhs as 'a nationality with a distinct religious, ideological, cultural and political character'. An autonomous Sikh state, therefore, was 'the unconditional, absolute and minimum demand and political objective of the Sikh Panth as a whole'. This proposed state was to be 'democratic in constitution': it was to have 'a socialistic economic structure'; and it was to give 'full protection' to the minorities.

Gurbachan Singh and Lal Singh go into the background of the demand for an autonomous Sikh state. Its origins could be traced to the 'historical traditions' of the Sikhs, their 'inner urges' and their 'political ideals'. So long as there was no discussion of 'any political future' there was no occasion for giving expression to the concerns of the Sikh Panth. With the Simon Commission, however, the situation began to change. The Muslims of the Punjab began to clamour for a permanent majority in the province and the Sikhs responded by suggesting to Mahatma Gandhi in 1930 that a new province should be carved out of the existing

Punjab. In 1931 they made the same suggestion to the Viceroys, Lord Irwin and Lord Willingdon. This demand was presented at the Second Round Table Conference by Sampuran Singh and Ujjal Singh.

However, the Sikh demands went unheeded, and the Communal Award was given. The Provincial Autonomy established on its basis caused terrible hardships to the Sikhs. Their religious rights were sought to be thwarted and their 'national' language, Punjabi, was sought to be suppressed. In 1940 came the Pakistan Resolution of the All India Muslim League. The Indian National Congress sought to appease the Muslims at the cost of the Sikhs. This disillusioned the Sikhs: 'in this situation emerged a further step in the old Sikh demand for splitting up the Punjab, called the Azad Punjab Scheme'. Its purpose was to ensure that the Sikhs held 'the balance of power' in the new province. They were canvassing support for this idea when 'Gandhi-Raja Formula' was floated. Its acceptance would have divided the Sikhs into two parts in two different states. Therefore, the Sikhs asked for a separate Sikh state. This was the only way in which they could survive 'in the midst of aggressive communalism'.

In the present-day world of total organization and mobilization of peoples no 'minority' could survive without 'political strength'. The aggressive communalism of Muslim and Hindu majorities presented a grave threat to the Sikhs and their identity. They needed a state in which they were free from aggression and in which they could make laws for themselves. 'The Sikhs do not seek to dominate anyone. They want to establish a secular democratic state, *in which the bulk of the Sikh population may be concentrated*. The economic basis of life in such a state is bound to be socialistic, in accordance with the traditions of the Sikh society, and the inner urge of the hardy, self-respecting Sikh peasantry.'

Sikh nationhood was essentially the product of Sikh history. Organized as 'the Khalsa', the Sikhs acted as a distinct and separate nation in the days of the *misls* and Ranjit Singh (late eighteenth and early nineteenth century). They established a theocratic political organization first, and then a monarchical system. They were now organizing their national life on the democratic principle. The Gurdwara Reform movement was a decisive landmark in the revival of the Khalsa. They began to run 'a kind of parallel Government' in the form of the SGPC which 'issued commands and ordinances, organized *jathas*, fought the bureaucracy and through its actions galvanized the entire Sikh people with a powerful feeling of their aroused nationhood'. With the emergence of the concept of the 'Indian Nation', Hindus, Muslims and Sikhs came to be treated as 'communities', with the result that these 'nations' were sought to be subordinated to the Indian Nation. The Sikhs had come out of this illusion 'fostered by the lust for domination by Hindu majority'. Having formed a true conception of their status, they demanded 'a National State for themselves'. No Sikh entertained any doubt about his nationality as being different from that of the Hindus. The latent nationhood of the Sikhs had reasserted itself.

Gurbachan Singh and Lal Singh give a whole chapter to the views of a number of political thinkers and leaders to prove their point that the Khalsa constituted a distinct 'nation'. They go on to argue that modern 'political theory has recognized in practice the principle of providing national states to the various nationalities'. More than forty new nation-states had emerged in Europe. The Jews had been promised a national home in Palestine, 'their sacred land'. The Sikhs were demanding nothing more than establishing themselves as 'a governing group, along with other groups in a democratic system'. The areas asked for the Sikh state were the areas covered by the Sikh homeland, 'a broad compact area of which the Central Punjab is the nucleus'. More specifically, this 'Sikh Zone' covered the Lahore and Jullundur Divisions, parts of the Ambala and Multan Divisions, the Sikh princely states and the state of Malerkotla, and certain hill areas in the north and north-east. 'It is in this land, which by virtue of proprietorship, development, historic-associations and religious sanctity already belongs to the Sikhs, where the Sikhs wish to find a safe home, free from interference'. More than 80 per cent of the Sikhs lived in this zone and owned more than a quarter of its land.

Gurbachan Singh and Lal Singh do not mention the percentage of Sikhs in the total population. Nevertheless, they refer to 'minorities' within the Sikh state to whom a free, prosperous, happy and contented life is promised. But if the Sikhs were to be politically dominant in the Sikh state, it could not have a democratic constitution, because the Sikhs could not form a majority in the area of the Sikh state. Or, was it simply assumed that there would be no absolute 'majority' in the Sikh state? If so, the Sikh state differed from the Azad Punjab only in being sovereign. In no sense could it be called 'a Sikh State'.

For a quarter of a century after the publication of *The Idea of the Sikh State*, there was no talk of Sikh state or Khalistan among the Sikh leaders. In October 1971, the idea of Khalistan was advertised by Jagjit Singh Chauhan in the *New York Times*. Four years earlier he had enjoyed a short spell of power as a minister in the Cabinet of Lachhman Singh Gill who remained Chief Minister of the Punjab for nine months in 1967-8. Living now in England, Chauhan had no following in the Punjab. Whenever he visited India he was treated well by some eminent leaders of the Congress. His idea of Khalistan was treated as a joke but it could embarrass the Akalis and tickle their opponents in politics. About a decade later, in June 1980, Balbir Singh Sandhu announced the formation of Khalistan, claiming himself to be the Secretary of the National Council of Khalistan with Jagjit Singh Chauhan as its President. But this organization existed only on paper. In March 1981, a US citizen, Ganga Singh Dhillon, who was known to Chauhan, addressed the annual session of the Sikh Education Conference organized by the Chief Khalsa Diwan, and put forth the view that the Sikhs formed a 'nation'. The implication was that any demand for independence could be justified on that basis. Soon afterwards, however, the Chief Khalsa Diwan dissociated itself from Dhillon's statement and reiterated its complete loyalty to the Indian State.

Besides the National Council of Khalistan, the White Paper on the Punjab published by the Government of India mentions another significant group which operated from overseas, the Dal Khalsa. It had been formed at Chandigarh in April 1978. Its President was a stenographer of the Panjab University who had published a pamphlet on Khalistan. The term 'Dal Khalsa' served as a reminder of the 'national army' of the Sikhs which had succeeded in establishing a sovereign Sikh rule during the late eighteenth century. The Dal was opposed to the Sant Nirankaris. In 1979 it contested elections for the SGPC, but without any success. In 1982 the responsibility for throwing the head of a cow in a Hindu temple was reported to have been claimed by the Dal Khalsa. The Dal was generally associated with Sant Jarnail Singh but he never acknowledged that it had anything to do with him. Indeed, the founding of the Dal Khalsa is attributed to Giani Zail Singh who paid the bill for its first meeting at the Aroma Hotel at Chandigarh and who used to ask journalists to give prominence to its activities. From the viewpoint of a movement for Khalistan, the activities of the Dal in the Punjab were hardly of any account.

The Khalistan movement has been associated with Sant Jarnail Singh more than with anyone else. What has been published on his life and of his speeches enables us to notice some of the relevant aspects of his activities and attitudes. He was initially a protagonist of religious reform. At the age of thirty, he assumed the headship of the Damdami Taksal in 1977 on the death of his predecessor, Sant Kartar Singh Bhindranwale. An open conflict with the Sant Nirankaris, who were looked upon as heretical by Sant Kartar Singh, was a legacy inherited by Sant Jarnail Singh. What happened on the Baisakhi day of 1978 at Amritsar was an extension of this legacy, underlining the religious dimension of Sant Jarnail Singh's outlook and attitude. Till his death in June 1984 he continued to declare that religion was his sole concern. For him, the *Adi Granth* was the only sacred scripture of the Sikhs; Guruship was vested in this *Granth*, giving it the status of *Guru Granth Sahib*. The Khalsa code of conduct provided the only valid mode of life for the Sikhs. He believed in fact that the antidote to external and internal threats to Sikhism was strict conformity to the Khalsa way of life. Insistence on the maintenance of the external form and hostility to drugs and alcohol appear to flow from his religious outlook. That this concern distinguished him in his own eyes from the other Sikh leaders comes out clearly in a statement he made in 1984 that he was responsible only to the cause of Sikhism, to uphold the symbols of the faith, to see that the beards of the Sikhs remained intact, their hair uncut, and that they did not go after the evil things in life, like alcohol and drugs.

However, there was another dimension of his religious outlook. To bear arms was a religious duty of the Sikhs. The choice of arms was not confined to the sword (*kirpan*) as one of the five obligatory Ks. The choice was extended to modern weapons, which also carried the implication that they were meant to be actually used. The use of physical force was for him a legitimate part of religion. The encouragement and the form which he gave to violence has to be seen in this context. If anything, his insistence on the use of arms went on increasing. Quite explicitly he told his audience from the roof of Guru Ram Das Langar when he was virtually confined to the Golden Temple complex:

> For every village you should keep one motorcycle, three baptized Sikhs and three revolvers. These are not meant for killing innocent people. For a Sikh to have arms and kill an innocent person is a serious sin. But, Khalsaji, to have arms and not to get your legitimate rights is even a bigger sin. It is for you to decide how to use these arms. If you want to remove the shackles of your slavery you must have a plan.

In other words, you had to be up in arms against the enemies of the faith. In his mind, hostility towards the government easily got transferred to 'Hindus': 'If you do not have the five 'ks', if you are not armed with a rifle and a spear, you will be given the beating of your lives by the Hindus.' The reference here is to the killing of Sikhs but even otherwise Sant Jarnail Singh could bracket 'Hindus' with the government. 'I only finish those,' he said on another occasion, 'who are enemies of the Sikh faith like policemen, government officials and Hindus.'

The language used by Sant Jarnail Singh has been generally interpreted to support the view that he was leading an armed struggle for Khalistan. Naturally, his movement is looked upon as 'secessionist' as well as militant. The White Paper issued by the Government of India refers to secessionist and anti-national activities which had the objective of establishing an independent state for the Sikhs with external support. The activities of Sant Jarnail Singh are included in this view of the situation. However, when he was asked by a journalist in 1983 whether or not he supported the demand for Khalistan, his reply was: 'I am neither in favour of it nor against it. If they give it to us, we won't reject it.' He repeated this in March 1984. In one of his morning *darbars* on the roof of the Langar he asked the audience if they wanted the Anandpur Sahib Resolution implemented in full. Hands were raised by the congregation and Sant Jarnail Singh was satisfied: 'You need not say anything more'. He warned the Akali leaders that if they accepted anything less than all the demands in the Anandpur Sahib Resolution he would expose them before the Sikhs. On the eve of the Operation Blue Star, when the Akali leaders were in favour of a settlement with the government, he refused to agree to anything less than the Anandpur Sahib Resolution. Thus, whereas his activities and his informal responses to questions on Sikh independence may seem to point towards Khalistan, his formal stand did not go beyond autonomy for the Punjab as a part of the Indian Union.

Articulation in favour of Khalistan became more pronounced after the death of Sant Jarnail Singh. For this development, it is possible to see the relevance of the Operation Blue Star and the Sikh massacres in Delhi in the wake of Indira Gandhi's assassination. Even more important was the failure of Rajiv-Longowal Accord. In any case the number of militant groups and the number of youngmen who joined them during seven years after the death of Sant Jarnail Singh appears to have been far larger than their number during the seven years of his own activity from 1977 to 1984. Many of the Sikhs living in Great Britain, Canada and the United States were vocal in favour of Khalistan. Many of the militants working in the Punjab too made no secret of their political objective. Continuity was provided by two important organizations: the All India Sikh Students Federation (which had been closely associated with Sant Jarnail Singh under the leadership of Bhai Amrik Singh, the eldest son of Sant Kartar Singh), and the Damdami Taksal. On their initiative, a meeting of the Sarbat Khalsa (in theory, the entire body of the Sikhs) was held at the Golden Temple on 26 January 1986. A flag of Khalistan was hoisted and the Akal Takht rebuilt by the government was demolished. Khalistan was proclaimed a few months later. In August 1987, at a convention called by the Acting Jathedar of the Akal Takht, Professor Darshan Singh, it was declared that the goal of the Sikh Panth was to have a political setup in an area in which the Sikhs could experience a glow of freedom (presumably within the Indian State). This did not satisfy the militants. They continued their activity for at least five years more.

V

In retrospect, we can see that the pamphlet on Khalistan had nothing to do with the Akalis. Its idea appealed to some Sikhs who were actually opposed to them. The Azad Punjab scheme involved reorganization to ensure that no religious community was in absolute majority in this reorganized politico-administrative unit of the Indian State. The relationship of this unit with the Indian State was not spelt out, but it may not be unsafe to assume that it was something like 'provincial autonomy'. The Sikh state conditionally demanded by the Akalis was different from the Azad Punjab essentially in being sovereign, rather than autonomous. This was true of their later demand for a sovereign state irrespective of whether or not Pakistan was created. With the Sikhs being no more than 20 per cent within the proposed state, this sovereign state was not really a 'Sikh' state. The proposal was unrealistic. There was no possibility of it being taken up seriously by the colonial administrators and politicians, even if some of them were sympathetic to the Sikhs.

Though unrealistic in terms of the situation on the ground, the Akali demand for a Sikh state underlined their concern for the future and gave trenchant expression to their political aspirations based on their self-image. The literature published in connection with this demand gave an elaborate rationale for Sikh 'nationhood' on which the demand for self-determination was based. The demand of the Akalis for political recognition on the basis of Sikh identity was the culmination of a process which had started half a century earlier. They have never relinquished the claim to represent the Sikh Panth. The form in which this recognition was sought in 1945-6, that is a sovereign state, was never forgotten by their opponents after 1947. The ultimate design of sovereignty, and therefore of secession, was seen in every important political move or demand of the Akalis, particularly by their opponents in the Punjab. Even at the national level there was a certain degree of distrust. The significance of the Akali demand for a sovereign Sikh state, which incidentally was supported by the Communist Party, was not merely negative. The idea could be revived by interested individuals or parties. Because of the changed demographic situation, the idea of a sovereign Sikh state or Khalistan acquired altogether a new significance and carried far different implications. That was why even the 'paper tigers' like Jagjit Singh Chauhan, the Dal Khalsa, and Ganga Singh Dhillon could create some political ripples.

Sant Jarnail Singh's initial concern was religious reform. His anti-Nirankari programme was an important implication of this concern. To look upon his advocacy or use of violence in this connection as a political programme is to do violence to the ordinary connotation of the word 'political'. But he used violence for other purposes as well, partly in reaction to violence used by others, which created a vicious circle. This circle was rapidly transformed into a spiral. It is absolutely clear that Sant Jarnail Singh would not have been able to do all that he did without the support and protection of some Congress leaders who had their own political designs and purposes. The failure of negotiated settlement with the Akalis and the known links of Giani Zail Singh with the Sant added much to his prestige and influence. Several other factors must be added to understand the influence and the 'authority' which the Sant came to exercise. For our immediate purpose, however, it is more relevant to know the stage at which his activity became 'political'. Even more relevant is to know whether or not Khalistan became his political objective. If he had this objective in mind he did not make a public declaration. Quite obviously, he did not mobilize people in the name of Khalistan. In the absence of a declared objective, his statements and his activities have to be interpreted more carefully.

This does not mean, however, that there was no movement for Khalistan, or that this movement had nothing to do with Sant Jarnail Singh. It is not possible to pinpoint the beginning of the movement, but it is safe to suggest the relevance of the Operation Blue Star, Operation Wood Rose, the anti-Sikh violence in Delhi, and the failure of the Rajiv-Longowal Accord for the emergence of a conscious objective and its pursuit by an increasing number of militant groups. They did not operate under the leadership of a single person, though they appear to have held Sant Jarnail Singh in high esteem. They were joined by individuals who were not politically committed. There was infiltration too. But they did have their sympathizers and supporters, not only outside the Punjab and in foreign countries but in the Punjab itself. On the whole, it may be valid to talk of a movement for Khalistan. Individuals professing affiliation to the Damdami Taksal and the All India Sikh Students Federation were more conspicuous in the movement than others. That is why the movement has been and can be associated with Sant Jarnail Singh. There are individuals, mostly abroad, who still subscribe to the idea of Khalistan. In an unguarded moment, K.P.S. Gill, the then Director-General of Police, expressed his gratification by saying that there would be no such movement for thirty years. The implication is that there was a movement.

The Akalis have never demanded a sovereign state for the Sikhs after 1946. There has been a demand for Sikh Homeland standing in a special relationship with the Centre and having a special internal constitution, but only by individuals or small splinter groups of the Akalis. Paradoxically, it is impossible to think of a 'Sikh Homeland' outside the Indian Union within which the 'Sikh Homeland' is to have its being. What the Akalis have insisted upon is autonomy for the Punjab and for other states in the country, a truly federal system – something like the system visualized by the Constituent Assembly before it became clear that Pakistan was going to be created. The Akalis have never resorted to armed militancy or violence for attaining any political objective. Their approach has been constitutional or agitational since 1920 and this is a very strong tradition. Their compromising gestures towards Sant Jarnail Singh and his followers changed neither the political objective nor the approach of the Akalis.

If we look at the development of Akali politics after Independence, it appears to have been marked more by agitational than constitutional approach, understandably because their smaller number and the adoption of the Indian Constitution did not leave them much choice. The government on its part, in the state and at the Centre, has pursued a policy of resistance and confrontation, punctuated at times by accommodation. We can think of two important demands of the Akalis for which they did not agitate. The first was for weightage and proportional representation which was not conceded. The second was about the recognition of Punjabi as the medium of school education, which was largely met by the Sachar Formula. The Regional

Formula was a result of negotiations but it had been preceded by agitation for a Punjabi-speaking state. However, the Regional Formula was not implemented. Logically, therefore, there was a second phase of agitation. This also meant a long delay in the creation of the Punjabi-speaking state. More important, however, was the difference in the form of this and the earlier linguistic states. This difference from the Akali viewpoint was discriminatory and it gave birth to new problems simultaneously with the creation of the new state. The Akali experience of government, marked by a feeling of interference in political terms and constraints in economic terms, added one more item to their agenda. Among other things, the political and economic demands of the Akalis were articulated in the Anandpur Sahib Resolution of 1973, and reiterated at Ludhiana in 1978. The Rajiv-Longowal Accord is the best example of accommodation on the part of the government. But it failed, partly because of the way in which it was formulated but largely because of the forces working against its implementation.

The Hindu-Sikh debate about identity has been a source of confusion. There are questions which are bound to get inadequate, if not wrong, answers. Whether or not Sikhs were Hindu was one such question. We can persist in asking this question but without getting any the wiser. Sikh identity, like every other identity, is a product of history. One can fruitfully go into the evolution of this identity, in all its complications. But one has to start at the beginning. To be a Sikh was to be a follower of Guru Nanak. It is necessary to fully grasp the meaning of this simple statement. Guru Nanak told his followers what to believe and what to do, not only through his sermons in prose but also through his poetic compositions. These compositions were used by his followers for worship in congregation. He told his followers that this mode of worship was the most efficacious for achieving liberation, and for them it was the only way. His successors wrote their own compositions, in the name of 'Nanak'. All these compositions were put together in the *Granth* compiled by Guru Arjan. The compositions of Guru Tegh Bahadur were added to it later. It is now known as the *Adi Granth*, and is regarded as *Guru Granth Sahib*. The doctrine of *Guru-Granth* can be logically and historically traced to Guru Nanak's theology. Similarly, the doctrine of Guru-Panth can be traced to his decision to establish a line of succession. The *dharmsal*, with the twin institutions of *sangat* and *langar*, which developed into the present-day Gurdwara, has come down to us from the days of Guru Nanak. The ideal of social commitment can also be traced to his ideas and practice. The adoption of new beliefs, practices and institutions made the Sikhs conscious of their identity quite early in their history, and this consciousness was reinforced by later historical developments. The institution of the Khalsa by Guru Gobind Singh appears to be a great landmark in this process precisely because it made Sikh identity externally and unambiguously conspicuous.

The real significance of *Ham Hindu Nahin* has been lost because of its preoccupation with the Hindu-Sikh debate. The Khalsa had established their power in the late eighteenth century through the force of arms and their political will. Bhai Kahn Singh's argument that the Sikhs should be recognized as a political community was based on reflection and on rational argument. Sikh identity was used as the basis for this recognition. This was altogether a new kind of development, which makes it relevant for the present. The Akalis and the followers of Sant Jarnail Singh invoke the same identity, but they differ in their purposes. Even on the use of force there is no difference between them in theory. They subscribe to the idea that it is legitimate to use force. Their representatives often quote the Persian couplet from Guru Gobind Singh's *Zafarnama*, which means that it is legitimate to take up the sword when all other means have failed. The difference lies in interpreting 'when all other means have failed'. For the Akalis, that time has not come. For the followers of Sant Jarnail Singh, as much as for him, the time for the use of physical force had come. It may be tempting to see the objective of sovereign rule as a logical and inevitable step from the objective of autonomy. Historically, however, there is no inevitable link between religious identity and political sovereignty.

NOTES

1. Atul Kohli, *Democracy and Discontent: India's Growing Crisis of Governability*, Cambridge: Cambridge University Press, 1991 (Indian Paperback Edition 1995 (rpt.), pp. 353-5.

2. Ibid., pp. 376-7.
3. Dipankar Gupta, 'The Communalising of Punjab 1980-1985', in *Punjab: The Fatal Miscalculation*, ed. Patwant Singh and Harji Malik, New Delhi, 1985, pp. 209-29.
   For a more detailed discussion of the issue, Dipankar Gupta, *The Context of Ethnicity: Sikh Identity in a Comparative Perspective*, New Delhi: Oxford University Press, 1996.
4. Gyanendra Pandey, *The Construction of Communalism in Colonial North India*, New Delhi: Oxford University Press, 1994 (Paperback, 2nd Impression), pp. 21-2, 241.
5. Gyanendra Pandey (ed.), *Hindus and Others: The Question of Identity in India Today*, New Delhi: Viking Penguin India, 1993, p. 20.
6. Paul Wallace and Surendra Chopra (eds.), *Political Dynamics of Punjab*, Amritsar: Guru Nanak Dev University, 1981, p. 3.
7. Rasheeduddin Khan, *Bewildered India: Identity, Pluralism, Discord*, New Delhi: Har-Anand Publications, 1995.
8. Partha Chatterjee, *The Nation and its Fragments*, New Delhi: Oxford University Press, 1994, p. 238.
9. Bhai Kahn Singh Nabha, *Ham Hindu Nahin* [We are not Hindus], Amritsar: Singh Brothers, 1995 (rpt.).
10. Pandey (ed.), *Hindus and Others*, p. 246.
11. Indu Banga, 'The Crisis of Sikh Politics (1940-47)', in *Sikh History and Religion in the Twentieth Century*, ed. Joseph T. O'Connell et al., Toronto: Centre for South Asian Studies, University of Toronto, 1988, pp. 233-55.
12. Sadhu Singh Hamdard, *Azad Punjab* (Urdu), Amritsar, 1943.
13. Gurbachan Singh and Lal Singh Giani, *The Idea of the Sikh State*, Lahore: Lahore Book Shop, 1946. Relevant in this context are also the following: G. Adhikari, *Sikh Homeland Through Hindu-Muslim-Sikh Unity*, Bombay, 1944. Harnam Singh, *Punjab: The Homeland of the Sikhs*, Lahore, 1945. Swarup Singh, *The Sikhs Demand Their Homeland*, London, 1946.

13

Five Hundred Years of the Sikh Educational Heritage

GURINDER SINGH MANN

The Sikh educational heritage is deeply rooted in Sikh beliefs and practice. After all, the very word Sikh means a disciple who discovers the truth from the compositions of the Gurus, the founding leaders of the Sikh tradition and then applies it to his or her life's activity.[1] The literary corpus that constitutes the core of this heritage began to form early in the sixteenth century and continued to expand until the middle of the nineteenth century.[2] In subsequent times, scholars have attempted to clarify, elaborate, and systematize the information enshrined in these primary sources, and the Sikh religious leadership has made concerted efforts toward its dissemination.

This essay is divided into three sections: the first traces the development of the Sikh educational heritage and addresses basic issues: its nature, composition, and significance. The second deals with the sites and modes that the Sikh community has created over time for the communication of the educational heritage to future generations. In the final section, the focus is on the challenges that have surfaced during the twentieth century and the opportunities that follow the migration of large number of Sikhs outside the Punjab, their historic home and sacred land. The Sikh community presents an interesting case study towards an understanding of how the content of educational heritage, the modes adopted for its transmission, and its scholarly understanding within a religious group evolved to meet the needs of changing times.

I

Guru Nanak (1469-1539), the founder of the Sikh tradition, believed that the most productive human conversation is the one that focuses on the divine.[3] Consequently his approximately five hundred poetic compositions sing about Vahiguru, the most commonly used designation for God in the Sikh tradition. He adopted Punjabi, the indigenous language of the region, associated with rustic people of the time, as the medium of his compositions, and inscribed them in a distinct script named Gurmukhi (of the Gurmukh/Sikhs).[4] Compiled in the 1530s, the Pothi (book/volume) including his compositions served as the first container of the Sikh educational heritage, and a significant marker of the new community's identity.

Guru Nanak's understanding of Vahiguru is centred on its unity and uniqueness. The divine nature is comprised of two aspects: the primal aspect includes Vahiguru's self-creation (*sambhau*) followed by an unrevealed phase (*gupat*) during which no divine attributes were developed (*nirgun*). Later, Vahiguru decided to bring the creation into being, manifested (*pargat*) itself in the universe and in the process acquired positive attributes.[5] About the primal aspect, human beings can only speculate and any efforts to describe it in words have to be restricted to negative terms, but it is the creative aspect of Vahiguru that constitutes the heart of Guru Nanak's reflections on the divine nature.

Guru Nanak believes that Vahiguru is the sovereign of the universe, which was created as the divine abode and Vahiguru watches over its activity with parental care and affection.[6] Given this context, Vahiguru is the sole object of human prayer, source of all human values, and the divine overseeing of the world provides the model for ideal living.[7] Guru Nanak calls Vahiguru Sachiar (*sach-achar,* one with truthful-conduct) and all this leads to the primary thrust of his message, which is not theological but ethical in nature.[8]

Guru Nanak expects that human beings must understand the details of divine activity and then attempt to adopt the values associated with it in their own lives. Translating these values into action constitutes the core of Guru Nanak's vision of a meaningful life, which manifests itself in values such as service to others, truthful conduct, and social productivity.[9] For him, the acquisition of abstract truth is not sufficient in itself, it must turn into truthful conduct.[10]

This basic dictum provides the starting point of the journey towards the attainment of liberation, a place of honour in the divine court and the ultimate destination of human life.[11] Guru Nanak is, however, emphatic that liberation is not only personal, but collective and includes family, congregation, and 'people' around.[12] This serves as the basis for the importance assigned to communal and social obligations in Sikh life.

How did Guru Nanak attain this knowledge? He believes that his compositions result from conversations with Vahiguru; conversation turns into questions at times.[13] The ideas enshrined in them represent the truth and contain all that his followers need to live their lives meaningfully.[14] His followers clearly agreed with his belief. His successor, Guru Angad (1539-51), was emphatic that those who had met Guru Nanak needed no further instruction.[15]

Guru Nanak accepts the existence of revelation prior to his own and that sacred texts of other religious traditions that enshrine these revelations have the potential to serve as a source of liberating knowledge.[16] Yet to meet this goal, these texts must meet the criteria of reasoning and rational enquiry.[17] For instance, Guru Nanak believes that the *Atharva Veda,* a sacred text containing magic spells, cannot offer any positive guidance toward how to orient human life and consequently cannot serve the role of a scripture.[18]

Guru Nanak supports the idea of a discussion (*goshati*) where questions are asked and answered in a spirit of helping each other learn as an important way to refine knowledge.[19] He spent over two decades travelling and meeting both Hindu and Muslim religious leaders and in the process refining his understanding of life, which later served as the foundation for the community of his followers at Kartarpur [1520(?)-39]. Guru Nanak's long composition reconstructing the discussion with the Nath Yogis, the Shaivite ascetics who dominated the religious landscape of the Punjab at that time, is the earliest composition in this genre of religious literature in north India.[20]

For Guru Nanak, knowledge is not abstract but has to have a practical thrust. Once acquired, it works like a sword that cuts through the cobwebs created by human instincts diverting human attention away from the goal of life, and it replaces egocentricity and arrogance with humility.[21] This personal cleansing further translates into a powerful yearning to do good to others.[22] Guru Nanak warns against intellectual arrogance that may come with the acquisition of knowledge, and expects the bearer of it to emanate light as he or she carries on the routine chores of life while simultaneously progressing toward liberation.[23]

As the tradition evolved, Guru Nanak's successors internalized the knowledge contained in his compositions, and the images, metaphors, and themes closer to his heart echo in the writings of five of his successors who created poetic compositions. Guru Angad and Guru Amardas (1551-74) came from outside the Sikh community and were exposed to Sikh ideas later in their lives, but from Guru Ramdas (1574-81) onwards, the remaining Gurus had grown up within Sikh settings and thus had ample opportunity to imbibe them from early childhood onward.

Guru Amardas emphasized the centrality of moral deeds in one's search for liberation.[24] For Guru Arjan, the performance of pure deeds and belief in Vahiguru represented the desirable religious path.[25] He also extended Guru Nanak's image of 'knowledge as the oil in the lamp' to knowledge as 'the lamp itself', the source of light.[26] He called it an eye cleanser, something that focuses and sharpens one's vision.[27] Knowledge also appears as a sword to cut down negative emotions.[28] He designated an ideal Sikh as a Brahmgiani (Knower of Vahiguru), an active participant in life who always yearns to do good for others.[29]

The Pothi containing Guru Nanak's compositions underwent expansion during the leadership of Guru Amardas and Guru Arjan. The compositions of the successor Gurus, bards at the Sikh court, and careful selections from some non-Sikh saints, both 'Hindu' and Sufi, which synchronized with the Sikh understanding of human life and the unity of the divine were appended to those of the founder. Guru Arjan also believed in the revelatory nature of Sikh sacred literature and described the Pothi as a ceremonial plate which carried food that contained all the elements required for a recipe for liberation.[30] It was the seat of Vahiguru and in this status, it becomes an object of reverence.[31]

Beliefs enshrined in the compositions recorded in the Sikh Pothi were not only to be recited and revered, but understood and translated in real life.[32] Guru Nanak's successors attempted to elaborate on his themes and the exegesis of Sikh sacred compositions began in earnest at the turn of the seventeenth century. The traditional view is that Bhai Gurdas (d. 1638) was given the duty to exegete these compositions so that all Sikhs could understand the knowledge contained in them. The structure of his ballads (*vars*), where he takes important themes and explains them on the basis of the Gurus' writings, reveals his commitment to providing a clear interpretation of Sikh tenets.[33]

For Guru Amardas, the superiority of the Sikh path was taken for granted and he exhorts the Muslim and Hindu leaders to recognize this.[34] Being the best path, it was on the rise and Guru Arjan refers to landmark achievements such as the establishment of the community at Ramdaspur; completion of the Darbar Sahib; the majesty of this Sikh centre and the spread of the community.[35] If Guru Nanak and Guru Arjan sang of the glory of the divine court, the bards at the Sikh court praised the majesty of the Gurus and their courts as a replica of the divine court on this earth.[36] The tensions with the Mughals enter the Sikh records as well.[37]

Furthermore, as the Gurus were understood to have lived out the content of their teaching, it was considered important to record the life story of the founder Guru. Bhai Gurdas composed an entire ballad on this theme, and the *janamsakhi* literature expanded on it. This genre served as an excellent venue to envision the life of the founder of the community as a special human being. For these storytellers, Guru Nanak was the leading teacher of the age (*jagat guru*), who was the bearer of the divine word enshrined in the Sikh Pothi. Following the prophets in Islamic literature that these people may have heard about, they presented Guru Nanak as having the ability to perform miracles. Focus of this literature remained on Guru Nanak, but the stories about Guru Amardas and other Gurus were developed as the time passed.[38] With this literature another dimension of learning entered the field, namely, Sikh history.

In about a century following Guru Nanak's death then, the Sikh educational heritage included the revelatory compositions enshrined in the scriptural text, and the stories about the Gurus and their courts. This heritage is characteristically manifested in a manuscript supposed to have been prepared for Bibi Rup Kunvar, the daughter of Guru Har Rai (1644-64). The opening section of the text contained Sikh liturgical compositions, and the second part included stories built around Sikh moral values and episodes from the lives of the Gurus.[39] These aspects of Sikh education continued to develop as the tradition matured.

The closing decades of the seventeenth century saw further expansion of this corpus of literature. We have references to the training of Gobind in the 1670s, who would later become Guru Gobind Singh (1675-1708). His education included the learning of Gurmukhi, Takari (script used in the Punjab hills to write local dialects), and Persian (the language of the Mughal administration). This demonstrates the importance that the Sikhs assigned to the larger context. While the learning of Gurmukhi was essential to immerse oneself in the Sikh sacred lore as well as other day-to-day communications, the Takari helped in dealing with the people living in the Punjab hills, and Persian being the language of the aristocracy of the time would be expected from a well-informed person.[40]

The future Guru's formal training also included the use of weaponry. The metaphorical sword of knowledge of Guru Nanak, and the double-edged sword of humility of Guru Arjan,[41] which were to trim the complications of life, had taken the form of a literal steel sword required to address the situation of political oppression of the Sikhs by the local Rajput chiefs and the Mughal rulers. With Guru Gobind Singh's decision to elevate the Sikh community to become the Khalsa (the pure community) in the late 1690s, the Sikh belief system expanded to maintain the body in its pristine form, by keeping bodily hair, and adorn it with symbols of royalty such as turban and arms. In this new look, the Sikhs emanated divine light (*didar*), and were assigned the destiny to establish the Khalsa/Sikh Raj, a sovereign state.[42] This vision of the Khalsa Raj was rooted in Guru Nanak's belief in divine justice and life of self-respect.

The Sikh literary heritage also expanded during this period.

Beginning with the late 1670s, we see poets and singers from the distant Sikh congregations as well as the courts of the local chiefs in the hills seeking Sikh patronage at Chak Nanaki, Paunta, and Anandpur.[43] The bulky literature of the period falls into three parts. The better known of these is a compilation that later came to be named the *Dasam Granth* (the tenth book or book of the tenth Guru). This includes Braj and Punjabi translations of Hindu mythological tales (*Bachittar Natak*) and Arabic and Persian literatures (*Mir Mehdi* and *Hikayat*), and stories about a medley of contemporary characters (*Charitro Pakhayan*).[44] The second part includes texts such as the *Sarab Loh Granth* (book of all iron), the *Pothi Prem Ambodh* (Book of Poets of Love), and so on, which claim to have been produced at Anandpur. Finally, there are references in eighteenth century sources to compilations such as the *Samund Sagar* (Sea of Seas), the *Vidya Sagar* (Sea of Knowledge), which are no longer extant.[45]

Finally, the elevation of the Sikh community into the Khalsa and the dissolution of the office of the personal Guru created a situation in which the *rahit,* the code of Sikh beliefs and practice, came into focus. The statements pertaining to *rahit* such as 'five dos and five donots' appear in the opening pages of scriptural manuscripts beginning with the turn of the seventeenth century, and these evolved into the new genre called the *Rahitnamas* (Manuals of Belief and Practice). The three early extant documents of this type are attributed to Nand Lal (1695), Prahlad Singh (1695/1705), and Chaupa Singh and a group of Sikh scholars (1700), who created a detailed statement on *rahit* supported with relevant quotes from the *Guru Granth* and claim that this had endorsement of Guru Gobind Singh.[46] The *janamsakhi* literature expanded to include a new auxiliary form called the praise of the Gurus (*gur sobha*/later *gur bilas*). Sainapat, a court poet at Anandpur, introduced this genre by writing a text about Guru Gobind Singh, which he completed in 1711.[47]

By the end of the Guru period then, the Sikh educational heritage contained literature in five different areas which had developed in the following order: (1) Sikh revelatory writings that began with those of Guru Nanak and reached their canonical form in the 1680s, and this sacred text attained the status of the *Guru Granth* (Guru manifested in the book) after Guru Gobind Singh's death in 1708; (2) the writings of Bhai Gurdas, the exegesis of the compositions in the *Guru Granth* and the ideas enshrined in them, served as the core of interpretive literature; (3) the rudimentary statements pertaining to *rahit* had started to be recorded around 1600 and by the turn of the eighteenth century they emerged as an autonomous genre called the *Rahitnamas*; (4) by the early seventeenth century, the *janamsakhi* literature began to be committed to writing and stories about the lives of Guru Nanak, Guru Amardas, Guru Arjan, and Guru Gobind Singh were created later; (5) finally, the poetry associated with the court at Anandpur was recorded in the *Dasam Granth* and *Sarab Loh Granth*, etc., and subsequently became part of the Sikh educational heritage.

The first category was represented in the form of a bounded text and remained unchanged. The next three genres by definition were open ended and expanded over time. The *rahit*-related documents multiplied as later writers addressed new issues facing the community at the time of their writing. Sikh writers retold stories about the lives of the ten Gurus; the life of Guru Hargobind became the subject of a *Gur Bilas;* a text celebrated the martyrdom *(Shahid Bilas)* of Bhai Mani Singh (d. 1738), the first Sikh to have been elevated to the level of becoming part of Sikh heritage (1800).[48] The early eighteenth-century beliefs in the special status of the Sikh community as the Guru Panth, and the resulting belief that it was divinely sanctioned to rule the Punjab reached its full development in Ratan Singh Bhangu's *Guru Panth Prakash* [Rise of the Guru Panth] completed in 1841. The status of the literary corpus produced at the Sikh court during the period of leadership of Guru Gobind Singh has been under dispute since the early eighteenth century and there seems to be no resolution in sight.[49]

By this point in time, the primary corpus of the Sikh educational heritage reached its completion and what follows can safely be considered as its elaboration and systematization. Later writers are larger in number, more prolific in production than their predecessors, and register a distinct consciousness of being scholars who engage with other people's ideas and views. Bhai Santokh Singh (d. 1843), who marks the transition to the new period, wrote on Guru Nanak and his successors, in over 6,500 printed pages, created the *Garbh Ganjani Tika* [pride breaking commentary] on the *Japji*, denouncing a contemporary interpretation of the same text, and sought patronage from three Sikh courts on the basis of his scholarly credentials.[50]

The annexation of the Sikh Raj by the British in the 1840s resulted in the introduction of Western education and the printing press to the Punjab. The Sikhs welcomed the press, the first printed edition of the *Guru Granth* was published in mid-1860s and numerous editions have come forth since then. In the process, its pagination became standardized at 1430, and the text is available in the standard size used in ritual worship and in smaller sizes for devotional and scholarly purposes at home. In the 1970s, the earlier tradition of manuscripts where the words were connected with each other was discontinued and as the words were separated the reading became easier. In addition to Gurmukhi, the sacred script, the text of *Guru Granth Sahib* is also available in Devanagari and Indo-Persian, and these are intended for those who can understand the language but cannot read the script. In the 1990s, a text with three columns including the Gurmukhi, its transliteration in Roman script, and its translation into English, respectively, was created. This is primarily for the use of Sikhs living in the West who may not have access to the Gurmukhi original.[51] At present an edition of the *Guru Granth* with Gurmukhi, Devanagari, and English translation is available on the internet (www.srigranth.org).

The tradition of commentaries on key sections of the *Guru Granth* also continued and we have a large bulk of writings available on the subject. Research has been conducted on both its structure and message. The annotated editions of the complete text of the *Guru Granth* began to be created in the closing decades of the nineteenth century and since then we have witnessed over half a dozen efforts in this direction. Several translations in English and one in French of the *Guru Granth* are also available. G.B. Singh's work in the 1940s developed an area of scholarship that focused on early Sikh scriptural manuscripts in an attempt to reconstruct the history of the canonical text, and the past decades have seen key strides in this direction.[52]

The *rahitnama* literature also underwent significant systematization during this period. This work began in the 1870s with an important compilation by Bhagwan Singh entitled *Bibek Bardhi*

Granth [Book of Wisdom], which included thirty-six early *rahit* related documents.[53] This was followed by Avtar Singh Vahiria's comprehensive statement on the *rahit*, *Sikh Dharam Shashtar* (1894). Working on the basic assumption that *rahit* is an evolving discipline, Sikh representative bodies such as the Panch Khalsa Diwan (*Khalsa Rahit Prakash*, 1908), and the Chief Khalsa Diwan (*Gurmat Prakash*, 1915), started the initiative toward creating an authoritative statement. Under the auspices of the Shiromani Gurdwara Prabandhak Committee (SGPC), this effort attained its final form as the *Sikh Rahit Maryada* (1950) [Sikh Way of Life]. The *Sikh Rahit Maryada* has successfully served as the authoritative statement for an overwhelming majority of the Sikh community since then.[54]

The *janamsakhi* and *Gur Bilas* literature began to be published in the 1870s and has continued to attract attention. Over time critical editions of various branches within this large corpus have been created and efforts have been made to assess their historical value. This literature continues to serve as the primary source for information imparted at the Gurdwara and other forums, and working within this broad genre, new versions of the stories continue to emerge. In the 1990s, Sant Jarnail Singh Bhindranwale (d. 1984), followed Bhai Mani Singh as the rightful subject of a *Shahid Bilas*.[55] Finally, the text of the *Dasam Granth* was printed in the 1890s for the first time and several printed editions have been published since then. In 2002, the management of the Takht Sri Hazur Sahib, Nander, released what it believed to be an authoritative edition of the text.

At the heart of Sikh literary corpus lies the *Guru Granth*, Sikh scripture, which serves as the repository of Sikh beliefs and practice, and numerous commentaries are available to understand its message. Scholars have attempted detailed reconstruction of the history of its making. Rooted in these teachings, the *Sikh Rahit Maryada* provides guidance for both the personal and corporate life of the Sikhs. Numerous editions of the *janamsakhis*, the *Gur Bilas,* and other historical documents such as that of Bhangu provide understanding of the lives of the Gurus and the destiny of the Sikh community. The literature produced during Guru Gobind Singh's period marks the phase of Sikh heritage whose literary and historical context is yet to be firmly understood.

II

Early Sikh literature provides us with a fairly good sense of the setting in which the educational heritage was transmitted during the formative stages of the Sikh community. At Kartarpur, Guru Nanak was the centre of the community, which looked upon him as the model for their own living. He guided their path by providing them with core beliefs and direction.[56] He structured the daily rhythms of their lives by inviting them to gather at his place at sunrise and sunset and assigned a prayer to be recited just before going to sleep. These prayer sessions comprised of listening to the recitation of the Guru's verses (*path*), their singing (*kirtan*), their exegesis (*katha*) in which the Guru himself must have clarified the complexities of his ideas and answered questions, and supplication (*ardas*).[57] Work in the fields seems to have filled the day in between these two prayer sessions.

The newly created Sikh rituals, ceremonies, and institutions marked another level of Sikh life, which would have served as an important mode of transmission of this heritage. Guru Nanak constructed ceremonies around his beliefs and their performance would have further reinforced these beliefs. From simple Sikh greetings such as Dhan Nirankar (the formless one is great), or Sat Kartar (the creator is true) to more complex rituals such as the *charan pahul* (the nectar of the feet), the initiation ceremony in the early Sikh community, would have served to educate Sikhs of their identity. For instance, in the Sikh *charan pahul*, the nectar was generated by the touch of the toe of the new entrant.[58] Those who participated in the ceremony could not have missed the significance assigned to humility in Sikh belief,[59] and the Guru or other officiating Sikhs would have clarified the distinct character of the Sikh ceremony from the one prevalent among the Vaishnavas. This was true of the role of Sikh institutions too. The *langar* (community meal/kitchen) enshrined Sikh values of equality, hard work, service, and charity.[60] Unlike the Nath Yogis who begged for food, and many Sufis who accepted land grants from the local chiefs to run their kitchens, the Sikhs provided for the *langar* themselves.

This model of transmission that began at Kartarpur continued throughout the early period. The Guru served as the primary source of knowledge and guidance, and as the community grew, the Masands, the Guru's nominees in distant congregations, replicated this model in their respective places. They were well versed in Sikh beliefs and practice and were able to provide guidance to their constituents. If there were any issues, they could ask the Guru when visiting the Sikh court during the Baisakhi and Diwali, the local festivals that became part of the sacred Sikh calendar. It seems that a letter could also be written seeking advice if there was some urgent matter. Prominent Sikhs such as Bhai Gurdas could also help in matters of belief and practice.

We do not know the literacy level within the early Sikh community, but there are interesting details that are worth mentioning. The respect assigned to scribal activity seems to have developed very early in the tradition. We do know that Lehina, later named Angad, when elevated to the office of Guru Nanak, was involved in scribal activity at Kartarpur. Bhai Gurdas, himself a scribe, mentions names of others who held position of leadership within the Sikh community.[61] It is also clear that the majority group that joined the early Sikh community came from a nomadic background and could not have had much exposure to reading and writing. During the seventeenth century, however, they seem to have become proficient in writing, and scriptural manuscripts inscribed by Bura Sandhu (1605), Gurdita Jateta (1653), and Pakharmal Dhillon (1688), who belonged to this segment of the society, are still extant. In later history, influential writers from within this group included Sainapat, Bhai Mani Singh, Koer Singh Kalal, and Ratan Singh Bhangu. We do not have their counterparts among the nomads who joined the Muslim and Hindu communities.

After the elevation of the Sikh community to the Khalsa and the resulting dissolution of personal authority, we see an interesting expansion of the modes of transmission of the Sikh educational heritage. Needless to say, the family setting had been an important arena of transmission since early times. Guru Nanak is emphatic that liberation has to be attained within the familial setting and the society at large.[62] With the turn of the eighteenth century, we begin to have concrete references to it. Chaupa Singh advises the woman of the house to visit the Gurdwara twice a day, memorize the verses of the Guru, and teach her husband the beliefs of the tradition.[63] In the *Prem Sumarg* (Path of Love), we see women moving closer to the centre of Sikh society and expected to undergo the ceremony of the *khande di pahul* (nectar of the double-edged sword), learn Sikh literature (Gurmukhi *vidia*), practise Sikh beliefs, and be able to transmit them to their children.[64]

Chaupa Singh also mentions the office of the Dharamsalia (the custodian of the *dharmsal*, the Sikh place of worship in early Sikh history), his qualifications, and the community's responsibility toward him. With the *Granth* becoming the Guru, the *dharmsals* became the Gurdwaras, the house of the *Guru Granth*, and its caretaker was named the *granthi/bhai*. In this role, the *granthi* oversaw the ritual routine at the Gurdwara, and being well versed in Sikh sacred lore officiated over ceremonies such as weddings, and also helped young Sikhs to learn how to read the *Guru Granth*. With the rise of Sikh political power in the second half of the eighteenth century, the Sikh numbers grew and as a result new Gurdwaras were built in villages with Sikh population. These served as places for the transmission of the Sikh educational heritage with the *granthi* as the primary teacher. This model was not unique to the Sikhs but synchronized well with the mosque and its school (*maktab*) and the Hindu temple with its facility to teach (*pathshala*).

In addition, we have an interesting eighteenth-century document which informs us that while leaving for south India in 1705, Guru Gobind Singh appointed Bhai Mani Singh and Bhai Fateh Singh to be the caretakers of the Darbar Sahib, Amritsar and the Damdama Sahib, Talwandi Sabo, respectively.[65] Their primary brief was to impart education to Sikhs. While Darbar Sahib remained in the eye of the storm during Sikh struggle for sovereignty with the Mughals, and the Afghans until the 1760s, the Damdama Sahib quickly developed as a place of Sikh learning (Guru ki Kashi), and traditions associate Baba Dip Singh with the inscribing of the manuscripts of canonical versions of the Sikh scripture and the sending of them to other historical Gurdwaras. Both these places expanded their work during the Sikh Raj (1765-1849) and served as centres where the *granthis* and itinerant Sikh scholars received training.[66]

Finally, we have references to Sikh savants, who took up an informal role of providing guidance. The learning of the *Guru*

Granth and/or earlier associations with the Guru and the Sikh court may have helped them in this role. Bhai Mani Singh is the most prominent figure in the early part of the eighteenth century. We have documents that claim to have been his answers to questions pertaining to matters of belief, practice, as well as history.[67] There are other writings attributed to Daya Singh, Desa Singh, Sahib Singh, only known to us by name who offered their views on issues of Sikh beliefs and practice confronting the community at various points in time. It seems that the answers these people offered were copied and circulated within the community. We come across numerous small size manuscripts (*gutkas*) from this period, which include Sikh liturgical compositions and the statements of *rahit* attributed to these people.

In the post-Guru period thus, the Sikh community managed to evolve a system that effectively met its educational needs. We see the transmission of Sikh heritage spreading out of the Sikh court to include the mother, the family, the village Gurdwara, large Sikh centres of learning at Amritsar and Talwandi Sabo, and even independent scholars who were available to teach. The British administration report of 1849-51 on popular education records an extensive system of Gurdwara-attached 'Gurmukhi schools' where 'sacred books' of the Sikhs were taught and it registers the presence of 'some females' among the student body. G.W. Leitner refers to 'a typical Sikh village' in Sialkot, in which everyone before annexation could read and write Gurmukhi.[68]

As referred to in the previous section, the Sikh community welcomed the arrival of the printing press in the Punjab. While it slowly eroded the tradition of Sikh calligraphy and manuscript production, it made the *Guru Granth*, its commentaries, *rahit* related documents, historical texts, and a host of other publications such as community newspapers, periodicals, etc., available to large numbers of people. The increasing accessibility of this literature enabled lay people to learn the basics of the tradition and then transmit them to their children.

The schools attached to the village Gurdwaras, however, came under pressure from the British educational system and were slowly phased out by the early twentieth century. Government schools were opened to impart secular education and teach subjects such as English, science, and mathematics, which were expected to prepare young people to obtain jobs in the administration. The fundamental shift of the goal of education from imbibing Sikh heritage to preparing students for a career in government service made the Gurdwara schools redundant. The education that the *granthi* was trained to impart was no longer helpful for job prospects in the changed circumstances.

The institution of the Gurdwara, however, continued to thrive and the need for *granthis* to oversee its activity grew. Consequently, the role of central places such as Amritsar and Talwandi Sabo in training these personnel did not diminish and these centres of learning continued to function. Scholars associated with Damdama Sahib created new branches such as at Boparai and Bhindran Kalan in Ludhiana district, and Mehta in Amritsar district. At all these places, Sikh children undergo rigorous training in reciting, singing, and exegesis of the *Guru Granth*, along with immersion in the *Dasam Granth*, *janamsakhi*, and *Gur Bilas* literature. After they complete their training, they move into positions of *granthis* in Gurdwaras now spread all over the world. The SGPC also took interest in training *granthis* and established institutions such as Sikh Missionary College, Amritsar. This mode of transmission of the Sikh educational heritage continues the eighteenth-century traditions in all their purity.

In the decades that followed the arrival of the British in the Punjab, Sikh leadership responded to the new developments in several ways ranging from complete rejection (Baba Ram Singh, 1816-85) to absolute fascination with modernity (Dyal Singh Majithia, 1849-98). The mainstream Sikh leadership floated a middle alternative that had profound impact on Sikh education.[69] These leaders were fully committed to preserving the Sikh heritage while simultaneously expanding its boundaries to incorporate the content of Western education, which was not deemed to conflict with Sikh beliefs and practice. New subjects such as science, mathematics, and English were added to help the general progress of the community, and pave the way for Sikh youth to avail themselves of employment opportunities in the police force and civil service. The Sikhs had learnt Persian earlier and they took to the learning of English in their stride. This thinking manifested itself in the creation of places of learning such as

Khalsa College, Amritsar. The attempt was to blend the Sikh educational heritage with new areas of knowledge.

Khalsa College with its boarding facilities was seen to provide a congenial and an effective environment for the inculcation of Sikh beliefs and practice in the younger generation while training future leadership. In 1892, a command (*hukamnama*) was issued from the Darbar Sahib, Amritsar, which initiated the fund-raising drive that made it possible to establish the college. Keeping with the tradition of sponsoring the cause of Sikh education, Sikh chiefs and common folk alike contributed handsomely in cash and kind and the college was founded the very same year. The Sikhs whole-heartedly supported the college, and in return expected it to nurture the religious and political leadership of the community.[70] It continues to enjoy a special status within the Sikh communitarian thinking. In 2000, the buildings needed conservation work and Sikhs from neighboring villages came in their own tractor-trolleys and offered free labour to accomplish this task.

The Gurdwara on the campus served as the centre of Sikh religious life, where the students gathered for morning and evening prayers, and to listen to experts on the Sikh tradition. The special hour for Gurmat (Sikh teachings), which was a formal part of the curriculum, completed the transmission of Sikh education. Prominent Sikh intellectuals of the twentieth century such as Teja Singh (1895-1958), Bhai Jodh Singh (1882-1981) and Sahib Singh (1892-1977), to name only a few, served as Gurmat teachers at Khalsa College. In teaching these classes, they created syllabi that were later developed by Dharm Prachar Committee (committee for the propagation of religion) of the SGPC in the form of elaborate teaching materials (*Dharam Pothis*) for use in Sikh schools.

Khalsa College, Amritsar, was only open to men but female education was not neglected, and the first college for women, another community-supported project, was established at Ferozepur the same year, i.e. in 1892. Both Bhai Takht Singh, the leading light behind the project, and Bibi Harnam Kaur, his wife, were interested in formally educating Sikh women in their heritage, so that they could effectively nurture Sikh children and provide religious guidance within the context of the Sikh family. Like the

Khalsa College, the motive behind the Sikh women's college was an emphasis on the transmission of Sikh values to the younger generation. Bhai Takht Singh went out of his way to keep the college a community venture and did not accept government grants.[71]

As the Sikhs moved into the twentieth century, other institutions of higher learning were founded along similar lines, and with the same supporting agencies. The Sikh National College, Lahore, was built on land donated by Dehra Sahib, the historic Gurdwara in Lahore. When B.R. Ambedkar, an influential untouchable leader, considered converting to Sikhism along with his large following in the middle decades of the twentieth century, the Sikh leadership built Khalsa College, Bombay, to welcome them; this time funds came from the Gurdwara at the birthplace of Guru Nanak at Nankana Sahib.[72]

Beginning in 1908, the Sikh community developed the forum of Sikh Educational Conference, which effectively responded to the Sikh community's concern for education. When the Sikh Educational Conference started, there were only seven Khalsa schools, but by 1947, three hundred and forty Sikh schools had been established. The mode of operation was simple. An educational conference would be called under the auspices of a local Gurdwara. Sikh intellectuals gathered there would make speeches, emphasizing the need for Sikh education, and an appeal would be made to the congregation to donate money. The Gurdwara would add the required amount to donations that had already been collected, and a school would be started. The number of schools that were founded through this method indicates the vigorous response given by local communities to these appeals in the cause of Sikh education.[73]

After the partition of the Punjab in 1947, Sikh concern for education has got translated into the founding of the Punjabi University, Patiala (1962), and Guru Nanak Dev University, Amritsar (1969). Whatever be the official understanding about these places, the Sikh community regarded them as Sikh institutions. The credentials of the first Vice-Chancellors, Bhai Jodh Singh at Patiala and Bishan Singh Samundri at Amritsar, clearly suggest that both these Sikh educationists had long and fruitful association with Sikh education before they moved to head these new universities.[74]

In addition to these major universities, numerous Khalsa colleges and schools were established with the help of the local Gurdwaras and grants from affluent Sikhs. Such grants were not confined to the Punjab. Principals of colleges in the Doaba region, which has sent so many Sikhs overseas, frequently made trips abroad to collect donations from Sikhs who had previously resided in their particular areas or had been students at their colleges. Between 1966 and 1975 the centenaries of the births of Guru Nanak and Guru Gobind Singh, and of the martyrdom of Guru Tegh Bahadur, provided appropriate occasions for the opening of new Sikh educational institutions. Many Sikhs saw the building of a college or a school as the right tribute to the memory of their Gurus. Though often overlooked, the significance of these twentieth-century educational institutions, and the forums that created them, is immense.

In the context of such forums, it was at the Sikh Educational Conference held in March 1981 that Ganga Singh Dhillon, a naturalized American Sikh reiterated the claim that the Sikhs were a distinct nation and therefore entitled to an independent state, called Khalistan.[75] Similarly it was the Khalsa colleges, as places of religio-political learning, which served as the main setting for the Sikh Students Federation. Of course, not all of the formidable Sikh resistance to the political structure in the Punjab during the 1980s and the early 1990s can be attributed to forces that grew up as a consequence of the educational legacy of the past century. The indigenous Sikh system that preceded the colonial period survived in all its purity in the centre at Mehta from which Sant Jarnail Singh Bhindranwale emerged. To them, their institution represents a continuum of over two and a half centuries of Sikh learning, and Sant Bhindranwale found his direct descent from Baba Dip Singh to be a major source of inspiration. Yet Sant Bhindranwale may never have achieved what he did if he had not become closely associated with the Sikh Students Federation, whose members were educated in the Sikh colleges of the Punjab that fulfilled the dream of blending modern education with the Sikh heritage. Had these two visions of Sikh education not coalesced, we might never have seen the drive for greater Sikh autonomy in modern Punjab.

The arrival of modernity coincided with Sikh emigration from the Punjab and the community's spread all over the globe in the past century and a half. The Sikhs, like any other first-generation immigrant community were initially concerned with establishing themselves in a basic way. The first indication of the establishment of a Sikh community, however small, was the founding of a Gurdwara. The Gurdwaras at Kalindni, East Africa (1898), Hong Kong (1901), Vancouver (1908), London (1910), and Stockton (1912) mark the early spread of the Sikh community, and as we write, there are over six hundred Gurdwaras outside South Asia. Once established, the Gurdwara serves as the centre where collective thinking and action take shape. It also functions as the place for social activity and provides a natural environment for the transmission of the Sikh educational heritage to each new generation. In large congregations, the Gurdwara has a school where the teaching of Gurmukhi, the compositions of the Gurus, and Sikh history are taught. Many devoted individuals offer their service to this cause, but the general feeling persists that this is not enough and that more disciplined training is required.

This has resulted in the organization of residential summer camps, which offer an opportunity to teach young Sikhs a complete Sikh way of life. Each day begins with the recitation of morning prayers (*Japji*) and ends with the traditional thanksgiving prayer (*Sohila*). All through the day children are taught Sikh history and religious ideas. The Sikh children I have spoken to seem to enjoy these camps. They easily make friends with other Sikhs, friendships for which they have often yearned for in the local schools where no other Sikh children are in attendance. They return home having learned much more in a group setting than their parents could teach them in individual family settings.[76]

At the turn of the twenty-first century, the community overseas has established three schools: Thai Sikh International School, Bangkok (1985, www.thaisikh.com/index.htm), Khalsa School with branches at Vancouver and Surrey (1986, 1992, www.khalsaschool.ca/page124.htm), and Guru Nanak Sikh Secondary School, Hayes, Middlesex (1993, www.axcis.co.uk/26996.html), and their settings create provisions for local Sikh children to have a total immersion in Sikh education during the regular school year.[77] Recognized by local educational authorities, these schools offer a regular academic programme that is supplemented by an extra hour of Sikh teachings daily. From my conversations with students and their parents in the past years, it emerged that these children are far more comfortable in Sikh schools and happy to learn about their religious beliefs while not having to explain Sikh religious symbols such as uncut hair and the turban to those who do not understand them. These schools are thus an important response to the need for Sikh education overseas.

The issue of the transmission of Sikh heritage has been a high priority of several private Sikh organizations. The Sikh Education Foundation of Singapore has done seminal work in both imparting the Sikh educational heritage to children in Singapore and creating teaching materials for Punjabi and the 'Sikh Way of Life', which can be used anywhere in the world. The Sikh Foundation of Palo Alto, California, has helped establish Sikh Studies programmes at the University of California (Santa Barbara, Riverside, and a research programme at Irvine). The Sikh Heritage Foundation, West Virginia, has been instrumental in the establishment of Sikh Heritage Gallery at the Smithsonian Museum of Natural History, Washington D.C., in 2004.

The period following the Indian army's attack on the Darbar Sahib, Amritsar, in 1984, is often interpreted as a time when the overseas Sikhs took a leading role in demanding Khalistan, a separate state for the Sikhs, and advanced issues of Sikh human rights in international forums.[78] This view rightly emphasizes their initiative but fails to take full account of the ways in which such Sikhs responded to these events. The single most significant result of the happenings in the Punjab was the incredible boost they provided to overseas efforts to articulate, define, consolidate, and perpetuate the religio-political identity of the Sikhs. The work of earlier decades has gathered considerable momentum since 1984 as new ways and means to improve the teaching of a Sikh way of life to Sikh children were devised.

This context also demanded the projection of a clearer image of the community beyond its own boundaries. As a result, Sikh leadership began to develop liaisons with leading North American universities, prodding them to introduce Sikh Studies into their academic programmes. Such efforts have met with considerable success. Within a brief span the teaching of Sikhism was introduced at Toronto University (1986-92), the University of British Columbia (1987-97), Columbia University (1989-99), the University of Michigan (1989-), the University of California, Santa Barbara (1999-), and Hofstra University, New York (2001-). Other ways such as participation in interfaith forums, holding Sikh Day parades in cities like New York, were developed to reach the mainstream and be able to explain the Sikh way of life.[79]

In the past five centuries then, the Sikhs created sites and modes to impart the Sikh educational heritage to its future generations. These evolved to meet the needs of changing historical circumstances ranging from religious persecution, political supremacy, confrontation with modernity, to active participation in the process of globalization. Historically, the Sikhs have kept a relatively open mind toward new developments. If the late eighteenth century saw the Sikh community adopting Persian, as the language of administration, the present-day Sikhs are happy to put up the text of the *Guru Granth* on the Internet, and their forums are keenly debating issues confronting them around the globe.[80] In the intermittent period, they welcomed the printing press, the electrification of the Darbar Sahib in the 1880s, the use of loud speakers in places of worship, the making of the audio cassettes, and more recently the televising of the ritual opening of the *Guru Granth* in the morning and evening service at the Darbar Sahib, Amritsar. While this provides the other Gurdwaras the opportunity to follow the routine at the Darbar Sahib, the presence of the camera has also brought a new level of precision to the activity itself. Sikhs who may never have had the chance to be at the Darbar Sahib during these times can watch the ceremony from their homes, and receive the command of the day (*hukam*) on the Internet.

III

As referred to earlier, the literary corpus that enshrines primarily the Sikh educational heritage attained its final shape by the middle of the nineteenth century and since then the community has labored hard to clarify, systematize, and disseminate it. The hallmark of this literature is the assortment of interpretations of Sikh beliefs, and practice, history and vision of the future.[81] This scholarly tapestry contains five broad strands emerging from the training of scholars, medium of expression, primary purpose of writing, and targeted audience.

The products of the indigenous Sikh education constitute the primary strand. It began with Bhai Santokh Singh and can be traced through Tara Singh Narotam (d. 1895), Giani Gian Singh (d. 1921) and Sant Gurbachan Singh (d. 1969) to Jathedar Joginder Singh, the current Jathedar of the Akal Takht. Sant Gurbachan Singh was based at Bhindran Kalan, a branch of the Sikh centre of learning at Damdama Sahib. His writings emerged from his lectures to prospective *granthis* at his centre and Sikh audiences during his extensive tours of the region. They belong to the *katha* tradition as he spoke and wrote to inspire his listeners and encourage them to follow a Sikh way of life. There are fine insights scattered all over in his writings and it is interesting to understand his version of Sikh beliefs and history.[82] Jathedar Joginder Singh was also educated at Bhindran Kalan, became a *granthi* at the Darbar Sahib and eventually rose to the position of the Jathdar of the Akal Takht. In addition to being an exegete of the *Guru Granth* he did important scholarly work that included comparing the various editions of the *Guru Granth* and an edition of the *Gurbilas Patshahi Chhevin*.[83]

There are others who are products of indigeneous Sikh education but had the opportunity to move out of the purely religious setting. The most prominent among this group were Kahn Singh Nabha (1861-1938), Shamsher Singh Ashok (1903-86), Piara Singh Padam (1921-2001). Padam, for instance, was educated at his village school but later worked for the SGPC (1943-50), Punjab Languages Department, Patiala (1950-65), and Punjabi University (1966-83) during his long career. His writings range from the lives and teachings of Guru Nanak and Guru Gobind Singh to the history of Gurmukhi script and Punjabi literature. Well versed in early Punjabi sources, Padam's contribution to scholarship goes far beyond inspiring Sikhs to include the first publication of early Sikh writings and an important interpretation of Sikh beliefs and practice. His essay on Guru Gobind

Singh's *Zafarnama* [Letter of Victory] is the best statement on this important Sikh document.[84]

Then there are scholars such as Bhai Jodh Singh, Sahib Singh, and Teja Singh, who started with indigenous Sikh education but went on to join institutions run along Western educational lines. Teja Singh, the most prominent among them, started education at the Gurdwara and mosque schools in his village, and went on to do his B.A. (1914) and M.A. (1919) from Gordon Missionary College, Rawalpindi. From 1919-46, he worked at the Khalsa College, Amritsar, and produced an annotated edition of the *Guru Granth*, which stands unchallenged since its publication in the 1940s. A deeply committed Sikh, he did not feel comfortable in even putting his name as the editor of this seminal work. His writings which include commentaries on Sikh liturgical texts, first-hand records of events leading to the Gurdwara Reform movement in the 1920s, etc., were geared to meet the challenges of modernity, mentoring young scholars, and providing guidance to Sikh religious and political leadership.[85] Here we see writers who largely use Punjabi as their medium of expression but had the facility to write in English.

This takes us to the next strand – scholars who had different readership in mind than just the Sikhs, and wrote only in English. The first authoritative figure in this group is J.D. Cunnigham (d.1851), a British administrator-cum-scholar, who wrote a history of the Sikhs in the late 1840s. Ernest Trumpp (d. 1885), a German philologist hired by the British authorities, prepared an English translation of the *Guru Granth* and other sacred Sikh writings in the 1870s. Max Arthur Macauliffe (d. 1913), another British administrator, wrote a multi-volume history and translations of sacred writings. This strand reached its climactic hue in the works of W.H. McLeod (1930-). A New Zealander, McLeod, has written extensively on the origin, evolution, and modernization of the Sikh tradition, prepared critical editions of the *janamsakhi* and *rahit* literature, and has significantly contributed toward introducing the Sikh tradition to the Western world.[86]

During the twentieth century, this strand expanded to include Sikh scholars who were trained in Western modes of education and wrote only in English. Beginning with the late 1960s, J.S. Grewal (1927-) emerged as the central figure in this genre of scholarship. Trained at the School of Oriental and African Studies, London University, he has practised what he calls 'methodological atheism', and the seal of his scholarship lies in his precise interpretation and rigorous use of the sources at his disposal. His wide range of scholarly interests, fresh interpretations of existing materials, introduction of a large set of primary sources will remain an object of emulation for future historians, and his *Sikhs of the Punjab* is a classic in the field.[87]

Finally, the past two decades have seen the emergence of a new variety of scholarship. It began with Richard Fox, a brilliant cultural anthropologist, who used Sikh history to support his theory of cultural changes under colonialism. The others who followed him include scholars such as Harjot Oberoi and more recently Brian Axel.[88] Their primary interest lies in theory and they are keen to examine contemporary Western ideas about religion and society by applying them to the Sikh tradition. In the past years, these writings have been in considerable fashion and even the American Academy of Religion put its seal of approval on Oberoi's work in 1996. As for these scholars' grasp of Sikh history and their contribution toward a better understanding of the Sikh tradition, it is an open question.[89]

Given this diverse background and interests of scholars, it is natural to have differences of interpretation. At times, these academic differences have spilled into public debates. A quick survey of these storms points to the complexity of the situation. The twentieth century began with the publication of a commentary of the *Guru Granth* which was understood to be in response to Ernest Trumpp's misinterpretation of the *Guru Granth* in 1877, by a group of Sikh scholars under the leadership of Giani Badan Singh.[90] Later debates that evolved into major controversies were as follows:

Years	*Author*	*Title*	*Issues under discussion*
1920s	Teja Singh Bhasaur	*Sanchian Guru Granth Sahib*	Text of *Guru Granth*
1930s	G. S. Preetlari	*Param Manukh*	Life of Guru Gobind Singh
1940s	G.B. Singh	*Prachin Biran bare*	The Kartarpur *Pothi*

1970s	Giani Bhag Singh	*Dasam Granth Darpan*	Authorship of *Dasam Granth*
1970s	Fauja Singh Bajwa	*Guru Tegh Bahadur*	Death of Guru Tegh Bahadur
1990s	Amarjeet Singh Grewal	*Guru Granth & Modernity*	Message of *Guru Granth*
1990s	Pashaura Singh	*Guru Granth*	History of *Guru Granth*
1990s	Piar Singh	*Gatha Sri Adi Granth*	History of *Guru Granth*
2000s	G.S. Kala Afghana	*Dasam Granth*	Authorship of *Dasam Granth*
2000s	Jathedar Joginder Singh	*Gurbilas Patshahi Chhevin*	Life of Guru Hargobind
2000s	Giani Gurdit Singh	*Mundavani*	Text of *Guru Granth*[91]

A detailed discussion of these controversies is beyond the scope of this essay but some basic observations are in order. The third column above shows that the issues under discussion include the teachings, text, and history of the *Guru Granth* (Bhasaur, G.B. Singh, Giani Gurdit Singh, Grewal, Pashaura Singh, Piar Singh), the lives of the Gurus (Bajwa, Jathedar Joginder Singh, Preetlari), and the authorship of the *Dasam Granth* (Giani Bhag Singh, Kala Afghana). Fauja Singh Bajwa and Pashaura Singh wrote in English, all others wrote in Punjabi.

The background of these writers is considerably diverse. They include community activists (Bhasaur and Grewal), and retired government officials (G.B. Singh, Kala Afghana), singers of the verses of the *Guru Granth* (Giani Bhag Singh), scholars trained in indigenous Sikh modes (Giani Gurdit Singh, Jathedar Joginder Singh), university professors (Bajwa, Pashaura Singh, Piar Singh), public intellectuals (Preetlari). Furthermore, the people who raised objections against these writers also came from a wide range of backgrounds, including singers of the verses of the *Guru Granth*, university professors, intellectuals, community activists, retired government officials – their criticism appeared both in Punjabi and English.

Finally, the role of Sikh religious authority/the SGPC in these debates needs to be understood clearly. As mentioned earlier, at the heart of these debates lie differences of interpretation. Those who argued against the above-mentioned publications interpreted the academic differences in religious terms where they supposedly spoke for the Sikh tradition while the books under discussion presented a threat that needed to be contained. The SGPC leadership is often left with no option but to get involved when someone complains against a book as challenging Sikh beliefs. Being a community institution, it has its constraints and cannot keep aloof when approached. It has not created any system to oversee scholarship and thus ends up seeking help from its Dharm Prachar Committee, which has the responsibility to propagate Sikh beliefs. Based on the recommendation of the Dharm Prachar Committee, the SGPC leadership reached decisions that ranged from excommunicating Bhasaur (1927) and Kala Afghana (2003) to assigning religious penance to Piar Singh (1993), Pashaura Singh (1994), and Giani Gurdit Singh (2005), temporarily suspending the sale of Jathedar Joginder Singh's book, an SGPC publication (2002), and exonerating Amarjeet Singh Grewal (1994).

The result of these controversies may have offered a temporary sense of power for some and personal agony to others but the fact stands that this strategy has not succeeded in putting an end to any of these debates. The current storm around Giani Gurdit Singh's work echoes the Bhasaur episode in the 1920s. The issue at stake is the authenticity of the *Ragmala* (rosary of musical measures), a composition of twelve verses recorded at the closing of the text of the *Guru Granth*. Bhasaur dropped this from his multi-volume text of the *Guru Granth*, and Giani Gurdit Singh recently argued that the *Ragmala* is not available in the early scriptural manuscripts he has examined. The SGPC is well aware of the issue at stake and the absence of an easy solution. In the 1940s, after prolonged deliberations the SGPC leadership left it to the discretion of each congregation to decide whether to read the *Ragmala* or not in its ritual worship.[92]

To interpret these happenings as an attempt of Sikh religious authority to re-assert itself, or representing these debates as conflict between traditional versus historical scholarship, does not fully explain the complex interplay of people and points of view represented here.[93] These explanations lose sight of the overall context. First and foremost, Guru Nanak's emphasis on the role of human reasoning and rational investigation (*akl*) in one's beliefs has historically manifested itself in Sikh openness to new ideas and influences. Some Sikhs have raised the flag of 'blasphemy', but (there is no Punjabi or Sikh word for it). Resulting from this openness, the SGPC has not created any system to oversee scholarship and the fact that the sale of its own publication had to be suspended temporarily needs to be carefully registered. As for historical scholarship, Sikhs have practised it themselves for over a century now, and these controversies cannot be interpreted as Sikh rejection of the so-called new methods of research.[94] The reasons for these debates going out of hand range from academic differences in interpretation, and anxiety by some for the implications of these works for the community to downright desire to control Sikh scholarship.

In any case, these continuous debates sap the energy of the community and divert the SGPC leadership's attention away from broader issues of the transmission of the Sikh educational heritage. In my own experience, a lot needs to be taken into account by the SGPC. Many educated Sikh families find it more fashionable to speak Hindi at home, send their children to non-Sikh schools that are considered better preparatory places for successful careers. The Khalsa schools do not seem to be able to afford to offer classes in Gurmat anymore. The position of the Gurmat teacher at Khalsa College, Amrtisar, is a case in point. It has been in suspended animation for several years now and the department of Guru Granth Studies at Punjabi University is virtually closed down. Sikh leadership is in the process of planning the establishment of a new Sikh university, a worthy cause, but it might not hurt to look into revamping the existing structures of Sikh education. Finally this is the first time in the history of the Dharm Prachar Committee when none of its nominated members has any scholarly credentials.

The globalization of the Sikh community, however, brings interesting opportunities. The Sikh community overseas, now numbering two million and steadily increasing, is in an interesting historical situation. Unlike the situation in the Punjab, these communities cannot take the transmission of the Sikh heritage to the children for granted. This situation would require a wide range of changes such as parents' acquiring accurate information about Sikh beliefs and practice, a new type of *granthi* who can communicate with children in their first language as well as participate in the inter-faith activities in the neighbourhood and the Gurdwara architecture undergoing change to demarcate Sikh religious beliefs from Punjabi culture. Furthermore, living in a post-Operation Blue Star phase, when the Western world first took notice of the Sikhs, and now the post-11 September 2001 world, it is imperative that the mainstream people of the countries the Sikhs have adopted are provided with some basic knowledge of who the Sikhs are.[95]

This new phase of Sikh history has thus created circumstances that require a new level of elaboration of the Sikh educational heritage expressed in an idiom that is understood by Sikh children growing up in the new homes of their parents as well as the mainstream people living there. The Sikh community in North America has taken the lead and responded to this need by establishing programmes in leading universities where a new generation of scholars and teachers of Sikhism can be trained. In the future, young scholars from the Punjab may also be interested in participating in these activities. In their routine functioning, such programmes will generate up-to-date translations of Sikh texts and produce other source material required for teaching Sikhism. Projects like the Sikh Heritage Gallery at the Smithsonian Museum, Washington D.C. will help toward defining what constitutes Sikh material heritage and how best to present it to both the Sikh and non-Sikh public. As the community continues to reflect on these issues, the Sikh tradition will advance further towards becoming a major actor on the stage of world religions, a status it rightly deserves.

NOTES

1. *Sikhi sikhia gur vichari*, M1, *GG*, 465; *Guri kahia sa kar kamavahu*, M1, *GG*, 933. M1 stands for Mahala 1, Guru Nanak, M2 for Guru Angad and so on; *GG* for the *Guru Granth* and all page references are from *Shabadarth Sri Guru Granth Sahib Ji* (Amritsar: Shiromani Gurdwara Prabandhak Committee, 1969). The pagination being uniform these references would apply to any standard edition of the *Guru Granth*.

2. I consider Ratan Singh Bhangu's *Guru Panth Prakash* as the cut off point for primary Sikh heritage. The earliest manuscript of the *Guru Panth Prakash* that I know is dated Phagan, Sammat 1898 (1841CE) and is inscribed by Dayal Singh. This manuscript records both the *Guru Panth Prakash*, and *Sri Guru Panth Prakash*, as the title. For the sake of consistency I follow the *Guru Panth Prakash*. For the recent printed edition, see Ratan Singh Bhangu, *Sri Guru Panth Prakash*, ed. Balwant Singh Dhillon, Amritsar: Singh Brothers, 2004.
3. *Mai gunh gala ke siri bhar, gali gala sirjanhar,* M1, *GG*, p. 351.
4. Guru Nanak's compositions 'are in the language of the Jatts of the Punjab. "Jatt" in the dialect of the Punjab means a villager, a rustic': *Dabistan-i Mazahib*, ed. J.S. Grewal and Irfan Habib, New Delhi: Tulika, 2001, p. 63.
5. *Avigato nirmailu upje nirgunh te sargunh thia,* M1, *GG*, p. 940.
6. *Qudrati takhati rachaia sachi nibherhanhharo,* M1, *GG*, p. 580; *Sache takhat nivasu,* M1, *GG*, p. 1279; see also M1, *GG*, pp. 1035-43: *Rainhi dinasu duai dai daia jagu khelai khelai he*, M1, *GG*, p. 1021.
7. *Eki ravi rahia sabh thai, avaru na dise kisu puj charhai*, M1, *GG*, p. 1345.
8. *Ohu ape takhat bahai Sachiara*, M1, *GG*, p. 1026; *Tu sacha sachiar jinni sachu vartia*, M1, *GG*, p. 1279.
9. *Jaha karanhi taha puri mati, karanhi vajhahu ghate ghati*, M1, *GG*, p. 25; *Karanhi kaba, karanhi kalama,* M1, *GG*, pp. 140-1; *Sachi rahit sacha sukhu pai,* M1, *GG*, p. 1343; *Ghali khai kichhu hathau dai,* M1, *GG*, p. 1245.
10. *Sachau urai sabhu ko upari sachu achar,* M1, *GG*, p. 62.
11. *Vichi dunia sev kamaiai tan dargah baisanhu paiai*, M1, *GG*, p. 26.
12. *Api tarai janu pitra tarai,* M1, *GG*, p. 1026; *Api tarai sangati kul tarai,* M1, *GG*, pp. 353, 1039; *Api tarai sagalai kul tarai,* M1, *GG*, pp. 622, 877; *Api tarai tarai bhi soi,* M1, *GG*, p. 944.
13. *Jaisi mai avai khasam ki banhi taisarha kari gianu, ve Lalo,* M1, *GG*, p. 722; *Saha kia gala dar kia bata tai ta kahanhu kahaia,* M1, *GG*, p. 878; *Eti mar pai karlanhe tain ki darad na aia,* M1, *GG*, p. 360.
14. *Sach ki banhi,* M1, *GG*, p. 722; *Sabhi nad Bed gurbanhi,* M1, *GG*, p. 879; *Sunhi sunhi sikh hamari,* M1, *GG*, p. 154; *Sunhi sikhvante Nanaku binavai,* M1, *GG*, p. 503.
15. *Tin kau kia updesiai jin Guru Nanak deau,* M2, *GG*, p. 150.
16. *Pothi Puranh kamaiai,* M1, *GG*, p. 25.
17. *Akali parh kai bughiai akali kichai dan, Nanaku akhai rahu ehu hori galan Saitanu,* M1, *GG*, p. 1245.
18. *Banhi Brahma Bedu Atharbanhu karanhi kirati lahaia,* M1, *GG*, p. 903.
19. *Rosu na kijai utaru dijai kiau paiai gurduaro,* M1, *GG*, p. 938.
20. M1, *GG*, pp. 938-46.

21. *Gian kharhgu le man siu lujhe,* M1, *GG*, p. 1022; *Saram,* M1, *GG*, p. 7; *Sifati saram ka kaparha mangau,* M1, *GG*, p. 1329.
22. *Vidia vichari tan parupkari,* M1, *GG*, p. 356.
23. *Ved parhahi te vad vakhanhai bine hari pati gavai,* M1, *GG*, p. 638; *Ihu telu diva iau jalai, kari chananhu sahib tau milai,* M1, *GG*, p. 25.
24. *Sachu kamavai sachi rahai sachai savi samai,* M3, *GG*, p. 560.
25. *Sarab dharm mahi sreshat dharm, hari ko namu japi nirmal karamu,* M5, *GG*, p. 266.
26. *Binu tel diva kiau jale,* M1, *GG*, p. 25; *Gur gian dipak ujiaria,* M5, *GG*, p. 210.
27. *Gur gian anjanu sachu netri paia,* M5, *GG*, p. 210; *Gian anjanu guri dia agian andher binasu,* M5, *GG*, p. 293.
28. *Gian kharhgu kari kirpa dina dut mare kari dhai he,* M5, *GG*, p. 1072.
29. *Parupkar umaha,* M5, *GG*, p. 273; M5, *GG*, p. 816.
30. *Dhur ki banhi,* M5, *GG*, p. 628; *Mahali bulaia prabhu amritu bhuncha,* M5, *GG*, p. 562. *Thal,* M5, *GG*, p. 1429.
31. *Pothi parmesar ka thanu,* M5, *GG*, p. 1226.
32. *Dithai mukati na hovai jicharu sabadi na kare vichar,* M3, *GG*, p. 594; M3, *GG*, p. 560.
33. Bhai Gurdas, *Varan*, ed. Gursharan Kaur Jaggi, Patiala: Punjabi University, 1987, is the standard edition of the text.
34. *Sekha chauchakia ... eharh teharh chhadi tu gur ka sabadu pacchanhu,* M3, *GG*, p. 646; *Brahmu bindahi te brahamanha je chalahi satigur bhai,* M3, *GG*, pp. 849-50.
35. *Mai badhi sachi dharamsal hai gursikha lahada bhali kai,* M5, *GG*, p. 73; *Mera gharu bania banu talu bania prabhu parase hari raia ram,* M5, *GG*, p. 782; *Mandar mere sabh te uche. ... Kirati hamari gharighari hoi, bhagati hamari sabhani loi,* M5, *GG*, p. 1141.
36. M1, *GG*, p. 6; M5, *GG*, pp. 1235-6. Bhatts, *GG*, pp. 1385-1409.
37. M4, *GG*, p. 306; M5, *GG*, p. 199.
38. For this literature, see Kirpal Singh, ed. *Janam Sakhi Prampara,* Patiala: Punjabi University, 1990; Rai Jasbir Singh, ed., *Guru Amardas Srot Pustak,* Amritsar: Guru Nanak Dev University, 1986; Piara Singh Padam, *Prachin Punjabi Gadd,* Patiala: Kalam Mandir, 1978. For English translation, W.H. McLeod, *The B40 Janam-Sakhi,* Amritsar: Guru Nanak Dev University, 1980, and for critical discussion of this literature see his *Early Sikh Tradition,* Oxford: Clarendon Press, 1980.
39. The manuscript was extant at Kiratpur until recently. Anne Murphy and I examined and photographed this manuscript in 1999.
40. For these details, see *Chaupa Singh Rahit-Nama,* ed W.H. McLeod, Dunedin: University of Otago Press, 1987, p. 79; *Apani Katha* in *Shabadarth Dasam Granth Sahib,* ed. Bhai Randhir Singh, Patiala: Punjabi University, vol. 1, pp. 76-7. For *rahit* literature, Piara Singh

Padam, *Rahitname*, Amritsar: Singh Brothers, 1995, and W.H. McLeod, *Sikhs of the Khalsa*, New Delhi: Oxford University Press, 2003.

41. *Garibi gada hamari khana sagal ranu chhari*, M5, *GG*, p. 628.
42. McLeod (ed.), *Chaupa Singh Rahit-Nama*, p. 88
43. Ibid., p. 82. Chaupa Singh mentions that the Guru sent letters asking scribes to reach the Sikh court.
44. *Shabadarth Dasam Granth Sahib* does not include the *Charitro Pakhayan*.
45. *Sarab Loh Granth*, ed. Harnamdas Udasi, Anandpur: Guru ka Bagh, n.d. *Pothi Prem Ambodh*, ed. Davinder Singh Osahan, Patiala: Punjabi University, 1989. For references to other texts, see *Chaupa Singh Rahit-Nama*, p. 82.
46. The dates appear as follows: Nand Lal: Maghar 9, Sammat 1752 (1695); Chaupa Singh et al.: Jeth 7, Sammat 1757 (1700); Prahlad Singh, Magh Vadi *thit panchami*, Virvar, Sammat 1762 (1705)/the one that is popular in printed texts is Magh Vadi *thit panchami*, Ravivar, Sammat 1752.
47. Sainapat, *Sri Gur Sobha*, ed. Ganda Singh, Patiala: Punjabi University, 1988 (the standard edition of the text).
48. Kavi Seva Singh, *Shahid Bilas*, ed. Garja Singh Giani, Ludhiana: Punjabi Sahit Academy, 1961.
49. For two opposing positions on this text, Piara Singh Padam, *Dasam Granth Darshan*, Patiala: Kalam Mandir, 1990, and Ratan Singh Jaggi, *Dasam Granth da Karatritava*, New Delhi: Punjabi Sahit Sabha, 1966. A partial discussion of the related issues and the translations of some sections from the text are available on the Internet (www.dasamgranth.org/dasamgranth).
50. For a brief introduction to this interesting figure, see Piara Singh Padam, *Mahan Kavi Santokh Singh*, Patiala: Kalam Mandir, 1990.
51. G.S. Mann, *Making of Sikh Scripture*, New York: Oxford University Press, 2001, pp. 121-36.
52. G.B. Singh, *Sri Guru Granth Sahib dian Prachin Birhan*, Lahore: Modern Publications, 1944. Later works include Swami Harnamdas Udasi, *Adi Sri Guru Granth Sahib dian Puratani Birhan te Vichar*, Kapurthala: Kantesh Pharmacy, n.d. (1969?). Piar Singh, *Gatha Sri Adi Granth*, Amritsar: Guru Nanak Dev University, 1992. Balwant Singh Dhillon, *Early Sikh Scriptural Tradition*, Amritsar: Singh Brothers, 1999. Pashaura Singh, *The Guru Granth Sahib*, New Delhi: Oxford University Press, 2000; G.S. Mann, *The Making of Sikh Scripture*, and Giani Gurdit Singh, *Mundavani*, Chandigarh: Sahit Prakashan, 2003.
53. I am grateful to Punjabi University for permitting me to photograph this manuscript (MS 228) presently available at Dr Balbir Singh Sahitya Kendra, Dehradun.
54. However, it is important to register the presence of variants: Bhai

Randhir Singh, *Gurmat Bibek,* Ludhiana: Published by author, 1946; Jathedar Joginder Singh, *Sri Hazuri Maryada Prabodh,* Nander: Sri Takhat Abchal Nagar, 1967; Giani Gurbachan Singh Khalsa, *Gurmat Rahit Maryada,* Amritsar: Khalsa Brothers, 1986; *Khararha Sikh Rahit Maryada* (Sant Samaj, 1994).

55. Gurtej Singh and Swaranjeet Singh (eds.), *Shahid-Bilas Sant Jarnail Singh Bhindranwale,* Chandigarh: Satsandhi Publications, 2001.
56. *Bhule sikh guru samjhae ujharhi jade maragi pai,* M1, *GG*, p. 1032; *Guru kahia sa kar kamavahu,* M1, *GG*, p. 933; *Sacha arazu sachi ardasi,* M1, *GG*, p. 355.
57. *Guruduarai hoi sojhi paisi,* M1, *GG*, p. 730.
58. *Dabistan-i Mazahib,* pp. 78, 84.
59. *Mithatu nivi Nanaka gunh changaia tatu,* M1, *GG*, p. 470.
60. *Sa jati sa pati hai jehe karam kamai,* M1, *GG*, p. 1330.
61. Bhai Gurdas, *Varan,* p. 137; Chaupa Singh also refers to the presence of Sikh scribes: *Chaupa Singh Rahit-Nama,* pp. 65, 82.
62. *Ghari rahu re man mughadh iane,* M1, *GG*, p. 1030.
63. *Chaupa Singh Rahit-Nama,* p. 115.
64. *Prem Sumarg,* ed. Bhai Randhir Singh, Jalandhar: New Book Company, 2000 (1953), pp.13-14. The text is yet to be firmly dated, the earliest manuscript that has come to my notice was prepared in 1807.
65. Gurdwara *Gazette* (November 1965), pp. 274-5.
66. Madanjit Kaur, 'The Contribution of the Bungas to the Education of the Punjab', *Proceedings Punjab History Conference,* 1978, pp. 94-101. For references to Dip Singh, see Ratan Singh Bhangu, *Sri Guru Panth Prakash,* pp. 210, 334; Giani Gian Singh, *Tawarikh Guru Khalsa,* Patiala: Punjab Languages Department, 1987, vol. II, p. 262.
67. *Sikhan di Bhagatmala,* ed. Tarlochan Singh Bedi, Patiala: Punjabi University, 1994.
68. G.W. Leitner, *History of Indigenous Education in the Punjab*, Patiala: Punjab Languages Department, 1971 (rpt.), pp. 36, 155-6. For details regarding schools, see part III, pp. 1-13.
69. G.S. Mann, *Sikhism,* Prentice Hall, 2004, pp. 58-9.
70. Khushwant Singh, *A History of the Sikhs,* Princeton: Princeton University Press, 1966, vol. II, p. 144.
71. For primary documents, Dalwinder Singh, *Bhai Sahib Bhai Takhat Singh Ji,* Ludhiana: Sikh Missionary College, 2003.
72. Durlab Singh, *The Valiant Fighter,* Lahore: Hero Publishers, 1942, pp.153, 157.
73. Amrit Walia, 'Achievements of Sikh Education Conference', *Proceedings Punjab History Conference,* 1975, pp. 205-12.
74. Sikhs saw the founding of Guru Nanak Dev University, in particular as a major event. It was understood as the fulfilment of the dream that

the Khalsa College could develop into a full-fledged university. The physical proximity of the two institutions and the appointment of Bishan Singh Samundri, who at that time was the Principal of Khalsa College, as the first head of the university supported this general communal understanding of the issue.

75. Paul Wallace and Surendra Chopra, eds., *Political Dynamics and Crisis in Punjab,* Amritsar: Guru Nanak Dev University, 1988, p. 37.
76. *The New York Times,* 18 July 1998.
77. Guru Nanak Sikh School in Hayes was opened as an independent school but in 1999 became the first school to receive public funding. Primarily a secondary school, catering for 11-18 year olds, this school has a very good reputation and was almost at the top of table of schools 'adding value' to student education, i.e. getting higher qualifications relative to their socioeconomic background. Lea Junior School, in Slough, Berkshire – further west from London and Heathrow, is almost set to become the second Sikh school. This will be a primary school, i.e. catering for 4-11 year olds.
78. Darshan Singh Tatla, *The Sikh Diaspora,* Seattle: University of Washington, 1998.
79. G.S. Mann, 'Sikhism in the United States of America', in *The South Asian Religious Diaspora in Britain, Canada, and the United States,* eds. Harold Coward et al. Albany: SUNY Press, 2000, pp. 259-76.
80. See, for example, Ramandeep Kaur Grewal and T. Sher Singh, 'Same Sex Marriage', *The Sikh Times* <sikhtimes.com>, 17 February 2005.
81. My position here is different from that of Harjot Oberoi who argues that toward the end of the nineteenth century, the Tat Khalsa imposed a singular reading of Sikh beliefs and history, etc., *Construction of Religious Boundaries,* New Delhi: Oxford University Press, 1994. In my view, this reading of Sikh history neither shows a clear understanding of early Sikh sources, nor does it register the diversity of views that are available in the twentieth century Sikh writings.
82. Giani Gurbachan Singh Ji Khalsa, *Gurbandhi Path and Darshan,* Bhindran Kalan: Gurdwara Akhand Prakash, 1990s.
83. Jathedar Joginder Singh and Amarjit Singh (eds.), *Gur Bilas Patshahi Chhevin,* Amritsar: SGPC, 1998.
84. The special issue in his honour of the *Punjabi Dunia,* Patiala: Punjab Languages Department, April 2002.
85. For his life story, see S.S. Amol, *Professor Teja Singh*, Patiala: Punjabi University, 1977.
86. See Joseph D. Cunningham, *A History of the Sikhs*, Delhi: S. Chand and Company, 1985; Ernest Trumpp, *The Adi Granth*, Delhi: Munshiram Manoharlal, 1978; Max Arthur Macauliffe, *The Sikh Religion.* New Delhi: S. Chand and Company, 1985; Hew McLeod,

Discovering the Sikhs: Autobiography of a Historian, Delhi: Permanent Black, 2004.

87. J.S. Grewal, *The Sikhs of the Punjab*, New York: Cambridge University Press, 1990. For his seminal contribution to scholarship, see *Five Punjabi Centuries*, ed. Indu Banga, New Delhi: Manohar, 2000, pp. 11-41.
88. Richard G. Fox, *Lions of the Punjab: Culture in the Making*, Berkeley: University of California Press, 1985. Harjot Oberoi, *Construction of Religious Boundaries: Culture, Identity and Diversity in the Sikh Tradition*. Brian K. Axel, *The Nation's Tortured Body: Violence, Representation, and the Formation of Sikh Diaspora*, Durham: Duke University Press, 2001.
89. J.S. Grewal's judgement goes as follows: Harjot Oberoi, despite his sophisticated conception of historical methodology, can come up with highly inadequate interpretation of the known evidence. See Grewal's *Contesting Interpretations of the Sikh Tradition*, New Delhi: Manohar, 1998, p. 305.
90. Giani Badan Singh, *Adi Sri Guru Granth Sahib Ji Satik*, Patiala: Punjab Languages Department, 1970 (rpt.). For an interesting critique of this project, *Sikh Concept of the Divine*, ed. Pritam Singh, Amritsar: Guru Nanak Dev University, 1985, p. 9.
91. I have not mentioned debates around the research of W.H. McLeod, Harjot Oberoi, and to some degree my own, for the simple reason that the SGPC was not directly involved in these cases.
92. Shamsher Singh Ashok, *Shiromani* Gurdwara *Prabandhak Committee da Punjab Sala Itihas*, Amritsar: SGPC, 1982, p. 228. It is important to recognize that Bhai Manjit Singh, who had the singular feat of dealing with three controversies during his brief stint as the Acting Jathedar of the Akal Takht reached the right conclusion: it was not useful to enter these debates. Though these controversies were raging there is no reference to them in the World Sikh Meet-1995, Amritsar: SGPC, 1995, pp. 5-11.
93. Pashaura Singh, 'Recent, Trends and Prospects in Sikh Studies', *Studies in Religion* (1998), and W.H. McLeod, 'Discord in the Sikh Panth', *Journal of American Oriental Society*, vol. 119, part 3, 1999.
94. Karam Singh Historian, *Katak ke Visakh*, Ludhiana: Lahore Book, 1912, was the first work in this area and a whole tradition has developed since then.
95. Sikh leadership overseas is well aware that the rumblings such as 'we need to tell the Americans that Sikhs are not Muslims', which followed 11 September 2001, were neither useful nor justified. Simultaneously, there is a relative openness on the part of mainstream forums to include Sikhism in their activity. For instance, Oxford University Press' new series on Religion in American Life includes a section on Sikhism, etc.

Glossary

Adi Granth: the Sikh scripture, compiled by Guru Arjan in 1604 (containing the compositions of the first five Gurus and a number of *bhaktas, sants* and *sufis*) and authenticated by Guru Gobind Singh with the compositions of Guru Tegh Bahadur. Now known as *Guru Granth Sahib*.

Adi Purkh: Original Being, God.

ahimsa: non-violence, non-injury to living beings.

Akali: the militant followers of Guru Gobind Singh who regarded themselves to be the guardians of the faith, also called Nihang; a protagonist of Gurdwara reform in the 1920s; now a member of the Shiromani Akali Dal.

Akhand Path: an uninterrupted reading of *Guru Granth Sahib*.

akhara: a wrestling ground; used generally for the establishments of Udasis and Nirmalas.

akl (*aql*): rational investigation.

amrit: the nector (conferring immortality), ambrosia.

amritdhari: the Sikh who has taken *amrit* (baptism of the double-edged sword).

anjan: collyruim applied to the eyes.

ardas: the Sikh prayer.

ardasia: one who offers *ardas*; the Sikh priest employed by Sikh rulers and *jagirdars* for the purpose.

bani: utterance, inspired verses, sacred poetry.

bhakti: devotion; a devotional mode of worship.

bhet: an offering to a deity; land given in charity.

bhog: mortuary rites; the end of a performance.

burhiya: an old woman.

chanani: a ceremonial cloth spread overhead, a shelter and symbol of authority or sanctity.

charan pahul: the nectar of the feet; the practice of drinking the water in which the toe of the *guru* has been dipped, symbolizing humility and dedication on the part of the initiate.

chauki: a four-legged low stool or table.

chela: a disciple; an attendant.

chhal: deceit.

dan: charity; emphasis in the Sikh tradition is on giving something to others rather than receiving anything from them.

deepak: the earthen lamp that can be blown out.

Dhan Nirankar: 'Great is the Formless one'(used as a salutation).

Dhanak: the lowest category of untouchables.

dharma: a set of duties expected of a member of a particular caste or sect.

dharmsal: Sikh sacred space or the Sikh place of worship in early Sikh history; synonymous with Gurdwara.

Dharmsalia: one who looks after a *dharmsal*.

dharmyudh: war of righteousness; a mode of agitation among the Akalis.

dhoti: a sheet of cloth worn around the waist in varying styles to cover the lower portion of the body.

fan-i tufangandazi: the art of musketry.

ghazis: fighters; holy warriors.

gilja: an epithet commonly used by the Sikhs for Gilzai Afghans, especially for Ahmad Shah Abdali; in Punjabi it refers to the carrion-eating male vulture.

golak: one among several categories of offerings; a receptacle kept for voluntary cash offerings in *dharmsals* or Gurdwaras.

granthi: the professional reader of *Guru Granth Sahib*; the functionary in charge of a Gurdwara.

Gurbachan: literally, what is uttered by the Guru; Gurbani.

Gurbani: composition of the Guru, especially in the Sikh tradition; refers to *Guru Granth Sahib* too.

Gurdwara: the door of the Guru; a Sikh place of worship, generally a centre of social activity too.

gurmaryada: the ethical principles and practices in accordance with the teachings of the Guru; the tradition set by the Gurus for the Sikhs.

gurmata: resolution of the Guru; the collective decision taken before the *Guru Granth Sahib* at a gathering of Sikhs.

Gurmukhi vidia: learning based on the compositions of the Gurus, and on Sikh literature in general.

gutka: a small collection of texts from the compositions of the Gurus.

halal: the traditional Muslim mode of slaughtering animals for meat; anything lawful, as opposed to *haram* (prohibited).

haumai: I-ness; self-centredness; pride.

hukam: an order; the divine order operative in the natural and the moral world.

Jampur: the city or the abode of Yama; hell.

janamsakhi: a genre of Punjabi literature related to the life of Guru Nanak and his teachings.

Japji: a composition of Guru Nanak used for the morning prayer; in *Guru Granth Sahib*, this composition includes a *shalok* of Guru Angad at the end.

jatha: a group of volunteers for a specific purpose.

jaulan kunan: galloping.

jhatka: the mode of slaughtering an animal for meat with one stroke of the sword or some other instrument; probably the traditional non-Muslim mode of slaughtering in India.

jogi: one who pursues the objective of union with the deity; a Shaiva renunciant belonging to one of the twelve Gorakhnathi orders.

kalal: a brewer or distiller by caste; one who served liquor.

kaljug: the fourth cosmic age, associated with utter degeneration in all walks of life.

kangha: the comb supposed to be kept by a baptized Singh as one of the five Ks.

kara: the iron bangle worn by a baptized Singh as one of the five Ks.

karaha: cauldron; the sacred food (*prasad*) prepared in it, was called *karha prasad*: its three ingredients are wheat flour, sugar and *ghee*.

katha: exegesis of the Guru's verses.

kesh: the hair of the head.

keshdhari: a baptized Singh who maintains long unshorn hair.

Khalsa: an epithet used for the Sikhs directly affiliated to the Guru rather than through a *masand*; Guru Gobind Singh declared that he would recognize only the Khalsa as Sikhs; those who volunteered to have baptism of the double-edged sword became Khalsa Singhs.

khande di pahul: nectar of the double-edged sword.

Khangi Karobari: the minister in-charge of the royal household.

khidava: a person employed for keeping a child busy in one kind of play or another; a male wet nurse.

kirpan: a sword; carried by a baptized Sikh as one of the five Ks.

kirtan: corporate singing of divine praises, both in the morning and the evening.

langar: the kitchen attached to a Gurdwara from which food is served to all, regardless of caste or creed; a community meal.

mahant: head of a religious establishment; the Udasi custodian of a Gurdwara.

maryada: limit, boundary; bounds (of law, usage); custom; convention; traditionally correct behaviour; decorum.

Masand: the Guru's representative in a distant congregation; introduced by Guru Amar Das and developed as an important link in the organization of the community by Guru Ram Das and Guru Arjan; removed by Guru Gobind Singh when the office holders became a source of weakness and disharmony.

misl: a band.

misaldar: the leader of a *misl*; in combination, these Sikh leaders occupied territories to rule.

mlechh: an uncouth barbarian; an outsider with whom no association is desirable; a foreign invader; an untouchable.

moksh: release from death and rebirth; deliverance, emancipation.

morcha: a battle front; an agitation in protest.

mukti (*moksh*): release, emancipation, liberation.

nadar (from *nazr*): kind notice; divine grace.

Nam: the Name; a conception of God in Sikh philosophy; God in his absolute state, without any attribute other than *hukam*; the path and the way of life promulgated by Guru Nanak.

namaz: the Muslim prayer.

nirgun: without attributes or qualities.

nitnem: the verses for daily recitation; the daily routine of religious worship.

pahul: Sikh baptism, especially that of the double-edged sword; also *amrit*.

Panth: a path; the people following a particular path; collectively the followers of the Gurus; the Sikh community.

paranda: thick cotton threads with knots, used by women for tying their hair to hang on the back as a tail.

par-dristi: to look at 'another woman' or things belonging to others.

pargat: manifest, revealed, no longer concealed.

parikrama: the path around a temple for circumambulation.

par-tirya: literally, another woman; appears to carry the import of a woman other than one's wife.

path: recitation of Gurbani or *Guru Granth Sahib*.

Pothi: a book.

prashad: sacred food; simply food.

qazi: the official who administered civil and criminal justice according to the Islamic law.

rahit: way of life, used especially for the Sikh way of life in accordance with the philosophic and ethical principles advanced by the Gurus.

Ramdasias: the leather tanners (*chamars*) affiliated to the Sikh faith.

sabha: a society or an association.

sach-achar: truthful living and conduct, emphasized by Guru Nanak.

sachcha padshah: the true king, used metaphorically for God and the Guru.

sahaj: the state of union with God.

sahajdhari: a Sikh not initiated afresh through the baptism of the double-edged sword.

sambhau: self-sufficient, God.
sangat: association, congregation; a local Sikh community.
sant: a saint; generally a follower of the figures like Namdev, Kabir, Ravidas and Dadu; equated with Sikh in the *Guru Granth Sahib*, and now with an eminent Sikh known to be pious.
Sarbat Khalsa: the entire body of the Sikhs meeting for a particular purpose.
sardar: a leader; a Sikh ruler; any Khalsa Sikh.
Sat Kartar: 'the Creator alone is true' (used as a form of salutation).
satnam: the true Name (refers to God).
satsang: true association; singing hymns in praise of God in congregation.
sewa: service; service of the Guru, a deity, a person; voluntary service of others.
shabad: the word; a hymn; verses from *Guru Granth Sahib*.
shaikh: the head of a Sufi order; a respectable Muslim.
shradh: the practice of feeding Brahmans in the name of one's ancestors.
siddha: a person who has attained to high spiritual state so as to command supranatural powers.
simarna: a rosary for counting beads.
sloka: a popular form of verse, also pronounced as *salok* or *shalok*.
Sohila: a composition of Guru Nanak recited especially at the end of a ceremony.
sultan: the ruler, the king.
takht: a throne; one of the five important religious centres of Sikhism.
taksali: true, staunch.
tikka (tilak): the sacred mark on the forehead.
ulama: plural of *alim*, a learned man among Muslims; the representatives of orthodox Islam.
Vaishnava: a devotee of Vishnu or his incarnation as Rama or Krishna.
var: a literary genre, generally used for heroic poetry; Guru Nanak used it for his religious compositions; the most famous *vars* in Sikh literature were composed by Bhai Gurdas in the early seventeenth century in praise of the Sikh Gurus and their teachings.
Yama: Death.
zimmi: the people of the book who paid *jiziya* (tax) in a Muslim state in lieu of protection of life and property; the non-Muslim subjects of a Muslim state in India were generally treated as *zimmis* (and not as infidels who had no right to protection).

Bibliography

Abul Fazl, *Akbarnama*, vol. III, ed. Agha Ahmad Ali and Abd al-Rahim, Calcutta, 1873-7.

Adhikari, G., *Sikh Homeland Through Hindu-Muslim-Sikh Unity*, Bombay, 1944.

Ali, Imran, *The Punjab under Imperialism*, Princeton: Princeton University Press, 1988.

Amol, S.S., *Professor Teja Singh*, Patiala: Punjabi University, 1977.

Archer, W., *Paintings of the Sikhs*, London: HMSO, 1966.

Aryan, K.C., *Punjab Painting*, Patiala: Punjabi University, 1975.

Ashok, Shamsher Singh, *Shiromani Gurdwara Prabandhak Committee da Punjahsala Itihas*, Amritsar: SGPC, 1982.

——— (ed.), *Shri Gur Sobha*, Amritsar: SGPC, 1967.

Ashton, S.R., *British Policy towards the Indian States, 1905-1939*, New Delhi: Select Book Service Syndicate, 1985.

Axel, Brian K., *The Nation's Tortured Body: Violence, Representation, and the Formation of Sikh Diaspora*, Durham: Duke University, 2001.

Bal, Sukhmani, 'Politics of the Central Sikh League, 1919-1929', *Punjab History Conference Proceedings*, Patiala, 1982.

———, 'Politics of the Central Sikh League', M.Phil. dissertation, Jawaharlal Nehru University, Delhi, 1982.

Ballard, Roger, 'The Context and Consequences of Migration: Jullundur and Mirpur Compared', *New Community*, vol. 11, part 4, 1983.

Banga, Indu, 'The Crisis of Sikh Politics (1940-47)', in *Sikh History and Religion in the Twentieth Century*, ed. Joseph T. O'Connell et al. Toronto: University of Toronto, 1988.

——— (ed.), *Five Punjabi Centuries*, New Delhi: Manohar, 1997 (rpt. 2000).

Bardhan, P., 'Trends in Land Relations: A Note', *Economic and Political Weekly*, Annual No. 1970.

———, 'Variations in Extent and Form of Agriculture', *Economic and Political Weekly*, 18 September 1976.

Barr, William, *Journal of a March from New Delhi to Peshawur and from thence to Cabul, including travels in the Punjab*, London, 1844; Patiala: Punjab Languages Department, 1970 (rpt.).

Barrier, N. Gerald, *The Punjab Land Alienation Bill of 1900*, Duke University, Monograph No. 3, 1966.

———, *The Sikhs and Their Literature*, New Delhi: Manohar, 1970.

———, 'Muslim Politics in the Punjab 1870-1890', *The Panjab Past and Present*, vol. V, 1971.

Bedi, Tarlochan Singh (ed.), *Sikhan di Bhagatmala*, Patiala: Punjabi University, 1994.

Bhai Gurdas, *Varan*, ed. Gursharan Kaur Jaggi, Patiala: Punjabi University, 1987.

Bhangu, Ratan Singh, *Sri Guru Panth Prakash*, ed. Balwant Singh Dhillon, Amritsar: Singh Brothers, 2004.

Bhardwaj, H., 'Tenurial Conditions and Mode of Exploitation: A Study of Some Villages in Orissa', *Economic and Political Weekly*, Annual No. 1975.

Bhim Sen, *Nuskha-i Dilkusha*, British Library, Or. MSS 23.

Brack, Bruce La, 'The New Patrons: Sikhs Overseas', in *The Sikh Diaspora: Migration and the Experience beyond Punjab*, ed. N. Gerald Barrier and Verne A. Dusenberry, Delhi: Chanakya Publications, 1989.

Buchignani, Norman, Doreen M. Indra and Ram Srivastava, *Continuous Journey: A Social History of South Asians in Canada*, Toronto: McLelland and Stewart, 1985.

Calvert, H., *The Wealth and Welfare of the Punjab: Being Some Studies in Punjab Rural Economics*, Lahore: Civil and Military Gazette Press, 1922.

Caveeshar, Sardul Singh, 'Progress of the Sikhs', *Sikh Review*, vol. IV, no. 20, 1916.

Chadha, G.K., *The State and Rural Economic Transformation: The Case of Punjab, 1950-1985*, New Delhi: Sage, 1986.

Chatterjee, Partha, *The Nation and its Fragments*, New Delhi: Oxford University Press, 1994.

Chattopadhyaya, Harprasad, *Indians in Africa, A Socio-Economic Study*, Calcutta: Bookland Private Limited, 1970.

Chayanov, A.V., *The Theory of Peasant Economy*, Homewood (Illinois), 1966.

Coomaraswamy, Ananda, *Rajput Painting*, Oxford, 1916.

Copland, Ian, *The British Raj and the Indian Princes: Paramountcy in Western India, 1857-1930*, Bombay: Orient Longman, 1982.

Cunningham, J.D., *A History of the Sikhs from the Origin of the Nation to the Battles of the Sutlej*, London, 1849; ed. H.L.O. Garrett, Delhi: 1915; Delhi: S. Chand and Company, 1985.

Dabistan-i Mazahib, ed. Nazar Ashraf, Calcutta, 1809; Lucknow: Nawal Kishore, 1904.

Dantwala, M.L. and C.H. Shah, 'Pre-reform and Post-reform Agrarian Structure', *Indian Journal of Agricultural Economics*, July-September 1971.

Darling, M.L., *The Punjab Peasant in Prosperity and Debt*, London: Oxford University Press, 1925; Delhi, 1977 (rpt.).

Davis, Kingsley, *The Population of India and Pakistan*, Princeton: Princeton University Press, 1951.

Deol, Jeevan, 'Eighteenth Century Khalsa Identity: Discourse, Praxis and Narrative', in Christopher Shackle, Gurharpal Singh & Arvind-Pal Singh Mandair (eds.), *Sikh Religion, Culture and Ethnicity*, Richmond: Curzon, 2001.

Desai, Rashmi, *Indian Immigration in Britain*, London: Oxford University Press, 1963.

Dewey, C. and A.G. Hopkins (eds.), *The Imperial Impact : Studies in the Economic History of Africa and India*, Athlone Press for the Institute of Commonwealth Studies, 1978.

Dhillon, Balwant Singh, *Early Sikh Scriptural Tradition*, Amritsar: Singh Brothers, 1999.

Foster, W. (ed.), *Early Travels in India (1583-1619)*, London, 1927; Delhi (rpt.) 1968.

Fox, R., *Lions of the Punjab: Culture in the Making*, Cambridge University Press, 1988.

Gill, S.S., 'Migratory Labour in Punjab Agriculture', *PSE Economic Analyst*, vols. 1 and 2, 1986.

Gosal, G.S. and A.B. Mukerji, 'The Religious Composition of India's Population – A Spatial Analysis', *Tijdschrift voor Economische en Sociale Geografic*, vol. 16, pp. 91-100.

Goswamy, B.N., 'Pahari Painting: the Family as the Basis of Style', *Marg*, vol. xxi, no. 4, 1968.

———, 'Of Patronage and Pahari Painting', in *Aspects of Indian Art*, ed. Pratapaditya Pal, Leiden, 1972.

———, *Painters at the Sikh Court*, Weisbaden, 1975.

———, 'Painting at Patiala', *Pushpanjali*, Bombay, 1980.

———, 'A Matter of Taste: Some Notes on the Context of Paintings in Sikh Punjab', *Journal of Regional History*, Amritsar: Guru Nanak Dev University, 1981. Reproduced in *Paroksa*, ed. Gulam-mohammed Shaikh and Kapila Vatsyayana, Delhi, 1984.

———, *Nainsukh of Guler : A great Pahari Painter from a small Hill State*, Zurich, 1997.

Goswamy, B.N. and Eberhard Fischer, *Pahari Masters: Court Painters of Northern India*, Zurich: Artibus Asiae, 1992.

Goswamy, Karuna, 'Frescoes in the Sheesh Mahal, Patiala', *Roopalekha*, vol. xxxviii, nos. 1-2.

———, *Kashmiri Painting*, New Delhi: Aryan Books International (for the Indian Institute of Advanced Study, Shimla), 1998.

Grewal, J.S., 'The Prem Sumarg: A Theory of Sikh Social Order', *Punjab History Conference Proceedings*, Patiala: Punjabi University, 1965.

———, *Guru Nanak in History*, Chandigarh: Panjab University, 1969.

———, *The Sikhs of the Punjab*, Cambridge: Cambridge University Press, 1990.

———, *Contesting Interpretations of the Sikh Tradition*, New Delhi: Manohar, 1998.

Grewal, J.S. and Irfan Habib, eds., *Sikh History from Persian Sources*, New Delhi: Tulika/Indian History Congress, 2001.

Grewal, Ramandeep Kaur and T. Sher Singh, 'Same Sex Marriage', *The Sikh Times* <sikhtimes.com>, 17 February 2005.

Griffin, Keith, 'On the Emigration of the Peasantry, *World Development*, vol. 4, 1976.

Griffin, Lepel, *Rajas of the Punjab*, Patiala: Punjab Languages Department, 1970 (rpt.; 1st pub. 1873).

———, *Ranjit Singh*, Oxford, 1905.

Gulati, K.C., *The Akalis Past and Present*, Delhi: Ashajanak Publications, 1979.

Gunther, John, *Inside Asia*, London: Hamish Hamilton, 1939.

Gupta, Dipankar, 'The Communalising of Punjab 1980-1985' in *Punjab: The Fatal Miscalculation*, ed., Patwant Singh and Harji Malik, New Delhi, 1985.

———, *The Context of Ethnicity: Sikh Identity in a Comparative Perspective*, New Delhi: Oxford University Press, 1996.

Habib, Irfan, *The Agrarian System of Mughal India (1526-1707)*, Bombay: Asia Publishing House, 1963.

Hamdard, Sadhu Singh, *Azad Punjab* (Urdu), Amritsar, 1943.

Helweg, A., *Sikhs in England*, Oxford University Press, 1986.

Hess, Linda and Shukdev Singh (trs.), *The Bijak of Kabir*, San Francisco: North Point Press, 1983.

Hirashima, Shigemochi, *The Structure of Disparity in Developing Agriculture*, Tokyo: Institute of Developing Economies, 1978.

Hugel, Baron Charles, *Travels in Kashmir and the Punjab, Containing a Particular Account of the Government and Character of the Sikhs*, London, 1845.

Husain, Khalifa Muhammad, *Tarikh-i Patiala* (Urdu), n.p., n.d.

Indra, Doreen, 'The Portrayal of South Asians in the Vancouver Press, 1905-1976', *Ethnic and Racial Studies*, vol. 2, part 2, 1979.

Irwin, William, *Later Mughals*, ed. J.N. Sarkar, New Delhi, 1971 (rpt.).

Jaggi, Ratan Singh, *Dasam Granth da Karatritava*, New Delhi: Punjabi Sahit Sabha, 1966.

Kang, D.S., 'Environmental Problems of the Green Revolution with a focus on Punjab, India', in *International Dimensions of the Environmentalist Crisis*, ed. Richard Barrett, Westview Press, 1982.

Kang, Kanwarjit, 'Mural Paintings in 19th Century Punjab', Ph.D. thesis, Panjab University, Chandigarh, 1978.

Karam Singh Historian, *Katak ke Visakh*, Ludhiana: Lahore Book, 1912.

Kaur, Madanjit, 'The Contribution of the Bungas to the Education of the Punjab', *Punjab History Conference Proceedings*, 1978, pp. 94-101.

Ker, James Campbell, *Political Trouble in India, 1907-1917*, Calcutta: 1973 (rpt., 1st pub. 1917).

Kessinger, T.G., *Vilyatpur, 1848-1968: Social and Economic Change in a North Indian Village*, University of California Press, 1974.

Khalsa, Giani Gurbachan Singh, *Gurbani Path Darshan*, Bhindran Kalan: Gurdwara Akhand Prakash, n.d.

———, *Gurmat Rahit Maryada*, Amritsar: Khalsa Brothers, 1986.

Khan, Iqtidar Alam, 'Indian Response to Firearms (1300-1750)', *Proceedings Indian History Congress*, Bangalore, 1997.

———, 'The Matchlock Musket in the Mughal Empire – An Instrument of Centralization', *Proceedings Indian History Congress*, Patiala, 1998.

———, 'The Khalsa of Guru Gobind Singh: Its Soldiers and their Arms', in *The Khalsa and the Punjab*, ed. Himadri Banerjee, New Delhi: Tulika/Indian History Congress, 2002.

Khan, Rasheeduddin, *Bewildered India: Identity, Pluralism, Discord*, New Delhi: Har-Anand, 1995.

Kohli, Atul, *Democracy and Discontent: India's Growing Crisis of Governability*, Cambridge: Cambridge University Press, 1991, Indian Paperback Edition 1995 (rpt.).

Krishan, Gopal, 'Distribution of the Sikhs outside the Punjab (India)', *Indian Geographical Journal*, vol. 46, nos. 1&2, 1971, pp. 35-41.

———, 'Demography of the Punjab', *Journal of Punjab Studies*, vol. 11, no. 1, 2004, pp. 77-92.

Ladejinsky, W., 'Green Revolution in Punjab: A Field Trip', *Economic and Political Weekly*, June 1969, Bombay.

Lee-Warner, William, *The Native States of India*, London: Macmillan and Co., 1910.

Leitner, G.W., *History of Indigenous Education in the Punjab since Annexation and in 1882*, Patiala: Punjab Languages Department, 1971 (rpt.).

Lenin, V.I., *Complete Collected Works*, 45 vols., Moscow: Progress Publishers, 1980.

———, *The Development of Capitalism in Russia*, Moscow: Progress Publishers, 1977.

Loehlin, C.H., 'The Sikhs in California', in, *Punjab Past and Present: Essays in Honour of Dr Ganda Singh*, ed. Harbans Singh and N. Gerald Barrier, Patiala: Punjabi University, 1996 (2nd. edn.), pp. 291-301.

Lord, John, *The Maharajas*, London: Hutchison, 1971.

Macauliffe, M.A., *The Sikh Religion: Its Gurus, Sacred Writings and Authors*, 6 vols., Delhi, 1998 (rpt.).

Mann, Gurinder Singh, 'Sikhism in the United States of America', *The South Asian Religious Diaspora in Britain, Canada, and the United States*, ed. Harold Coward et al., Albany: SUNY Press, 2000.

———, *The Making of Sikh Scripture*, New York: Oxford University Press, 2001.

———, *Religions of the World: Sikhism*, London: Laurence King Publishing Ltd., 2004.

Mansukhani, Gobind Singh, 'Sikh Rahat-Maryada and Sikh Symbols', in *Advanced Studies in Sikhism*, ed. Jasbir Singh Mann and Harbans Singh Saraon, Irvine, CA: Sikh Community of North America, 1989.

Marenco, Ethne K., *The Transformation of Sikh Society*, New Delhi: Heritage Publishers, 1976.

McLeod, W.H., *Guru Nanak and the Sikh Religion*, Oxford: Clarendon Press, 1969.

———, *Early Sikh Tradition*, Oxford: Clarendon Press, 1980.

———, *The B40 Janam-Sakhi*, Amritsar: Guru Nanak Dev University, 1980.

———, *Textual Sources for the Study of Sikhism*, U.K.: Manchester University Press, 1984.

———, *The Chaupa Singh Rahit-Nama*, New Zealand: University of Otago Press, 1987.

———, *Historical Dictionary of Sikhism*, London: The Scarecrow Press, 1995.

———, *Sikhism*, Penguin Books, 1997.

———, 'The Khalsa Rahit: The Sikh Identity Defined', in *Exploring Sikhism: Aspects of Sikh Identity, Culture, and Thought*, New Delhi: Oxford University Press, 2000.

———, 'The Problem of the Punjabi Rahitnamas', in *Exploring Sikhism: Aspects of Sikh Identity, Culture, and Thought*, New Delhi: Oxford University Press, 2000.

———, *Sikhs of the Khalsa: A History of the Khalsa Rahit*, New Delhi: Oxford University Press, 2003.

———, *Discovering the Sikhs: Autobiography of a Historian*, Delhi: Permanent Black, 2004.

Nabha, Kahn Singh, *Gurshabad Ratnakar Mahankosh*, Patiala: Punjab Languages Department, 1999 (rpt.).

———, *Ham Hindu Nahin* [We are not Hindus], Amritsar: Singh Brothers, 1995 (rpt.).

Nadkarni, M.V., 'Tenants from the Dominant Class: A Developing Contradiction in Land Reforms', *Economic and Political Weekly*, Review of Agriculture, December 1976.

Narang, K.S. and P.C. Saxena, *History of the Punjab* (revd. H.R. Gupta), Delhi, 1953.

Natwar-Singh, K., *The Magnificent Maharaja: The Life and Times of Maharaja Bhupinder Singh of Patiala, 1891-1938*, New Delhi: HarperCollins, 1998.

Nayar, Baldev Raj, *Minority Politics in the Punjab*, New Jersey: Princeton University Press, 1966.

Nikolinakos, M., 'Notes Toward a General Theory of Migration in Late Capitalism', *Race and Class*, vol. XVII, part 1, 1975.

Nur Muhammad, *Jang-nama*, ed. Ganda Singh, Amritsar, 1937.

O'Dwyer, Michael, *India as I Knew it, 1885-1925*, London: Constable, 1925.

Oberoi, Harjot, *The Construction of Religious Boundaries: Culture, Identity and Diversity in the Sikh Tradition*, New Delhi: Oxford University Press, 1994.

Osahan, Davinder Singh (ed.), *Pothi Prem Ambodh*, Patiala: Punjabi University, 1989.

Padam, Piara Singh, *Prachin Punjabi Gadd*, Patiala: Kalam Mandir, 1978.

———, *Dasam Granth Darshan*, Patiala: Kalam Mandir, 1990.

———, *Mahan Kavi Santokh Singh*, Patiala: Kalam Mandir, 1990.

——— (ed.), *Rahitname*, Amritsar: Singh Brothers, 1995 (rpt.).

Pandey, Gyanendra (ed.), *Hindus and Others: The Question of Identity in India Today*, New Delhi: Viking Penguin India, 1993.

———, *The Construction of Communalism in Colonial North India*, New Delhi: Oxford University Press, 1994 (Paperback, 2nd impression).

Parkin, Raleigh, *India Today*, New York: John Day, 1945.

Patnaik, Utsa, *Peasant Class Differentiation: A Study in Method with Reference to Haryana*, New Delhi: Oxford University Press, 1987.

Rahi, J.S. and Rita Chaudhry (trs.), *Tree and The Sage*, Delhi: Ajanta, 2000.

Raj, K.N., 'Ownership and Distribution of Land', *Indian Economic Review*, April 1970.

Raj, V.M., 'Village Lease Markets for Agricultural Land: Some Approaches for Analysis', *Economic and Political Weekly*, Review of Agriculture, June 1974.

Randhawa, M.S., *Kangra Paintings of the Gita Govinda*, New Delhi, 1963.

———, 'Kehar Singh and Kapur Singh: Two Punjabi Artists of the 19th Century', *Chhavi*, Benares, 1971.

Remple, H. and R.A. Lobdell, 'The Role of Urban to Rural Remittances in Rural Development', *Journal of Development Studies*, 1978.

Rose, E.J.B. and Associates, *Colour and Citizenship: A Report on British Race Relations*, Oxford University Press, 1969.

Sahni, Ruchi Ram, *Struggle for Reform in Sikh Shrines*, Amritsar: 1965.

Sainapat, *Sri Gur Sobha*, ed. Ganda Singh, Patiala: Punjabi University, 1968.

Sanehi, Swaran Singh, 'Rahitnamas of the Sikhs', *Journal of Sikh Studies*, vol. XI, pt. 1, 1984.

Shiva, Vandana, 'The Green Revolution in the Punjab', *The Ecologist*, vol. 21, part 2, 1991.

Singh, Avtar, *Chehrah Dekhan Da Shisha* (Punjabi), Amritsar: Gurmat Press, 1911.

Singh, Baba Bishan, *Aise Ko Taisa* (Punjabi), Lahore: Sri Gurbax Press, 1911.

Singh, Bawa Narain, *Sikh Hindu Hain* (Punjabi), Amritsar: Public Service Printing Press, n.d.

Singh, Bhai Jodh (ed.), *Kabir Bani Steek*, Patiala: Punjabi University, n.d.

Singh, Bhai Randhir, *Gurmat Bibek*, Ludhiana: Bhai Randhir Singh, 1946.

——— (ed.), *Apani Katha in Shabadarth Dasam Granth Sahib*, vol. 1, Patiala: Punjabi University.

——— (ed.), *Prem Sumarg*, Jalandhar: New Book Agency, 2000 (rpt.).

Singh, Daljeet, *Essentials of Sikhism*, Amritsar: Singh Brothers, 1994.

Singh, Dalwinder, *Bhai Sahib Bhai Takhat Singh Ji*, Ludhiana: Sikh Missionary College, 2003.

Singh, Darbara, 'Historical Geography of the Colonial Punjab 1849-1947', Ph.D. thesis, Chandigarh: Panjab University, 2004.

Singh, Durlab, *The Valiant Fighter*, Lahore: Hero Publishers, 1942.

Singh, Fauja, 'The Effects of Land Transfers on Rural Economy During the Later Half of the 19th Century', *Punjab History Conference Proceedings*, Patiala: Punjabi University, 1979.

Singh, G.B., *Sri Guru Granth Sahib dian Prachin Birhan*, Lahore: Modern Publications, 1944.

Singh, Ganda, *Bhai Jodh Singh : Abhinandan Granth* (Punjabi), Patiala, 1962.

———, 'Scholars of History', *Bhai Vir Singh Shatabadi Granth*, ed. Harbans Singh, Delhi, 1972.

——— (ed.), *Some Confidential Papers of the Akali Movement*, Amritsar: SGPC, 1965.

——— (ed.), *Hukamname Guru Sahibaan, Mata Sahibaan, Banda Singh and Khalsa ji De*, Patiala: Punjabi University, 1967.

——— (ed.), *Bhai Nand Lal Granthavali*, Patiala: Punjabi University, 2000 (rpt.).

Singh, Giani Badan, *Adi Sri Guru Granth Sahib Ji Satik*, Patiala: Punjab Languages Department, 1970 (rpt.).

Singh, Giani Gian, *Tawarikh Guru Khalsa*, vol. II, Patiala: Punjab Languages Department, 1987.

Singh, Giani Gurdit, *Mundavani*, Chandigarh: Sahit Prakashan, 2003.

Singh, Giani Hazara (ed.), *Varan Bhai Gurdas*, Amritsar: Khalsa Samachar, 1962.

Singh, Giani Mahan, *Bhai Sahib Bhai Vir Singh Da Gurmukh Jiwan*, Amritsar: Khalsa Samachar, 1977.

Singh, Gurbachan, and Lal Singh Giani, *The Idea of the Sikh State*, Lahore: Lahore Book Shop, 1946.

Singh, Gurdarshan, 'Character and Impact of the Singh Sabha Movement on the History of the Punjab', Ph.D. thesis, Patiala: Punjabi University, 1973.

Singh, Gurtej and Swaranjeet Singh (eds.), *Shahid-Bilas Sant Jarnail Singh Bhindranwale*, Chandigarh: Satsandhi Publications, 2001.

Singh, H.K. Manmohan, 'Population Pressure and Labour Absorbability in Agriculture and Related Activities: Analysis and Suggestions

Based on Field Studies Conducted in Punjab', *Economic and Political Weekly*, 17 March 1979.

Singh, Harbans, 'Origin of Singh Sabha Movement', *The Panjab Past and Present: Essays in Honour of Dr. Ganda Singh*, ed. N.G. Barrier and Harbans Singh, Patiala: Punjabi University, 1976.

——— (ed.), *The Encyclopaedia of Sikhism*, Patiala: Punjabi University, 1998.

Singh, Haribhajan, *Rukh te Rishi*, Delhi: Navyug Publishers, 1992.

Singh, Harnam, *Punjab: The Homeland of the Sikhs*, Lahore, 1945.

Singh, Jathedar Joginder, *Sri Hazuri Maryada Prabodh*, Nanderh: Sri Takht Abchal Nagar, 1967.

Singh, Jodh, *Guru Sahib Ate Veda*, Amritsar: Wazir Hind Press, 1912.

——— (tr.), *The Dasam Granth*, vol. IV.

Singh, Joginder, 'The Sikh Resurgence 1849-1947', M. Phil. dissertation, Amritsar: Guru Nanak Dev University, 1980.

Singh, Kavi Seva, *Shahid Bilas*, ed. Garja Singh Giani, Ludhiana: Punjabi Sahit Academy, 1961.

Singh, Khushwant, *The Sikhs*, London: George Allen & Unwin Ltd., 1953.

———, *A History of the Sikhs 1469-1988*, 2 vols., Princeton: Princeton University Press, 1963-6.

——— (ed.), *Janam Sakhi Prampara*, Patiala: Punjabi University, 1990.

Singh, Mohindar, *The Akali Movement*, New Delhi: Macmillan, 1978.

Singh, Nihal, 'The triumph of the Indians in Canada', *Modern Review*, August 1909.

Singh, Nripinder, 'Rahitnamas and Aggrandizement of Khalsa Tradition', in *Sikhism and Secularism: Essays in Honour of Professor Harbans Singh*, ed. Dharam Singh, New Delhi: Harman Publishing House, 1994.

Singh, Pashaura, *The Guru Granth Sahib*, New Delhi: Oxford University Press, 2000.

Singh, Piar, *Gatha Sri Adi Granth*, Amritsar: Guru Nanak Dev University, 1992.

Singh, Rai Jasbir, 'Rahitnamas: Their Period of Writing', *Punjab History Conference Proceedings*, Patiala: Punjabi University, 1980.

——— (ed.), *Guru Amardas Srot Pustak*, Amritsar: Guru Nanak Dev University, 1986.

Singh, Ranjit (ed.), *Principal Teja Singh Abhinandan Granth* (Punjabi), Patiala, 1956.

Singh, Sahib (ed.), *Asa di Var Steek*, Amritsar: Singh Brothers, 1991 (17th edn.).

——— (ed.), *Steek Bhagat Bani (Kabir)*, Amritsar: Singh Brothers, 1994 (6th edn.).

Singh, Sant Visakha, *Malwa Itihas*, 4 vols., Kishangarh: Author, 1970.

Singh, Shubha, *Overseas Indians The Global Family*, Delhi: Shipra Publications, 2005.

Singh, Swarup, *The Sikhs Demand Their Homeland*, London, 1946.

Singh, Teja, 'The Singh Sabha Movement', *The Panjab Past and Present*, vol. IV, 1973.

———, *Essays in Sikhism*, Lahore, 1941.

Singh, Teja, *Jivan Kahani, Raj Yogi Sant Atar Singh Ji Maharaj de vrosae sewak Sant Teja Singh ji di apni kalm ton likhi hoi*, 2 vols., Barhu Sahib: Kalgidhar Trust, 2000.

Srivastava, S.P., *Art and Cultural Heritage of Patiala*, Delhi, 1991.

Suri, Sohan Lal, *Umdat-ut-Tawarikh*, vol. III, tr. V.S. Suri, Delhi, 1961.

Talbot, I. and S. Thandi (eds.), *People on the Move, Punjabi Colonial and Post Colonial Migration*, Oxford: Oxford University Press, 2004.

Tatla, Darshan Singh, *The Sikh Diaspora*, Seattle: University of Washington, 1998.

Tatla, Darshan Singh and Ian Tablot, *Punjab*, Oxford: Cilo, 1997.

Trench, C.C., *Viceroy's Agent*, London: Jonathan Cape, 1987.

Trumpp, Ernest, *The Adi Granth*, Delhi: Munshiram Manoharlal, 1978 (rpt.).

Tupper, C.L., *Indian Political Practice*, vol. I, Delhi: B.R. Publishing House, 1974 (rpt.; 1st pub. 1895).

Tuzuk-i Jahangiri, ed., Saiyid Ahmad, Ghazipur and Aligarh, 1863-4.

Udasi, Swami Harnamdas, *Adi Sri Guru Granth Sahib dian Puratani Birhan te Vichar*, Kapurthala: Kantesh Pharmacy, n.d.

——— (ed.), *Sarab Loh Granth*, Anandpur: Guru ka Bagh, n.d.

Venkat Narayan, S., 'Poor Millionaires', *Sunday Times*, London, 18 January 1975.

Vinayak, Ramesh, 'The Price of Prosperity', *India Today*, New Delhi, 15 July 1992.

Vyas, V.S., 'Tenancy in a Dynamic Setting', Review of Agriculture, *Economic and Political Weekly*, June 1970.

Walia, Amrit, 'Achievements of Sikh Education Conference', *Punjab History Conference Proceedings*, April 1975, pp. 205-12.

Walia, Ramesh, *Praja Mandal Movement in the East Punjab States*, Patiala: Punjabi University, 1972.

Walker, Benjamin, *Hindu World*, London: George Allen & Unwin Ltd., 1968.

Wallace, Paul and Surendra Chopra (eds.), *Political Dynamics of Punjab*, Amritsar: Guru Nanak Dev University, 1981.

Ward, A., 'European Capitalism's Reserve Army', *Monthly Review*, vol. 27, part 6, 1975.

Index

Contributors

J.S. GREWAL: former Vice-Chancellor, Guru Nanak Dev University, Amritsar, and Director, Indian Institute of Advanced Study, Shimla, is now Chairman of its Governing Body. He has written extensively on the history of India, the Punjab and the Sikhs. Among his works on Sikh history are *Guru Nanak in History* (1969), *The Sikhs of the Punjab* (1990) and *Contesting Interpretations of the Sikh Tradition* (1998).

KARAMJIT K. MALHOTRA: Research student, Department of History, Panjab University, Chandigarh.

IQTIDAR ALAM KHAN: retired Professor of History, Aligarh Muslim University, has written extensively on Mughal India. Among his publications are *Mirza Kamran: A Biographical Study* (1964) and *Political Biography of a Mughal Noble: Munim Khan, Khan-i-Khanan, 1497-1575* (1973).

B.N. GOSWAMY: retired Professor of History of Fine Arts, Panjab University, has written extensively on painting and art. His major publications include *Pahari Painting: The Family as the Basis of Style* (1968), *Pahari Masters: Court Painters of Northern India* (1992), and *Piety and Splendour: Sikh Heritage in Art* (2000).

ANURUPITA KAUR: Research Fellow, Department of History, Panjab University, Chandigarh, working on 'Social Transformation in the Punjab: A Study of the Sikhs under British Rule 1849-1919'.

JOGINDER SINGH: Professor Namdhari Guru Ram Singh Chair, Guru Nanak Dev University, Amritsar, has published articles and books, including *The Sikh Resurgence* (1997), *The Sikh Leadership* (1999) and *Sikh Militancy in Punjab* (forthcoming).

DARSHAN SINGH TATLA: Director, Institute of Sikh Diaspora Studies, Lyallpur Khalsa College, Jalandhar, has published useful bibliographies, including *Sikhs in North America* (1991) and *A Guide to Sources Ghadar Movement* (2003).

MOHINDER SINGH: Director, National Institute of Punjab Studies, New Delhi, has published *The Akali Movement* (1978), and *The Akali Struggle: A Retrospect* (1988). Currently he is engaged in locating, photographing and cataloguing Sikh relics and historic personalities.

KULDEEP K. GREWAL: Research Fellow, Department of History, Panjab University, Chandigarh, is working on 'Paramountcy and Patiala, 1880-1947'.

GOPAL KRISHAN: Senior Professor and Honorary Director, Population Research Centre at the Centre for Rural and Industrial Development, Chandigarh, has published extensively on urbanization and demography; he has been awarded D.Sc. (honoris causa) by the University of Pecs (Hungary).

SHINDER S. THANDI: Senior Lecturer in Economics, Coventry University (U.K.), has published a number of papers in the area of development economics.

GURINDER SINGH MANN: Kundan Kaur Kapany Professor of Sikh Studies, University of California, Santa Barbara, has published extensively on Sikh history and Sikhism; notable among his publications are *The Making of Sikh Scripture* (2001) and *Sikhism* (2004).